COMPOSITION, CHROMATICISM AND THE DEVELOPMENTAL PROCESS

Composition, Chromaticism and the Developmental Process

A New Theory of Tonality

HENRY BURNETT and ROY NITZBERG
Queens College, The City University of New York, USA

ASHGATE

© Henry Burnett and Roy Nitzberg 2007

Published by
Ashgate Publishing Limited
Gower House
Croft Road
Aldershot
Hampshire GU11 3HR
England

Ashgate Publishing Company
Suite 420
101 Cherry Street
Burlington, VT 05401-4405
USA

Ashgate website: http://www.ashgate.com

British Library Cataloguing in Publication Data
Burnett, Henry
    Composition, chromaticism and the developmental process : a new theory of tonality
    1. Tonality 2. Composition (Music) – History and criticism 3. Chromaticism (Music)
    I. Title II. Nitzberg, Roy
    781.2'58'09

Library of Congress Cataloging-in-Publication Data
Burnett, Henry.
    Composition, chromaticism, and the developmental process : a new theory of tonality / by Henry Burnett and Roy Nitzberg.
        p. cm.
    Includes bibliographical references.
    ISBN 978-0-7546-5162-8 (alk. paper)
    1. Tonality. 2. Chromaticism (Music) I. Nitzberg, Roy. II. Title.

    ML3811.B87 2007
    781.2'58–dc22

                                            2006036163
ISBN 978 0 7546 5162 8

Printed and bound in Great Britain by TJ International Ltd, Padstow, Cornwall.

Bach musicological font developed by © Yo Tomita.

Contents

List of Figures

List of Diagrams

List of Music Examples

Notes on Authors

Henry Burnett is Professor of Music at the Aaron Copland School of Music, Queens College of the City University of New York, where he is also the Associate Director. A musicologist, Prof. Burnett specializes in music history, including style criticism and theory, primarily of the seventeenth, eighteenth, and nineteenth centuries. In addition, he is noted for his work in the field of traditional Japanese music, including its performance – Prof Burnett is a licensed master (Natori) of shamisen and koto. His articles have appeared in *Music Theory Spectrum*, *Perspectives of New Music*, *International Journal of Musicology*, *The New Grove Dictionary of Music and Musicians*, *Asian Music*, *American Organist*, and *American Choral Review*.

Roy Nitzberg received his Ph.D. in music theory from the City University of New York Graduate Center in 1999; the title of his dissertation was "Voice Leading and Chromatic Techniques in Expositions of Selected Symphonies of Joseph Haydn, Introducing a New Theory of Chromatic Analysis." He studied Schenker analysis with Carl Schachter and Charles Burkhart. He coedited *Hogaku*, the journal of the Traditional Japanese Music Society, between 1984 and 1989 and was the Associate Director of the Center for Preparatory Studies in Music, a children's music program at Queens College (City University of New York), from 1987 until 1995. Dr Nitzberg also teaches music theory, ear training, and music appreciation at Queens College, Hunter College, and Hofstra University.

Preface

Henry Burnett

This book is meant primarily for the educated music public that has a thorough grounding in music theory with at least a modicum of historical perspective, and that is interested in another way of looking at aspects of musical composition that will not be found in any other analytical treatise. Although not a textbook, this book is also meant for my students, both undergraduate and graduate, who take my undergraduate music history sequence, or my various graduate courses, all of which are predicated, in some way or other, on a knowledge of the theory of chromaticism and modal/tonal composition set forth in the following chapters. For those who are skeptical about the efficacy, or indeed, "truth" of the theories presented here, I would strongly urge the reader, after reading the book in its entirety, to apply this theory to pieces of your own choosing, and then decide how much may be of value towards your own musical understanding. However, just as in any well-considered theory, the understanding comes about as a result of its continuous practical application.

The following example, taken from an article by Joseph Straus, is an illustration of the efficacy of this theory in clarifying chromatic issues, as well as other difficult analytical problems. Within a much wider topic of the "disability in music," Straus discusses Schoenberg's analysis of the C minor String Quartet of Brahms, op. 51 no. 1.[1] In general, Schoenberg speaks of a "tonal problem" which is raised at the start of a piece, but which must then be solved by the end of the composition. Straus then illustrates Schoenberg's concept using Schoenberg's discussion of the Brahms quartet as an example. Straus states:

> Schoenberg himself never defined "tonal problem" in a comprehensive or systematic way and provided no complete analytical demonstration. The closest approximation is his discussion of Brahms's String Quartet, Op. 51, no 1, first movement, which focuses on the rhetorically charged F♯ in measure 20. This F♯, a "tonal problem" in the key of C minor, a "far-reaching digression," as Schoenberg calls it, has the local effect of destabilizing and unbalancing the tonality and the long-range effect of leading to remote keys, including E-flat minor (or which the F♯, now spelled as G♭, is the diatonic third degree).[2]

If one analyzes this movement according to the theory presented here, one immediately realizes why F♯ creates "a tonal problem" in the key of C minor, the reason for which neither Schoenberg nor Straus addresses. A main tenet of this theory is that each key exists within a total pitch field of eleven pitch classes; the twelfth, or "missing pitch" as I have labeled it, forces a shift out of the prevailing pitch field

---

1   Joseph N. Straus, "Normalizing the Abnormal: Disability in Music and Music Theory," *Journal of the American Musicological Society*, 59/1 (Spring 2006): 136–40 in particular.

2   *Ibid.*, 140.

into another eleven-pitch-class field (the exact reasons for how and why pitch fields modulate is detailed in Chapters 1 and 2). According to the theory, C minor exists within an eleven-note, 3♭ pitch field, or "system," whose root pitch is E♭ and whose missing pitch is, in fact, F♯. When F♯ is introduced, it causes a system shift out of a 3♭ system into its symmetrical system complement, C (or "0"), the system of its parallel major. Thus F♯ acts as a "system-shift motivator" whose presence will disrupt the harmonic surface, as Schoenberg discovered, without knowing the reason why. Similarly, G♭, the enharmonic equivalent of F♯, and its symmetrical opposite, when introduced, will cause a system shift to a pitch field of six flats, thrusting the harmonic surface into E♭ minor. Knowing how F♯ and G♭ function as system-shift motivators, and their consequent effect in informing important harmonic events, can greatly increase our awareness of the compositional/developmental process *from the inside out*, as it were.

The method of analysis presented in the following pages is the culmination of many years of investigation centering on music history and analysis courses, on both the graduate and the undergraduate level, taught by me at Queens College, City University of New York, in the Aaron Copland School of Music. At first, when I started my teaching career in the early 1970s, I was encouraged by my music history students to delve ever deeper into the workings of the pieces we studied in class instead of just confining my lectures to material that was of a more circumstantial nature. Perhaps I overdid it, but I was soon questioning the very foundations of musical composition, in particular how the developmental process informs the design and harmonic structure of pieces from the late Middle Ages right into our own era. I was able to do this at that time since I was teaching the entire undergraduate music history sequence, then a three-semester sequence but now four semesters, and could view, more easily, long-range developments along with a class whose personnel remained more or less consistent throughout. With each rotation of the sequence, new ideas, new formulations, and new insights multiplied and stimulated my own musical growth, aided also by my study of authors who searched for the same understanding: Charles Rosen, Carl Dahlhaus, David Epstein, among many others. Having the same student body for each rotation of the sequence also allowed me to test the relevance of my ideas on music of various periods without the necessity of re-educating from scratch a different enrollment of students every semester.

However, it was only on the graduate level that I could get the necessary feedback, mostly in the form of penetrating questions, that I needed to further progress my analytical concepts. Indeed, if anyone should be the dedicatee of this book, it should be those students who were not afraid to ask the right questions at the right time. I was very fortunate to be teaching the very course that could most benefit me in terms of student feedback, and total freedom of content. That was the "Proseminar in Style Criticism and Analysis," an intense graduate course that I had been teaching almost without break since the early 1980s. The way I had originally set up the content for this course was to start with late Renaissance pieces and take the class, through one semester, right through to the end of the nineteenth century, hopefully ending with Debussy (there simply was not enough time to go any further historically). I would first give a lecture on the analytical/stylistic features of a given music period and then the students would be given a piece, or a comparison of two or more pieces from this same period, to analyze on their own, presenting their ideas in a formal typewritten paper. It was in this course, as well as other graduate courses given over the intervening years, that the present ideas concerning chromaticism, its relationship to tonality, and its function within the larger developmental processes of a musical composition were systematized into the theories that finally generated this book.

The organization of the book is basically teleologic; after an opening chapter that explains the basic tenets of the theory, the chapters that follow trace the development of my theory of eleven-pitch tonality through the various historical periods, beginning with the diatonic modal music of Josquin Desprez followed by the chromatic music of the later sixteenth century, then moving through the seventeenth century and the tricky question of the transition from modal to tonal thinking and how this transformation applies to eleven-pitch-class analysis. Further aspects of the theory, specifically an explanation of *primary chromatic* and *primary diatonic arrays*, are next discussed, along with previous tenets of the theory, as they apply to the concerto, quartet, and symphony genres of the eighteenth century, concentrating on Haydn, Mozart, and Beethoven. Subsequent chapters focus on the innovations and stylistic changes inherent in the music of the nineteenth century; namely, in the music of Schubert, Mendelssohn, Schumann, Brahms, and Chaikovsky, ending with a final chapter detailing how the theory could be applied to the more extreme chromatic music of Liszt and Debussy and concluding with a look at the atonal music of Schoenberg. The material presented in Chapters 3 to 7 is of my own devising (with editorial emendations by my co-author, Roy Nitzberg), with Chapters 1 and 2, which present the basis of the theory, composed by Dr Nitzberg, who is also the sole author of the final chapter.

The book is intended to be cumulative; that is, it is meant to be read from beginning to end, as various aspects of the theory are revealed along the way in conjunction with the evolving historical landscape. While the chapters dealing with sixteenth- and early seventeenth-century music concentrate on vocal music, the later chapters deal exclusively with instrumental music, solely for matters of expediency, covering both the symphonic and chamber music repertories. Genre notwithstanding, this theory applies equally to all modal/tonal and even atonal, non-serial music, vocal or instrumental, from at least the sixteenth century onwards, the possible exception being music composed before the sixteenth century since this repertory awaits further study.

Naturally, so vast a topic can cover only so much material in its first presentation, and we have had to limit the scope of the book to the music of only a sampling of composers and their works. Owing to limitations of space, many important composers have had to be left out of our discussion, even those whose works support our theoretical postulates. For instance, we were not able to include Berlioz, a composer noted for his daring use of chromaticism. In addition, the entire area of opera had to be omitted, yet its often dramatic key changes also reflect system sensitivity. Not surprisingly, even the interaction of characters, identified by certain specific tonalities (*Rigoletto* and *Turandot* come to mind here), can often be further musically understood by applying this theory to their individual key centers. In addition there are many other important topics that still await further investigation, and which also could not be included in this study. For example, the role of rhythm in relation to system shifts from one eleven-pitch-class area to another, or, just as importantly, a more detailed study of enharmonicism and how it effects system modulation. In fact, as we begin to explore the seemingly unlimited number of potential topics this theory generates, we believe that we have only begun to understand the nature of our tonal system and the overwhelming part that chromaticism plays in the compositional process.

A word or two about my co-author, Dr Roy Nitzberg. Among all of my former and present students who have traveled the path that I have set forth here, Dr Nitzberg is perhaps the one person who has followed and understood my theories since their inception, has sacrificed his professional standing for his belief in these theories, and has been steadfast in disseminating these concepts to his students. It is only fitting, therefore, that he should join me as co-author in presenting this complex theory to the general musical community. Dr Nitzberg has also been throughly trained in other analytical methodologies, most significantly, Schenkerian analysis. In fact, both of us have had extensive training in Schenker's theory and that is why we have always maintained that our theoretical approach can coexist with other analytical systems. In fact, Dr Nitzberg did just that for his doctoral dissertation on Haydn's Paris symphonies, analyzing the first movement expositions of each symphony both from a Schenkerian and from an eleven-pitch-class perspective. We feel that no one theory can explain every aspect of musical composition, and that the informed musician should ideally be open to any number of philosophical and analytical approaches, if only to avoid being overly dogmatic and thereby denying himself or herself the opportunity to understand a composition from more than a single viewpoint.

Acknowledgments

The authors would like most especially to acknowledge Ashgate Publishing and their editorial staff for their support of this project. In particular, we would like to offer our greatest appreciation to Heidi May, Commissioning Editor for Music Studies at Ashgate, for her belief in and staunch support of the validity of what is a highly controversial theoretical undertaking. If it were not for her tireless efforts, our book would never have been published. In addition, we would like to express our gratitude to the City University of New York Research Foundation for two research grants that enabled us to expand the scope of the book to almost twice its original size. We would also like to express our gratitude to Elliott Antokoletz and Michael von Albrecht, editors of the *International Journal of Musicology*, for allowing us to reprint extensive diagrams, figures, and text from previous articles written for the journal by Henry Burnett that laid the groundwork for the theoretical constructs articulated throughout the present study. During the years that this theory was being formulated in the graduate classes taught by Henry Burnett at the Aaron Copland School of Music, a number of graduate students, through their pointed questioning of Burnett's work, and their tireless efforts to understand the basics underlying this complex theory, helped considerably in refining the final stages of the theory as it is now conceived. In particular, we would like to thank Anthony Iandolo and Paul Madden for their support of Burnett's work, and the pointed questions they asked that eventually led to the completion of this theory. Lastly, we would like to thank two students, in particular, who studied with Henry Burnett at the Aaron Copland School of Music, Queens College, City University of New York, and whose help in compiling the manuscript was of vital importance. First and foremost is Thomas Lin (presently a Ph.D. candidate at Harvard University) for creating all the musical examples in the book in Finale, and for his comments on textual and editorial matters. Second is Sina Kiai, whose in-depth knowledge of Chopin and Debussy, especially in regard to our present theory, helped us in clarifying our analyses of the works of these composers.

Prologue: A Personal Reflection

Roy Nitzberg

I first met Henry Burnett in 1976 as the teacher for an elective I was taking at Queens College called "Music 45: Bach." After three years of pre-med, I decided that I missed music so much and that I despised the doctors of the future so much that some change had to occur in my life. As a pianist, I had already played many of Bach's preludes and fugues, a toccata, a partita, and had listened intently to Nikolaus Harnoncourt's new period-instrument LP recording of the Brandenburg Concertos, which I considered to be revelatory. I listened to it over and over again while trying to make sense of the facsimile of the score that accompanied the records. As my first course ever in the field of music, I believed that taking one on the music of Bach both was necessary and was probably going to be a lot of fun. Of course, having transferred from the Cornell University School of Agriculture to the City University of New York, I would never again have the opportunity to take the next class in the biology sequence, "Sheep 380" (it was a toss-up that semester between "Sheep 380" and "Horses 265"), but I figured that, somehow, I would get along without it.

Anyway, back to Henry Burnett. As the semester progressed, I realized that I knew nothing about Bach and nothing about much of anything else. I also noticed that I was writing more per day in "Bach 45" than I had ever written in "Human Genetics 110." I also noticed some students in the class using these new cassette-recording devices to tape Prof. Burnett's lectures. Looking back at that experience now, three decades later, I still think that the amount and, particularly, the depth of material imparted to us was incredible, especially to a class of mostly undergraduates. But it was the quality of the information and the manner in which it was presented that had me thinking after a few weeks that I should probably take every single course offered by Henry Burnett ... and it didn't matter very much what the topic was. And then it happened: one of the student's cassette-recorders got to the end of its 45-minute side and let out a nice, loud "pop." Without missing a beat, Burnett turned to the student, said "Your toast is ready," turned back to the class and continued the lesson. Yes, definitely, anything Henry Burnett taught I would take.

And so, over the course of the next few years, I took some other electives with Henry Burnett (yes, music students took electives in the 1970s and 1980s) including courses he taught in non-Western music, particularly in the chamber music of the Tokugawa and Meiji periods in Japan. I also made sure that the instructor for my required music-history sequence at Queens College was Prof. Burnett. One of the things from my history courses that seemed important was that all the compositions we discussed in class were accompanied with middleground Schenkerian graphs. Henry Burnett, who had studied the theory of Heinrich Schenker with Felix Salzer, was certain that the historical significance held by a piece of music could successfully be addressed only in conjunction with its theoretical groundwork. I also noticed as a graduate student some years later that theorists apparently did not like the idea of a music-historian having something innovative to say about music theory. Eventually, by the mid-1980s as a doctoral student in music theory, I found myself working as associate editor with Henry, a Natori shamisen master, on *Hogaku*, a journal he founded that was devoted to traditional Japanese music and was published by the Traditional Japanese Music Society of the City University of New York at Queens College. At the same time, we kept discussing aspects of Western music, particularly Classical-period symphonies by Joseph Haydn and the ways in which certain seemingly insignificant details of Haydn's chromaticism in the opening passages of a work kept returning in various ways as the composition took shape. I'll add that the reason these details seemed "insignificant" was that we all knew that chromaticism was only "musical pizza sauce," to quote another Queens College professor. Or so we thought: but if it were only "pizza sauce," why did those gestures keep returning?

Prof. Burnett's innovation of a new theory of symmetrical divisions in tonal music began by questioning the nature of the development process in these Haydn symphonies; more specifically, by relating that process to the exploration of long-range relationships between diatonic pitch classes and their chromatic inflections. These inflections created an association of consonant and dissonant conflicts that became the basis of a working-out process that consumed entire movements of Classical symphonies, if not entire works. It seemed that what Haydn was up to was not all that different from what Mozart was up to. Or Beethoven ... Henry began to treat such conflicts between the diatonic and the chromatic as part of the lifeblood of the composition; dissonances created by the introduction of chromaticism almost seemed to be the *raison d'être* of a piece, almost as if Haydn, Mozart, and Beethoven were informing their listeners of a hitherto undisclosed aspect of the compositional process that had been missed by traditional music theory. The primary dyadic conflict, a conflict between a diatonic tone and its chromatic counterpart, told us what the music was "about," so to speak. Furthermore, the recognition of the dyadic conflict also provided insight into the way that Classical-era composers unfolded the entire chromatic aggregate as the issues involving the primary dyad were slowly and carefully expanded and, therefore, developed. Prof. Burnett and Shaugn O'Donnell eventually co-authored an article on this subject, published in *Music Theory Spectrum* (Spring 1996) and entitled "Linear Ordering of the Chromatic Aggregate in Classical Symphonic Music."

By 1998, Prof. Burnett had written a new article on the organization of chromaticism in a diatonic context for the *International Journal of Musicology* (2000) called "Levels of Chromatic Ordering in the First Movements of Haydn's London Symphonies: A New Hypothesis" that discussed his conception of a *Principal* (later changed to *Primary*) *Chromatic Array* (PCA). This was the first time that Prof. Burnett had offered a theoretical explanation of how a composition's dyadic conflicts could be understood as part of a large-scale and methodical unfolding of all twelve pitch classes. The theory also described how the PCA was woven into the harmonic and formal fabric of a work.

At this point, my curiosity about Prof. Burnett's theories was reaching a critical mass, and I was becoming increasingly uncomfortable with the thought that there may have been a very important aspect of the compositional process that had never been discussed, or, for that matter, explored by any of the theorists I had worked with at Queens College or at the City University of New York Graduate Center. By this time, there were already rumors floating around the Graduate Center, particularly among the Schenkerians – the self-appointed arbiters of refined musical taste and decency – that if Burnett's theories (which no one really knew since they wouldn't discuss the theories with him) had any validity, then Schenker himself would have already discovered them. And had they not been worth anything, Schenker would have torn them to shreds long ago in *Das Meisterwerk* as another "negative example." Meanwhile, at Queens College, most of the theorists had stopped talking to Henry. Nothing like what Henry was proposing had ever been conceived of in the theoretical writings of the nineteenth century or the early twentieth century. In fact, a theory postulating a far more structurally significant role for chromaticism than simply a decoration or embellishment of the diatonic background had never been proposed by anyone, with the possible exception of David Epstein, who, in the 1970s, was one of the first theorists to speculate about the power of a single dissonant pitch to determine large-scale motion. But we all knew that chromaticism was a lower-level appendage of the diatonic and, according to Tovey, Rosen, Riemann, Schenker, or anyone else, nothing could alter that ... maybe. In his "Levels of Chromatic Ordering," Burnett had argued that the chromatic was not something structurally trivial, but that the chromatic was at least as significant as the diatonic and that the interaction between the two may have been responsible for the manner in which the entire Classical period evolved. I thought that this might certainly be worth delving into, particularly since I had finished my class work, had passed my exams for the Ph.D. in Music Theory at the Central University of New York Graduate Center, and was ready to start writing my dissertation on the voice-leading aspects of Joseph Haydn's symphonies. But I also believed that I could not honestly pursue this project without evaluating the new theory. Many graduate students I knew had been studying Prof. Burnett's ideas in his Pro-Seminar classes and many had indicated that here was something new and exciting, and something to which they, as theorists, composers, and musicologists, could relate.

I finally sat down with Henry and we discussed his new approach in considerable detail. He also agreed to be the primary reader for my dissertation, "Voice-Leading and Chromatic Techniques in Expositions of Selected Symphonies of Joseph Haydn, Introducing a New Theory of Chromatic Analysis," which was successfully defended in 1999. The "new theory of chromatic analysis" included the application of the primary chromatic array and Burnett's newest contribution, eleven-pitch-class systems analysis, in conjunction with extensive Schenkerian voice-leading graphs to the two groups of Haydn's Paris symphonies. What had been most interesting about the project for me was Burnett's new ideas about how the tonic key of a composition could be expressed in terms of a collection of eleven notes, meaning a pitch field consisting of all the notes of the tonic diatonic scale and all the chromatics except for the one note written either as a minor third or as an augmented second above the tonic. This part of the theory was the most recent and the one that was the most difficult to prove consistently and convincingly, since it ultimately was derived from modality and the distinction between *musica recta* and *musica ficta* pitch classes in the Medieval/Renaissance gamut. Burnett and I had met quite a number of times and communicated via email and telephone about how the "missing pitch" would alter the gamut of eleven notes from its primary collection into a complementary collection of eleven notes with its own "missing pitch." I remember how painstaking it was to figure out how this whole process worked, and the most difficult aspect for both of us, I think, was trying to solve the problem without resorting to the standard harmonic interpretations we had both learned as students at Queens College. At the point when Henry had finally solved the problem, I had already begun to analyze my symphonies and eventually incorporated this newest aspect of the theory into the dissertation.

By now, both of us had been attempting to apply rules of eleven-pitch-class analysis or, as we started to call it, "systems analysis," to music other than that of the Classical era. Henry was now organizing his Pro-Seminar lecturers around the music he would normally use for that class but was now incorporating aspects of his new theory to explain facets of the music that had previously never been discussed, much to the annoyance of the theory faculty, but to the delight of the composition majors in the class, who invariably grasped the relevance of Henry's ideas as they pertained to their own compositions.

We also found it startling, and, may I add, somewhat unnerving, that systems analyses could be successfully applied to music of the Romantic period, to Schoenberg's free atonal period, music of the Baroque, and now, most shocking, music of the sixteenth century. I began to think that Henry Burnett had done something unprecedented in the history of Western music theory: he had uncovered a common principle underlying all art music from the Renaissance up to World War I. In fact, much to the consternation of some of our colleagues, I started referring to Henry's theory as the first and only "unified field theory" in the history of the discipline, although I'll add that Felix Salzer had attempted the articulation of a broad theory, too, in his *Structural Hearing*, applying the theory of Heinrich Schenker to compositions from Gregorian chant to Hindemith piano sonatas.

The point cannot be made too strongly: Henry Burnett had uncovered a single principle that draws together all styles of art music from sixteenth-century chromatic modality to early twentieth-century atonality. Previously, we had been taught that modality had (somehow mysteriously) evolved into tonality, and had reached a pinnacle in the late works of Beethoven, and then, through the successful experiments of Wagner, Liszt, and Richard Strauss, tonality had (somehow mysteriously) dissolved into atonality. What we were not taught was that the evolving composition process was not and had never been contingent upon the artificial boundaries of discrete style periods.

Burnett noticed that certain scholars, particularly Eric Chafe, had begun to discuss the tonal language of Claudio Monteverdi using hexachordal analysis to help describe the harmonic properties of seventeenth-century composition. Burnett's contribution to the discussion was his contention that the issue of mode was not as pivotal as the issue of gamut, particularly as it related to eleven-pitch-class systems in Monteverdi's madrigals. His article "A New Theory of Hexachord Modulation in the Late Sixteenth and Early Seventeenth Centuries" was published in the *International Journal of Musicology* in 1999. Of course, by this time, we had already noticed that the same (or similar) principles explained not only Monteverdi's tonal language, but also Corelli's, Handel's, Bach's, Sammartini's, Haydn's, etc., and therefore, a sensitivity to the issues surrounding *prima* and *secunda* compositional techniques had persisted in the music of later periods.

In 2000, Henry and I decided that the best way to proceed was to author jointly an extensive article that drew together my Haydn symphony analyses and speculations about eleven-note gamuts in Bach's keyboard works plus Henry's now-extensive analyses of Schubert's C major String Quintet. The article would have to begin with the simplest ideas of the primary chromatic array and continue through systems analysis and the concept of the missing pitch. By this time, these new ideas included a theory of complementary tritone symmetries to explain the circumstances surrounding the missing pitch and alternative eleven-note gamuts, diagrams of systems analysis coordinated with the circle of fifths (which we now thought of as a "circle of tritones"), and some of Henry's extensive note-to-note analyses of Schubert and Mozart. The article, called "Eleven Pitch-Class Tonality: A New Theory of Symmetrical Divisions Underlying 'Key-Centered' Tonality," which we originally conceived as being about 50 pages long, was already close to 120 pages not including musical examples, making it increasingly unlikely that any of the American theory journals would pick it up. Around the same time, I presented a conference paper entitled "Hidden Thirds Behind the Quinten's Fifths: Symmetrical Properties and Formal Organization in Haydn's String Quartet in D minor, op. 76 no. 2" at New York University for the April 2000 meeting of the New York State Music Theory Society. Although there was resistance to the theory, there was also much interest on the part of theorists, who were intrigued by the prospect of a new theory of tonality that potentially had such far-reaching consequences.

But not all aspects of the theory had yet reached completion. In late 2001, Henry finally discovered his long-sought-after theory of counterpoint to explain the coincidence of the primary chromatic array and the formal organization of sonata form. Henry's concern was still to comprehend how one might proceed compositionally. After all, all the composers whose music was keeping us busy had studied and taught species counterpoint. But, at least in school, counterpoint was usually taught almost as something autonomous and divorced from harmony, while the study of theory was very often taught as primarily a harmonic discipline with contrapuntal appendages. Henry was suggesting that both were part of a much larger compositional process that was intricately related to the evolution of sonata form in the eighteenth and nineteenth centuries, and which could better explain unusual harmonic goals in the more problematic works of Beethoven, Schumann, and Brahms. For example, Henry discovered that the seemingly off-the-wall motion from D minor to C major as a structural area in the first half of the Scherzo from Beethoven's Ninth Symphony was accomplished by simply expanding the D♮–A♮ tonic fifth to a sixth, D♮–B♮, and then resolving the sixth to a C octave. In other words, the arrival to so distant a harmonic area was the result of a large-scale first- and second-species progression 5–6–8 operating on the deepest structural level. Unfortunately, this aspect of the theory is not covered in the present book.

The addition of all this new material to the already extensive existing body of work would have made publication as an article unwieldy and beyond the scope of most American theory journals. Colleagues at the Aaron Copland School of Music

(Queens College) suggested that a book would be a more appropriate publishing medium. What follow, then, are the basic ideas behind the theory which we now believe can be addressed completely and fully only within the proportions of a book, and I am honored to be part of the theory's dissemination. We both hope that the publication of this book will generate a considerable amount of interest, discussion, and much-needed flat-out controversy in the increasingly complacent world of music theory. Personally, I think that Henry's theory is the most important contribution to Western music theory since Schenker's *Die freie Satz* and may be far more revolutionary since it is based on a new understanding of the role played by chromaticism in composition over the past several hundred years and is, therefore, a theory that offers new insight into a broad palette of musical styles.

Chapter One

Introduction

I. Why is a New Theory of Tonality Necessary?

The present study seeks to explore the nature of chromaticism in modal and tonal music from the sixteenth century to the opening of the twentieth. Beginning in the early part of the 1980s, with the help of several outstanding students and colleagues at the Aaron Copland School of Music, City University of New York, Henry Burnett has evolved a comprehensive theory of chromaticism and its role in all aspects of tonal and modal organization.[1]

Chromaticism, and in particular the completion of the chromatic aggregate, is endemic in all but the simplest of tonal pieces. In fact, the introduction of all twelve tones of the chromatic scale can hardly be avoided in any piece admitting to functional triadic tonality whose length is of any consequence. The simple harmonic movement of applied dominants will introduce most of the five chromatic tones, the ones absent usually found as a result of a motion in the opposite direction, in fourths. Since most tonal pieces move in exactly this manner, one is bound to hit all five chromatic tones at some point or other. The question is not whether the total aggregate will be completed – that is a given – but, rather, how the aggregate is partitioned as a future source of developmental material.

On the other hand, chromaticism applied against a diatonic background needs to be qualified and contained if the composer wishes to maintain the integrity of the key. Since a key is defined by certain harmonic progressions and voice-leading motions, a haphazard use of chromatic tones could easily disrupt one's understanding of the underlying tonal structure, and, as a result, negate any meaningful gesture or argument

---

1 Previous publications exploring this topic, used selectively in this book, are: Henry Burnett and Shaugn O'Donnell, "Linear Ordering of the Chromatic Aggregate in Classical Symphonic Music," *Music Theory Spectrum*, 18/1 (1996): 22–50; Henry Burnett, "Levels of Chromatic Ordering in the First Movements of Haydn's London Symphonies: A New Hypothesis," *International Journal of Musicology*, 7 (1998): 113–65; Henry Burnett, "A New Theory of Hexachord Modulation in the Late Sixteenth and Early Seventeenth Centuries," *International Journal of Musicology*, 8 (1999): 115–75. In addition to these must be added the work of Roy Nitzberg, the co-author of the present study. His was the first Ph.D. dissertation to combine traditional Schenkerian analyses with the chromatic theories of Burnett. See "Voice-Leading and Chromatic Techniques in Expositions of Selected Symphonies by Joseph Haydn, Introducing a New Theory of Chromatic Analysis," Ph.D. dissertation, City University of New York, 1999. Nitzberg also presented the new chromatic theory in a paper titled "The Hidden Thirds Behind the Quinten's Fifths: Symmetrical Properties and Formal Organization in Haydn's String Quartet in D minor, op. 76 no. 2," at the Music Theory Society of New York State's annual meeting at New York University, April 8, 2000.

the composer is trying to make working within those compositional parameters. The situation is comparable to painting. The painter deliberately chooses certain colors with which to depict a scene or an emotion. If the prevailing color scheme is pastel in the manner of Renoir, the painter's "key" in this instance, the insertion of dark opaque colors, indiscriminately applied, would draw one's attention away from the main focus of the painting and, indeed, would interfere with one's understanding of the painter's visual deployment, development, if you will, of the painting's primary color scheme.

In tonal music, no less than in art, the composer's choice of chromatic tones at any given moment must be carefully weighed. After all, these tones are perceived against a diatonic scale that is supported by a series of diatonic chords arranged in an asymmetrical hierarchy. If the key that is produced by this arrangement of scale tones and chords is to be understood at all, assuming that is the composer's intent, then certain steps must be taken by the composer to establish that key within the mind of the listener.

For reasons of tonal clarity, again assuming the composer's intent (not all composers seek tonal clarity in their works), most key-centered pieces will begin with relatively few harmonically significant chromatic tones in their opening phrase, or if chromaticism is introduced, care is taken to relegate it to the foreground level as embellishing or passing. Once the all-important tonic–dominant relationship that defines the key takes place, and is understood by the listener, the composer has a certain amount of liberty in increasing the chromatic spectrum. This may take place after only a few bars of music, so long as the key is established as a frame of reference. The situation is not unlike the Baroque concerto practice of beginning an allegro with the *Vordersatz*, a motive that clearly defines the key through the use of tonic and dominant chords in root position.

Naturally, there are mature Classical pieces that deliberately attempt tonal ambiguity at the beginning of a piece, such as Haydn's Quartet op. 33 no. 1 in D, but sooner or later, the key must be evident, or else large-scale prolongation, not to mention the formal design inherent in the sonata form, would be impossible to achieve and, as a result, the recapitulation and final resolution of dissonant issues would be rendered meaningless.

Chromaticism, by its very nature, increases tension, depending on how unstable it renders the prevailing tonality. It is no wonder then that composers tend to increase the density of chromatic material as a piece progresses, thus also heightening the effect of the formal restoration of the tonic, which may or may not occur at the moment of recapitulation. Considering the unstable nature of chromatic pitch classes projected against a diatonic background, it would seem natural that composers would choose their chromatic tones with great care, either as embellishments within the melody or motive, or as chord structures.

So why is a new analytical theory of tonality, form, and style necessary? Simply because traditional musicological/analytical methodologies have been unable to answer satisfactorily so many complex compositional questions, especially those regarding seemingly unexplainable chromatic digressions or substitutions, within the diatonic framework of a modal or tonal composition. One plausible reason for this is that previously musicology, as a scholarly discipline, has been historically transmitted as a compilation of disparate ideologies (for example, philosophy – including "feminism," "queer" musicology, and lately, "disability studies"[2] – archival musicology, theory and analysis, and factual history) that has long resisted any urge to impose a "unified field theory" to interpret the steady metamorphosis of Western art music from its earliest roots in late Medieval modality all the way through twenty-first century atonality. Consequently, the validity of any transformational model or idea concerning the natural evolution of styles is questioned and even frowned upon nowadays as epitomizing some kind of grotesque teleological bigotry. Going against current thought, we believe that the teleological approach aimed at the observation of stylistic change is still valid when considered from the purely compositional perspective.

II. The Concept of Development and its Relationship to the Compositional Process

We begin then by challenging the traditional understanding of development, which we believe to be the very backbone of Western art music uniting all musical periods. We find current definitions of the developmental process inadequate as most concern the manipulation of motives and limit the term to the music specifically of the high Classical and Romantic periods. For instance, Walter Frisch gives the popular definition of "development," as a process "in which the smallest elements of a theme – its intervals and rhythms – are continuously modified."[3] On the contrary, we believe that throughout music history, composers were always sensitive to a developmental process that concentrated on working out specific diatonic and chromatic pitch-class relationships that encompassed entire movements, if not entire compositions, and which resulted in a narration of carefully controlled events that guided the listener from one end of the composition to the other.

In a similar vein, Arnold Schoenberg's theory of the *Grundgestalt* takes the developmental process as a series of events emanating from surface details potentiating a string of incidents that turn motives into far-reaching organizational devices.[4] Charles Rosen's ideas of motivic transformation are also concerned with the manipulation of surface details.[5] Heinrich Schenker, too, believed that great compositions transformed simple foreground events through a series of compositional manipulations that potentially propel a simple motive into higher levels of middleground structure.[6] Schenker's understanding of structural levels and

---

2   See Joseph N. Straus, "Normalizing the Abnormal: Disability in Music and Music Theory," *Journal of the American Musicological Society*, 59/1 (Spring 2006): 113–84.

3   Walter Frisch, *Brahms and the Principle of Developing Variation* (Berkeley, 1984), p. 36.

4   Arnold Schoenberg, *The Musical Idea and the Logic, Technique, and Art of its Presentation: A Theoretical Manuscript by Arnold Schoenberg*, trans. and ed. Patricia Carpenter and Severine Neff (New York, 1995).

5   Charles Rosen, *The Classical Style: Haydn, Mozart, Beethoven* (New York, 1971–72, rev. edn, 1997), *Sonata Forms* (New York, rev. edn, 1988).

6   Heinrich Schenker, *Free Composition*, trans. and ed. Ernst Oster (New York, 1979).

voice-leading revolutionized music theory, finally enabling it successfully to dig beneath immediate foreground events. But even his most profound teachings, as well as the often startlingly original speculations of Riemann, Tovey, Dahlhaus, and others, still provide no comprehensive *theory of development*, and so are ultimately unable to unite the various tendrils of compositional organism into a unified whole. As early as the 1970s some authors attempted to go a step beyond traditional theory. For example, David Epstein courageously offered the idea that a single pitch may be responsible for initiating a whole chain of events that is played out over the course of a composition.[7] James Baker has extensively examined the notion that Classical-era composers seemed to be more than simply interested in composing out the entire chromatic aggregate; in fact, it may have been one of the most significant aspects of Classical-era composition.[8] Eric Chafe has discussed hexachords and the harmonic properties of Monteverdi's conception of modality/tonality.[9] But none of these authors has explored these issues in sufficient depth to develop a theory to support their conclusions.

We believe that the process of compositional development may be defined by a chromatic background that coexists with a diatonic contrapuntal background. In the music examples that follow, we see chromatic events initiated by simple dyad conflicts as foreground manifestations of the interactions of the chromatic and diatonic genera. These chromatic and diatonic events are the two genus expressions of slowly unfolding tonic octaves. In order to help clarify the new theoretical approach, let us briefly examine the way in which a very prominent D♭ is developed in the opening of Haydn's F minor String Quartet op. 20 no. 5. Within the opening harmonic area, the D♭ first appears twice quite innocently as appoggiaturas to C in the opening statement, then as an inversion of a B♭ minor triad, and finally as part of an augmented sixth sonority in the counterstatement/bridge. Gradually, a chromatic element, D♮, is played off the diatonic D♭, and this inflection becomes the basis of a dyad conflict that influences the very essence of the work: both the development section and coda open with D♭ major triads. In fact, we could assert that the D♭/D♮ dyad conflict is responsible for a series of chromatic events that branch outward from this axis, permeating the structure of the quartet. Or it could be argued that the D♭/D♮ dyad conflict, worked out on increasingly deep structural levels, informs the philosophical substance and meaning of the work since the entire composition is organized around events influenced by this simple chromatic event.

Another striking example of Haydn's manipulation of a single pitch-class to effect large-scale harmonic motions occurs in the first movement of his String Quartet op. 64 no. 3. This work has been the subject of extensive analytical discussion, but not a single author has remarked on the working-out process of specific pitch-class

---

7   David Epstein, *Beyond Orpheus: Studies in Musical Structure* (Cambridge, Massachusetts, 1979).

8   James Baker, "Chromaticism in Classical Music," in Christopher Hatch and David W. Bernstein (eds), *Music Theory and the Exploration of the Past* (Chicago, 1993), pp. 233–307.

9   Eric Chafe, *Monteverdi's Tonal Language* (New York, 1992).

material.[10] For reasons that will be elaborated upon later, we note that scale-degree ♭3 is a peculiarly disruptive force in the major mode. In particular, this pitch class often connotes the parallel minor, but may equally be disruptive of the tonal space under various harmonic conditions outside tonic harmony, as in the case of op. 64 no. 3. The first movement of this quartet is in B♭, but Haydn withholds introducing scale-degree ♭3 (D♭) until the "apparent" medial caesura in the dominant harmonic area at m. 33.[11] Instead of bringing the theme to full closure, Haydn undermines the dominant arrival by switching to the minor dominant, F minor. The A♭ thus introduced yields the even more distant D♭ as a harmony in its own right (m. 40). The D♭ has now become the controlling pitch, effectively bringing the entire period (meaning the first attempt to establish the second harmonic area and its extension into the parallel minor of the dominant) in line by turning itself into an augmented sixth chord that resolves to V/V. This prepares the structural arrival to the second harmonic area in m. 48. Haydn further develops this pitch in the development section proper. Here, the theme first presented in m. 33 reappears in B♭ minor (m. 87), D♭ now fulfilling a role that implies the parallel tonic minor. The harmonic area of B♭ minor remains in effect until m. 96, where D♭ now attaches itself to an E♭ triad, creating a dominant seventh and pushing the music into A♭. However, Haydn again thwarts expectations by switching mode and plunging the music into A♭ minor. It is only in m. 102 that D♭ finally relinquishes control of this entire flat-key harmonic progression by its transformation into its enharmonic equivalent, C♯. Once C♯ supersedes D♭, D♭s entirely disappear from the pitch-class landscape and the music begins to move toward sharper keys in preparation for the recapitulation. Thus, a substantial portion of the development section is devoted to an unfolding narrative about D♭ and its controlling influence over the harmonic middleground.

Beethoven's "Waldstein" Piano Sonata in C major op. 53, composed about three decades after the Haydn quartet, follows a "Haydnesque" procedure, but takes the simple dyad conflict and promotes it to new levels of developmental sophistication. Beethoven's first use of the chromatic E♭ within a C major context is presented within the first few measures so that the opening statement already contains the chief dyad conflict between the diatonic E♮ and the chromatic E♭. Compared with Haydn's use of D♮ in the op. 20 quartet, which first appears as a simple chromatic passing tone between D♭ and E♭ in the bridge, Beethoven's E♭ has more immediate consequences. Since the opening statement terminates with a cadential 6/4 chord *that includes E♭*, the E♮/E♭ dyad conflict frames the initial period of the sonata's first movement, pushing the chromatic envelope toward a new level of organizational inventiveness.

Yet E♭ is not the only chromatic consideration here, even if it may be the most conspicuous. Within the first couple of measures of the opening statement, both F♯ and B♭ appear in succession, both pitch classes emanating from the diatonic tritone F–B. The F♯ yields the next accidental, a C♯ appoggiatura that decorates the D–G descending scale passage in the upper voice. Just as F♯ and C♯ were generated from

---

10 For a comparative overview of analyses of this work see James Hepokoski, "Beyond the Sonata Principle," *Journal of the American Musicological Society*, 55/1 (2002): 120ff.

11 The terminology used here is from *ibid.*, pp. 123–4.

an implied F♮, the upcoming B♭ in the surprising ♭VII sonority is generated from an explicit B♮ in the bass. Similar to the image of a tree, with F–B as its trunk and with chromatics branching from it, the chromatics themselves now take on a life of their own, generating their own fifths cycles, as if Beethoven were expanding his primary tonal material (C major) with chromatics at both ends of the diatonic spectrum:

$$C\sharp - F\sharp / [F] \leftrightarrow B / B\flat$$

As the bass continues to descend from C to B♭, and then from B♭ to A♭, creating a modally mixed IV6 chord, a filling-in of the chromatic spectrum seems under way: E♭ now enters against the A♭ in the bass and the opening statement cadences on the dominant. The cadence is decorated with ♭6/4 – 5/3, again featuring E♭. The spectrum of notes now expands to

$$C\sharp - F\sharp / [F] \leftrightarrow B / B\flat - E\flat - A\flat$$

which gives us not only all twelve pitch classes within the opening statement but also five chromatic pairs and a plethora of secondary dyadic conflicts.

The pitch, E♭, with its enharmonic respelling as D♯ in the counterstatement/ bridge, becomes, in this new guise, the leading tone of the second harmonic area. In m. 14, a second period begins by repeating the opening statement with rhythmic diminutions. However, at the point where the parallelism between bridge and opening statement is abandoned in m. 18, a new note enters, the expected-next sharp G♯ (as part of a ♯4/2 chord), which initiates a series of enharmonic respellings in the sharp direction. Continuing in fifths, G♯ motivates D♯ (as an appoggiatura to E♮) and then A♯, presented as part of an augmented sixth chord that eventually tonicizes the major mediant in the third period as the second harmonic area of the sonata.

The continual interplay between E♭ and E♮, combined with more surprising enharmonic twists and turns, becomes the lifeblood of the last movement of the "Waldstein" as well. By the time the entire work has reached its conclusion, Beethoven has unfolded ten enharmonic pairs and has employed an array of 22 notes. Each of these events can be traced back to the manner in which Beethoven introduced E♭ in the exposition's opening period!

Traditional theory *à la* Piston would most likely be concerned with the unusual use of chords in the "Waldstein" and their unexpected presentations: actually, the piece is a compulsive chord-labeler's dream (or nightmare, depending upon your outlook). At the point where the second harmonic area would be parsed as V of V of V of V, many students of Piston's theory might run away screaming. Some Riemannian analysts might define the tonality of the second theme as mode mixture of the dominant relative. A motivic analysis might concentrate on the opening melodic gesture, E–F♯–G, following its iterations and transformations over the course of the sonata. A voice-leading analysis in the manner of Heinrich Schenker might also take the E–F♯–G motive as a jumping-off point, explain it as rising organically from scale-degree 3, the *Urlinie* E, and deal with its transformation to E–F♯–G♯ in the bridge after a chromatically delineated transfer of register. Such an analysis would undoubtedly concern itself, too, with the arrival of the second harmonic area in E representing a way station, so to speak, dividing the C–G fifth. Of course, all the chromaticism would be understood as embellishing the tonic background.

In each case, present-day theory attempts to deal with the work as a dry canvas, without concerning itself with the compositional and developmental process. "After all," theorists would undoubtedly argue, "how could we possibly *know* what was going on in Beethoven's head as this masterwork was conceived?" Of course, to claim the *correct* answer to that question would be folly and pretension. What is unique about this new theory, however, is its assumption that there *is* something underneath – perhaps conscious, perhaps unconscious – informing and controlling the compositional process that has never been unearthed. Ours is not a theory of voice-leading, nor is it one of chord-labeling, although it does assume a working knowledge of these important and necessary tools. Also, even though there is an interesting crossover between this theory and meantone tuning, this is not a theory of acoustics, and this area of inquiry will not be addressed in this volume. Our primary investigation is not simply motivic, but more specifically developmental. It is the chromatic element in music that creates the necessity for the developmental element since chromaticism needs both to flourish and to resolve; one way or the other, the tension of chromaticism must be both justified and ameliorated. There has always been a diatonic genus *and* a chromatic one as well. Simply describing the developmental process as one of motivic or thematic manipulation has its limitations; however, discussing chromatic content as part of the pre-compositional material of the musical process creates a new perspective with which to approach an analysis. We explore that dissonant element and how it is presented and resolved on the level of the pitch class. The pitch class determines arrays, conflicts, and inflections from diatonic to flat or sharp equivalents; these elements control the composition and teach us, as stated above, what the whole composition is "about."

The developmental process in classical music exists on many levels. Just as there are an infinite number of pieces, so are there countless ways of exploring the musical material of any one of them. The most obvious method of exploration is closely connected to thematic/motivic variation; meaning that the melodic contour, rhythm, or intervallic structure of a motive is manipulated in such a way that it becomes a source of unity over the course of the movement or work. Very often all the thematic material of a movement is derived from the opening statement; the composer systematically reveals, and works out, each musical element within the motive until all possible constructions seem to be exhausted. This method is closely associated with Beethoven, although the process is equally valid for Haydn and Mozart, not to mention earlier composers such as J.S. Bach. However, underlying the motivic manipulation there are other, subtler developmental procedures that may be revealed only through careful study of the scores. The reasons for these deeper, almost hidden structures is not always easily explained, but they seem to pervade all the major works of the period, most notably in those of Haydn, Mozart, and Beethoven.

The concept is not dissimilar to that used by composers in the later Middle Ages and the Renaissance, where a conspicuous foreground event was supported by a background structure which was not readily apparent. In the Middle Ages, isorhythm was the source of many hidden structures, the slow rate of the tenor and its relationship to *talea* and *color* being almost impossible to discern. In the Renaissance, complex canons, almost amounting to musical games, served the same purpose. For example, the prolation canons of Ockeghem, Josquin, and Pierre de la Rue, where imitations proceeded at different rates of prolation, were not meant to be overly conspicuous. The object was to achieve a perfectly smooth contrapuntal harmony and a regular rhythmic flow, despite the fact that all or some of the voices were moving at different metrical rates. It is virtually impossible to hear that two voices are always in a prolational canon during the Kyrie of Josquin's *Missa L'homme armé super voces musicales*, just as it is virtually impossible to hear that the borrowed *cantus*, the "L'homme armé" melody, begins on subsequent pitch levels of the natural hexachord in each movement of the same mass.

In the latter part of the eighteenth century and the early nineteenth century, these underground manipulations were still utilized, and were just as important to the overall progress of the composition. Disguised developmental procedures now became a deeper-level development within the more foreground, thematic development of the composition: thus while motivic/rhythmic manipulations were carried out on a foreground level, dissonant pitch-class relationships (chromatic tones foreign to the diatonic mode), both as fixed pitch-class configurations and as transpositions of an initial pitch-class configuration, operated concurrently, albeit more discreetly.

This particular developmental process arose from a need to resolve dissonant relationships within a given tonality. In terms of harmony, a dissonance refers to any pitch class that is foreign to the diatonic scale. (In pre-tonal music these pitch classes are derived from the relationship between *musica ficta* and *musica recta*.) In a Classical symphony, one without a slow introduction, dissonant tones appear, at first, embedded within the opening diatonic phrase, often within the immediate context of a chromatic trichord in which a diatonic tone is stated, inflected up or down a half step, and then locally resolved; for example, C as diatonic pitch → C♯ as chromatically inflected pitch → D as tone of resolution. The chromatically inflected tone often moves as a leading tone – and thus an inner voice of some dominant or dominant-related triad – or as a Neapolitan, or often as some kind of ♭VI, including chords of the augmented sixth. Chromatic trichords may appear in any voice and may form the initial articulations of chromatic aggregates.

The chromatic trichord is controlled by a more crucial chromatic pitch-class relationship based upon a "fixed dyad," a diatonic pitch inflected to its nearest half-step neighbor with the same "family" name, such as E♭ to E♯ or A to A♯. This, in turn, becomes the basis for a developmental process that is intricately linked to the completion of the chromatic aggregate. Thus the initial diatonic tone and its inflection become a dyadic seed undergoing growth and transformation over the course of the entire movement. The first movement of Mozart's Symphony no. 40 in G minor provides an excellent case in point. The E♭–D semitone, so prominent in the opening theme, is juxtaposed with an E♮ in the bass of m. 14; an F♮/F♯ is also a prominent dyad before this, but this relationship is a diatonic one in G minor.

The E♮ then descends to an E♭ that supports an augmented sixth chord in the next bar, the two pitch classes, E♮ and E♭, being heard as inflections of one another. More striking is the fact that E♮ in m. 14 is preceded by a B♭ in the same voice, the resulting tritone giving even more prominence to the sudden appearance of the E♮. This same juxtaposition returns 16 bars before the end of the movement, where the E♮/E♭ dyad is resolved into tonic harmony. The same E♭ augmented sixth returns, highlighted by a quarter rest in the line. Interestingly, all the other fixed dyads are resolved at the same time, each one carefully spelled as an inflection of the same pitch class. The E♭/E♮ dyad maintains its prominence throughout the symphony: at the opening of the second harmonic area it appears within a chromatic trichord, F–E♮–E♭, in the strings and is then expanded over the remainder of the exposition. Significantly, this dyad is fixed no matter which local harmony is functional at the moment. In the second movement the E♭/E♮ dyad is the last but most significant of a series of dyadic pairs that are in play throughout the movement. In the fourth movement, the E♭/E♮ dyad is prominent in the opening measures and, surprisingly, remains so until the very end of the symphony with E♮ maintaining its autonomy in rising melodic minor scales in the cellos and basses stated three times eight measures before the double bar. In fact, any expectations we might have had of E♮ finally resolving into its E♭ diatonic counterpart are never fulfilled, perhaps as a manifestation of Mozart's wit.

The effect of a dissonant tone or chord within a diatonic statement of a theme initiates a ripple effect similar to that described in chaos theory. In chaos theory a small, almost insignificant event assumes ever larger and larger proportions that causes a stable system in which it operates to undergo constant deflections and deviations, thus destabilizing that system. The technical name for this process is "sensitive dependence on initial conditions," and would seem to be valid for any situation, scientific or artistic, in which an ordered system is subjected to random variation stemming from an initial, often minuscule, event.[12] Thus, a dissonance implanted within a diatonic line at the outset of a composition assumes ever greater structural significance until it becomes the main preoccupation of the movement, conditioning every event in its course.

Chaos theory acknowledges, however, that what appears to be random is, in fact, pure scientific calculation, "order *masquerading* as randomness."[13] Similarly, what at first appears as a random romp through unrelated dissonant keys in a development section, or as an unusual harmonic gesture within a bridge that leads to a totally "wrong key" at the start of the second harmonic area of the exposition, turns out, after careful examination, to be part of a calculated design, fulfilling the possibilities of the initial chromatic gesture.

For tonal dissonance to operate as a developmental procedure, it must arise from the diatonic background, be worked out through motivic manipulation as well as through projection into deeper levels of structure, and then resolve into the diatonic pitch field from which it emerged. Often this means that the primal dissonance of the

---

12 James Gleick, *Chaos: Making a New Science* (New York, 1987).
13 *Ibid.*, p. 22.

movement, or the entire composition, must seek resolution into the tonic triad. This may not occur until the coda of the sonata-form movement.

Once a dissonant relationship is established at the outset, either as a dyad conflict or as part of a trichord, the natural procedure is then to "work out" the initial chromatic inflection, allowing it to become the focal point of the composition. This is only to be expected since dissonances appearing within an initial phrase tend to lead to their own expansion; a subsequent diatonic motion, without expanding upon the implications of the initial dissonance(s), would only dissolve the tension prematurely.

III. Postulates of the Theory

This study presents a new theory of art music that is a considerable departure from what is generally taught to our students and from what exists in prior treatises. A music theory predicated on an obligatory interaction of the diatonic and the chromatic is incompatible with pre-existing theories that interpret the diatonic as a foundation upon which the chromatic may or may not develop. The present theory can be reduced to a corpus of five essential postulates to delineate its most basic components. Each of these postulates will be subjected to detailed discussion in subsequent chapters.

1. Any tonal or modal composition past the middle of the sixteenth century will seek to unfold both a chromatic and a diatonic octave from the final or tonic of the mode or key over the course of the composition. Specifically, the tendency of the chromatic is to ascend by half step until the octave is completed at *ti–do*, while the tendency of the diatonic is to descend by scale degree until the octave is completed at *re–do*. The two lines are thus controlled by a contrapuntal progression that ultimately achieves octave completion via the major sixth moving to the octave. We call the octave ascent of the chromatic genus to the final or tonic the *Primary Chromatic Array* (PCA), and the descent of the diatonic genus the *Primary Diatonic Array* (PDA). Lesser chromatic orderings that do not seek tonic octave completion occupy a lower level of structure and are called *Secondary Chromatic Arrays* (SCAs).

2. Modes and keys are ultimately derived from larger gamut systems and therefore comprise more than just the seven notes of their respective diatonic octave species. In order for any composition, whether modal or tonal, to prolong its final or tonic through harmonic cadences occupying the middleground, chromatic alterations of diatonic degrees are mandatory. Thus any given mode or key will comprise both diatonic and chromatic pitch classes drawn from the larger gamut systems to which they pertain. However, no mode or tonality ("key") may have more than eleven diatonic and chromatic pitch classes. The twelfth or "missing pitch" of any mode or tonality is that which is not included in the respective gamut system of that mode or tonality. If the twelfth pitch class is included, this signifies a modulation of the gamut or system either up or down depending on how the pitch class is spelled and whether we are dealing with a mode or a key. The missing pitch, thus, is also a "system-shift

motivator;" that is, an individual pitch class that may provoke a modulation from one eleven-pitch-class system to another. Either way, the missing pitch or system-shift motivator is invariably the minor third or augmented second above either the central hexachord of the modal gamut (usually *naturalis* or *mollis*) or of the tonic system of a key (if the tonic system is minor, then the missing pitch is derived from the system of the relative major).

3. In common-practice tonality, any given eleven-pitch-class system is defined by its "consonant tritone;" meaning the tritone that is based on the tonic pitch class of the key and its octave divider (always spelled as a sharp). Again, a minor mode will use the octave divider of its relative major. The missing pitch of any given system will automatically form its own "dissonant tritone," based on its own tonic pitch and its own octave divider. The dissonant tritone forms a symmetrical complement to the consonant tritone of the system since one divides the other exactly at the halfway point. Both tritone complements therefore form a "systems matrix" of minor thirds/augmented seconds. Any composition that contains all twelve pitch classes will inevitably imply a modulation or shift from one tritone eleven-pitch-class area to another. However, no composition that maintains a background key can modulate outside its systems matrix; all modulations of systems relate to the tonic consonant tritone and its complement.

4. Since every mode or key is ultimately derived from a larger gamut system of overlapping hexachords, each gamut system or tonality is harmonically governed by its central hexachord reordered in fifths. Any minor mode key will depend on the hexachord of its relative major since no minor mode hexachord exists. Thus C major can be expressed as a reordered hexachord, F–C–G–d–a–e[14], in which all the strong chords (or harmonic areas) appear at the beginning of the hexachord and all the weaker chords (or harmonic areas) appear at the end of it. A minor, the relative minor of C, follows the same hexachord except that the ordering of keys is reversed (A minor appears at the end of the hexachord and its relative appears at the beginning).

5. Each of the above postulates may be understood ultimately under the control of a background that is organized by the strictest rules of counterpoint. Any valid analytical system must approach a composition within the framework of its basic contrapuntal structure. Both the PCA and the PDA may be viewed respectively as (1) the pairing of soprano and tenor voices of a fundamental two-part texture, and (2) a species contrapuntal reduction of the essential structure of any given composition. The length and complexity of the composition determine the ways in which its fundamental structure is fleshed out, creating a unique entity. Most compositions would display at least a subsidiary-level voice part between the soprano and tenor and, more often than not, another subsidiary-level voice part in the bass. Therefore, the developmental process, with all its diatonic and chromatic adjuncts in the form of its various arrays, is bound by the laws of counterpoint.

---

14 In abbreviated references to keys, upper-case letters and Roman numerals denote major keys; lower-case letters and Roman numerals denote minor keys.

By returning the chromatic to its rightful role with the diatonic as co-progenitor of the compositional process, we believe that music theory will have another, and perhaps, more successful methodology with which to interpret composition, chromaticism, and the developmental process. Subsequent chapters will flesh out the postulates of the theory and apply them to works from the literature.

Chapter Two

Eleven-Pitch-Class Tonality

I. A New Theory of Symmetrical Divisions Underlying "Key-Centered" Tonality

Conventional tonal theory interprets chromaticism as a diatonic adjunct that either embellishes the tonal surface or supports the coherence of higher structural goals in a voice-leading fabric.[1] In this context, chromaticism is understood to support and define the diatonic key. However, we propose a new construct where the roles traditionally assigned to the diatonic and chromatic are reconsidered. This theory places structural emphasis on tritone symmetries and eleven-pitch-class harmonic areas and, in so doing, uncovers common compositional approaches to specific chromatic relationships of seemingly divergent musical epochs. Therefore, the theory attempts to create a basis for a discussion of *commonality* among style periods whereas musical historiography has essentially focused upon *distinction*. In our view, changes in style occur as composers face the challenge of presenting the chromatic aggregate (the "commonality") in new ways within the diatonic surface, whether that surface is modal, tonal, atonal, or a hybrid of any of these. Further, we hope to accomplish something never before attempted on a large scale: to provide musical discourse with a "unified field theory" in a bid to tie together loose ends that have begun to form as the discipline has become more sophisticated and increasingly successful in determining the nuts and bolts of musical language. Again, our jumping-off point differs from that of conventional theory since we begin not with the diatonic, and the relationships among scale steps, but with the total gamut of, and wide variety of, compositional choices present in the chromatic. We offer this new theoretical approach as a means toward the explanation of the potentiating force of the chromatic pitch class within a tonal context and, in so doing, attempt to answer some problematic questions as yet unanswered by present-day music theory.

Our theory of eleven-pitch-class tonality encompasses two divergent but interrelated hypotheses that, when considered in tandem, form a larger and more meaningful construct: the first involves the consistent absence of a specific pitch class (referred to as "the missing pitch") from the total chromatic aggregate, yielding an eleven-pitch-class field; the second involves the Primary Chromatic Array (PCA), in which the total chromatic aggregate is linearized, in ascending half-step order, over the course of entire movements.

---

1   For example, see Edward Aldwell and Carl Schachter, *Harmony and Voice Leading*, 2nd edn (New York, 1989), p. 13, where the authors state: "chromatic elements embellish a basically diatonic substructure; the term *chromatic* (Greek *chroma*, color) clearly conveys the decorative character of these tones."

The term "eleven-pitch-class tonality" relates directly to the first of these concepts, that of the missing pitch. The nomenclature associated with an eleven-pitch-class field is the "system." A system comprises an eleven-pitch-class field or collection whose missing pitch determines the specific system. For example, a "0" system is an eleven-note collection whose root is C (C = 0) and which contains every chromatic note within that octave except E♭ or D♯. A root is defined here as the pitch class that generates any given eleven-pitch-class collection. The "root" of any given system is not to be confused with the "key:" a "0" system can accommodate any number of keys formed from the field of eleven pitch classes and ordered into a harmonic progression tonicizing a local harmonic area. If one numbers each note of a chromatic scale as an ordered sequence of pitch classes from 0 to 11, E♭ or D♯ is pitch class (pc) 3. In general terms, therefore, pc 3 is the missing pitch from the total chromatic aggregate. More specifically, in a "0" system, the missing pitch, pc 3, is spelled as either E♭ or D♯. Therefore, the missing pitch of any system is that pitch which is a minor third or augmented second above the root.

Other recent theories seemingly address the issue of structurally significant third relationships in chromatic contexts and as expressions of a tonic background. One branch of music theory that has contributed some of the most recent and most significant research on chromaticism in tonal music calls itself "Neo-Riemannian." It addresses music that maintains its formal tonal and triadic underpinnings, but whose tonal unity is often indefinite or ambiguous. Such music is represented in works of Wagner, Liszt, Scriabin, early Schoenberg, and others, but may also encompass unusual harmonic progressions by Beethoven, Schumann, or even Mozart. The Neo-Riemannians suggest that even though this music employs explicit tonal passages and even tonally conceived cadence formulas, its hybrid nature has left more traditional analytical methods with less-than-successful interpretations of a significant body of literature.

David Lewin is one of the first of the Neo-Riemannians to examine these problematic works.[2] Lewin suggests a contiguous line of major or minor thirds, derived from the alignment by thirds of two series of perfect fifths, where any three successive choices of notes will create a consonant triad. He employs the series b♭–D♭–f–A♭–c–E♭–g–B♭–d–F–a–C–e–G–b–D–f♯–A–c♯–E–g♯–B–d♯ as a tool to determine the relational properties of the harmonic organization of these works. This harks back to the mid-nineteenth-century theories of Hugo Riemann. Edward Lowinsky has referred to the harmonic language of this difficult music as "triadic atonality,"[3] while Richard Cohn has used the term "triadic post-tonality."[4] Such discussions recall previous efforts of Adele Katz,[5] Carl Dahlhaus,[6] and Gregory

---

2   David Lewin, "A Formal Theory of Generalized Tonal Functions," *Journal of Music Theory*, 26/1 (1982): 23–60.

3   Edward Lowinsky, *Tonality and Atonality in Sixteenth-Century Music* (Berkeley and Los Angeles, 1961).

4   Richard Cohn, "Introduction to Neo-Riemannian Theory: A Survey and Historical Perspective," *Journal of Music Theory*, 42/2 (Fall 1988): 167–80.

5   Adele Katz, *Challenge to Musical Tradition* (New York, 1945).

6   Carl Dahlhaus, *Between Romanticism and Modernism: Four Studies in the Music of the Later Nineteenth Century*, trans. Mary Whittall (Berkeley and Los Angeles, 1980).

Proctor.[7] Cohn points out that "both Neo-Riemannian and post-structuralist paradigms ... recognize the potential for tonal disunity in music that uses classical harmonies, and accordingly resists shoehorning all chromatic triadic music into the framework of diatonic tonality."[8]

It must be underscored, however, that the prevalent major-third or minor-third relationships described in traditional Riemannian and Neo-Riemannian theory have no affinity whatsoever to the present theory's identification of pc 3 as the missing note of an eleven-pitch-class area. While thirds are significant entities both in the present theory and in Neo-Riemannianism, the latter posits the third as an organizational feature of more foreground elements in relevant works related to the interaction of primary chordal harmonies and potential substitutions for them. The present theory, on the other hand, emphasizes fixed minor third relationships as a by-product of the equal subdivision of the tritone. These third relationships represent the interaction among background complementary eleven-pitch-class areas.

In our basic definitions of systems, we see that in a 1♯ system, a system that unfolds eleven notes above the root G, pc 3 is B♭ or A♯; in a 1♭ system, a system whose root is F, pc 3 is A♭ or G♯. The system, then, is defined by the root pitch class of the major-mode diatonic scale associated with that collection of notes. Consequently, a composition in G major or one in E minor would reside within a 1♯ system whose root is G, while a composition in D major or B minor would be said to be in a 2♯ system whose root is D. Notice, too, that the present theory views the diatonic key as a "subset" of an eleven-pitch-class collection identified by its key signature and by its missing pitch: a missing pitch of C♯ or D♭ would signify a piece of music whose diatonic key is B♭ major or G minor and whose operational system is defined by its signature; however, the note that generates a 2♭ system, meaning its root, is B♭. Therefore, we consider the minor mode as a reordering of the major mode. The consideration of the minor mode ultimately derived from the major has it roots in the earlier church modes, whose octave species, whether dorian or mixolydian, derive from reorderings of the natural gamut of overlapping major third (*mi–fa*) hexachords. This will be discussed more fully in Chapter 3.

The introduction of the missing pitch within the context of an eleven-pitch-class field (not an unusual occurrence since, after all, most compositions use all twelve pitch classes) indicates a transposition from one eleven-note pitch field to another. For example, the use of E♭ in a "0" system moves us into a 3♭ system. Why this must happen will be considered below in the discussion of the "system-consonant tritone;" however, for now, it must be noted that the employment of E♭ in C major is much more than a simple "borrowing" from the tonic minor since the E♭ is the root of a new eleven-pitch-class field that has a signature of three flats and which contains the C minor diatonic scale as a subset.

It must be emphasized that the missing pitch is only necessarily missing from *any given eleven-note field* when compared with the entire chromatic aggregate. The term "missing" should not be inferred to mean a pitch missing from *the composition*

---

7   Gregory Proctor, "Technical Bases of Nineteenth-Century Chromatic Tonality", Ph.D. dissertation, Princeton University, 1978.

8   Cohn, "Introduction to Neo-Riemannian Theory," p. 169.

or the last chromatic to enter the total pitch field; pc 3 will enter whenever the compositional argument demands its presence.

All eleven-pitch-class systems are constructed around a "system-consonant" tritone, meaning that tritone which divides the root or tonic octave at its midpoint. Again, in reference to the "0" system, C–F♯ is the system-consonant tritone since F♯ is the symmetrical axis of the C octave. Notice, too, that the missing pitch divides the system-consonant tritone at *its own midpoint*: in the "0" system, E♭ (or D♯) symmetrically divides C–F♯. Therefore, depending upon the way in which the missing pitch is introduced into a composition, in any of its enharmonic variants, pc 3 bisects the system-consonant tritone symmetrically. We will see later that the enharmonic choice within a compositional context for pc 3 determines the role of the missing pitch and the determination of the motion from one eleven-pitch-class system to another. Therefore, enharmonic equivalence has no place in this theory.

The division of the system-consonant tritone at its midpoint creates a consequent "system-dissonant tritone," which is defined as that tritone which includes the missing pitch (pc 3) and which further implies a complementary eleven-pitch-class system where that particular tritone would, thus, be "system consonant." In a "0" system, the system-dissonant tritone may be spelled as either E♭–A or A–D♯, depending upon the spelling of pc 3.

Notice that the tritone discussed here is *literally* a tritone (an augmented fourth) as opposed to the interval of a diminished fifth. Therefore, the system-consonant tritone of a "0" system will consistently be spelled C–F♯, not C–G♭. The tritone G♭–C would be system-consonant in a 6♭ eleven-note system. The missing pitch spelled E♭ in a "0" system would indicate that pitch as the root of its own 3♭ eleven-pitch-class system (whose system-consonant tritone is E♭–A), whereas the missing pitch spelled D♯ would indicate that pitch as the octave divider of a 3♯ system a tritone below it, one whose system-consonant tritone is A–D♯ (see Figure 2.1).

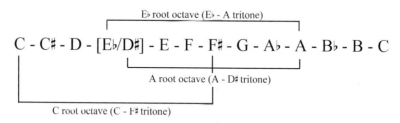

Figure 2.1 The system-consonant tritone and the two system-dissonant tritones of a "0" eleven-pitch-class system: note that the E♭/D♯ missing pitch is in brackets

Whereas prevailing music theories of the common-practice period, from Hugo Riemann to Heinrich Schenker, treat the chromatic aggregate as a colorfully fleshed-out diatonicism, the theory of eleven-pitch-class tonality treats the diatonic as a special case, or, as stated above, a subset, of the chromatic eleven-note system. Also, since this is not a theory of diatonicism, it is also not, nor can it be, a theory informed by voice-leading principles. As a result, individual pitch classes designated as structurally significant in eleven-pitch-class analysis may seem unusual choices to those conversant with modern diatonic theories. This will become particularly noticeable in analyses that utilize the PCA, the second hypothesis of eleven-pitch-class tonal analysis.

Simply defined, the term "Primary Chromatic Array," as we have described this organizational entity, describes a higher-level unfolding of each chromatic pitch class of the aggregate successively, starting from pc 0, the tonic pitch class of the composition, until the entire chromatic octave (including the missing pitch) has been unfolded over the course of a movement. Especially in sonata-form movements, large segments of the PCA (pcs 0–7, for instance, counting the tonic as pc 0) will repeat themselves before reaching octave completion, and within differing harmonic contexts. The total chromatic octave itself may be repeated, as it usually is in a recapitulation, depending on the length and complexity of the composition.[9] Significantly, the PCA may inform the harmonic structure of the movement through compositional choices of structural harmonic goals on both middleground and background levels.

Composers may or may not be conscious of this unfolding, since much of it happens as a condition of tonality regardless of whether the composer intends it or not. George Perle refers to the unconscious application of characteristic stylistic conventions as part of the toolbox of "precompositional" ideas that permeate all compositions within a given temporal vocabulary.[10] These are the concepts that are taught to undergraduates who still need to learn the basic "nuts and bolts" of music. We expect the symphonies of Mozart and Haydn to have a great commonality of harmonic, melodic, and formal features; but, on the other hand, it is less likely that the surface details of works by Mozart and Ravel will be as similar. As composers become increasingly separated in time, these precompositional ideas vary accordingly. On the other hand, Perle also discusses those issues that are composition-specific, those that surpass the ordinary and move into the realm of the true creative process where the composer attains an acute realization of the internal logic and rationale of his compositional material and is able to develop such material in a manner which is both internally rational and creative. He employs the term "reflexive reference" to describe this, a term originally utilized to describe poetry.[11]

The PCA, then, functions on both levels: we have yet to examine a chromaticized work where the PCA fails to operate convincingly. And yet, there also seem to be as many cases where the PCA acts as a determining compositional force within the

---

9   For a more detailed discussion of the derivation of the PCA (originally designated as the *Principal* [later changed to *Primary*] Chromatic Array) and its manifold presentations in sonata-form movements, see Henry Burnett, "Levels of Chromatic Ordering in the First Movements of Haydn's London Symphonies: A New Hypothesis," *International Journal of Musicology*, 7 (1998): 113–65.

10   George Perle, *Serial Composition and Atonality* (Berkeley and Los Angeles, 1977), p. 8 n. 12.

11   George Perle, *Twelve-Tone Tonality* (Berkeley and Los Angeles, 1977), p. 162; Perle cites Joseph Frank, "Spatial Form in Modern Literature," in Mark Schorer et al. (eds), *Criticism: The Foundations of Modern Literary Judgment* (New York, 1948), p. 383.

work, each successive chromatic entity becoming an apparently purposeful event as the composition moves from one structural goal to the next. We will see an example of this in the analysis of the Schubert C major String Quintet below. Also, some of Beethoven's more complex compositions lend themselves particularly well to PCA analysis. The emphasis that Beethoven often places upon the Neapolitan within the first period – for example, in both first movements of the "Appassionata" Piano Sonata in F minor op. 57 and the String Quartet op. 132 in A minor – dramatizes the position of pc 1 before it ascends to pc 2 by providing it with its own harmonic area. Especially in his late works, Beethoven seems to take great pains to articulate many of the PCA pitch classes, giving these tones not only harmonic support, but even more dramatically, their own harmonic areas.

Since the PCA operates on the deepest structural level, and is the slowest-moving in its unfolding, other chromatics, not in any particular order, may be presented around it, always moving at faster rates and occupying lower structural levels (such as foreground chromatic scales or segments thereof, etc.). These create secondary chromatic arrays (SCAs) that occupy the foreground.[12] This may be likened to the various functions of the dominant chord in Schenkerian analysis, whether one hears it locally as a foreground event or operating on a deeper background level, informing the design and structure of the movement. In voice-leading analysis, dominant triads will appear all over, but only one obtains the highest level of structural significance. So too do chromatic pitch classes operate within various levels of chromatic arrays depending on their own degrees of structural magnitude. This places the choice of a single note, even one that may appear to be quite secondary by the voice-leading criteria, in a potentially active, and therefore quite significant, position. Consequently, we have discovered that particular gravity is often accorded pc 3 at the point where it is unfolded in the PCA. We will see later that the interaction of the two possible enharmonic presentations of pc 3 in conjunction with the unfolding PCA becomes an exceptionally important compositional attribute.

II. Eleven-Pitch-Class Systems: Their Relevance and Application to Works in the Literature

A. The Bach Inventions and Well-Tempered Clavier, Book 1

We begin this part of the discussion with a simple observation: several of Bach's two-part inventions unfold only eleven pitch classes and the missing pitch class is invariably the same in each case. That is, if one catalogs all the notes used by Bach to write the Two-Part Invention in C major, only eleven are found; the notes of the C major scale plus C♯, F♯, G♯, and B♭. The note E♭ and its enharmonic, D♯, are absent. In each of the five inventions in C, D, E♭, F, and B♭, basically short, diatonic, single-issue compositions, the same eleven notes are used, in the movable-*do* sense. In the complete set of 15 inventions, eight are in major keys. (The minor

---

12 See Burnett, "Levels of Chromatic Ordering" for a more detailed discussion of secondary arrays.

mode, and the special considerations surrounding minor mode in reference to this theory, will be discussed later.) Of those eight, five have only eleven pitches and the same pitch class, pc 3, is missing from each of those five. The question may therefore be raised: does this indicate Bach's sensitivity to an obscure chromatic issue, or is it just coincidental?[13] Of the twelve available pitch classes in C major, pc 3, spelled as either D♯ or E♭, is the most difficult to unfold in a simple diatonic context without raising various chromatic voice-leading issues. One could argue that Bach omits pc 3 in these five instances, perhaps, to avoid even a very local tonicization of iii, where pc 3 would be spelled D♯, or even a short excursion into the minor mode where pc 3 would be spelled E♭. However, we believe such potential explanations to be inadequate. Instances of motions to iii within the major mode abound in Baroque compositions at least since the publications of Corelli's opp. 1–4 in the late 1690s. In particular, Baroque concertos often use iii as the penultimate goal before the tonic return. But these pieces are extensive and use the motion to iii to achieve harmonic climax, consequently necessitating "modulations" from one eleven-pitch-class system to another (this will be discussed fully in Chapter 3). One could argue, then, that Bach's decision to avoid the entry of a iii triad or to avoid the parallel minor could have been conditioned upon his purposeful avoidance of pc 3 within the context of a short composition.

Sensitivity to an eleven-pitch-class issue, with special attention paid to pc 3, continued well beyond the late Renaissance and Baroque eras. For example, the slow introduction to Beethoven's Symphony no. 1 in C major uses only eleven pitch classes, and the only one missing is pc 3; by the time it finally enters, we are already in the bridge passage of the exposition. On the other end of the compositional spectrum, the opening period (mm. 1–11) of Schoenberg's op. 11 no. 1 uses only eleven pitches and, consistent with its "key signature" of no sharps or flats, the missing pitch is E♭ or D♯ (this will be discussed in Chapter 8). Interestingly, E♭ emerges in a significant way in the following two periods, just before the central section.

Of course, the number of pitch classes a composer chooses to use will vary from one composition to the next depending on length, circumstance, and complexity; pieces may draw upon fewer than eleven pitch classes just as they may contain the total aggregate. Bach's other three major-mode inventions from this same collection vary in the total number of pitch classes they contain. For example, the Invention in

---

13 This is not the first time that questions about the supremacy of eleven notes have appeared in the theory world. Such observations have been made by theorists and composers such as Edward Lowinksy in reference to Renaissance motets (see his *Secret Chromatic Art in the Netherlands Motet* [New York, 1946], p. 100 n. 34). The composer Henry Weinberg, professor emeritus at the Aaron Copland School of Music, City University of New York, has often observed in his lectures and seminars that Orlando di Lasso consistently unfolds eleven pitch classes in his motets and madrigals. Henry Burnett has gone a step further by noting in his "A New Theory of Hexachord Modulation in the Late Sixteenth and Early Seventeenth Centuries," *International Journal of Musicology*, 8 (1999): 115–75, that in the vast majority of compositions in Monteverdi's madrigal collections (1) eleven notes are unfolded and sectional divisions of longer madrigals separate eleven-note gamuts, (2) at points of modulation, different eleven-note gamuts are unfolded, and (3) in each eleven-note gamut, the same pitch class, pc 3, is missing. This will be further discussed in Chapter 3.

G major uses only nine notes, the seven diatonic ones plus F♮ and C♯. The pitches B♭ and A♯, which would be the enharmonic variants of pc 3 in a 1♯ system (where G is the root and A♯/B♭ is the missing pitch), are not used. The designation "1♯ system" refers to a field of eleven notes where G is the root and where A♯/B♭ is the missing pitch.

In the Invention in A major, pc 3 is present, spelled only as B♯. Each time B♯, the system-shift motivator, is present (mm. 10–12), it occurs as a localized leading tone, part of an applied chord to C♯ minor (iii), first as V7/iii and afterwards as VII^07/iii. The second chordal form, the diminished seventh chord, particularly interests us here because the seventh of the chord, A♮, is present each time, just after pc 3 enters, effectively preventing the 3♯ root system from shifting up to a 6♯ system.

To clarify, in a 3♯ system, the system-consonant tritone is A–D♯. The system-dissonant tritone, F♯–B♯, includes the missing pitch of the 3♯ system. Therefore, we could say that the use of the missing pitch, B♯, functioning as a system-shift motivator, propels us three notches clockwise along the circle of fifths into a system whose tritone F♯–B♯ is system-consonant, and where F♯ is the root of a new eleven-note system. As a result, F♯–B♯ becomes the system-consonant tritone of the new 6♯ system. The missing pitch, pc 3, of the 6♯ system, is A♮ (a minor third above F♯), the root of the original 3♯ tonic system. (The other possibility would be G×, the enharmonic of A♮, a note which does not appear in this invention.) We contend, therefore, that the interaction of system-shift motivators between B♯ and A♮ in A major has both a dynamic disruptive *and* a stabilizing effect. Thus, in any major-mode tonality, a diminished seventh chord that contains pc 3 as one of its members (spelled as either a minor third or an augmented second above the tonic) simultaneously contains both system-shift motivators: the missing pitch of the tonic system and the missing pitch of the complementary dissonant system. The two pcs effectively "cancel each other out," preventing a system modulation. "System modulation" or "system shift" refers to the motion, either "real" or "implied," from one eleven-pitch-class field to another occasioned by the introduction of pc 3, the missing pitch of the prevailing eleven-pitch-class field. A real modulation will remain in the new eleven-pitch-class field whereas an implied modulation will immediately introduce the "correcting" missing pitch needed to return to the tonic system. The B♯ diminished seventh chord referred to in the A major invention would therefore be said to imply a shift of system but without realizing such a shift.

The relationship between systems and harmonic arcas needs to be briefly addressed here. The modulation from a 3♯ to a 6♯ system in the A major invention is locally articulated by the prolongation of, first, A major and, afterwards, C♯ minor. Although C♯ minor as a tonic entity would have four sharps in its key signature, here we find that the harmonic area around C♯ minor is subsumed under a briefly expressed 6♯ system; that is, C♯ minor as a localized harmonic area is a subset of a 6♯ system. As previously stated, it is important not to confuse the key signature of a diatonic prolongation (had it really been a tonic) with its system; only the key signature of the background tonic of a composition and that of its tonic system will be identical. Similarly in tonal voice-leading analysis, a brief – or even a lengthy – excursion into a non-tonic harmonic area does not usually signal a motion away from the background tonic sufficient to displace it tonally.

The final invention to be examined is the one in E major, the only one of the group of 15 that Bach organized in binary form. This invention is an excellent example of the dramatic interplay of opposing pitch classes of competing consonant and dissonant systems. Again, like the A major invention, the E major invention uses pc 3 spelled exclusively as an augmented second above the tonic. In E major, a 4♯ system with E as its root, the missing pitch may be spelled as either G♮ or F×; here, however, Bach consistently uses the F× spelling. Therefore, each use of F×, as a system-shift motivator, will propel us from the tonic 4♯ system to its complementary 7♯ system (F× divides the C♯ octave symmetrically), and, consequently, the tonic, E, will bring us back into the tonic system again.

Example 2.1 Bach, Invention in E major, mm. 21–42

Here, the missing pitch does not appear until the first part of the *B* section, after the first double bar, during a tonicization of G♯ minor (iii in E major) that succeeds a cadence on the dominant at the end of the *A* section (Example 2.1). An F× is presented as a leading tone in this area and, in m. 29, brings us into a 7♯ system; when E♮ finally enters uncontested in m. 32 (the effect of the E♮ in m. 30 is immediately negated by the F×s surrounding it), it momentarily restores the tonic 4♯ system. However, between mm. 37 and 43, a tug-o'-war between F× and E♮ is finally settled in favor of E♮ and the conclusive return to the tonic 4♯ system in m. 43 coincides with the uninterrupted final prolongation of tonic harmony. In fact, the cadence in G♯ minor in mm. 41–2 is directly followed by a return to the opening measures of the invention in invertible counterpoint; there is no B major dominant, nor is there, it seems, the need for any, to smooth over the transition from G♯ minor to E major: the return of E♮ is sufficient to restore both the tonic system and the tonic key without any further harmonic elaboration.

One can only speculate as to Bach's motivation for exclusively using the "sharp" spellings of pc 3 in the major-mode inventions that employ all twelve notes. However, two fundamental points need to be stated here: when a composition presents only eleven pitch classes, it will invariably be pc 3 that is absent; second, when that twelfth note appears, its deployment will initiate a chain of events that will figure prominently in the development of that composition.

We postulate, then, that the introduction of pc 3 creates a unique kind of chromatic dissonance which effects a disruption of the tonal fabric in the prevailing eleven-note pitch field. However, it is the crucial interaction between the system-consonant tritone and its system-dissonant complementary tritone that gives rise to a special affiliation between system-shift motivators – pc 3 of the tonic system and pc 3 of the complementary systems. In a "0" system, such a partnership of motivators would exist between the notes E♭ and F♯ (where the presence of E♭, pc 3 of the "0" system, would create an affiliation with F♯, pc 3 of the 3♭ system) or between the notes D♯ and C (D♯, pc 3 of the "0" system, would interact with C♮, pc 3 of the 3♯ system). It should be noted, too, that the intervallic relationship between these pairs of notes is either a *minor third* or an enharmonically respelled *minor third*. The two tritone pairs form a larger network of minor third relationships that *operates beneath the surface level of the tonic unfolding*; an equalizing of the interaction between the tonic unfolding on the one hand, and the tritone systems operating underneath on the other, becomes increasingly relevant toward the end of the nineteenth century and into the twentieth century.

In compositions where all twelve pitch-classes are present, pc 3 invariably appears in ways that are noticeably distinctive. We have examined some examples where pc 3 is written as an augmented second above the tonic. Now we will examine the Prelude in C major from Bach's *Well-Tempered Clavier*, Book 1 (Example 2.2), in which pc 3 is consistently spelled as a minor third above the tonic C. In m. 19, where the opening measure reaches its octave transposition point, Bach has already unfolded eleven notes and pc 3 has not yet entered. As the piece continues, however, E♭ finally enters in m. 22, but with the simultaneous appearance of F♯. As the music continues during the dominant pedal, E♭ enters one more time, again in conjunction with F♯. Significantly, the C major fugue that follows unfolds only eleven notes and, as you might guess, the missing note is pc 3. Incidentally, the C major Prelude and Fugue from Book 2 follow the same system organization as those in Book 1: the prelude uses pc 3 only in very close proximity to F♯, while the fugue has only eleven pitches, omitting pc 3.

Example 2.2 Bach, *Well-Tempered Clavier*, Book 1, Prelude in C major

Bach's use of E♭ raises the possibility of a modulation from a "0" system to a 3♭ system. However, E♭ appears with F♯, the missing pitch of a 3♭ system. The simultaneous deployment of both system-shift motivators, E♭ and F♯, effectively prevents any system modulation by presenting the missing pitch of the tonic system alongside the missing pitch of its complementary system. By having both E♭ and F♯ in the same diminished seventh chord, Bach simultaneously destabilizes and restabilizes the musical fabric. Without F♯, the potential for motion into the tonic minor would be far too strong, disrupting the purity of the tonic major, the presentation of which is the primary concern of the opening prelude. The F♯ thus effectively prevents us from hearing a stark major/parallel minor here. In addition,

Bach employs another strategy to highlight his missing pitch. In the 35-measure prelude, the E♭ appears in m. 22, which is approximately 62 per cent of the way through the music. The 22:35 ratio is the closest one can come to the Golden Section proportion where there is only one chord per measure. But there is more: the next entry of E♭ is in m. 28, which is the fifth measure of an eight-measure pedal point; 5:8 is also a Golden Section proportion.

The tritone symmetries that govern symmetrical divisions within the major mode can be condensed into a single illustration. Figure 2.2 illustrates "The tonic system matrix of symmetrical axes" (hereafter referred to as the "tonic system matrix") of a theoretical composition in either C major or A minor, since both keys share the same key signature, and therefore the same system matrix. Compare Figure 2.2 with Figure 2.3, "The circle of fifths." In Figure 2.2, if one starts with the note C (representing a C eleven-pitch-class system) and proceeds to the right, the introduction of E♭, borrowed from the parallel minor, moves the "0" system to a 3♭ system. Going up diagonally up to the left, F♯ (the tritone divider of the C octave and, of course, the missing pitch of a 3♭ system) is required to return us to the original "0" system. The upper member of any given tritone must be spelled as a sharp (or a natural in a flat system) since the note written as a flat does not appear within the chromatic octave of the eleven-pitch-class system. That is, within the C chromatic octave, G♭ could not functionally replace F♯ since G♭ cannot act as a leading tone anywhere on the usable circle of fifths (that is, allowing only for a usable circle of fifths between seven flats and seven sharps). In order for G♭ to appear, its presence would have to be prepared at least by E♭, the missing pitch of the "0" system.

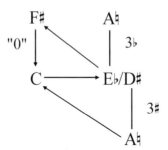

Figure 2.2   The tonic system matrix of symmetrical axes

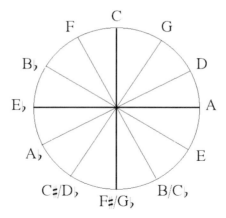

Figure 2.3   The circle of fifths

To reiterate, if pc 3 is spelled as D♯ in a "0" system, a set of similar, but "mirror-image," assumptions can be made. Since D♯ is the tritone divider of the A octave, its use in a "0" system will signify a move up three notches along the circle of fifths into a 3♯ eleven-pitch-class system with A as its root. The complementary dissonant tritone system to the A system will then be C–F♯, C♮ (or B♯) being the missing pitch of the A 3♯ system. However, in order to return to the original "0" system the missing pitch of the 3♯ system must be spelled C♮ (the minor third of the A 3♯ system), and not B♯ (the augmented second) since the modulation requires a move down three systems to "0," something that can be accomplished only if the missing pitch is spelled as a minor third. On the other hand, if B♯ were introduced instead of C, B♯ would indicate (or, rather, motivate) a modulation another three systems up (clockwise) from a 3♯ system to that of a 6♯ system, where B♯ symmetrically divides the F♯ octave.

We therefore postulate that the missing pitch of any tritone system, when spelled as a sharp, acts as the octave divider of a system whose root is a tritone below that sharp pitch class. However, if the missing pitch is spelled as a flat, that flat pitch class itself indicates its function as the root of its own tritone system. In addition to this, one may also consider, in a "0" system, that the missing pitch spelled E♭ is the root of the complementary 3♭ system; if the missing pitch is spelled D♯ (a pitch not on the usable circle of fifths), then it becomes the tritone divider of the 3♯ system. Notice in the circle of fifths (Figure 2.3) that relationships between systems may also be described as relationships between complementary tritones at right angles to one another. Using this diagram, one might quite accurately refer to a "0" system as *a C tritone system*; that is, an eleven-pitch-class system defined by its system-consonant C–F♯ tritone. (The terms "system" and "tritone system" have the same meaning, since both refer to eleven-pitch-class areas determined by a system-consonant tritone, and they may therefore be used interchangeably.) Similarly, the introduction of E♭ into the C tritone system would define a system delineated by the E♭ complementary tritone, E♭–A♮. Notice, too, that in order to get from one system to another, one will constantly move back and forth between the vertical and horizontal axes, or from the horizontal to the vertical.

These diagrams show that the use of pc 3 in any eleven-note field will invoke a system modulation along the circle of fifths by a minor third either in a clockwise direction or in a counterclockwise direction by 90 degrees depending upon the enharmonic spelling of the system's missing pitch; and that the enharmonic spelling of pc 3 is absolutely crucial to an understanding of the direction in which one moves around the circle. As a consequence, this theory is incompatible with any theory that espouses enharmonic equivalence. In Bach's C major prelude above, for example, the simultaneous employment of E♭ and F♯ was necessary to preserve the "0" system. Had F♯ not been used to counteract the system-modulatory potential of E♭, and had G♭ been used instead, that would have brought the systems further counterclockwise from a 3♭ system into a 6♭ system, opening up a Pandora's box of chromatic possibilities far more typical of Chopin than of Bach. Therefore, as discussed above, the concurrent use of E♭ and F♯ maintains the prevailing tonic system by provoking a system modulation and simultaneously negating it – or in other words, the simultaneous presence of the two system-shift motivators effectively cancels the potential for any system modulation.

Obviously, there are many ways of showing the symmetrical relationships of an eleven-pitch-class system graphically. As we have said, the simultaneous presentation of E♭ and F♯ (or the simultaneous presentation of D♯ and C♮) in a "0" system would stabilize the eleven-note environment and prevent it from modulating into either of its two complementary systems. This can more easily be seen in Figure 2.4.

In this figure, the middle line represents the tonic notes of the major-mode form of eleven-pitch class systems from 8♭ to 8♯; C is in the middle. Each note of the top line is the missing pitch of the system named directly underneath spelled as a minor third above the tonic of the major-mode form of that system. Therefore, the missing pitch of a 3♯ system may be spelled C. Each note of the bottom line is the missing pitch of the system directly above spelled as an augmented second above the tonic of the major-mode form of that system. In a 3♯ system, the missing pitch may also be spelled B♯.

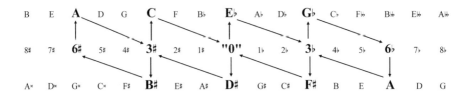

Figure 2.4 Table of eleven-note systems from 8♭ to 8♯

To determine the directions in which eleven-note systems move with the use of each system's missing pitch, the arrows must be followed in the directions indicated: the use of E♭ in a "0" system will move the pitch field to three flats. In the 3♭ system, F♯ must be used to return to the "0" system; however, the missing pitch in a 3♭ system spelled as G♭ will continue to move the pitch field further from the original "0" system, now into six flats. Notice that the motion from one eleven-note system to another is consistently three "notches" along the horizontal axes.

The long diagonals between the top and bottom lines are the system-consonant tritones for the eleven-pitch-class system in the middle line. Therefore, C (on the top line) and F♯ (on the bottom line) indicate the unique system-determining tritone of a "0" system, while E♭–A is the system-determining tritone of a 3♭ system and A–D♯ is the system-determining tritone of a 3♯ system.

One of the tenets of systems theory is that the tonic tritone system of any given movement operates on the deepest level of structure and interacts with more middleground harmonic expansions (that is, expansions involving symmetrically related tritone systems) that constantly play against it. Our thinking here is consistent with harmonic analyses that conceive of the second harmonic area (or second theme group) of a major-mode sonata exposition as V of a larger background tonic, not as a modulation that displaces the tonic key of the movement. We go a step further: *beneath the tonic key itself is an even deeper background system of minor thirds and augmented seconds comprising symmetrically related eleven-pitch-class tritone systems.* Consequently, we propose that tonality, along with its hierarchal structure, and its division into 24 major and minor keys, is ultimately derived from a chromatic gamut of all available pitch classes that is partitioned into diatonic scales of differing whole- and half-step patterns. Thus the chromatic aggregate actually underlies all tonal types and keys.

B. The Minor Mode as Reordered Root Octave

It was stated previously that the system analysis of the minor mode required special mention. In this analytical method, the minor mode takes the system of its relative major, just as in the circle of fifths a minor scale will always be plotted at the same locus as its relative major. Thus, a movement in D minor, such as the second movement from Beethoven's Piano Sonata op. 10 no. 3, would relate to a 1♭ system: both D minor and F major have the same tritone consonant/dissonant conditions that govern a 1♭ system and therefore must have the same missing pitch. This relationship of system to mode may help us to understand the minor mode's remarkable degree of tension: its tonic triad is not coordinated with its system's root, and always seeks to move toward its relative major (meaning the root of the key of its tonic system) in order to resolve this conflict. This is why second harmonic areas that are in the relative major in the expositions of minor-mode sonata-form compositions seem to have a harmonically stabilizing effect: the transition from the tonic minor to the relative major represents a motion toward the root of the system that is shared by both minor tonic and its relative and, therefore, a motion from instability toward stability.

We would therefore conclude that the minor mode derives from its relative major; that is, the minor mode is a rotation of the pitch classes that form the octave of the relative major: *do, re, me* of the minor thus equates with *la, ti, do* of the relative major. The major mode acts as a gamut of available pitch classes similar to the Medieval/Renaissance gamut from which it ultimately derives. Both gamuts support a number of tonalities, however; whereas the Medieval gamut gave rise to anywhere from eight to twelve different octave species, the tonal gamut (or system, as we choose to call it) supports only two, the major and its relative minor. Likewise, both gamut systems are constructed of major scalar patterns, there being no minor-mode equivalent of a major hexachord or scale.

Our view of the minor mode as a reordering of major is not without historical precedent. As evidence, on the title page of *Das wohltemperirte Clavier*, Book 1, Bach describes the content in this manner: "The Well-Tempered Clavier, or preludes and fugues through all the tones and semitones, both as regards the *tertia* major or Ut Re Mi and as concerns the *tertia* minor or Re Mi Fa ...".[14] Again, we see Bach considering the minor mode ("minor mode" itself was terminology that had yet to become popular) as deriving from the gamut of the major hexachord. In the revised version of his *Treatise on Harmony*, Rameau similarly considers the minor mode conforming to the intervallic structure of the notes within the *Re–re* octave or the *La–la* octave.[15]

In an advertisement by Carl Philipp Emanuel Bach in the *Critische Nachrichten aus dem Reiche der Gelehrsamkeit* of May 7, 1751, the son of the late composer writes about the upcoming publication of *Die Kunst der Fuge*, describing his father's compositional procedure for this work: "All these manifold fugues are composed upon one and the same principal theme, and in the same key, namely *D minor, or D La Re with the minor third* [our emphasis]."[16] One may conclude, then, that the theoretical derivation of the minor from the major continued even after the death of J.S. Bach.

In some minor-mode compositions, the composer may intend the transformation of the tonic minor into its parallel tonic major over the course of the entire piece, a motion involving two symmetrically related tritone systems. Haydn, for example, very often followed such a procedure. In the opening of the Symphony no. 83 in G minor of 1785, the first symphony of his Paris set, Haydn immediately begins an interplay between B♭ and C♯ within the opening melody: G, B♭, C♯, D. While C♯, the system-shift motivator of the G minor 2♭ system, would potentially move us up into a 1♯ system, the simultaneous presence of B♭ in the violas and cellos prevents any system modulation from occurring. The simultaneous presence of these two pitch classes prevents any system modulation from the prevailing 2♭ system throughout most of the first movement's exposition and development. However, by the end of the recapitulation's opening statement, the system-modulatory potential of the missing pitch is realized when, in m. 144, C♯ moves us unequivocally into a 1♯ system in the absence of any further instances of B♭. A couple of measures later, at the beginning of the bridge in m. 146, Haydn accordingly alters the key signature to one sharp, and the remainder of the recapitulation, with its absence of the missing pitch – in either of its enharmonic variants – maintains both a G major tonality and

---

14 Hans T. David and Arthur Mendel, *The New Bach Reader*, rev. and enlarged Christoph Wolff (New York, 1998), p. 97.

15 Jean-Philippe Rameau, *Treatise on Harmony*, trans. Philip Gossett (New York, 1971), p. 263.

16 David and Mendel, *The New Bach Reader*, p. 257.

its associated 1♯ system for the rest of the movement. Haydn later duplicates this procedure almost exactly in the only minor-mode symphony of the London set, no. 95 in C minor of 1791. After the recapitulation in the tonic C minor, Haydn, in a manner similar to that of his earlier G minor symphony, changes key signature to that of the parallel major for the second harmonic area (m. 129, "Maggiore" is indicated in the score at this point). From here to the end, E♭ is entirely absent, allowing F♯ to maintain the "0" system throughout. However, Haydn does offer the enharmonic equivalent, D♯ in place of E♭, balancing the flat-system tendency of the previous minor mode. In order to maintain the "0" system, however, the modulatory potential of D♯ is consistently negated by the simultaneous presence of C♮. Significantly, not only do the first movements of both symphonies end in the opposite major-mode system, but both of their finales are entirely in the parallel major, confirming the system modulation to the complementary system already accomplished at the end of their respective first movements.

C. Further Consequences of System Interactions

Among the more interesting consequences of system modulations (implied or real) are the foreground dyad conflicts that result and that are developed, or worked out, over the course of an entire composition. In the case of Haydn's Symphony no. 83 in G minor, besides the tug-o'-war between C♯ and B♭ raised early on, a B♭/B♮ dyad conflict in the bridge results from the constant pull toward the parallel major (G major) and away from the prevailing tonic minor (G minor).[17] Such pitch-class conflicts, which often become the deepest-level gambits in a composition, form one of the most important developmental processes in music of the eighteenth and nineteenth centuries (and perhaps even the twentieth). The very fact that eleven-pitch-class systems comprise tritones organized around minor third cycles naturally raises chromatic pitch classes that are inflections of diatonic ones belonging to the key. Every time a diatonic pitch class is inflected to its chromatic neighbor (either flat or sharp), a conflict arises which eventually must be resolved either with the chromatic inflection returning to its diatonic counterpart or, as in the case of Symphony no. 83, with the chromatically inflected pitch "winning out," as it were, displacing the initial diatonic pitch class altogether, supported by a true modulation to the alternate system – here, from a 2♭ system to a 1♯ system.

But what if "a true modulation to the alternate system" does not happen when, indeed, it is truly expected? The transformation of C minor into C major in Beethoven's Symphony no. 5 is often heralded as one of the most ecstatic artistic expressions of the ultimate triumph of will over fate ever conceived in a musical setting. Yet at least one commentator has suggested that Beethoven maintains a guarded skepticism

---

17 Within the body of the text, we make a distinction between a slash and a dash between adjacent pitch classes depending on function. A slash refers to a dyad confict in which one pitch class is the chromatic inflection of the other. On the other hand, a dash between two or more adjacent pitch classes refers to their harmonic relationship, either within a progression or as part of a larger tonal motion.

about that victory right up to the last note of the last movement.[18] Using system analysis to verify the musical content of the transformation, however, we find that Owen Jander may have stumbled upon an idea that has an uncomfortable validity.

The first scheme that offers the potential transformation of C minor into C major occurs at the second harmonic area of the first movement's recapitulation, in m. 303, where the thematic material that had previously been in E♭ major in the exposition is now transposed to C major. Thus, Beethoven has generated a dyad conflict between E♭ and E♮. The F♯s in m. 296 prepare for this potentiality by moving the tonic 3♭ system up to a "0" system; the "0" system is maintained throughout the rest of the recapitulation, and we are led to believe that C major has triumphed over C minor, in a manner procedurally similar to that of Haydn's minor-mode symphonies mentioned above. However, the coda, beginning in m. 374, begins a process that undermines such a contention. Both E♭ and F♯ enter in m. 390, still delaying the return of the 3♭ system. However, by m. 400, E♭ "wins" uncontestedly because of the absence of F♭. Of course, Beethoven, even during the short excursion into C major, never alters the key signature; the return to C minor, and, of course, to a 3♭ system, is no surprise.

The opening thematic material of the second movement resurrects the E♭/E♮ dyad conflict. Harmonically, the positive outbursts of C major later in the movement always succumb to the prevailing A♭ tonality: E♮ is always displaced by E♭.

By the end of the C minor third movement (the scherzo), the tonic 3♭ system has been stabilized again after the trio's short excursion into C major. This is the point where we would expect uncontested F♯s to change the system from the prevailing 3♭ system to a "0" system; *but this is just what Beethoven avoids.* In m. 324, the timpani ostinato on C begins and the lower strings gradually move from A♭ to G, and then, in m. 344, to F♯. We would expect that this F♯, or perhaps the one just before it in the violins, would be sufficient to maneuver us finally from a 3♭ system back into a "0" system, but it cannot since the E♭ in the first violins prevents such a system modulation. In fact, each time F♯ occurs now, there is always an E♭ afterwards to sustain the tonic 3♭ system. And, if we take Beethoven's "attacca" at the end of the third movement as an indication of the continued domination of the 3♭ system even into the fourth movement, we find ourselves gloriously in C major, with no sharps or flats in the key signature, *and still stuck in a 3♭ system.*

The same impasse is reached in the fourth movement. Certainly, within the context of a C major tonality, Beethoven, had he wanted, would have had no problem in adjusting the prevailing system up from a 3♭ system, thus coordinating the key signature and the system. Just after the opening of the exposition's bridge (m. 26), F♯s permeate the terrain, so that by the time the second harmonic area enters in m. 44, in G major (with its F♯ leading tone), we are now in the expected "0" system. The continual presence of F♯s in the closing period and coda simply stabilizes the "0" system. However, the development turns back to the 3♭ system (m. 106) and continues in the flat direction to a 6♭ system (m. 109). The A♮ in m. 134 brings

---

18 Owen Jander, "'Let Your Deafness No Longer Be a Secret – Even in Art': Self-Portraiture and the Third Movement of the C-Minor Symphony," *Beethoven Forum*, 8 (2000): 25–70.

us back to a 3♭ system, and the F♯ in m. 143 transfers us up into a "0" system during the development's retransition. But then there is that short, menacing recall of the third movement between the end of the retransition and the opening of the recapitulation; and with it there is an unequivocal return to the 3♭ system since not a single uncontested F♯ is present to return us successfully to a "0" system before the recapitulation – the modulatory potential of each F♯ is canceled each time by E♭. Therefore, at the recapitulation (m. 207), we just carry on in that fateful 3♭ system. The last attempt for the "0" system to displace the 3♭ system occurs in m. 349. At this point, we are in the coda, just before the Più allegro and Presto. And again, the promise of F♯, that single note that should have proclaimed the triumph of will over fate, is dashed each time by an omnipresent E♭. Not a single F♯ enters again before the movement closes. In fact, E♭'s inability to be successfully displaced by E♮ may explain Beethoven's saturation of the C major surface details with numerous A♭s and B♭s even in the Più allegro and Presto. Contradicting the final bombast of unrelenting C major harmony, the symphony actually ends in a 3♭ system; Beethoven's seeming victory over his fate – his deafness – may not be as convincing as we may be led to believe, with a slight element of doubt encrypted into a hardly noticeable but very present misalignment of diatonic key and eleven-note system.

In his Symphony in C minor, we see Beethoven's potential for optimism always offset by an underlying sense of pessimism related to his worsening deafness and, perhaps, an ever-pervasive cynicism about his future. Our interpretation thus supports Jander, who analyzes the movement as a manifestation in sound of Beethoven's attempt to describe his deafness compositionally.

D. Major-Third Relations within Diminished Systems

A question that often arises in systems analysis concerns compositions that unfold major thirds more prominently on the foreground than minor thirds. Beethoven's "Waldstein" Sonata op. 53, for example, subdivides the exposition of the first movement by major thirds and, consequently, raises some interesting enharmonicism. The sonata's first enharmonic issue occurs with the introduction of pc 3 within the prevailing "0" system. Initially presented as E♭ in the opening statement (sending the systems down to three flats), the counterstatement/bridge quickly raises F♯ (bringing us back into the "0" system) and soon introduces the D♯ that effects the modulation to E major, the movement's second harmonic area. The D♯, however, not only signals the arrival of E major, but also shifts the "0" system up to three sharps. Beethoven's achievement here is striking: by evoking a 3♯ system without reintroducing its missing pitch, C♮, until the very end of the exposition (thus restoring the original "0" system), he has effectively modulated from one tritone system to another, *the new system displacing the old over a substantial area*. The 3♯ system remains in effect almost until the end of the exposition. What is revolutionary here is the fact that the new system remains in control and is uncontested for so long.

Unlike diatonic analysis, which would define the second harmonic area in terms of a key signature of four sharps, chromatic system analysis would subsume the E major harmonic area under the prevailing 3♯ A–D♯ tritone system. The transposition of the E major second harmonic area to VI (A major) in the recapitulation, heard within the tonic "0" system, would tend to bolster this interpretation. To return to the exposition, C♮ is reintroduced in the closing period in m. 70 (against a D♯ which prevents a system modulation), and again in m. 74 (this time without the D♯) at the codetta to effect a return to the original "0" system. This whole exercise, in which the 3♯ system is effectively kept from materializing, is necessary, apart from its dramatic intensity, in order to prepare for the repeat of the exposition, which must naturally be in the tonic system. Additionally, ending the exposition in the tonic system creates a neutral pitch field from which Beethoven can now explore the most wide-ranging system modulations in the development section. Again, from the standpoint of system analysis, even a division by major thirds will have an underlying minor-third organizational imperative behind it.

Whereas a voice-leading analysis of the first movement of the "Waldstein" would emphasize the role of the E as dividing the space between C and G, and thus relegate the E to a secondary role, system analysis views as significant the harmonic area of E in respect to its role within the symmetrical tritone divisions of a "0" system, with Beethoven playing off the system-consonant C–F♯ tritone against the system-dissonant quality of the A–D♯ tritone. The A–D♯ 3♯ system introduces its own symmetrical properties that are ultimately used to re-establish the tonic "0" system at the end of the exposition. Therefore, another of the many things one can derive from this method of analysis involves an understanding of the system-modulatory potential of enharmonicism.

Sometimes, in music that is decidedly diatonic, the notation of the twelve-note aggregate may involve only twelve spellings. That is, in a simple C major symphony, the use of the chromatics C♯, E♭, F♯, A♭, and B♭ may be sufficient to create a chromatic environment that is capable of modulating out of system, but is equally capable of returning quickly to the tonic tritone system without intervening system modulations. However, in a more chromatically involved composition, F♯ could be associated with its enharmonic G♭. If pc 3 (again in a "0" system) is spelled as E♭, and there is no F♯ present, this will shift the system down to a 3♭ system. However, if G♭ (instead of F♯) is presented after E♭, the 3♭ system will then continue the motion downward and in a counterclockwise direction along the circle of fifths toward a 6♭ system. In order to restore the "0" system, an A♮ must enter, returning the system to 3♭ system, and, finally, F♯ must re-enter to return the tonic to its original "0" system.

In his earlier works, Beethoven was reasonably content to unfold three symmetrically related systems: the tonic and one on either side of it. For example, the Cello Sonata in F major op. 5 no. 1 uses only the 1♭ system (F), the 4♭ system (A♭), and the 2♯ system (D), according a limited spectrum of enharmonic pairs. However, remaining within the same key and genre, in Brahms's Cello Sonata in F major op. 99, the chromatic texture becomes sufficiently involved to traverse five systems: 7♭ (C♭), 4♭ (A♭), 1♭ (F, the tonic system), 2♯ (D), and 5♯ (B). In many of Brahms's other works, however, the authors have noticed that he may go through eight or nine system changes before returning to the tonic system. In the Debussy Cello Sonata, also in a 1♭ system (and, in this case, in D minor), we find that the first movement uses three systems: 4♭, 1♭ (tonic), and 2♯; the second movement goes through four systems: 7♭, 4♭, 1♭ (of course), and 2♯; and the third movement uses five systems: 10♭, 7♯, 4♭, 1♭, and 2♯.

One may then surmise that as triadic tonality began gradually to dissolve toward the end of the nineteenth century, what remained was the same eleven-pitch-class symmetrical mechanism that had always been beneath the surface of diatonic key-centered tonality, and perhaps modality as well. By the time of Bartók (for example, in his *Music for Strings, Percussion, and Celesta*), the situation had reversed itself to the extent that the composer's triadic sonorities were now completely subsumed under the symmetrical rubrics of unfolded tritone systems.[19]

E. Tonality as Hexachordal Reordering

Key-centered tonality is often referred to as a hierarchal system that is articulated by progressions of major and minor triads prolonging structurally significant harmonic areas that support a background tonic. The exact nature and relationship of these large-scale harmonic progressions has not, as yet, been fully explained or explored in the literature other than to say that they project a cadential progression on the background level. So long as tonality is heard as nothing more than a progression based on the relationship of tonic to dominant, with the subdominant lying somewhere in between, a full realization of the unique interrelationships of harmonic areas controlled by the background tonic will remain undisclosed.

What we propose is nothing less than a redefinition of tonality itself as something more than just an octave species which supports chords of fixed quality (major and minor). If we accept a tonality as comprising an eleven-pitch-class field or gamut from which harmonic areas are derived, we have considerably extended the definition. But what determines the ordering of harmonic areas? Although this concept will be expanded greatly in subsequent chapters, we will introduce the essential points of this issue here.

Part of a potential answer lies in the origins of the tonal system, which is ultimately derived from the medieval gamuts of overlapping hexachords.[20] The tonality of C major is thus the last step in a long evolutionary process that converted the C *naturalis* gamut, itself allowing eleven pitch classes, to the key of C major. The same could be said for all the other keys: the F *mollis* gamut became F major, the G *durus* gamut became G major, and so on. In fact, the C hexachord (the central hexachord of the *naturalis* gamut), which originally controlled the harmonic motions of modally derived composition, never really disappeared, but simply evolved into the first six

---

19 As an interesting corollary to this discussion, see Ernó Lendvai, *The Workshop of Bartók and Kodály* (Budapest, 1983), pp. 270–317, 757–62. In his theoretical descriptions of the music of Bartók, Lendvai also indicates his interest in minor third and tritone relationships. However, Lendvai's starting point is a decidedly Riemannian one where keys related by minor thirds to a tonic, and their tritone implications, are all defined as relatives along symmetrical axes. Thus, according to Lendvai, any member of the minor third cycle based on the tonic pitch (e.g. C–E♭–F♯–A) may substitute for the tonic itself, a position decidedly at variance with the theory of tritone systems presented here.

20 See Burnett, "A New Theory of Hexachord Modulation."

notes of the C major scale. Throughout the entire sixteenth and seventeenth centuries, notes of the C hexachord (or the F hexachord, depending on the signature), reordered in fifths, F–C–G–D–A–E, provided most, if not all, of the harmonic motions within a single composition, often in direct contrast to the prevailing modality. However, instead of these fifths supporting a background tonality, they were often related more locally, one fifth progressing to the next, moving both up and down the reordered fifths of the hexachord. (See Chapter 3 for a more detailed discussion of the modal hexachord and its harmonic implications.)

A diagram of the C major hexachord reordered as fifths follows. On either side of the primary hexachord are single and double bars respectively separating tones outside the main hexachord and indicating differing tonal functions. Starting at the left, the B♭ followed by a single line represents the added flat seventh degree, and is the only allowable flat in the C major hexachord system (more fully explained in the next chapter, this pitch class derives from the subdominant hexachord of the medieval untransposed gamut). Since B♭ is the only allowable flat, its harmonic significance ties it to the subdominant side of the key, and may be used as a root-position chord in its own right as IV/IV and not simply as an added seventh. Harmonically, however, B♭ would be an unlikely structural goal in C major since this pitch does not relate directly to the tonic, but to the subdominant. Therefore, our diagram indicates the pitch separated by a single line:

									D♯
B♭	/	F –	C –	G –	d –	a –	e	‖	b	B
♭VII	/	IV	I	V	ii	vi	iii	‖	vii⁰	V/iii

The pitch class that follows the double line at the end of the reordered hexachord is another matter entirely. B♮ is the next fifth up from E, the terminus of the reordered C hexachord. It therefore does not exist within the C hexachord and cannot function as a goal in its own right unless the entire system is transposed. Thus a B major chord with D♯, the missing pitch of the "0" system, would imply a motion up three key signatures to a system of three sharps on A (the reason for a shift up three signatures in a tonal composition, as opposed to a modal one, is fully explained in Chapter 4). However, if B is used as a contrapuntal chord, without a major third, it can exist within the "0" system as a diminished harmony. Thus a major advantage of perceiving any given key as a reordered hexachord is that its reordering in fifths provides the harmonic relationships that characterize the large-scale harmonic plans of most eighteenth-century music.

As the reordering shows, the primary harmonies in C major are located at the beginning of the reordered hexachord, and these are the ones most likely to be tonicized as harmonic areas closest to the prolonged tonic: C initiates the composition and G is the first goal away, whether the piece is Baroque or Classical in origin. Likewise, IV is most likely tonicized to maintain tonic stability, as in a recapitulation or a coda of a sonata-form movement, or as part of a larger movement back to the tonic after the dominant area has been explored, as in a development section. The other three triads are all minor, and they usually occur as points furthest removed from the tonic. In many major-mode eighteenth-century symphonies, for instance, either vi or iii appears only at the climax of the development section as the penultimate harmonic area before the tonic return. As one might expect, given the nature of eleven-pitch-class systems, vi is more often encountered as the penultimate goal since a tonicization of iii would require the introduction of the missing pitch, effectively modulating the tonic eleven-pitch-class area up three systems in the sharp direction. In the first movement of a C major string quartet in sonata form, for example, the development section ending on an E minor triad would virtually require a D♯ before the end of the retransition, thus introducing the missing pitch spelled as an augmented second above the tonic and, thus, propelling the systems three notches clockwise on the circle of fifths. Such a note would move the music into a 3♯ system. However, at the outset of the recapitulation, the appearance of the note C, most likely immediately present in the first chord of the recapitulation, would restore the tonic system since C♮, the missing pitch of the 3♯ system spelled as a minor third above A, would move us three systems counterclockwise on the circle of fifths.

It was mentioned previously that such a procedure was very common in Baroque concertos, where entire movements built toward this climax and in which the return of the tonic automatically restored the original eleven-pitch-class system. The return to the tonic after prolonging iii was usually "unprepared," with no structural dominant preceding the restoration of the tonic.[21] It may be concluded that the mere appearance of the tonic pitch, the corrective pitch that restored the tonic system from that of three sharps (in the case of C major), was deemed sufficient to convince the hearer that the tonic was now structurally regained.

Oddly enough, after the middle of the eighteenth century, one often finds iii (or even III♯) as the penultimate goal only in symphonies composed in the last two decades of the century, especially works by Joseph Haydn. Here too, Haydn sometimes omits the dominant retransition at the end of the development, and simply connects iii to the tonic recapitulation, as in the first movement of his Symphony no. 94 in G major. Again, the original system is always restored with the return of the tonic pitch class. What is significant, then, is that composers (at least before the later nineteenth century) generally seem reluctant to go beyond the limits of the tonic hexachord in plotting the background harmonic scheme of a movement, or even within subsections of a movement, and will generally not exceed those limits. Thus one simply does not find B major as the penultimate goal in the development of a C major symphony, just as one would not find E major in a symphony in F. In addition to the fact that a system modulation based on the seventh scale degree would so destabilize the tonic system that it would be extremely difficult to restore it convincingly at the point of recapitulation, the seventh scale degree supports diminished harmony and is therefore incapable of acting as a localized tonic unless completely changed into a major triad, thus losing its association with the tonic on any level since it no longer acts as a leading-tone chord.

---

21 See the reference to Corelli's opp. 1–4 above. Among countless examples of this procedure, we cite: Bach's Brandenburg Concertos no. 2 in F (first movement) and no. 4 in G (first movement), Handel's op. 3 no. 1 in B♭/G minor (first movement), and Vivaldi's op. 4 no. 1 in B♭ (first movement).

The minor mode viewed as a reordered hexachord is equally revealing. Since the minor mode is derived from the gamut of its parallel major, a reordering of C minor, for example, would follow that of an E♭ hexachord:

									F♯
D♭	/	A♭ –	E♭ –	B♭ –	f –	c –	g	‖	d	D
♭II	/	VI	III	VII	iv	i	v	‖	ii⁰	V/V

In the case of the minor mode, the chords that define the key are all minor and they are placed toward the end of the sequence. All the "strong" chords (those that are major) appear at the beginning of the sequence. These are the harmonies that provide stability within the key, while the tonic, subdominant, and dominant chords are all minor and therefore inherently unstable.

Minor modes are unstable compared with their parallel majors because of several factors. First, there is no minor third over the fundamental in the overtone series (this fact may be the reason why there were only major hexachords in the gamut). Second, there is no major dominant, and thus no voice-leading V in the minor mode; the mode must be adjusted to create one by adding a leading tone. Third, the minor third, as an interval, has the tendency to collapse into a unison, but the major third may remain as it is without further contrapuntal motion.

No wonder then that the tendency of the minor mode is toward the relative major in place of the dominant. Because of its inherent instability, the minor tonic constantly seeks to move either to its parallel major (via the missing pitch of its system; here, in C minor, the missing pitch is F♯), or simply to rotate its bass to that of the tonic of its eleven-pitch-class system, here three flats. Because the relative major of the mode is contained within the opening trichord of the hexachord, occupying a position of strength, its appearance neutralizes the instability of the tonic, *but it also robs the area of tension*. Thus the motion to III is inherently a stabilizing one that quite defeats the whole premise of large-scale form, that is, to create harmonic tension by moving to areas that are dissonant in relationship to that of the tonic in order to justify a return to that very tonic as a source of resolution. It would seem, then, not too much of a surprise that composers of the late eighteenth century tended to view the minor as a special case – it was just too volatile. Why else would Haydn write only one minor-mode symphony in his late-period London group (Symphony no. 95 in C minor, discussed above), and Mozart write only two minor-mode symphonies in his whole career, both in G minor?

Notice, too, that the next fifth beyond G, the last fifth of the E♭ hexachord, is D, supporting a diminished chord (here ii⁰) within the key of C minor, and, in this state, unable to function as a tonal center. However, in the minor mode, the missing pitch, here F♯, is also the leading tone of the dominant, the last pitch class of the series. Since both tonic and dominant occupy positions at the far end of the reordered hexachord, and are inherently unstable as minor chords, the missing pitch now relates to the very chords that purport to establish the key. In major mode, the missing pitch relates to a harmonic area that is clearly distantly related to the tonic. The minor mode, on the other hand, is characterized by a constant fluctuation between minor tonic and parallel major every time the missing pitch is introduced. That is,

F♯ would relate to C major as its system-consonant tritone, just as an E♭ would relate to A♮ as its system-consonant tritone. Of course, in C minor, the modulatory potential of F♯ is constantly negated ("corrected") by E♭, the third of the tonic triad, the two pitch classes remaining at odds with each other over the course of the composition. Perhaps this explains why Haydn (as well as J.C. Bach and Beethoven, to mention just two) always sought to "resolve" the minor mode into its parallel major, either by the end of the first movement (the second harmonic area material being transposed from the relative major of the exposition to that of the tonic major in the recapitulation) or, at the very least, by the last movement.

It is interesting to note that the original ordering of J.S. Bach's Two-Part Inventions (which first appeared as a series of *praeambula* in the *Klavierbüchlein* for Wilhelm Friedemann) was C (major), d (minor), e, F, G, a, b, B♭, A, g, f, E, E♭, D, and c.[22] It would appear that Bach was thinking of presenting the pitch classes of the C hexachord as tonics for the first six inventions, with each invention corresponding to its proper mode within the C hexachord: the inventions in C, F, and G are thus in major, while the ones in d, e, and a are in minor. Further, these six inventions share similarly constructed subjects that arpeggiate the tonic triad exclusively (the other inventions arpeggiate other chords as well), thus forming a unified set within the total work.

Throughout the eighteenth century composers and theorists alike recognized that modulation within any given key was normally confined to the roots of the first six notes of the tonic major scale. Georg Joseph Vogler (1749–1814) in his *Tonwissenschaft und Tonsetzkunst* (Mannheim, 1776) clearly follows contemporary thought when he defines the limits of modulation within the key as follows:

> There is only one single law for modulation, but it is a general one: that there should be no going beyond a step that is one ♯ or one ♭ removed from the key signature ... Every piece of music ... is named by reference to a certain key. In order to preserve its unity, it must not modulate to a key more than one step away ... From this is it clear that in any one key there are only *six* [emphasis mine] that can appear as principal or primary keys: e.g. in C: C major, A minor; F major, D minor; G major, E minor.[23]

In other words, any structural goal beyond the roots of the tonic hexachord would constitute a motion that would disrupt tonal coherence. More specifically, a modulation beyond the tonic hexachord to a key area of more than one flat or sharp would, in fact, lie within the tonal orbit of *another tonic hexachord*, unrelated to the original tonic key; in our terms, a hexachord from another tritone system.

---

22 See Johann Sebastian Bach, *Inventionen und Sinfonien*, ed. Georg von Dadelsen (Kassel, 1972), vol. 3.

23 Georg Joseph Vogler, *Tonwissenschaft und Tonsetzkunst* (Mannheim, 1776), pp. 70–72, quoted in Ian Bent (ed. and trans.), *Music Analysis in the Nineteenth Century*, vol. 1: *Fugue, Form and Style*, Cambridge Readings in the Literature of Music (Cambridge, 1994), p. 143.

Chapter Three

The Modal Gamut in the Sixteenth Century

I. Introductory Remarks

In this chapter we will trace the origins of eleven-pitch-class tonality in the modally inflected music of the sixteenth century, particularly in the works of the Mannerist composers, beginning with Cipriano de Rore, through to the works of Orlando de Lasso.[1] These composers consciously sought to express ever more highly emotional poetry (both secular and sacred) through their interpretation of the Greek diatonic and chromatic genera. The chapter then continues with a detailed discussion of selected madrigals by Claudio Monteverdi, whose music is emblematic of the evolving modal language of the early to middle seventeenth century.

The inexhaustible diversity and richness of the harmonic style that typifies the music of these influential composers, and that of the early to mid-seventeenth century in general, would seem to militate against the formation of a unified theory appropriate to this music. Part of the problem lies in the very nature of the music itself, which seems, on the surface at least, to be forever fluctuating between a chromatically extended modal system and an emerging "key-centered" diatonic one; the two systems often, even deliberately, work in opposition, even within the same composition. Such ambiguity of harmonic language often results in anachronistic analyses whose mixture of modal and key-centered terminology is an expedience that is at best an uneasy alliance of two quite different theoretical constructs. Some modern-day theorists have even gone so far as to discard the modal element altogether in favor of a purely tonal, Schenkerian graphic approach that attempts to equate the music with the key-centered tonality of the eighteenth century.[2]

---

1   Parts of this chapter were previously published in Henry Burnett, "A New Theory of Hexachord Modulation in the Late Sixteenth and Early Seventeenth Centuries," *International Journal of Musicology*, 8 (1999): 115–75. However, since writing that article, we find that our interpretation of the music in relation to our theory has changed drastically. Therefore this present chapter supersedes all analytical discussions contained in the previous article.

2   There are not many in-depth harmonic analyses of Monteverdi's music, nor of the music of his contemporaries, beyond the purely descriptive. Wherever they exist, the musical discussion tends, more often than not, to support other more literary and/or poetic concerns. For example, John Whenham, "Five Acts: One Action," in John Whenham (ed.), *Claudio Monteverdi: Orfeo*, Cambridge Opera Handbooks (Cambridge, 1986), pp. 42–77, employs an anachronistic modal-key-centered terminology (that is, referring to modes as if they were keys in the modern sense – e.g., G minor instead of G dorian) in discussing the harmonic plan of the opera. Jeffery Kurtzmand does likewise in his "A Taxonomic and Affective Analysis

Undoubtedly, each of these various analytical approaches has something to offer, but none seems to confront the music in a way that both respects the music's integrity as a composition of its own time and place and, at the same time, is meaningful to modern-day theorists. We believe, on the other hand, that the theory we offer is entirely compatible with constructs known to composers and theorists alike during the sixteenth and seventeenth centuries: specifically, one that is based on hexachordal modulations of eleven-pitch-class areas. Further, we believe that a precise understanding of modal hexachordal gamut modulation, that is, the shift from one eleven-pitch-class gamut to another, will explicate our explanation of similar operations in the tonal and even the atonal music of later centuries.

II. Sixteenth- and Early Seventeenth-Century Approaches to Chromaticism and Eleven-Pitch-Class Modality

Ever since the early eleventh century, when Guido of Arezzo described the total pitch universe of the eight church modes in terms of a gamut of overlapping hexachords, hexachords and modes were irrevocably linked as separate-but-equal functions within a harmonically fluid modal system, which survived well into the seventeenth century. Originally Guido's gamut consisted only of two white-note hexachords on C and G, thus omitting B♭. However, it soon became apparent that a flat accidental, and consequently a flat hexachord on F, was necessary to avoid the tritone – designated as the "diabolus in musica" by theorists of the late Middle Ages.[3]

Right from the start, then, hexachords – in particular, the *mi–fa* half-step within their initial tetrachords – were necessary to explain pitch classes not found in the purely white-note octave species of the modes. Aside from the added B♭, derived from the *molle* hexachord, the gamut was expanded by inflected modal degrees needed to prepare the cadence, that is, the major sixth moving outward to the octave. Since B♭ was the only allowable flat within the natural gamut, the appearance of the next flat, E♭, also sung as *fa*, could be explained only as a transposition of the entire gamut down a fifth, there being no hexachord in the natural gamut containing an E♭.[4] Starting with Willaert in Venice in the 1530s, composers began to investigate the potential of chromaticism as a musical expression of the emotionally laden

---

of Monteverdi's 'Hor che'l ciel e la terra'," *Music Analysis*, 12/2 (1993): 169–96. The same is true for Gary Tomlinson, *Monteverdi and the End of the Renaissance* (Los Angeles, 1987). At the other extreme are the few Schenkerian analyses, which seem to follow the pioneering efforts of the late Felix Salzer. See Salzer's "Heinrich Schenker and Historical Research: Monteverdi's Madrigal *Oimè, se tanto amate*," in David Beach (ed.), *Aspects of Schenkerian Theory* (New Haven and London, 1983), pp. 135–52; and David Gagné, "Monteverdi's *Ohimè dov'è il mio ben* and the Romanesca," *The Music Forum*, 6 (New York, 1987), pp. 61–92.

3   The origin of Guido's hexachords as a system of deductions is fully explained in Karol Berger, *Musica Ficta: Theories of Accidental Inflections in Vocal Polyphony from Marchetto da Padova to Gioseffo Zarlino* (Cambridge, 1987), pp. 2–11. Also, see Dolores Pesce, "B-flat: Transposition or Transformation," *The Journal of Musicology*, 4/3 (1985–86): 330–49.

4   Andrew Hughes, *Manuscript Accidentals: Ficta in Focus 1350–1450*, Musicological Studies and Documents, 27 (n.p., 1972), pp. 47–51.

poetry chosen for the texts of secular madrigals (and of some sacred motets, too). To accomplish this, it became increasingly necessary to adopt a procedure not only for moving by fifths in the flat direction, but for moving in fifths in the sharp direction as well, as often violent poetic conceits required wild juxtapositions of flats and sharps. It became increasingly likely that the choice of notes in the flat direction would move beyond B♭ and E♭, including A♭ and even D♭ and beyond occasionally. The choice of notes in the sharp direction also continued beyond G♯ to D♯. However, a signature (meaning the *cantus*) remained confined to either *durus* (no accidentals), *mollis* (one flat) or, more rarely, two flats throughout the sixteenth century and into the first half of the seventeenth. The practice of indicating sharps as transpositions to the *durus* side of the fifths cycle began to appear only in the 1640s.

The chromatic expansion of the gamut was also due in part to the increased interest in the chromatic genus of the ancient Greeks. Pure theoretical modality had now to contend with a great many more chromatic inflections of diatonic pitches, introduced within a much smaller time span, than had ever been the case before. As a result, the older diatonic modal system metamorphosed into an *extended modal system* capable of supporting ever more overtly emotional texts.

Not surprisingly, a number of conservative theorists deplored what they thought to be the insidious encroachment of chromaticism into traditional modality. Ghiselin Danckerts, detailing the events and defending his position as judge in the famous Vicentino–Lusitano debates (Rome, 1551), emphatically states:

> I shall not leave out the account of the abuse that was introduced in our time, not many years ago, by certain greenhorn composers in composition of polyphonic works. Having scorn for all good laws, orders, and ancient rules (persuading themselves that with their new laws and rules they will take away the fame from other composers), they show that they do not know the orders of the authentic and plagal modes that have to be necessarily observed in diatonic compositions so as not to enter into disorders because of which everything goes to ruin, or if they know them they show that they do not want to observe them, busying themselves only with sharpening and flattening notes beyond their ordinary intonation ... They do it without giving any reason, except that they compose in such way in a new manner. They like to do it, since they see that also others do it, and thus, one blind man leading another, they all tumble down into the ditch.[5]

The inevitable result of introducing ever more varied pitch-class material into the diatonic mode was to weaken the power of the modal final to represent the sum of all its parts, and, consequently, to weaken pure modality as a viable theoretical system.

Consequently, the whole subject of modal definition, and how far that definition would accommodate modernist tendencies, became the subject of further heated debates among conservative theorists, progressive composers, and enlightened aristocrats in northern Italy around the turn of the sixteenth century. The most famous of these, the Artusi–Monteverdi controversy, is perhaps the most germane to the present topic. Among the many contrapuntal solecisms Monteverdi is accused

---

5 Ghiselin Danckerts, *Trattato sopra una diffentia musicale*, c. 1560s, trans. Karol Berger as *Theories of Chromatic and Enharmonic Music in Late Sixteenth-Century Italy*, Studies in Musicology, 10 (Ann Arbor, Michigan, 1976), p. 34.

of having committed in his madrigals, Artusi mentions the fact that Monteverdi's setting of *Cruda Amarilli* (1600) contains more cadences in C (mode 12 according to Zarlino's classification) than in G (mode 7), the madrigal's final. In his *Discorso secondo musicale* (Venice, 1608), Artusi becomes quite explicit on the subject of modal purity:

> If Monteverdi wished to write a composition in a single mode (*Tono*) such as the First, he could not, because perforce there would be a mixture of modes. For when a composer constructs a piece in the First Mode, he must keep to the following order. The tenor should proceed or "modulate" by way of the notes of the First natural Mode or whichever mode he intends to construct it in ... and the bass by way of its collateral [the plagal mode] as the tenor. The contralto regularly corresponds to the bass, but an octave higher. So all vocal compositions are mixtures of the authentic and plagal. But the mixtures of Monteverdi are not regular like these, but irregular. If he sets out to give one form to his composition, he ends up giving it another, because he exceeds the bounds of mixture. Therefore one may say that he throws the pumpkins in with the lanterns.[6]

Even more relevant are Vincenzo Galilei's comments in his *Il primo libro della prattica del contrapunto* (1591) regarding the modern tendency toward extended modality:

> [T]he best and most famous contrapuntists have used cadences on any step at all [of the mode] in their vocal compositions. Moreover ... the sure identification of the mode is derived from the last note in the bass. That this is true is obvious every time this last note is hidden from the sight of the person studying the piece ... With the eyes, therefore, and not with the ears, do modern practitioners know the modes of their pieces ... Moreover, take any modern vocal piece in whatever mode and remove or add one or two notes at the end to make it terminate in other notes than the previous ones (without going to extremes, though), and practitioners today will say that there has been a mutation of mode ... And when Zarlino too would wish to persuade me again of the simplicities he writes, saying that among our modes one has a quiet nature, another deprecatory, others querulous, excited, lascivious, cheerful, somnolent, tranquil or infuriated and others yet different natures and characters, and finally that the modes as practitioners use them today have the same capacities as those he mentioned the ancient modes possessed, I would answer, convinced by experience, which teaches us the contrary, that these are all tales intended to confuse dunderheads. If our practice retains the smallest part of these aptitudes it does not derive them from the mode or the final note or the harmonic and arithmetic divisions but from the way contrapuntists make the parts progress in any of the modes according to what suits them best.[7]

From the above quotations, it would seem plausible to assume that the more progressive composers of the period did not limit their choice of auxiliary cadential areas only to those associated with any given mode; instead, these composers seem to have been guided by some other harmonic imperative. Especially in the works of the greatest composers of the period, cadential arrivals were carefully planned, and

---

6   Quoted in Claude V. Palisca, "The Artusi–Monteverdi Controversy," in Denis Arnold and Nigel Fortune (eds), *The New Monteverdi Companion* (Oxford, 1985), p. 145.

7   *Ibid.*, p. 146.

were natural conditions of both text syntax and an innate desire to create a sense of large-scale form. Composers felt too constricted when confining themselves to cadencing on the structurally significant pitch classes of the pure mode only; they obviously wanted enough freedom of expression to interpret musically the emotions occasioned by the Petrarchan and Tasso-esque poetry of the period. The pursuit of a new freedom of expression could be satisfied only by an expanded chromatic vocabulary, one which quickly outgrew the limitations of the language of diatonic modality.

III. The Medieval Gamut and Three-Hexachord-System Modulation

Figure 3.1 shows the evolution of the untransposed (or *naturalis*) Guidonian gamut from its linear inception in the eleventh century, as a pitch field of seven overlapping hexachords, to its final stage, beginning in the 1540s, as a harmonic system capable of functioning as a series of fifth-related triads supporting either a major or a minor third. Starting at the top of the figure, the Guidonian gamut, although constructed entirely from hexachords, contains within its ambitus all the pitch classes necessary to formulate the eight (and eventually twelve) church modes, the authentic finals of which are indicated by the roman numerals in the figure. Within the *recta* gamut the only "accidental" allowed was B♭, for purposes discussed previously. The three original hexachords comprising the untransposed gamut are indicated next. These three hexachords form the three-hexachord system of the natural gamut with the hexachord on C (*naturale*) at its center. The hexachords on G (*durum*) and F (*molle*) are exact transpositions of the C hexachord, and are further related to the latter by their position a fifth above and a fifth below the C hexachord respectively. To simplify, the hexachord occupying the upper fifth position of any one system, regardless of transposition level, will herein be called the *dominant* hexachord; similarly, the hexachord occupying the position of the lower fifth will herein be called the *subdominant* (literally, the "lower dominant") hexachord of the system. The hexachord governing the system (comparable to the *naturale*) will be referred to as the *central* hexachord, regardless of transposition level. A primary property of the central hexachord of any three-hexachord-gamut system is that when it is reordered as fifths, it provides all the possibilities of the composition's harmonic structure. As a background harmonic pitch field, the central hexachord contains within it all of the structurally significant root pitch classes (that is, all those modal pitch classes capable of supporting triads as well as providing all the essential cadential points within a single composition) of all eight or twelve modes of the untransposed or transposed gamut.

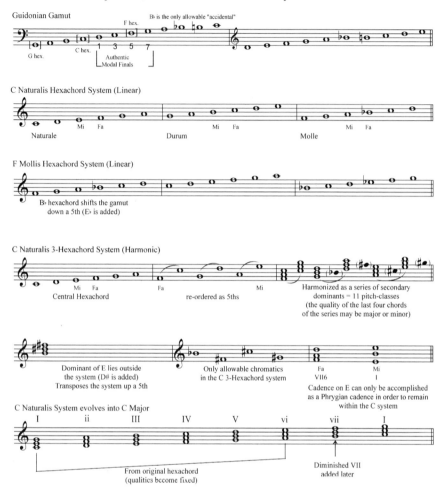

Figure 3.1 Evolution of hexachord-system modulation

Since transposition of the gamut was recognized by the addition of the next flat, the presence of E♭ would be understood as a note whose presence indicates a transposition of the central hexachord down a fifth. An E♭ would now occupy the same position as B♭ had previously occupied in the natural gamut; that is, as *fa* within the F, or *molle*, hexachord. If every added flat were sung as *fa*, then each new flat would require its own hexachord starting on *ut*. Thus, E♭ would be sung as *fa* within a B♭ hexachord (B♭ being *ut*). Since there is no B♭ hexachord in the C gamut, E♭ would naturally be viewed as *fa* within the subdominant hexachord of the *mollis*, or F gamut. In Figure 3.1, the new hexachord on B♭ would then place the new F hexachord at the center of the new system with the hexachords on C and B♭ as the dominant and subdominant hexachords respectively. In this context, the introduction of E♭ as part of the B♭ hexachord within the new three-hexachord system would be considered *musica recta.*[8]

To summarize, the addition of flats thus continues along the subdominant side of any three-hexachord-gamut system: for example, B♭ is found only within the subdominant hexachord of the *naturalis* system. Through exact transposition, each flat added after B♭ is derived from the subdominant hexachord of the next three-hexachord system transposed down a fifth, E♭ from the subdominant hexachord of the F (*mollis*) system, A♭ from the subdominant hexachord of the B♭ (2♭) system, and so forth.

The concept of a possible connection between hexachord and harmony is not new. Besides the several theorists of the seventeenth century who discuss this topic, and who will be examined later in the chapter, three studies published in the 1990s and devoted to the works of Monteverdi and Schütz emphasize the importance of hexachord mutation and transposition as a determinant of form and harmonic organization.[9] In particular, Eric Chafe's innovative theory proposes an intimate relationship between *cantus* (a system equated with signature), either *durus* (no signature) or *mollis* (a signature of one flat), and a four-hexachord framework – B♭, F, C, and G – that comprises two overlapping hexachord systems (that is, C, F, G and F, B♭, C) which operate within one or the other of the two signatures. Each hexachord system contains the equivalent of the untransposed *naturale*, *durum*, and *molle* hexachords on C, G, and F respectively.

Chafe writes: "... the expanding tonal range of early seventeenth-century music might be described as the beginnings of a circle of transposable systems, each comprising three hexachords" (p. 29). To Chafe, then, transposition implies either harmonic motion within a given hexachord system (what might best be described as a *mutation*) or a wholesale shift of system to another pitch level (meaning a *transposition* of system that necessitates a change in *cantus*). Chafe delimits the total pitch content of both untransposed and transposed gamuts to a four-hexachord range; the hexachords starting from lowest to highest are B♭, F, C, and G respectively. Each hexachord carries with it harmonic implications as well since every pitch class may serve as the root of a triad, either major or minor. Chafe maintains that the governing hexachord of each system is that which corresponds to the *naturale*; however, the six notes of any one of the hexachords within the four-hexachord framework may form the root of a complete triad, either major or minor. What Chafe explains next about the harmonic organization of the hexachord deserves a full quotation since it

---

8   See Margaret Bent, "Musica Recta and Musica Ficta," *Musica disciplina*, 26 (1972): 73–100. Our conclusions regarding what constitutes *musica recta* are similar to Bent's, although we arrive at them from a different perspective that seems, if anything, to support her arguments further.

9   Most relevant to the present study are Eric Chafe, *Monteverdi's Tonal Language* (New York, 1992), and two studies by Eva Linfield: "Formal and Tonal Organization in a 17th-Century Ritornello/Ripieno Structure," *The Journal of Musicology*, 9/2 (1991): 145–64; and "Modulatory Techniques in Seventeenth-Century Music: Schütz, a Case in Point," *Music Analysis*, 12/2 (1993): 197–214. Linfield's own work is centered on the music of Heinrich Schütz, but is nevertheless indebted to Chafe. Chafe's own theory is ultimately derived from Carl Dahlhaus (Chafe, *Monteverdi's Tonal Language*, p. 25).

forms the crux of his theory. Referring to the individual pitch classes of any given hexachord, he states:

> Five of these may be preceded by their dominants, while the sixth – the sharpest or phrygian degree – usually is not ... Usually altered from minor to major, the sixth degree serves as the final for phrygian cadences and as the dominant of the fifth cadence degree, but when it appears as the final of a dominant–tonic cadence (that is, preceded by *its* dominant) the hexachord has shifted in the sharp direction. Likewise, when major chords are altered to minor it is usually an indication either of hexachordal shift in the flat direction or an incidental expressive device (p. 27).

In other words, Chafe conceives the six notes of the individual hexachord as a reordering of fifths in which the *mi–fa* degrees form its outer perimeters. Thus the C hexachord may be rearranged F–C–G–d/D–a/A–e/E, where the upper- and lower-case letters indicate the major or minor quality of the triad. Since there is no fifth beyond E, there can be no triad built on B to act as a functional dominant without shifting hexachords (however, Chafe seems to contradict this statement by including a major triad on B within the G hexachord, as indicated in his diagram on page 27).

Although Chafe's general approach is valid for this repertory, his explanation of what constitutes a "system" is confusing. Chafe states that "... we are justified in describing the system (i.e., *cantus durus* or *mollis*) of any given madrigal as normally comprising up to three hexachords (very often two, sometimes three, very rarely fewer than two or more than three ..." (p. 28). This statement seems to contradict his four-hexachord framework mentioned above – is Chafe's definition of a "system" one that comprises two, three, or four hexachords? Chafe then continues: "The key signature, then, expresses the tonal content of the 'central' hexachord, F in the 1♭ system and C in the natural, while the work itself may introduce up to three contiguous hexachords without any necessity of key signature shift." But Chafe's theory is simply not rigorous enough to explain system modulations *within* a given *cantus*, and *without* a key signature change.

Explained in greater detail later in this chapter, the present theory differs substantially from that of Chafe's in that we specifically define a harmonic area (derived from the total number of pitch classes associated with any given three-hexachord system) as one containing eleven pitch classes, and, therefore, we fundamentally disagree with Chafe's four-hexachord framework (p. 27) since what he designates as allowable triads in both the natural and "sharp" hexachords results in overlapping hexachord systems of twelve pitch classes each. By this arrangement, each of Chafe's three-hexachord systems would contain all twelve notes of the chromatic scale, and thus would be inherently incapable of transposition because of its theoretical redundancy. Chafe's assertion that a major triad can exist on B, and therefore support a D♯ in what he calls a "sharp hexachord" (itself a misnomer since no F♯ exists in a G hexachord) within the untransposed gamut, is theoretically impossible without the entire gamut being transposed up a fifth. The sharp would then appear within the D hexachord as *mi*, the D hexachord itself being the dominant hexachord of a G system, with the C hexachord occupying the subdominant position. The same condition holds true for the 1♭ system. Here Chafe allows for a triad on E major, which too is theoretically impossible if the system is to remain untransposed (see Figure 3.1). Finally, because he limits the transpositional capabilities of the system, both within a single composition and among related pieces, Chafe is forced to drop hexachordal terminology altogether halfway through his book when he discusses Monteverdi's later madrigals.

Distinct from Chafe, we believe that we have developed a more cogent theoretical construct which effectively addresses issues either left unanswered by Chafe or avoided by him altogether. Our theoretical model is based on a transposable three-hexachord system – *in effect, a system capable of modulation*. We use the term "modulation" in its modern connotation as harmonic motion in which one harmonic area (that is, one three-hexachord system) is displaced by another: both areas have identical intervallic content. Modulation is therefore analogous to *transposition* in that both processes achieve the same results of moving the gamut, albeit temporarily, from one pitch level to another.

More specifically, the analytical methodology presented here is intended to provide a more comprehensive theory of large-scale harmonic unfolding, based on the transposition of eleven-pitch-class areas (that is, the total pitch material, both diatonic and chromatic pitch classes, associated with a given three-hexachord system) than has previously been attempted by scholars. As a result, our theoretical model of the harmonic workings of modally constructed music can be systematically applied to both secular and sacred music composed at least as early as c. 1542 (the date of Cipriano de Rore's first book of madrigals) at least to the 1670s, when the older modal system gives way to a "key-centered tonality," and thus to the works of Heinrich Schütz and his contemporaries.

IV. The Properties of the Central Hexachord as Harmonic Background

Three-hexachord systems provided all the necessary pitch material for a harmonic expression of the modes: they allowed for internal cadences to be clearly defined through the addition of leading-tone accidentals and expressive melodic embellishments, and even for tonal ambiguities through the introduction of chromatic pitch classes not found in the diatonic mode that seemingly contradicted the prevailing modality.

The reason for the apparent ambiguity arising between mode and hexachord system is easily enough explained. Each three-hexachord system is governed by its central hexachord, which, when reordered in fifths, provides all the chord formations inherent in the system. For example, the *naturalis* system is governed by the C hexachord. This means that the C hexachord, reordered in fifths, becomes the harmonic basis of any composition in which it is operational. In fact, each note of the central hexachord may become a cadential goal in its own right regardless of mode; the quality of the triad built on each root pitch of the reordered hexachord can be adjusted to allow for a leading tone.

Within the *naturalis* system, it is only the central hexachord on C, reordered in fifths, that will accommodate all of the cadential goals contained within the eight (or twelve) untransposed church modes; therefore, it is only this hexachord – and here we differ from Chafe's interpretation – that will assume harmonic control over the course of the composition, unless a modulation occurs to another system that is sustained long enough to establish a new central hexachord. Only two pitch classes differentiate the pitch material of the central hexachord from its dominant and subdominant partners; in the case of the *naturalis* system, the pitches are B♮ and B♭, from the *durum* and *molle* hexachords respectively. Neither of these pitch classes may be *goals* of motion within the *naturalis* three-hexachord system, although a triad on B♭ functioning contrapuntally as an upper neighbor to A, or as part of a fifths cycle to F, would be allowable and is seen often enough; after all, B♭ is the only allowable flat in the C system. However, as a harmonic goal, B♭ would be impossible unless it were associated with one of the transposed *mollis* systems, since this pitch class does not exist in any of the church modes of the untransposed gamut. As a pitch class within the *naturalis* system, B♮ functions as a leading tone to the triad built on the first note of the central C hexachord. Its function is therefore similar to that of other sharps of the system; all of these sharp accidentals are contrapuntally derived, and none may form the root of a triad and still remain within the system. The only exception to this, at least by the time of Monteverdi, would be a first-inversion diminished triad on B♮ as a contrapuntal leading tone chord resolving to C, although any triad on B♮ (with or without the missing pitch, D♯) still remains an impossibility as a harmonic goal within the system.

As shown below, each pitch class of the central hexachord may form root-position triads of various qualities (major or minor, or both). Altogether, the system comprises exactly eleven pitch classes: the six of the central hexachord, the added flat from the subdominant hexachord, one added natural (or sharp) from the dominant hexachord, and three sharps needed to form the major sixth at cadences:

Quality of third:	A	E	B♭/B♮	F♮/F♯	C♮/C♯	G♮/G♯
C hexachord:	F –	C –	G –	d –	a –	e

Taking each triad in turn, the triad on F must be major if it is to be a cadential goal; an F minor triad is possible, but highly improbable since an isolated A♭ without an E♭ preparation would seem an unlikely occurrence and would imply the addition of flats beyond the *naturalis* system. Alternatively, an A♭ as an inflected passing tone for poetical or textural reasons would also be a possibility. The next triad in the cycle, C, can only be major since an E♭ would modulate the system down a fifth into *mollis*. A G triad may occur as either major or minor. Likewise, the triads on D, A, and E may also support a raised or lowered third, depending upon harmonic function. Note also that the E triad may utilize a G♯ in order to act as a secondary dominant to A; consequently, in the *naturalis* three-hexachord system, G♯ as a chord tone is preferred to its enharmonic A♭.

Examining the literature of the period confirms the above pitch-class preferences. For instance, in Giaches de Wert's madrigal publications Book 7 (1581), Book 10 (1591), and Book 11 (1595),[10] there is not a single instance of an A♭, a A♯, or a

---

10 Giaches de Wert, *Opera omnia*, ed. Carol MacClintock and Melvin Bernstein (17 vols, n.p., 1961–77).

D♯; instead, these tones are invariably spelled G♯, B♭, and E♭. To be precise, each madrigal, in all three books, unfolds only one flat accidental – either B♭ in *cantus durus* or E♭ in *cantus mollis* – the rest of the chromatics are sharps. If fewer than eleven pitch classes are unfolded (and these instances are rare), then only sharps are presented. It is not improbable therefore to assume that Giaches de Wert considered the chromatic spectrum of the *naturalis* gamut and the *mollis* gamut (that is, one transposition level down a fifth) not to exceed two flats (B♭ and E♭), depending on the governing three-hexachord system, with the remaining four accidentals as sharps only. Most keyboard music of the period reflects the spelling of these tones in the *naturalis* and *mollis* gamuts as described: the "black keys" are invariably labeled B♭, C♯, E♭, F♯, and G♯. It is only when fully chromatic keyboards are discussed by theorists, in particular Vicentino and Zarlino, that we find all enharmonic equivalents included. These experimental keyboards were, however, devised in order to make the gamut transposable at all levels, thus going beyond the normal C and F three-hexachord systems generally in use.[11]

To continue our discussion of the harmonic properties of the central hexachord, the above diagram of the reordered *naturalis* hexachord shows the E triad as the terminus of the fifths cycle; a triad built on the next fifth would, therefore, be out of the *naturalis* system altogether. A triad on B, acting as dominant to E, would necessitate a D♯, the enharmonic equivalent of E♭. Just as E♭ would signal a transposition down a fifth from the *naturalis* to the *mollis* three-hexachord system, so would D♯ signify a transposition up a fifth from the *naturalis* to the *durus* three-hexachord system. Each hexachord system, as stated earlier, contains a total of eleven pitch classes; the presence of the missing pitch class implies a transposition (or modulation – the two terms are synonymous here) either up or down a fifth depending upon how the pitch class is spelled. In defining "modulation" as a motion from one eleven-pitch class area to another within a single piece, the pitch classes acquired as part of the new three-hexachord system must be considered *musica recta*. The new gamut thus formed displaces the previous one, even if temporarily. (In more chromatic pieces, there may, in fact, be more than one system modulation – see the discussion of Rore's *Da le belle contrade* below). Further, the chromatic material of each hexachord system may contain any, but not necessarily all, of the eleven pitch classes of that system, including the one flat from the subdominant hexachord and one sharp (or natural) from the dominant hexachord, along with the remaining three chromatic tones spelled as sharps, used as *subsemitonia modi* (leading tones). Gioseffo Zarlino's comment concerning the need to adjust the chord quality of modal pitch classes to create a leading tone is particularly relevant here. He states: "[E]very

---

11 See Karol Berger, *Theories of Chromatic and Enharmonic Music in Late Sixteenth-Century Italy*, Studies in Musicology, 10 (Ann Arbor, Michigan, 1980), pp. 51–6. Elsewhere, Berger cites Pietro Aaron's treatise *Toscanello in musica* (Book II, ch. 40), as well as his *Lucidario in musica* of 1545. Aaron plainly states that the Italian twelve-step monochord and Italian organs in general include G♯, but consistently omit both A♭ and D♯ (Karol Berger, "The Common and the Unusual Steps of Musica Ficta: A Background for the Gamut of Orlando di Lasso's *Prophetiae Sybillarum*," *Belgisch tijdschrift voor muziekwetenschap*, 39–40 (1985–86): 69.

progression from imperfect to perfect consonance should include in at least one part the step of a large semitone, expressed or implied. To this purpose the chromatic and enharmonic steps will be found very useful, provided they are written in the manner to be described elsewhere."[12] From a historical perspective it is interesting to note the following: before the sixteenth century, compositions tended to present eight or nine different pitch classes at most within any given three-hexachord system, but, by the end of the next century, composers were consistently unfolding eleven. As far back as the 1940s, Edward Lowinsky made a similar observation:

> It has not been observed yet that all seven Psalms [referring to Lasso's *Penitential Psalms*] work with exactly the same tone material. Each Psalm uses eleven tones. If we examine these eleven tones, we find that each time they fit into the pattern of a scale comprising two chromatic tetrachords. The only chromatic tone missing is the one between the tetrachords, or in other words the tritone. To give one example: Psalms 1 and 3 have no key signature and employ the notes of this scale: A – G♯ – G♮ – F♯ – F♮ – E – D – C♯ – C♮ – B – B♭ – A ... [13]

Even though Lowinsky recognized that the missing pitch of the *cantus durus* system Lasso employed was D♯/E♭, he never extended his findings – relegated to a footnote! – beyond Lasso's *Penitential Psalms*, nor did he theorize about the significance of eleven-pitch-class areas as a harmonic system applicable to a much larger repertory.

Eventually, by the end of the seventeenth century, the emerging conception of key-centered tonality required that the variable quality (either major or minor) of the triads contained within any given three-hexachord system, or "key," be fixed (see Figure 3.1, last system). For example, within the C *naturalis* system a triad on G would only be major while a triad built on D would only be minor. At the same time, the three hexachords of any given system began to realize a large-scale harmonic relationship – the pitch material associated with the subdominant hexachord became fixed within a larger harmonic progression as "pre-dominant" harmony and assumed its position as IV within the tonic progression. No longer were B♭ and B♮ indiscriminately interchanged within a purely linear context without harmonic justification. The result of these fixed associations was the formation of major "keys:" the C *naturalis* system became C major, the F *mollis* system became F major, and so on.

---

12 Gioseffo Zarlino, *The Art of Counterpoint. Part Three of "Le istitutioni harmoniche,"* *1558*, trans. Guy A. Marco and Claude V. Palisca (New Haven and London, 1968), p. 83.

13 Edward Lowinsky, *Secret Chromatic Art in the Netherlands Motet* (New York, 1946), pp. 100–101 n. 34.

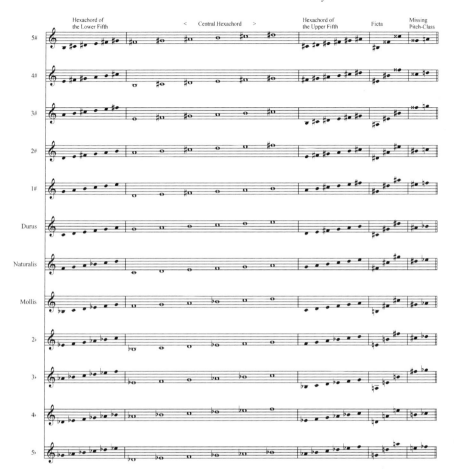

Figure 3.2 Three-hexachord systems

The entire three-hexachord theoretical system and its most common transpositions are presented in Figure 3.2. Reading from left to right, each grouping of three hexachords forms its own self-contained system comprising a central or governing hexachord, after which the particular three-hexachord system is named, and which, when reordered as fifths, is capable of harmonic potential, and its associated hexachords that flank it a fifth below and a fifth above. Next to this basic diatonic pitch material are indicated the leading-tone accidentals needed to form formal cadences. In the figure, these leading-tone accidentals are labeled *ficta*. We use this term in its original sense to mean those pitch classes that exist outside the *diatonic* gamut. In addition, for these notes to belong to any given eleven-pitch-class area, they must be written into the music, not simply implied as an editorial or performance emendation. Besides, the addition of flats or sharps by the performer would rarely if ever result in a system change; not only would one usually allow the tritone to prevent a system modulation, but also the addition of consecutive flats would eventually destroy any sense of tonal organization.

Figure 3.2 identifies the four chromatics associated with each three-hexachord system (the "added flat" found in the subdominant hexachord, the "added sharp" (or natural) from the dominant hexachord, plus the three sharp accidentals) resulting in a harmonic area or region of eleven pitch classes. Each eleven-pitch-class area is associated with a missing pitch class indicated at the end of each line of the figure. As stated above, the *naturalis* three-hexachord system (named after its central hexachord) represents the untransposed Guidonian gamut and is associated with the missing pitch class D♯/E♭. Similarly, the *mollis* 1♭ system omits G♯/A♭. When a composer moves from one eleven-pitch-class area to another within a single composition, a new pitch class is acquired and a previously present pitch class is omitted. As we will demonstrate, a relationship exists between the linear accumulation of new *ficta* pitch classes (which become *recta* in the gamut of the new transposition) and harmonic movement at deeper structural levels. The sharp and flat enharmonic identity of the missing pitch class signifies direction (up or down) when it appears through the process of modulation, defined here as the movement from one eleven-pitch-class region to another. It is interesting to note, however, that with rare exceptions, only two signatures, *cantus durus* (natural) and *cantus mollis* (one flat), govern any given transposition level, no matter how many sharps of flats may be contained within the system.

Theorists of the first decades of the seventeenth century, if not earlier, alluded to only certain chromatic pitch classes as being acceptable within the untransposed and transposed gamuts. For instance, in chapter 32 of his treatise *L'antica musica ridotta alla moderna prattica* (Rome, 1555),[14] Nicola Vicentino presented polyphonic four-voice cadences on different scale degrees in each mode (see example 32 in the translated edition), including those of lesser structural significance (those not on the final, repercussion and mediant degrees). In all modes in *cantus durus*, Vicentino's "♮ quadro" (hard hexachord), the only *ficta* used were C♯, F♯, G♯, and B♭; while in *cantus mollis* (specifically the lydian and hypolydian modes, which Vicentino pointed out were usually written "per ♭ molle" [in the soft hexachord]), the *ficta* he used were F♯, C♯, B♮, and E♭. Thus in *cantus durus* (the *naturalis* three-hexachord system), both E♭ and D♯ were omitted, leaving the D as a natural before the final cadence in both authentic and plagal phrygian modes. Similarly, in *cantus mollis*, Vicentino had no operable cadence at all on A in modes 5 and 6 in order to avoid the missing pitch G♯ (the leading tone of A) or its enharmonic equivalent A♭.

A contemporary theorist of relevance to this discussion is Adriano Banchieri (1567–1637).[15] In both his *L'organo suonarino* (Venice, 1605)[16] and his third edition

---

14 Chapter 32 of Book 3 is entitled in the original "Dimostratione di molte cadentie che si usanò ne gli otto Modi, à quattro voci, della Musica participata, e mista" (translated as "Demonstration of Many Four-Voice Cadences Used in the Eight Modes of Tempered and Mixed Music"); see fols 55r–57r. See Rika Maniates's translation of the entire Book 3 as *Ancient Music Adapted to Modern Practice* (New Haven and London, 1996), pp. 173–80.

15 Banchieri was particularly an ardent admirer of Monteverdi's works and even quotes the *cantus* part of "non più guerra, pietate" from Monteverdi's Fourth Book in his own *Cartella musicale* of 1614 (see Paolo Fabbri, *Monteverdi*, trans. Tim Carter [Cambridge, 1994], pp. 106, 138). Banchieri also sent Monteverdi a letter congratulating the composer on his acceptance into the Bologna's famed Accademia dei Filarmonici (*ibid.*, pp. 193–4).

16 Facsimile edn (Bologna, 1969).

of *Cartella musicale* (Venice, 1614),[17] Banchieri clearly presents the allowable cadences for each of the eight church modes, five in *cantus durus* and three in *cantus mollis* (see Figure 3.3).[18] The chromaticism found at Banchieri's cadential points (chromaticism arising from the use of *subsemitonium modi*) in those modes in *cantus durus* is identical to the chromaticism associated with the *naturalis* three-hexachord system illustrated in Figure 3.4.

Figure 3.3   Banchieri's modes

17 Facsimile edn (Bologna, n.d.).

18 Figure 3.3 is taken from Banchieri's earlier treatise, *L'organo suonarino*, p. 41, reproduced in Walter Atcherson, "Key and Mode in 17th-Century Music Theory Books," *Journal of Music Theory*, 17 (1973): 219. Banchieri discusses the church modes from the standpoint of a practicing seventeenth-century musician; that is, he transposes several of them (indicated in Figure 3.3) into *cantus mollis*, reflecting what was probably current practice on the part of church choir directors and organists; see Joel Lester, *Between Modes and Keys: German Theory 1592–1802* (New York, 1989), pp. 78–9.

Significantly, D♯ is not used in the cadence for either of Banchieri's phrygian modes (modes 4 and 5) even though half-steps occur at all other cadential points in this *cantus*! Only three accidentals are indicated by Banchieri – G♯, C♯, and F♯ – in *cantus durus*. The B♭, however, while not included in the diagram (since it does not function as a leading tone), is included in Banchieri's contrapuntal illustrations of the *cantus durus* modes (cf. Banchieri's illustration of D dorian counterpoint in the *Cartella musicale*, p. 72 of the facsimile edition). Similarly, E♭s are added in *cantus mollis* modes as a matter of course (see Banchieri's mode 2 counterpoint, p. 73). The three modes in *cantus mollis* likewise contain only three sharps, C♯, F♯, and B♮. The G♯ is omitted as a leading tone from the modes in this *cantus*; all the lower neighbor Gs in modes 6 and 7 are left natural. It would therefore seem reasonable to assume that, for Banchieri, only eleven pitch classes were available within any given *cantus* without undertaking a transposition of the entire gamut.

A contemporary of Banchieri is the equally important German theorist Otto Siegfried Harnisch, whose discussion of monophonic and four-voice polyphonic cadences in his *Artis musicae delineatio* (Frankfurt, 1608) also supports an eleven-pitch-class gamut.[19] Figure 3.4 presents Harnisch's monophonic cadences in all twelve modes. Typical of most sixteenth- and early seventeenth-century theorists (including Banchieri), Harnisch recognizes the final, third, and fifth of the mode as being structurally significant. He then applies figurations to four-voice polyphonic cadences, with the addition of several "rare" or irregular cadential points in some of the modes.

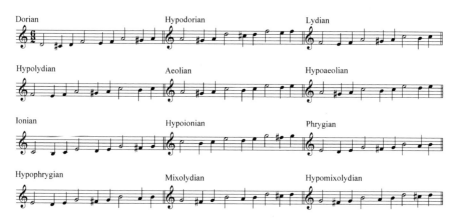

Figure 3.4   Harnisch's monophonic cadences

No polyphonic cadences utilize accidentals beyond those available within the untransposed gamut, so their depiction here would be redundant. Also, since only the cadence of each mode is illustrated, Harnisch has no need to include the B♭ of the untransposed gamut – which is why his diagram only includes ten pitch classes.

---

19 The following relies heavily on a detailed discussion of Harnisch's treatise in Benito V. Rivera, *German Music Theory in the Early 17th Century: The Treatises of Johannes Lippius* (Ann Arbor, Michigan, 1980), pp. 210–15. Our Figure 3.4 is taken from this source.

Additionally, his twelve modes are not "church keys" in the manner of Banchieri, but are the traditional eight modes augmented by those four proposed by Glarean and Zarlino, who added the regular and hypo forms of the ionian and aeolean modes. We are therefore dealing with only the untransposed gamut. However, even here Harnisch is careful to include only accidentals associated with the *naturalis* three-hexachord system – C♯, F♯, and G♯ – even if the illustration of the mode shows cadence points on E or B. Harnisch's phrygian, hypophrygian, mixolydian, and hypomixolydian cadences consistently avoid both D♯ and A♯, resulting in whole-tone lower neighbors to the *final* and *fifth* degrees of the phrygian and hypophrygian modes, and to the third degrees in the mixolydian modes. Yet within these same modes, both F♯ and C♯ are clearly indicated (see Figure 3.4).

In Harnisch's polyphonic settings of the phrygian modes, the cadences to E are all of the phrygian type, with F moving to E in the bass voice. In these modes there is also no root-position cadence to B; the monophonic formula is absorbed into a plagal cadence on E, with B forming the fifth of the E triad. In fact, Harnisch disregards a polyphonic cadence on B altogether in hypophrygian, mixolydian, and hypomixolydian modes, stating that such a cadence appears only in phrygian mode – and exclusively as a melodic formula – and is currently "not in use" by contemporary composers.[20]

Last, and perhaps most important for this study, is the *Musurgia universalis* (Rome, 1650) of Athanasius Kircher, the primary theorist whom Eric Chafe calls upon to support his own conception of hexachord modulation.[21] Kircher gives four-voice polyphonic cadences in all eight modes, as do Banchieri and Harnisch before him, followed by an additional four; each modal cadence is complete with accidentals necessary to function as leading tones. Interestingly, Kircher ends each modal cadence on a full triad with a major third, no matter whether the mode is minor or major, the only exception being the final triad in the hypophrygian mode (discussed below). Kircher illustrates polyphonic cadences in more than one section of the *Musurgia*; however, the cadential group that is most relevant to this discussion (and not addressed by Chafe) occurs in Book 8 of the second volume (pp. 63–4). Under the heading "Systema universale quo assumptum thema per XII tonos mutatur essentialiter" ("Universal system in which a given theme is completely changed [transposed] through the twelve modes"), Kircher demonstrates how a four-voice polyphonic cadence can be constructed in all modes, in both *cantus durus* and *cantus mollis*. His use of modal transposition to illustrate certain authentic–plagal pairings is similar to Banchieri's "church keys," although Kircher expands the number to twelve. Figure 3.5 summarizes Kircher's "systema."

---

20 *Ibid.*, p. 213.

21 Athansius Kircher, *Musurgia universalis, sive Ars magna consoni et dissoni in X libros digesta*, repr. edn, ed. Ulf Scharlau (Hildesheim, 1970). Chafe's discussion of Kircher and his particular approach to hexachord modulation is quite thorough, and the reader is referred to that source for further information (see Chafe, *Monteverdi's Tonal Language*, pp. 41–53).

Mode (& Final)	Cantus	Accidentals	Comments
I. Dorian (D)	durus	C♯, F♯, B♭	
II. Hypodorian (G)	mollis	F♯, B♯, E♭	
III. Phrygian (A)	durus	G♯, C♯	
IV. Hypophrygian (E)	durus	D♯	Kircher states: *in hoc tono non valet clausula* ("no good cadence can be made in this mode")
V. Lydian (B♭)	mollis	E♭	
VI. Hypolydian (F)	mollis	none	
VII. Mixolydian (G)	durus	F♯	
VIII. Hypomixolydian (C)	mollis	none	
IX. Ionian (D)	mollis	C♯	
X. Hypoionian (A)	durus	G♯, C♯	
XI. Iastian (C)	durus	none	
XII. Hypoiastian (B♭)	mollis	E♭	

Figure 3.5   Kircher's "Systema universale"

The pitch content illustrated in Figure 3.5 confirms that Kircher's cadential progressions, similar to Banchieri's and Harnisch's, operate within eleven-pitch-class areas associated with either *cantus durus* (which omits D♯/E♭) or *cantus mollis* (which omits G♯/A♭); thus a major triad on B (supporting a D♯), in *cantus durus*, is avoided altogether. Kircher's "Systema" supports this fact by illustrating an authentic cadence in the hypophrygian mode (IV) on E in *cantus durus*, with a D♯ as leading tone. However, Kircher warns the reader, as does Harnisch before him, that such cadences "are not well made in this mode" (see Figure 3.5). This curious comment seems, on the surface, to be puzzling: what harm can a D♯ do other than strengthen a cadence to E? The only viable explanation would be that these theorists believed that in *cantus durus* D♯ was simply not a usable pitch, and that E was the terminus of the *naturalis* C hexachord and, therefore, could not be articulated by an applied dominant on B.

V. The Music of the Early Sixteenth Century and Three-Hexachord Gamut Systems

While theorists of the sixteenth and seventeenth centuries directly or indirectly acknowledge a gamut of eleven pitch classes – comprising the pitch material of the three diatonic hexachords (*naturale*, *durum*, and *molle*, with their octave transpositions) and their additional *ficta* – and state that this gamut was transposable either up or down by fifths, what proof is there that *composers* deliberately thought in terms of three-hexachord systems?

Evidence that composers, at least by the sixteenth century, if not earlier, were conscious of three-hexachord systems, and, indeed, deliberately sought to incorporate these systems into their compositions, can be verified by numerous examples. The following illustrations, starting with the motet *Dominus regnavit* of Josquin des Prez, may be used as exemplars. *Dominus regnavit* is written in a *mollis* 1♭ system, the hexachords of which are represented by the two conflicting signatures: B♭ in the *discantus* and tenor, circumscribing hexachords on F and C; and B♭ and E♭ in the *altus* and *bassus*, delimiting hexachords on B♭ and F (see Example 3.1).[22] The three hexachords together comprise the *mollis* transposed diatonic gamut whose central hexachord is on F. Reordered as fifths, the 1♭ system of *Dominus regnavit*, with F as *finalis*, has the following properties:

Quality of third:	D	A	E♮/E♭	B♭	F	C
Hexachordal pitch classes	B♭ –	F –	C –	g –	d –	a
	IV	I	V	ii	vi	iii

E♭ (the flat seventh degree) is the allowable flat in this gamut system. This pitch, like the others of the F hexachord, can either function as the root of a triad or be a chord tone of C. In addition, Roman numerals are indicated below each hexachord pitch class. Their presence is solely for the convenience of showing the harmonic relationship of the final to the other pitch classes in the system: the numerals are not intended to indicate tonal relationships in the sense of a modern-day key-centered tonality.

---

22 Josquin Desprez, *Werken*, ed. Albert J. Smijers (Amsterdam and Leipzig, 1921–56), vol. 17, pp. 33–40.

Example 3.1 Josquin, *Dominus regnavit* (opening)

By depicting the pitch material of the motet in this manner, one can easily see how Josquin has ordered his motet in terms of its pitch content and cadence structure. Also, the localized relationship of the hexachord tones to each other can tell us a great deal about Josquin's compositional choices and how he perceived chordal relationships. For instance, in the case of *Dominus regnavit*, the above hexachord diagram shows that Josquin confined himself to the diatonic gamut, with no modulation of system, a procedure typical of the music of the early sixteenth century; the only chromatic relationship found in the work is that between E♭ and E♮. Harmonically, Josquin emphasizes the first three hexachord pitches for all the structurally significant cadences in the motet. What is striking about this particular work is that only the first two hexachord pitches, B♭ and F respectively, consistently support a major third in their triads. All the others, with the exception of C, which is the only hexachord pitch class that supports either a major or a minor third, are invariably minor chords (shown by the lower-case Roman numerals). It is significant that the minor triads of the hexachord never become harmonic goals in this motet. Instead, they function contrapuntally with respect to the first three fifths of the central hexachord, B♭–F–C, as neighboring or deceptive motions (mm. 101–2) that create a continuous contrapuntal texture aided by diatonic 5–6 exchanges (see, for example, m. 69, where E♭ major exchanges with C minor). The latter technique is especially important in this work since a rising chromatic segment is derived from the progression E♭–c–C–F; namely, E♭–E♮–F is worked out motivically, thus creating a *dyad conflict*, a conflict which arises when a diatonic pitch is inflected to its immediate chromatic neighbor. In this case, the dyad conflict is between E♭ and E♮, the one chromatic alteration in the *mollis* hexachord.

On a deeper structural level, the harmonic organization of *Dominus regnavit* is based upon the interrelationship of two conjunct diatonic tetrachords spaced a fifth apart, F–G–A–B♭ and B♭–C–D–E♭, that govern the paired canonic imitation of the opening 28 measures. These two tetrachords are derived from the central and subdominant hexachords of the 1♭ system on F and B♭ respectively, whose tones – not coincidentally – are also the first two of the reordered *mollis* hexachord. All the diatonic pitch material of the *discantus* (soprano) and tenor voices relates to both the F and C hexachords, the C hexachord being that of the upper fifth of the system. Consequently, these voices never sing an E♭; this is the reason for the one-flat signatures. However, the *altus* and *bassus* contain pitch material from the B♭ and F hexachords exclusively, and thus E♭ is found only in their parts, which is the reason for the two-flat signatures in the original publication. The result of these interactions between the two voice pairings, often leading to formal cadences on F, allows Josquin to develop the E♭/E♮ dyad conflict that permeates the motet.

Josquin concludes the work, fittingly, with an authentic cadence followed by a plagal cadence. The last two triads thus summarize the relationship of the two hexachords on F and B♭, now interpreted as a harmonic function within the F lydian mode in *cantus mollis*. What is of considerable interest here is that E♭ is not a diatonic pitch within the modal octave of *mollis* lydian. Josquin seems to be more preoccupied with exploring the horizontal and vertical relationships of the two seminal F and B♭ hexachords – or, more precisely, their initial tetrachords – than with prolonging, or even expressing, an idealized F mode. Noticeably, cadences on either the third or the fifth degree are absent. More to the point, however, it is questionable whether or not mode should even enter the analytical discussion at all in works of this kind.

A knowledge of the governing three-hexachord system is essential when applying unwritten flats, either editorially or in performance, to correct non-harmonic relations. In a 1♭ three-hexachord system, for example, the only available flat beyond the B♭ already in the system would be E♭, *fa* of the subdominant hexachord. To go beyond this would mean a transposition out of the gamut system altogether, since A♭ is missing in a 1♭ system. Invariably, the composer will indicate if and when a transposition is to take place by actually writing in the new accidental at the appropriate moment.

Some modern musicologists support the notion of hexachord systems which are strictly defined by the number of flats allowed in each system, if only by implication. For instance, Karol Berger, in discussing the theory of "chain reaction," flats that are employed in order to correct vertical relations (a theory with which he is in total disagreement), states the following:

If the normal way of correcting melodic and vertical relations was by means of flats, and if "chain reactions" whereby one flat provoked the next were not practiced, it follows that pieces in which all internal accidentals were introduced in order to avoid melodic and vertical non-harmonic intervals would use at most one more flat than the number of flats in the key signature of the voice with the largest number of flats in the signature. Pieces in which all parts had no flats in the signature would require *at most* [our emphases] the use of B♭, pieces in which at least one part had a B♭-signature would require at most the use of B♭ and E♭, and pieces in which at least one part had a B♭/E♭-signature would require at most the use of B♭, E♭ and A♭.[23]

Berger's comments regarding the limits of possible *ficta* based on the number of flats in the signature would seem to follow general practice; however, a much more reliable method of determining the greatest number of possible flats is to first determine the three-hexachord system upon which the piece is based. The subdominant hexachord of the system always contains the greatest number of flats of that system. There are pieces in which the signature does not always reflect the actual system, however, since Renaissance composers seemed reluctant to go beyond two flats as a signature.[24]

Albert J. Smijers, editor of Josquin's *Werken*, reduces the conflicting signatures of the 1539 Nuremberg edition of *Dominus regnavit* to one flat in all voices, preferring to write in the missing E♭s. By doing so, he tacitly agrees that the governing system is a 1♭ system even though both *altus* and *bassus* have two flats in their original signatures. Carl Dahlhaus took exception to Smijers's liberality, emphatically stating that the piece was controlled by a 2♭ system in which the *secunda pars* "modulates" to a 1♭ system for 36 measures before returning to a 2♭ system for the remainder of the piece.[25] While Dahlhaus's criticism of Smijers's edition is correct in editorial terms, Dahlhaus's assertion of a 2♭ three-hexachord system, as opposed to a 1♭ system, is unsupportable. First, not a single A♭ – a pitch class that would have confirmed a 2♭ system – is either indicated or implied; and, second, E♮s abound, functioning as both *subsemitonum* to F, and as *mi* within the C hexachord – the hexachord of the upper fifth of the 1♭ gamut system.

It is rare to find pieces composed during the late fifteenth and early sixteenth centuries that indicate more than a single flat in their signatures, but compositions with two flats do exist. One outstanding example of such a work is the famous motet *Absalon fili mi*, once attributed to Josquin, but now thought more probably to be by Pierre de la Rue.

Despite the glaring scribal errors contained in MS Royal 8 G VII (in particular, the incorrect placement of flats in the tenor and bass signatures), the principal source for this work, it is almost certain that two flats, B♭ and E♭, were meant in all four voices.[26] That being the case, a 2♭ system governs the motet, and is also an indication

---

23 Berger, *Musica Ficta*, op. cit.: 121.

24 Op. cit.

25 Carl Dahlhaus, *Studies on the Origin of Harmonic Tonality*, trans. Robert O. Gjerdingen (Princeton, New Jersey, 1990), pp. 252–3.

26 Robert Toft, "Pitch Content and Modal Procedure in Josquin's *Absalon, fili mi*," *Tijdschrift van de Vereniging voor Nederlandse Muziekgeschiedenis*, 33 (1983): 7–8. Toft has proved conclusively that the low octave D♭ in the bass is a scribal error for a low octave E♭.

of its mode – transposed lydian *mollis* on B♭. What makes this particular motet so unusual is its modulation of systems that plunges the piece into a 4♭ system by its end, reflecting King David's ever-deepening despair over the loss of his son. Not only do the hexachord systems change – with each new system introducing its own missing pitch spelled as a flat – but the mode changes as well, beginning in major (transposed lydian) and ending in minor (transposed dorian *mollis*). In both cases the final of the *mode* remains the same, B♭. However, as the *quality* of the B♭ triad changes, starting in m. 36, this produces what may be music history's earliest example of a piece that begins in major and ends in its parallel minor.

Compositionally, the opening of *Absalon* is not unlike that of Josquin's *Dominus regnavit*, discussed above. That is, the answering voice enters on the subdominant hexachord of the 2♭ system, which presages the downward thrust into ever flatter hexachords that pervade the motet. The background modal final, B♭, is not convincingly confirmed as such until it is asserted by a series of structurally significant cadences in mm. 21, 24, and 36, culminating, finally, on an incomplete B♭ triad at the end of the motet. The following diagram shows the reordered 2♭ hexachord system that governs the motet:

Quality of third	G	D	A♮/A♭	E♭	B♭	F
Central hexachord:	E♭	B♭	F	c	g	d
	IV	I	V			

(A♭, the flat seventh degree, is the allowable flat in this system)

As in *Dominus regnavit*, all cadences fall on either the tonic or the subdominant of the mode so long as the 2♭ hexachord remains in effect. Note too, that only the dominant carries an inflected third degree while the other pitch classes of the central hexachord remain fixed as to chord quality. In m. 51, D♭ enters and shifts the 2♭ system down a fifth to a 3♭ system with E♭ as its central hexachord. Significantly, the text at this point reads "Non, vivam ultra" ("Let me not live longer"). We might infer that perhaps the composer no longer believed that the primary 2♭ system was still "alive." The new hexachordal arrangement now has a B♭ minor triad available since B♭ is now in the dominant position within the new hexachord:

Quality of third	C	G	D♮/D♭	A♭	E♭	B♭
Central hexachord:	A♭	E♭	B♭	f	c	g
	IV	I	V			

(D♭ is the allowable flat in this system)

Within the confines of the new hexachord, triads on D♭ (the flat seventh degree of the system) appear frequently, along with triads on E♭ and B♭ (both as minor and without the third). The new system remains in effect until the next missing pitch,

---

The motet has received a decidedly more accurate transcription with two flats in all voices (see Pierre de la Rue, *Opera omnia*, vol. 9, ed. Nigel St John Davison [Neuhausen-Stuttgart, 1996], where it is found among the *opera dubia*). All analytical references are based on this edition.

G♭ (the missing pitch of the 3♭ system), is added. This occurs in m. 66 on the word "plorans" ("weeping"). As a result, the previous 3♭ system now shifts down another fifth to a 4♭ three-hexachord system on A♭, with G♭ – used both as a minor third of the E♭ minor triad and as a root-position chord in its own right – the allowable added flat within the 4♭ system:

Quality of third:	F	C	G♮/G♭	D♮/D♭	A♭	E♭
Central hexachord:	D♭	A♭	E♭	b♭	f	c
	IV	I	V			

(G♭ is the allowable flat in this system)

This last hexachordal system remains uncontested; that is, there is no B♮, the missing pitch of the 4♭ system spelled as an augmented second, to revert the system up to three flats, nor is there a C♭ to transpose the system further down in the flat direction. The presence of G♭ not only confirms the new and last system, but also plays an important role in the final cadence, acting as the flat sixth degree within the B♭ dorian *mollis* mode. Only in the last 4♭ system do we see two hexachord pitch classes that carry an inflected third, those on E♭ and on b♭. Note too that the opening B♭ major sonority, spelled in upper case, has now become minor and spelled in lower case since that is the position it now occupies within the 4♭ system.

To sum up this area of the discussion, composers during the fifteenth century and well into the first half of the sixteenth century expanded the theoretical confines of traditional modality by operating simultaneously within two theoretical paradigms: the older church modality expressed within a governing three-hexachord system. As a result, modal finals were sometimes relegated to the sidelines of the piece, acting primarily as an ultimate point of resolution at the conclusion. However, within the body of the piece itself, harmonic and melodic organization revolved around mutation within the background three-hexachord system, the number of allowable flats added being contingent upon the number of flats contained within the subdominant hexachord of the system. Transposition of the system, either up or down a fifth, as part of the internal organization of the composition, was uncommon (*Absalon* is one of a few exceptional cases) until the 1540s, when composers, especially the madrigalists of northern Italy, deliberately incorporated an increased chromatic pitch field into their music. Pure modality, if there ever were such a thing, gave way to what we call *extended modality*, a harmonic/modal system that had to contend with many more chromatic pitch classes presented at a faster rate than had ever been the case previously. Similarly, the increased chromaticism affected the concomitant three-hexachord system, which now took on an added harmonic dimension of its own, in effect displacing an ever more weakly defined modality. It is the three-hexachord system and its emerging harmonic organization – analyzed by reordering of the hexachord in fifths – that directly informs the present theory.

Even with the extensive system modulations that characterize *Absalon*, its modal language still remains basically consonant; there are no sharp accidentals in the piece, and there is no attempt to apply direct chromaticism. For that, we must now turn to the chromatic composers of the next generation.

VI. Modulation of Gamut Three-Hexachord Systems in Chromatic Modality

We now turn our attention to specific pieces that contain a transposition (or modulation) of system within them. Before we look at specific pieces, however, we need to review what determines a particular eleven-pitch three-hexachord gamut system. Our determination is based on the following four criteria: (1) the signature, or *cantus*, of the composition which identifies the initial gamut system: a natural signature indicates a *naturalis* system, a 1♭ signature indicates a *mollis* system, a 2♭ signature indicates a 2♭ system, and so on; (2) the absence of the missing pitch class associated with a particular three-hexachord system; (3) the presence of the missing pitch class of the three-hexachord system spelled as the minor third degree above the root of the central hexachord of the prevailing gamut system, effectively transposing the system down a fifth; (4) the presence of the missing pitch class of the three-hexachord system spelled as the augmented second (the enharmonic equivalent of the minor third degree) above the root of the central hexachord of the prevailing gamut system, which would effectively transpose the system up a fifth. Once the composition has begun, and the governing three-hexachord system has been determined, the introduction of the missing pitch from that system will effect a modulation of that system either a fifth up or down, depending upon its spelling. Compositions may remain within one gamut system throughout, unfolding only eleven pitch classes, or they may have fewer than eleven pitch classes, or they may modulate systems once or more than once, depending upon compositional factors such as text-setting or even a composer's desire to complete a chromatic aggregate. The following analytical discussions should clarify how gamut systems and their modulations inform the background structures of so many vocal pieces of the mid-sixteenth century to early seventeenth century.

Giulio Cesare Monteverdi, in his defense of his famous brother, Claudio, in his appended "Declaration" to the latter's *Scherzi musicali* of 1607, mentions that Claudio Monteverdi acknowledged Cipriano de Rore (1516–1565) as the originator of the *seconda prattica*.[27] Cesare Monteverdi names certain madrigals of Rore which, he feels, approximate his brother's new practice. Among these is *Da le belle contrade* from Rore's Fifth Book (1566).[28]

The madrigal, based on an Italian sonnet by an unknown poet, is set in an F mode in *cantus mollis,* that is, in a 1♭ three-hexachord system. The form of the piece is that of a classic mid-sixteenth-century madrigal in that it is clearly divided into three sections, the outer sections diatonic and remaining within the 1♭ system, and the middle section chromatic with numerous hexachordal system shifts (see Figure 3.6).[29] Both outer sections, with text recited by the narrator, unfold eleven pitch

---

27 Giulio Cesare Monteverdi, "Dichiaratione della lettera stampata nel quinto libro de suoi madrigali," in Claudio Monteverdi, *Scherzi musicali a tre voce* (Venice, 1607), repr. in Claudio Monteverdi, *Tutte le opere*, ed. G. Francesco Malipiero, vol. 10 (Vienna, 1929), pp. 69–72.

28 Cipriano de Rore, *Opera omnia*, ed. B. Meier, vol. 5 (n.p., 1971). The work is also found in A.T. Davison and W. Apel (eds), *Historical Anthology of Music*, vol. 1, no. 131 (Cambridge, Massachusetts, 1959), pp. 142–3.

29 The translation of the text is taken from Allan W. Atlas, *Renaissance Music: Music in Western Europe, 1400–1600* (New York, 1998) p. 635. Altas also analyzes this piece in some detail.

classes that omit G♯/A♭, the missing pitches of a 1♭ system. While the chromatic middle section begins in m. 25 with the change in tense from narrator to female lover, it is in m. 36, at the words "Che sara qui di me" ("What will become of me here?"), that Rore disrupts the prevailing *mollis* system by introducing a G♯, suddenly shifting the 1♭ system up a fifth into *naturalis*. Within this short area of only five bars (mm. 36–40) eleven pitch classes are unfolded, omitting only E♭/D♯, the missing pitches of the *naturalis* system. The dramatically wrenching setting of the words "Ahi crud'amor!" on a C minor triad in m. 41 plummets the previous *naturalis* system down again to one flat and initiates a steady descent of increasingly flat hexachords that mirrors the increasing frustration of the jilted lover. Thus, in m. 46, A♭ enters on the word "dubbose" ("uncertain"), shifting the 1♭ system down to a 2♭ system. A D♭ follows next as the root of its own major triad (m. 48) on the word "dolcezze" ("pleasures"), bringing the system further down to a 3♭ system.

Text	*3-Hexachord System*	*Measures*	*Missing pc*
Da le belle contrade d'oriente	Mollis (1♭) F lydian	1-35	G♯/A♭
From the beautiful regions of the East	(11 pcs)		
Chiara e lieta s'ergea Ciprigna, et io			
Clear and joyful rose the morning star, and I			
Fruiva in braccio al divin idol mio			
Was enjoying, in the arms of my divine idol,			
Quel piacer che non cape humana mente			
That pleasure that transcends human understanding,			
Quando sentii dopo un sospir ardente:			
When I heard, after a passionate sigh:			
"Speranza del mio cor, dolce desio,			
"Hope of my heart, sweet desire,			
T'en vai, haime, sola mi lasci, adio.			
You go, alas, you leave me alone, farewell!			
Che sarà qui di me scura e dolente?	Naturalis (G♯ enters, 11pcs)	36-40	E♭
What will happen to me here, gloomy and sad?			
Ahi crudo Amor,	Mollis 1♭ (E♭ enters)	41-45	A♭
Alas, cruel Love,			
dubbose e corte	2♭ (A♭ enters)	46-47	D♭
how uncertain and short-lived			
Le tue dolcezze, poi ch'anchor ti godi	3♭ (D♭ enters)	48-52	F♯
Are your pleasures, for it even please you			
Che l'estremo piacer finisca	2♭ (F♯ enters)	53-55	C♯
That the greatest pleasure should end			
in pianto."	1♭ (C♯ enters, 11 pcs)	56 -to end	A♭/G♯
in tears."			
Nè potendo dir più, cinseme forte			
Unable to say more, she held me tightly,			
Iterando gl'amplessi in tanti nodi,			
Repeating her embraces in more entwinings			
Che giamai ne fer più l'edra o l'acanto.			
Than ivy or acantus ever made.			

Figure 3.6   Cipriano de Rore, *Da le belle contrade*

Example 3.2 Cipriano de Rore, *Da le belle contrade*

Example 3.2 Cipriano de Rore, *Da le belle contrade* continued

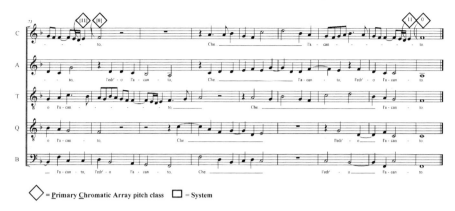

◇ = <u>P</u>rimary <u>C</u>hromatic Array pitch class   ☐ = System

In addition to associating the drama of the text with harmonic motions at the deepest level of structure, Rore distinguishes the lovers' voices by associating their individual speeches with different harmonic areas (see Example 3.2). At m. 41, for instance, where Venus expresses her sorrow, Rore modulates to the *mollis* 1♭ system, which initiates a series of hexachordal system shifts in the flat direction culminating on the word "dolcesse" with a modulation into a 3♭ system. Toward the end of her words "poi ch'anchor ti godi, che l'estremo piacer finisc'in pianto," the systems reverse and move back up in fifths starting with the introduction of F♯ on the syllable "mo" of "l'estremo" ("extreme"). The F♯ in m. 53 (see Figure 3.6) moves the 3♭ system up to a 2♭ system and, consequently, the C♯ in m. 56 on the syllable "to" from "pianto" ("tears") returns the system to *mollis*. The C♯ not only redresses the system to its original *mollis* state, but also signals the return of the male narrator's voice. Interestingly, C♯ appears in the same A triad that was heard at the end of the first *mollis* section (m. 33), and again at the end of the *naturalis* system in m. 40. The presence of C♯ finally restores the 1♭ system. The F triad that follows in the same bar is a reminder that A was indeed the furthest harmonic point from F within the reordered 1♭ hexachord; now F regains its status as modal final and center of its own gamut system. With the return of the 1♭ gamut system, all further modulation ceases as there is no A♭ or G♯ from here to the end of the madrigal.

Rore's *Da le belle contrade* also exhibits another aspect of chromaticism that will pervade the compositional process from here onwards: the desire of the composer to complete the chromatic aggregate by unfolding the tonic modal octave through rising chromatic half steps over the course of the entire composition. Rore's madrigal starts to climb chromatically from F in the alto voice of m. 22. Since F is the final of the madrigal, F must initiate the chromatic ascent. If we assign the Arabic number 0 to this first pitch class, the F♯ that follows in m. 25 (same voice) is then pc 1, and its resolution to G (pc 2) occurs in the same measure. The other chromatic ascending pitch classes follow in an ordered succession, primarily in the upper voice, often coinciding with important gamut system shifts. For instance, in m. 36, G♯ in the soprano voice (the madrigal's *cantus*) – and therefore the next chromatic pitch – enters over an E major triad. The G♯ is pc 3, the missing pitch of the 1♭ gamut system, shifting the system up a notch into the sharp direction to *naturalis*. The G♯

resolves to A, pc 4, in m. 37, and A, in turn, moves up to B♭, pc 5, in m. 38. Since the system shifts now move to the flat side of the fifths cycle, B♮, pc 6, must wait until the flat systems modulate up into the sharp direction. An expected B♮ enters on the last beat of m. 51 in the tenor as the raised third of an applied dominant chord to C, pc 7 (m. 52). Pc 8, C♯, appears next in the alto of m. 56, returning the previous 2♭ system up to the 1♭ system that governs the madrigal. Pc 9, D, follows soon enough, but pc 10, E♭, is omitted from the series simply because Rore wishes to keep the last section of the madrigal completely diatonic, thus excluding even the allowable additional flat of the 1♭ system. The deceptive cadence in m. 73, which is repeated as an authentic cadence in the last two bars of the madrigal, gives us the last two pitch classes, pc 11, E♮, and pc 0, F.

We have called the slow linear unfolding of the tonic chromatic octave ascending over the course of an entire composition the *Primary Chromatic Array* (PCA); this will be discussed more fully in later chapters. But sixteenth-century music is not concerned only with the unfolding of the chromatic tonic octave. The diatonic nature of the mode, which motivates all contrapuntal motion in the piece and, thereby, the treatment of consonance and dissonance, must also be taken into account. Just as the chromatic pitch classes within the tonic octave seek to ascend to the final octave in the soprano voice through the PCA, there is a concomitant diatonic unfolding of the modal octave in the tenor that descends to the modal final. This diatonic descent is called the *Primary Diatonic Array* (PDA).

The justification for the interaction of these two octave unfoldings, the chromatic ascending and the diatonic descending, is derived from the nature of Renaissance counterpoint itself. Sixteenth-century counterpoint is based upon the intervallic interaction of two structural voices, most often the soprano and tenor, although the alto and bass, and even the bass and soprano, may also assume structural significance. A formal cadence is formed through a 6–8 intervallic contrapuntal progression in which the upper voice ascends to the modal final via a leading tone forming a major sixth with the tenor. The two voices then resolve outward in stepwise motion to the octave; in effect, *ti* moves up to *do* and *re* resolves down to *do*, to use modern movable-*do* solfège terminology.

In Rore's madrigal *Da le belle contrade*, the tenor voice carries the PDA against the PCA in the upper voices. At first the tenor begins on the fifth degree of the mode before descending to the first structural pitch of the PDA, F, in m. 2. Since the first part of the madrigal is basically diatonic with many cadences on F, the tenor voice has no need as yet to descend further on a deeper structural level. Only in the second part, that part of the madrigal which is more intensely emotional, and therefore more chromatic, does the PDA begin to descend. In m. 38, the tenor's F has now been shifted up an octave, and descends in m. 40 from F to E♮. The next diatonic pitch in the descending diatonic array is D, but because of chromatic inflections in the tenor, D is first approached by an upper neighbor E♭ in mm. 41–2. In m. 43, D's diatonic descent to C is emphasized by a subordinate cadence on a C major triad in m. 52. The PDA pitch C is now sustained in the tenor voice on a higher structural level until its final descent begins in mm. 79–80. Measure 80 sees the tenor initiate its final descent, B♭–A–G. The G now forms the major sixth with the soprano's E♮, and both voices resolve to the F octave, giving *ti–do* in the soprano against *re–do* in the tenor.

Since we believe that our understanding of the contrapuntal unfolding of the diatonic and chromatic pitch classes of the modal octave can reveal important stylistic characteristics, our attention is drawn particularly to those individuals in the sixteenth century whose compositional interests included the exploitation of the modal octave's chromatic potential. Among those composers who followed Cipriano da Rore, Orlando de Lasso (1532–1594) had the approach to chromaticism that most informed the compositional techniques of the succeeding generation.

Lasso was the most published composer of the sixteenth century and his works were often cited by contemporary theorists as models of their kind. For examples, see the numerous citations in Joachim Burmeister, *Musica poetica* (Rostock, 1606); in Adam Gumpeltzhaimer, *Compendium musicae* (Augsburg, 1591); and in Maternus Beringer, *Musicae, der freyen lieblischen Singkunst* (Nuremberg, 1610). Studies, such as those of Wolfgang Boetticher and others, have shown that the late works of Lasso anticipated not only many of the stylistic innovations of the Florentine monodists but Monteverdi's *seconda prattica* as well.[30] Lasso had a strong influence on composers working in Venice, especially the Gabrielis, and consequently on Monteverdi, who succeeded Giovanni Gabrieli at San Marco. Significantly, Lasso's music exhibits the same affective use of eleven-pitch-class areas as does Rore's. For example, the *Prologo* to Lasso's *Prophetiae Sibyllarum* (Example 3.3) dramatizes the text through a series of three-hexachord-system modulations.[31]

---

30 See Wolfgang Boetticher, "Anticipations of Dramatic Monody in the Late Works of Lassus," in F. Sternfeld et al. (eds), *Essays on Opera and English Music: In Honour of Sir Jack Westrup* (Oxford, 1975), pp. 84–102.

31 Our analysis of the *Prologo* is yet another interpretation among many of this intriguing piece. It is interesting to note that all the following discussions differ in their fundamental methodologies, not to say their conclusions: William J. Mitchell, "The Prologue to Orlando di Lasso's Prophetiae Sibyllarum," *Music Forum*, 2 (1970): 264–73; Klaus K. Hübler, "Orlando di Lassus Prophetiae Sybillarum oder Über chromatische Komposition im 16. Jahrhundert," *Zeitschrift für Musiktheorie*, 9 (1978): 29; Karol Berger, "Tonality and Atonality in the Prologue to Orlando di Lasso's *Prophetiae Sibyllarum*: Some Methodological Problems in Analysis of Sixteenth-Century Music," *The Musical Quarterly*, 66 (1980): 484–504; Berger, "The Common and the Unusual Steps of Musica Ficta: A Background for the Gamut of Orlando di Lasso's *Prophetiae Sybillarum*," *Belgisch tijdschrift voor Muzickweienschap*, 39–40 (1985–88): 61–73.

Example 3.3 Lasso, *Prophetiae Sibyllarum, Prologo*

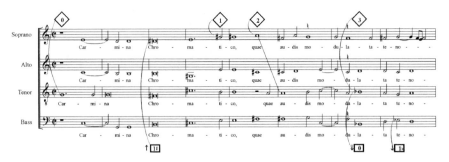

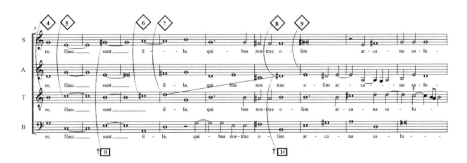

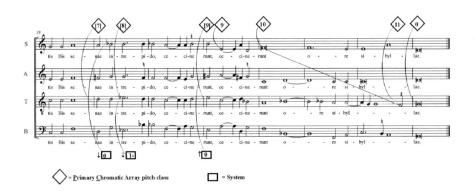

While structural cadences on G predominate in the *Prologo*, the association of the pitch classes of the G triad as cadential points within the mixolydian modal octave is of less concern than the forward drive and momentum, and of course the expressive character, created by the number and relationship of three-hexachord system shifts. Here too, the modulation of gamut systems works within the unfolding G chromatic octave. As shown in Example 3.3, the opening two bars clearly establish a C *naturalis* gamut in *cantus durus* (natural signature) and introduce the first pc of the PCA, G♮ (pc 0), in the tenor. In the third measure, on the syllable "Chro" of "Chromatico", an unexpected D♯ suddenly enters in the soprano voice, shifting the system up a fifth to the G gamut (*durus*). This modulation allows Lasso to introduce the next two rising PCA pitch classes (pcs 1 and 2), G♯ (m. 4) and A♮ (m. 5). Since the A♮ would next move to B♭, Lasso needs to shift the system down to accomplish this motion. He does so in m. 7: note that the A♮ has shifted into the tenor voice in m. 6 so that that voice can now move up to B♭ (pc 3) in the next measure. The B♭ shifts the system down a fifth from G *durus* to C *naturalis*, but Lasso goes even further by introducing E♭ in m. 8 (bass voice), shifting the system down another fifth to 1♭ (*mollis*) to articulate the text, "modulata tenore" ("in measured verses"). The B♭ next moves to B♮ (m. 9), pc 4, in preparation for the cadence on C (pc 5), in the same measure. M. 10 brings the system up again to *naturalis* with the G♯ in the soprano. This allows the next two PCA pitches to unfold: C♯ (pc 6, tenor, m. 11) acts as a leading tone to D (pc 7, m. 12, same voice). To move the PCA further, D♯ must be introduced next. This can be done only through another system shift, which occurs in m. 14. Here the D♯ in the alto voice brings the system up another fifth to *durus*, acting, at the same time, as leading tone to E, pc. 9, in m. 15. All that are necessary to complete the PCA chromatic octave are pcs 10, 11, and 0, that is, F♮, F♯, and G, respectively. The alto voice first introduces these notes in mm. 18–19, but they do not actually become significant until the approach to the final cadence in the last four measures of the motet. Thus, the soprano's F♮ in m. 22 is inflected up to F♯ in the tenor voice in m. 24 – the F♯ is understood as a necessary *ficta* note even though it is not indicated in the manuscript copy – before the ascending octave to G is finally completed in the last measure.

Along the way, Lasso returns the system to *naturalis* by first shifting out of *durus* in m. 19 with the return of B♭ in the soprano. The B♭ brings the system down to *naturalis*, but Lasso intensifies the modulation by going another fifth down to *mollis*, as he did previously in mm. 7–8, with E♭ entering in both tenor and bass voices in m. 19. The only way to return to the original *naturalis* system from the present 1♭ system is to introduce a G♯; this happens in the alto of m. 21. From this point to the end of the motet, the system remains in C *naturalis*.

In summation, while the G major triad serves as a point of reference, the internal harmonic scheme is not controlled by the *diatony* of G mixolydian; rather, the relationship of three-hexachord gamut systems yields an extreme chromaticism which supports the underlying affect of the motet, *carmina chromatico* heard in *modulata tenore* (chromatic songs that we hear in smooth-flowing modulations).

After the *Prologo*, the succeeding motets relate the oracles of the twelve Greek Sibyls, particularly those oracles that foretell the life and death of Christ. While a full discussion of Lasso's *Prophetiae Sibyllarum* would be impractical here, we can at least look at the first two motets of the cycle. *Sibylla Persica*, the first motet, foretells the birth of Christ (Example 3.4). It is written in G mixolydian mode in *cantus durus* and therefore begins in the *naturalis* three-hexachord system. Lasso immediately unfolds the first three pitch classes of the PCA in the soprano voice: G, G♯, A (pcs 0, 1, and 2 in mm. 1–3). On the syllable "de" of "residebit" ("will sit") in m. 6 (the opening text reads: "Born of a virgin mother, he *will sit* on the crooked back of an ass"), a D♯ enters as part of a B major triad, as an applied dominant of E, the last pitch class of the reordered C central hexachord. As a result, the system shifts up temporarily to G *durus*. The next system shift occurs in m. 13, where B♭ is introduced, followed immediately by E♭ (the text reads: "The joyful prince who alone *will bring salvation*"). The B♭, pc 3 of the PCA, brings the system back down to *naturalis*, but the E♭ that follows on the word "salutem" ("salvation") brings the system further down to a 1♭ system. Before the next system shift takes place in m. 17, the PCA continues to rise in half steps: pc 4 (B♮) appears in the tenor voice in m. 15, followed, in the same voice, by pcs 5, 6, and 7 (C, C♯, and D), articulated by a harmonic area around D, the dominant of the mode. In m. 17 the *mollis* system shifts up to *naturalis* with the entrance of G♯ on the word "lapsis" ("fleeting"). Pc 6, C♯, is reiterated in m. 26 as part of a phrygian cadence on A. Pc 7, D, is also reiterated in m. 30 on the word "solo" ("this *one* prophecy"), sung by the soprano voice alone. Pc 8, D♯, next appears in m. 33 in the alto voice as the third of a B major triad, set to the verb "est" ("this one prophecy *is* different"). The D♯ raises the *naturalis* system to *durus* again, and at the same time moves to E, pc 9, in m. 34. The PCA rise continues in mm. 35–7, in the soprano voice, with E moving to F and F♯, but this segment of the PCA must be understood as an anticipation of the structural completion of the chromatic octave, all in the soprano voice, that follows. Pc 8, D♯, is enharmonically respelled as E♭ in m. 39. The E♭, coming after an E♮, is heard as an expressive passing tone to D, highlighting the text at this point ("*He*, God, will be born of a virgin"). The E♮ returns in m. 41 (pc 9) and does not ascend to the next pitch in the series until F♮, pc 10, is reached in m. 47. Along the way, the system reverts to *naturalis* in m. 41 with the presence of B♭. From this point on, there are no further system changes and the motet ends in its background "C" system. The last two measures have F♮ move up to F♯ in preparation for the final authentic cadence to G, ending the chromatic ascent in the last measure.

Example 3.4 Lasso, *Prophetiae Sibyllarum*, motet 1, *Sibylla Persica*

Example 3.4 Lasso, *Prophetiae Sibyllarum*, motet 1, *Sibylla Persica* continued

The second motet in the cycle, *Sibylla Libyca* (Example 3.5), is also written in G mixolydian in *cantus durus*; therefore, its background gamut system is also *naturalis*. The text of this motet concerns the vindication of Christ against the calumnies of His enemies and His eventual eternal life in heaven. As in the first motet, there is a complete PCA rise in the upper voice, conditioning a number of gamut system changes. Also, the working-out of the ascending chromatic line differs from that of the first motet in several respects, not the least of which is the large-scale repetition of pcs 0–7 before the octave is completed. The opening of the motet up to the downbeat of m. 14 unfolds all eleven pitch classes of the *naturalis* "C" gamut system. When the text turns to "the charges so cheerfully laid against Him," E♭ enters, shifting the "C" system down to a 1♭ system. The 1♭ system harmonically focuses upon the F central hexachord, and the note F now acts as a large-scale lower neighbor to G, the final of the mode. Lasso has already prepared this relationship at the very opening of the motet by allowing G in the bass to be contrapuntally prolonged on a middleground level by F in m. 4 before returning to G in m. 6. The composer now takes this gesture and works the contrapuntal relationship between G and F into the deeper structural levels of system modulations.

Example 3.5 Lasso, *Prophetiae Sibyllarum*, motet 2, *Sibylla Libyca*

Example 3.5 Lasso, *Prophetiae Sibyllarum*, motet 2, *Sibylla Libyca* continued

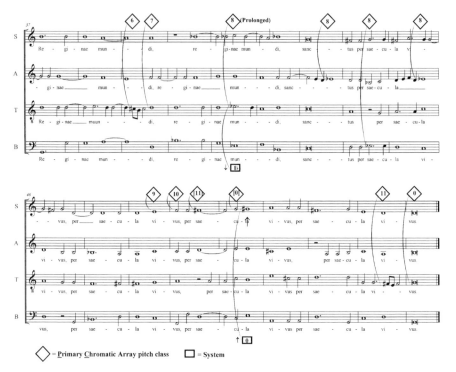

◇ = Primary Chromatic Array pitch class   □ = System

The 1♭ gamut system remains in effect until G♯ enters in m. 29, restoring the original *naturalis* system. Lasso's expression of the 1♭ system (mm. 14–28) is invigorated by a daring enharmonic shift which reinterprets the allowable flat of the system, E♭, as a D♯! While the E♭ that initiated the system shift into the 1♭ system (m. 14) has prepared us to accept D♯, the latter pitch still remains a very unlikely choice within a *mollis* system, especially when it is supported by a B major triad! Here again, Lasso is working out a contrapuntal detail first heard in the opening measures of the motet, namely the relationship between E and D. The second bass note after the initial G is E, and while its immediate resolution is up to F in m. 4, the E is, in turn, prolonged by a lower neighbor D in m. 5 which moves up to E in m. 7 (see Example 3.5). As dominant of the mode, D becomes a first goal of motion, albeit within a 1♭ gamut (mm. 23–6). As part of the dominant prolongation, E becomes a prominent upper neighbor in m. 26, supported, in turn, by that B major triad: thus the D♯. Note that the E triad in m. 26 is kept minor in order not to introduce a G♯ too early; Lasso saves that pitch for m. 29 as part of the cadence that ends the third line of the quatrain. The dominant prolongation that leads up to the G♯, and the return of the *naturalis* system, is also the structural arrival of the PCA at pc 7 (D).

The G♯ in m. 29, an inflection of the G♮ just before it, now begins another PCA rise from pc 0 (G♮). Pcs 0, 1, and 2 (G♮, G♯, and A) cover mm. 28–9. Pcs 3, 4, and 5 occur in mm. 25–7, the B♭ (pc 3) appearing in the tenor and bass voices, and the B♮ and C (m. 26) in the alto voice as part of a cadence on C. Pcs 6 and 7, C♯ and

D, next occur in the tenor in m. 39, forming a cadence on the dominant. The next pitch is E♭, the missing pitch of the *naturalis* system. By introducing this pitch in m. 41, Lasso shifts the system once more to a 1♭ system. The persistent E♭s in the alto and bass voices in the following measures preserve the 1♭ system until G♯ is once again introduced to return the system back up to *naturalis*. At the same time, E♭ is displaced by E♮, pc 9, in m. 48, in preparation for the final ascent to the *finalis*, thus completing the chromatic G octave. The E♮ moves immediately to F, pc 10, and then to F♯, pc 11, all within the soprano voice (mm. 48–9). While F♯ does move up to G♮, even going past it to G♯ and to A, the structural completion of the octave does not occur until the final authentic cadence, and in the tenor voice (F♯ up to G, pc 0). As it happens, the full PCA chromatic rise of all twelve pitch classes is not confined to one voice in this motet as in the previous one, but moves steadily downward from the upper voices (alto and soprano) and finally into the tenor.

Why does Lasso anticipate the final completion of the octave in the soprano in m. 50? One notices that this gesture is but one of several chromatic ascents involving the same pitch classes, as if Lasso were deliberately thinking of developing this chromatic fragment, or at least using it as a unifying gesture. The initiation of the PCA chromatic rise in the alto voice in mm. 6–7 concentrates on the trichord G♮– G♯–A. The same trichord reappears in the soprano voice in mm. 28–9, at the repeat of the first seven pitch classes of the PCA. Here the G♯ is necessary to revert the system to *naturalis*. These same pitch classes now recur at the end of the motet, and for the same reason: the soprano's G–G♯–A trichord (mm. 50–51) effectively shifts the system up to *naturalis* for the last time.

Another issue is of particular significance here: E♭, the missing pitch of the *naturalis* system, motivates the recurrence of the G–G♯–A trichord segment. Lasso is, in fact, anticipating a common developmental ploy used by composers in later style periods: the manipulation, or "working-out," of a chromatic trichord over the course of an entire composition.

Contemporaries of Lasso were also interested in developing chromatic events in their music, often working them into background system changes, although none was quite as consistent in their chromatic language as Lasso. The output of Luca Marenzio (1553 or 1554–99) is a case in point. Marenzio was, after Lasso, perhaps the second most revered madrigalist of the late sixteenth century, noted for his highly sensitive and emotional text settings. However, Marenzio's use of chromaticism and system modulation is stylistically distinct from that of Lasso, as an examination of Marenzio's madrigal *Solo e pensoso* will demonstrate (the opening measures of this work are presented in Example 3.6).[32]

---

32 Luca Marenzio, *Il nono libro de madrigali a 5 voci* (Venice, 1599).

Example 3.6 Marenzio, *Solo e pensoso* (mm. 1–24)

Solo e pensoso is taken from a sonnet by Petrarch (1304–74), one of several favorite authors whose poetry (sonnets and *canzoni*) was much favored by late sixteenth-century madrigalists. Petrarch was especially admired for the wide variety of contrasting emotions and images portrayed within a single sonnet, which gave the composer numerous opportunities for thematic and textural contrast, and therefore numerous occasions for chromatic inflection. The opening madrigalisms in *Solo e pensoso* are a case in point. There are two thematic ideas unfolded simultaneously which support the poetic imagery of the text. The soprano's "solo" rising chromatic line suggests the opening phrase of text, "Alone and pensive," while the lower voices "tread" along with their descending thirds in imitation, deliberately, it seems, breaking every rule of third-species counterpoint to bring out the poetic conceit of the rest of the line: "the deserted fields I tread with deliberate and slow steps."

The soprano's complete ascending chromatic line within the first 15 measures, a kind of accelerated PCA, is quite unusual. Such an accelerated chromatic unfolding is never found in other composers of the period, including Lasso. Lasso is more deliberate, with the entrance of each chromatic pitch placed slowly enough so that the entire chromatic octave (or at least the eleven pitch classes of a single system) covers a longer musical space. In other words, Lasso does not exhaust all his available pitch-class material before the piece ends; thus, he avoids diatonic stasis in the middle of the composition. Marenzio is more concerned with maintaining the modal structure of his piece, whereas Lasso, and Rore before him, seem to have had little concern about modal definition, both being more inclined toward working out the properties of the background gamut three-hexachord system of the madrigal. After an extraordinary chromatic opening, Marenzio reverts to pure diatonic mixolydian mode for long stretches of music.

Even so, Marenzio does utilize system modulation on a deeper structural level and in a unique way. The opening hexachord system is *naturalis*, supporting the mixolydian mode of the composition. But the nature of the soprano's steadily rising chromatic line forces a system change to *durus* at the entry of D♯ on the syllable "ti" of "deserti" ("deserted") in m. 9. However, the soprano, after completing the chromatic octave, descends chromatically to D♮, the fifth degree of the mode, in parallel sixths with the alto voice. It is the alto voice that restores the *naturalis* system with a B♭ on the word "passi" ("steps") in m. 17. All this works out well, but the soprano has not yet finished the chromatic descent to D. What was once a D♯ ascending to E now becomes an E♭ (on "lenti," "slow") descending to D in m. 21, causing another system shift, this time in the opposite direction, down to *mollis* (1♭). In order to return the system to *naturalis*, Marenzio would have to introduce a G♯, the missing pitch of the 1♭ system, spelled as an augmented second; Marenzio never uses an A♭ in this madrigal. The G♯, supported by E, does not appear until m. 65, implying a half cadence in A minor which never materializes, and which articulates the text at this point: "Because when joy is gone from actions ...". Thus, a very long time is spent within the 1♭ system (mm. 21–65) even though G mixolydian is clearly expressed by structural cadences on the *finalis* and dominant of the mode during this period. G mixolydian can function within a 1♭ system so long as G♯ or A♭ is absent. Indeed, the lengthy time spent in the 1♭ system finds its consequence within the second half of the madrigal.

With the return of the *naturalis* system in m. 65, the rest of the first half of the madrigal remains in that system and concludes on a full cadence on the dominant of the mode (m. 87). The second half of the madrigal starts in m. 88, still in the *naturalis* system, and contains a number of pictorial madrigalisms. But our concern is with the transposition to *mollis* in m. 118. This is a particularly restless part of the madrigal, the poetry depicting the lover's flight from Cupid since he wants no more unrequited love affairs. The text at this point (mm. 111ff.) reads in translation: "Yet neither such rough nor wild paths can I find where love does not seek me out ..." ("Ma pur sì aspre viene sì selvagge ..."). At the mention of "rough nor wild paths," E♭ enters (prepared by B♭) and forms the root of its own chord on the downbeat of m. 118. The lover's flight from Cupid is here reflected by a "flight" of systems, the 1♭ system remaining in force throughout the rest of the madrigal, while the G♯ needed to revert the system is totally absent. In fact, Marenzio avoids chromatic pitch classes altogether after m. 121, except for the F♯ leading tone at the final cadence. So while the madrigal ends on the final of the mode, G, the system remains *mollis*.

Marenzio's contrast of natural and flat systems enhances the poetic conceit of the lovers' distress. Notice too that the two systems balance each other: *naturalis, mollis, naturalis, mollis*; the first transposition to the *mollis* 1♭ system (mm. 21–65) balances and prepares for the 1♭ system that concludes the madrigal (mm. 118–39). Similar to Lasso, Marenzio also unfolds the complete PCA chromatic octave; however, the first structural chromatic pitch class does not occur until m. 65, when G♯ enters, reverting the previous *mollis* to *naturalis*. The G♯ (pc 1) does not immediately resolve to A (pc 2), but A does occur in m. 67 (tenor), and B♭ (pc 3) follows in the next measure (bass). Pc 4, B♮, articulates a brief motion to C, pc 5 (m. 70). The next pitch, C♯, pc 6, in turn articulates the cadence on D, pc 7, as part of the dominant cadence (mm. 86–7). After D, the next pitch class in the series, pc 8, is the missing pitch of the system, E♭, which enters in m. 118, effecting a transposition to *mollis*. Pc 9, E♭, follows in the upper voices in m. 120, and passes up to F, pc 10, in m. 122 (tenor). The last pitch of the PCA, F♯, pc 11, articulates the final G cadence, with G itself completing the octave in the last measure.

Our final examples of gamut systems in modality come from the madrigals of Claudio Monteverdi, a composer whose works straddle the stylistic tendencies of the late sixteenth and early seventeenth centuries and who leads us into the early Baroque period. Monteverdi's invention the *concertato* madrigal, supported by an instrumental basso continuo, articulates vertical progressions of the harmonies as never before. Because of the basso continuo's rhythmic function in articulating the rate of harmonic rhythm of the chord progression, the reordered pitch classes of the central hexachord now assume a more significant harmonic function, the instrumental bass often progressing in fifths, closely following the order of fifths within the reordered hexachord. As in earlier vocal music, the harmonic potential of the central hexachord can either support a background modal final by emphasizing through structurally significant cadences the first, fifth, and third degrees of the mode, or ignore it altogether. In the latter case, the hexachordal fifths become localized relationships giving little or no support to a background modal final. Especially within those madrigals from Book 5 on (after 1605), one often sees the bass moving in fifths progressions and leading to cadences that do not support the modal final at all, but do articulate hexachordal degrees (see, for instance, Artusi's comments on Monteverdi's *Cruda Amarilli* quoted above).

A case in point is Monteverdi's *Eccomi pronta ai baci* from the Seventh Book (Venice, 1619, text by Marino). Here is an example of a madrigal that remains in a *naturalis* system throughout, unfolding only ten pitch classes (there is no D♯/E♭, the missing pitch of the system, or B♭/A♯). The mode itself, D mixolydian, emphasizes the sharp side of the *naturalis* hexachord, whose harmonic reordering is given below:

Quality of third:	A	E♮	B♮	F♮/F♯	C♮/C♯	G♮/G♯
Hexachordal degree:	F –	C –	G –	D –	A –	E
			IV	I (final)	V	

From the above diagram, we can see that Monteverdi limits himself to only sharp accidentals with no flats present at all, not even the allowable B♭ of the "C" system.

The arrangement of the basso continuo line clearly outlines the properties of the C central hexachord; in fact, the bass line for the entire madrigal seems to be conditioned on the fifth relationships inherent in the C hexachord. Owing to the relationship of the hexachordal fifths to each other, harmonic progressions may or may not support a background tonic. When they do, one perceives the madrigal's short-term tonal progressions and harmonic relationships to be adumbrations of the harmonic language of later periods. For instance, the opening of the madrigal (see Example 3.7) clearly presents D as "tonic" within the first four measures, A acting as dominant at the close of the phrase. The next period repeats the phrase, this time on G, the subdominant of the mode. Through transposed repetition, this second phrase also forms a complete progression, supported by its dominant (mm. 5–8). Both D and its fifth A, followed by G and its fifth D, directly relate to their respective positions within the C hexachord from which they are derived.

As seen in the above diagram of the reordered hexachord for this madrigal, D is flanked by two fifths on either side of it, G and A, and this relationship now forms the higher-level harmonic progression of the opening of the madrigal. However, although the two tonic and subdominant phrases on D and G respectively may, within themselves, form complete harmonic progressions (in particular, I–V–I), large-scale prolongations of the modal tonic often do not adhere to later common-practice tonality – nor should they, considering the era. In the complete period from mm. 1–13 (see Example 3.7), the underlying progression is D–G–a, with the a triad kept always as minor. This is hardly a normal tonal progression, but it does conform to the nature of the reordered hexachord. By keeping the dominant as minor (see m. 10), the fifths both above and below D gain an equal status that is quite unlike their relationship in common-practice tonality, where the major dominant has a stronger hierarchal position than does the subdominant. Thus, in this instance, D can relate to G as much as it can to A. In addition, owing to the nature of the eleven-pitch-class gamut system, the quality of third above each hexachord pitch is variable, again emphasizing localized fifth relationships that do not necessarily relate to a background final of the mode. For example, the dominant cadence in m. 13 moves to a D major triad in m. 14, initiating a diatonic 5–6 sequential progression leading to a D dorian cadence in m. 19. Note that this sequential progression is based on the fifths of the hexachord, and that the only note within this progression which is not a root within the hexachord is B (m. 14, beat 3). The B is never harmonized as a major triad, but instead remains minor, thus preventing a system shift out of *naturalis*.

What is behind the move into D dorian? Monteverdi's sensitivity to the *concetto delle parole* of Marino's text obviously plays a major role in his choice of mode at this point. The poem concerns the amorous flirtations of a female lover who teases her male partner by demanding a kiss – rather "quickly" it seems – only to instruct him not to leave any unsightly red marks on her face by doing so. What makes the madrigal setting so humorous is that two male tenors and a bass are singing the part of the female lover, thus presenting the text from a male viewpoint, satirizing the fickleness of the woman's sexual desires.

Example 3.7 Monteverdi, *Eccomi pronta ai baci*

◇ = <u>Primary Chromatic Array pitch class</u>   ○ = <u>Primary Diatonic Array pitch class</u>

The motion to a pure dorian cadence in m. 19, with its prominent F♮, raises the fundamental compositional issue in this madrigal, which is the dyad conflict resulting from the major/minor inflected third degree over the D final, F♮/F♯, with the F♮ derived from D dorian and the F♯ derived from D mixolydian. Monteverdi is working out D in both its major and its minor modal variants. This relationship has already been forecast in m. 11, where, for the first time, F appears as F♮ and not as F♯. For the first time, too, the text mentions the male lover's name, Ergasto, but his name is set to D minor instead of the expected D major. D major returns in m. 14 as the female lover entices her male lover with the words "baciami Ergasto mio" ("kiss me, my Ergasto"). The F♮ now prepares for the extended D dorian cadence in mm. 17–19. D dorian remains in effect during the next section of the madrigal, reflecting the determined admonition of the female lover that her Ergasto "kiss so that your biting teeth leave no signs etched on my face ...". D mixolydian returns with the next line of text in m. 34 ("perchè altri non m'additi in essa poi" – "because others might point at me"), the D preceded by a fifths progression (mm. 32–4): E–a (again, kept minor)–D major. Again, D is flanked on both sides, first by A as minor dominant and, in m. 35, by G as subdominant.

The equality of sonorities, so typical of modal progressions of this period, can often lead to confusion as to what harmony is being prolonged at any given moment. The D major chord in m. 34 goes to G, momentarily emphasizing G as a temporary tonic with D seemingly its dominant, but in actuality D is the more important harmony and is confirmed as such at the end of the period with an authentic cadence (mm. 42–3). Again, a knowledge of the reordered hexachord and its localized fifth relationships allows us to understand the nature of such progressions: any member of the hexachord can act as either an applied dominant or as the "tonic" resolution of that applied dominant, regardless of the background modal final.

The next line of text (mm. 44ff.), "Ahi, ahi, ahi, tu mordi e non baci" ("Ah!, you're biting, not kissing!"), retains the F♯ as the harmonic rhythm accelerates and the vocal rhythms subdivide into smaller and smaller units. In mm. 52–5, at the words "tu mi segnasti, ahi, ahi!" ("you've scarred me, alas, alas!"), the madrigal reaches its climax, the F♯ now being almost violently juxtaposed with F♮ in the soprano voice and the F♮ supported by a minor cadential 6/4 in m. 54. The minor 6/4 chord resolves to a 5/3 in the next measure, ending the line. Immediately, in m. 56, F♯ returns as the female lover exclaims in no uncertain terms that "I'll die before I'll ever kiss you more!" In this way, the background dyad conflict of the piece, F♯/F♮ informs the structure of the composition, centering its climax on the close juxtaposition of the pitch classes of the dyad conflict.

The harmonic motion of the rest of the madrigal simply follows the ordering of the *naturalis* system's hexachordal fifths, first unfolding A (now major)–D–G (mm. 56–7), which is followed again by A–D–G, with the addition this time of C (m. 59); and so it goes until the final D mixolydian cadence. Since a harmonic ostinato governs the last 13 measures of the madrigal, A–D–G is stated several times. Thus the opening progression that pitted A and G against D within a symmetrical relationship now finds its resolution at the end of the madrigal, where the progression finally resolves into the final D authentic cadence. Monteverdi has thus unified the madrigal by composing out both a semitonal dyad conflict on the melodic/motivic level, and a harmonic relationship on a deeper one. The working-out process exhibited here is no less exacting, then, than that used by later Baroque and Classical composers and is indeed quite similar.

Our last example for this chapter is Monteverdi's *Ecco vicine o bella Tigre*, a setting of a text by Achillini.[33] This madrigal is also from the Seventh Book (see Example 3.8), and it too is set for male voices, this time for two tenors without vocal bass, accompanied by the basso continuo. What is interesting about this particular work is that it, like *Eccomi pronta ai baci*, works the relationship of both major and minor variants of the mode, this time G mixolydian against G dorian, raising a B♮/ B♭ dyad conflict. However, unlike the previous madrigal, *Ecco vicine* composes out the dyad conflict to encompass system modulations: G with B♭ (G dorian) appearing within the *naturalis* system, and G with B♮ appearing within the G *durus* system.

---

33 The music for this and the following madrigal examples is taken from Monteverdi, *Tutte le opere*, ed. G.F. Malipiero, vol. 7 (Vienna, 1928).

Example 3.8 Monteverdi, *Ecco vicine o bella Tigre*

Example 3.8 Monteverdi, *Ecco vicine o bella Tigre* continued

◇ = Primary Chromatic Array pitch class   ☐ = Missing Pitch

The madrigal opens in a *naturalis* C system whose hexachord formation is as follows:

						Durus shift
Quality of third: A	E	B♭/B♮	F♮/F♯	C♮/C♯	G♮/G♯	D♯
C hexachord: F –	C –	G –	D –	A –	E –	B
		I	V			

Monteverdi utilizes all eleven pitch classes of the *naturalis* system, but singles out the one allowable flat of the system, B♭, for special emphasis. Instead of beginning the madrigal in G mixolydian, the composer does the unexpected by introducing a B♭ over a G pedal, turning the mode into dorian, and at the same time creating an air of expectancy occasioned by the text "Ecco vicine o bella Tigre l'hore" ("The hour is near, O beautiful tigress").

It is interesting to note how Monteverdi structures the harmonic background of this madrigal. Monteverdi begins by unfolding the fifths of the *naturalis* hexachord in an ordered progression opening with the final, G, which moves to a half cadence on D in m. 11. The period that follows actually prolongs dominant harmony and leads to a formal cadence on A in m. 23, acting temporarily as V/V. Monteverdi's long-range fifths motion away from the G final reflects the *concetto* of the text, the musings of a worshipful lover about a woman who remains at a distance, in fact fleeing from him, he imagines, over mountains and valleys, with him eager to follow. After the A cadence, the fifth motion temporarily retreats to the tonic as the A moves to D (major), which subsequently moves to the final, G in m. 30, the whole period ending with a half cadence on D in m. 36.

Monteverdi's fifths motions also reveal an underlying chromatic rise (PCA) to the dominant of the mode from G to D, pcs 0–7. In fact there are two 0–7 rises, both incomplete, and each omitting different pitch classes, a condition that is not unusual in these compositions. The goal of the first rise is to C♯ (pc 6), the leading tone of the dominant. Beginning in the first measure, G ascends to B♭ (tenor 1), omitting G♯/A♭ (pc 1). Since Monteverdi does not want to inflect the B♭ to B♮ within the opening period (G is kept dorian), B♭ passes to C♮ in the same voice at the end of m. 6. Ultimately, this C♮ will have to be displaced by C♯, pc 6, in order to effect the cadence on the dominant in m. 11 (D is pc 7). Thus the PCA may omit pitch classes depending upon compositional factors. However, in such cases there is invariably a second rise which fills in the missing pitch classes of the first ascent. Thus in m. 12, on a first-inversion G triad, the series repeats from pc 0. This time pc 1, G♯, does appear in tenor 1 (m. 17) and passes on to A, pc 2 (same voice), in m. 20. However, within this PCA rise A does not pass on to B♭, a pitch already given within the first PCA ascent, but moves instead to B♮, pc 4, in m. 30, tenor 2. The B♮ ascends to pc 5, C♮, in m. 33 (again, tenor 2 and continuo bass) before it is again displaced by C♯ (m. 34, tenor 1) in preparation for the half cadence on D (pc 7) in the next measure. All of the music up to this point has remained within the C *naturalis* system; D♯ has yet to appear.

Significantly, Monteverdi saves the D♯, pc 8, for the midpoint of the madrigal (m. 37) and the start of a new line of text. With its introduction as the major third of a B triad, indicated by the sharp sign below the B in the basso continuo, D♯ effects a system shift up to G *durus*. All this supports the new sentiment in the text: "ma potess'io sequir solingo errante ..." ("But if I could follow, wandering alone ..."). At this point the next fifth of the background series can now be unfolded, namely E (A, in m. 23, was the previous fifth in the series). As it happens, E, pc 9, is also the next pitch in the ascending PCA. The G *durus* system remains in effect until m. 59, when B♭ (in the basso continuo) reverts the system to *naturalis*. During the *durus* modulation, the PCA climb continues with F♮, pc 10 (m. 46, tenor 1) ascending to F♯ in m. 47 (tenor 2). The F♯ at this point has not gained structural significance since it appears only as the fifth of the B major triad that articulates the E major cadence in m. 48. Monteverdi's fifths cycle actually concludes with the B major dominant of E, the cycle then reversing itself and rapidly returning to G, the final of the mode. Thus the E triad in mm. 48 and 49 moves to A in m. 50, D in m. 51 as structural dominant, and, finally, G in m. 52. The F♯ in tenor 1 in m. 51 is the structural PCA pc 11, and the subsequent G, now clearly in mixloydian mode, ends the sequence as pc 0. The PCA has thus encompassed the entire G chromatic octave from G as dorian to G as mixolydian, its "opposite" mode.

But this is not yet the end of the story. The return to G in m. 52 initiates another PCA rise, again starting from pc 0, but now all the operations are accelerated, supporting the image of the lover trying vainly to follow the footsteps of his beloved as she flees from him over mountains and valleys. Thus m. 58 begins the ascent from G, skipping over pc 1, G♯, and rising instead to B♭ in the next measure (with its system shift), all in the continuo bass. The same rise, in diminution, was seen at the opening of the madrigal when tenor 1 sang the identical pitch-class collection, G–A–B♭, in dotted rhythm. Tenor 1 now takes up the PCA from the continuo bass, and in the same measure, with B♮, pc 4. B♮ passes to C, pc 5, within the same voice, but then transfers the PCA line into tenor 2 with its C✕ as pc 6 (still in the same register, however). Naturally, C♯ moves to D as pc 7 in m. 61. As the lover intensifies his expression of adoration for his beloved ("e col cor devoto Amante"), D♯ enters the pitch field tossing the system back up to *durus* (m. 64 on the word "Amante"). D♯ is pc 8 and is supported harmonically by a B major triad, which once again moves to E in m. 68. E is pc 9, which now passes directly to F♯ (there is no pc 10 in this ascent) as pc 11. Only at the last moment does the system revert back to C *naturalis* when B♭ is introduced in m. 76. Here is the last juxtaposition of the primary dyad conflict of the piece, B♭/B♮. B♭ is once again heard within G minor ("dorian"). But as the last pitches of the PCA unfold, namely F♯ and G as pcs 11 and 0, Monteverdi deliberately ends the piece on octave Gs. Perhaps we are meant to hear the G octave as implying B♮ since the overtone series on G as fundamental would imply the major third. If that is the case, then the previous B♭ should be understood to have resolved itself once and for all to B♮, implied within the context of the octave G♮s in the final cadence.

Monteverdi's harmonic procedures, in terms of the unfolding PCA, system modulations, and hexachord as both harmonic foreground and background, are not unique to his time period, nor even to his nationality. We find very similar compositional concerns in the works of Heinrich Schütz, who most likely studied with Monteverdi in 1628; unfortunately, limitations of space prevent us from exploring these works. The major difference between Schütz and Monteverdi is in the German composer's somewhat greater interest in large-scale prolongations of structurally significant harmonic areas, especially in his later works. But there are many other composers doing this as well; in fact, it would be hard to find a composer whose harmonic language tends toward the chromatic and who does not unfold the chromatic octave or who does not follow the fifths orderings of a system's central hexachord. When modality finally yields to a stronger tonal harmonic organization around the latter part of the seventeenth century, these conditions are still present, and may now be reinterpreted in light of an encroaching common-practice tonality, which is the subject of the next chapter.

Chapter Four

Tonality and Systems in the Seventeenth and Early Eighteenth Centuries

I. Introduction: The Emergence of Key-Centered Tonality in the Instrumental Music of the Latter Half of the Seventeenth Century

During the 1670s and 1680s, northern Italian composers undertook the first bold steps to standardize an instrumental style that had gradually evolved over the course of the previous half-century. The north Italian cities of Rome, Venice, and Bologna, including the surrounding areas under their political and artistic influence, cultivated thriving instrumental traditions that complemented their already famous operatic and sacred music institutions. This new emerging style soon influenced all major musical capitals of Europe and established Italy as the focal point of a progressive school of instrumental composition.

Under the strong and vital influences of opera and cantata, all three Italian cities created instrumental works which, by the end of the seventeenth century, featured a cogent sense of tonal organization in which a tonic triad was prolonged over the course of an entire movement by functionally significant auxiliary cadences. The general interest on the part of Italian composers (and, to some extent, French composers as well) to create works with greater tonal clarity – specifically, compositions in which all harmonic motions within any given movement related directly to a background tonic – supported a new approach to phrase structure and rhythmic unity that reflected the new attitude toward mode (*tonus*) and hexachordal harmonic organization. The results allowed composers greater freedom to expand and develop thematic material and thus to enlarge the breadth and scope of each composition.

Previously, composers had relied on a number of compositional techniques inherited from the Renaissance to create pieces of any considerable length. Mosaic designs that ran together short, contrasting movements in the style of the canzona, for example, were especially popular in Venice during the first half of the seventeenth century. Such techniques appear in the violin canzonas and sonatas of G.B. Fontana (d. c. 1630), Tarquinio Merula (c. 1594–1665), and Biagio Marini (c. 1587–1663). Composers also attempted to create larger works through the use of other forms and procedures first established in the sixteenth century: for example, they favored variations upon a given theme or bass, multi-sectional toccatas characterized by contrasting fantasia (meaning, freely contrapuntal) and strictly imitative sections, and the ricercar, with its series of imitative subjects. However, without the aid of a text, whose presence would have allowed for a more expressive chromatic language, and consequently for more frequent shifts of eleven-pitch-class hexachordal systems, composers of instrumental music during the first half of the seventeenth century restricted themselves to movements of only moderate length and of only limited harmonic scope. The brevity of the individual sections, whether dance-derived in free counterpoint or strictly imitative, did not provide opportunities for large-scale modulations capable of supporting non-tonic harmonic areas. Such a modulatory process would require a complete harmonic progression in order to stabilize the "new key," a process that would not be fully established until the advent of ritornello form some time in the late 1680s. As a result, each section of these earlier canzona-like structures remained clearly within the tonic with cadences restricted to hexachordal pitches of the prevailing system. However, these points of cadential articulation did not in turn motivate full progressions within their respective harmonic areas; rather, the tendency was to return immediately to tonic harmony.

Until the advent of large-scale tonal modulation at the end of the seventeenth century, composers of instrumental music who wished to explore harmonic areas that existed outside the prevailing tonic hexachord system did so by shifting into contrasting eleven-pitch-class gamut systems. Perhaps owing to their improvisatory nature, pieces based on the toccata principle were more motivated than others to shift hexachordal systems, often with startling results. On the other hand, pieces in canzona form, such as early chamber sonatas, and keyboard canzonas were more likely than not to remain within one hexachordal system throughout. As an example of the former, consider Frescobaldi's *Toccata ottava* (see Example 4.1).

Example 4.1 Frescobaldi, *Toccata ottava* (mm. 1–7)

The toccata is composed in the F mode in *cantus durus* and therefore assumes a *naturalis* system. What makes the piece harmonically interesting is the conflict that arises between what appears to be pure F lydian as the background mode, with a natural signature and with frequent B♮s, and a tendency toward lydian *mollis* with written-in B♭s. However, F as a tonal center (either modal or tonal) is hardly established in the first measure before the harmony immediately veers toward the subdominant, the passing E♭ in the top voice effectively turning the F triad into an applied dominant of IV. As a result, the *naturalis* system shifts down a fifth to *mollis* and remains within a 1♭ system until G♯ enters in m. 6, returning the system to *naturalis*. Significantly, from m. 6 on there are no E♭s or D♯; the eleven-pitch-class area of the *naturalis* system remains uncontested until the end of the toccata. However, while the *naturalis* system remains intact throughout, the underlying harmonic progressions, rather than supporting an F tonic, relate more to pitch classes that form the roots of the *naturalis* hexachord:

Quality of third:				B/B♭	F/F♯	C/C♯	G/G♯
Hexachordal pcs:	F –	C –	G –	d –	a –	e
	I	V	II	vi	iii	vii
			V/V			V/iii

(B♭ is the allowable flat in this system and acts as IV/F)

As in the Monteverdi vocal examples cited in the previous chapter, Frescobaldi's harmonic motions tend to be localized; that is, the bass moves in fifths (not always in root position, but sometimes in inversion) following the fifths of the reordered *naturalis* hexachord. In Example 4.1 above, note the bass progression starting from the A⁶ chord on the third half note in m. 2: A⁶–D–G (downbeat of m. 3) –C. Instead of C now moving to F to reaffirm the tonic of the piece, C moves to another A⁶ to begin another series of fifths, and so on. In addition, the modal language of the period allows for any number of degree-inflected thirds within any particular fifths progression. Thus, the third half note of m. 6 supports an E minor triad, the third of which is inflected to G♯ on the fourth half note of the measure. Not only is E minor inflected to E major, but G♯ reverts the previous *mollis* system to *naturalis*. In this case, however, the E major triad does not then proceed immediately to the next fifth, A, but instead reverts to E minor on the downbeat of m. 7. Only then does the implied E minor harmony move to A⁶ once more, followed by d⁶ as the next fifth relation.

The rest of the toccata moves along the C hexachord in similar fashion, its fifths relationships pointing always toward D minor as a potential terminus. Only the last measure of the toccata redirects the harmony to F, with B♭ reintroduced in the bass as part of a ii6 chord, the measure ending emphatically with the dominant C moving to the F, the final of the mode.

As the seventeenth century progressed, composers of solo and trio sonatas came increasingly to rely on the one specific compositional form that had always manifested an inherent tonal structural coherency since its inception: the dance – either non-sectional or binary. Individual sonatas usually comprised one dance movement, sometimes with an introductory prelude, or they alternated brief, imitative, or through-composed movements for contrast. The *sonate da camera*, as a collection or suite of dance movements, is rare until Corelli's op. 2 of 1685.[1] Apart from their appearance in the *sonate da camera*, dance movements were often incorporated into the church sonata, although not labeled as such. Further, typical rhythmic patterns and typical phrasing of dance rhythms increasingly permeated other through-composed movements of the sonata.[2] These dance influences would soon affect the concerto grosso.

From their inception, dance forms had clear-cut phrasing supported by strong rhythmic accents. Both phrasing and accent combined to create a fuller sense of tonal direction. But, during the seventeenth century at least, dance movements did not allow for thematic expansiveness, for development of motives, or for much textural contrast within their relatively short sections. On the other hand, pieces of considerable length were in existence, though their overall structures were relatively shapeless – sometimes even rambling. As many of the toccatas, ricercars, and fantasias of Sweelinck, Scheidemann, Tunder, and Frescobaldi attest, composers were primarily interested in the individual moment or section (for example, a so-called "point of imitation") and in its surface detail. Frescobaldi confirms the mosaic character of these pieces when he states in his Preface to *Il secondo libro di toccate, canzone, versi d'hinni ...* (Rome, 1637):

> In the Toccatas I have not only paid regard to the fact that they are rich in varied passages and ornaments but also that *the individual sections may be played separately from one another* [our emphasis], in order to enable the player to make a conclusion at will, without having to end the Toccata.[3]

The restricted thematic scope of the dance forms and the disunited structures of the through-composed pieces were both a condition of the modal/tonal system then in use, a system in which internal harmonic progressions could just as easily relate to a background tonic as they could to the fifths of a reordered central hexachord. In either case, there was no established method to create a convincing long-term modulatory harmonic scheme where every harmonic goal could support and relate to an underlying background tonic triad.

In particular, what was missing from the stagnant tonality of the period was any consistent use of large-scale modulatory dominant progressions. What is meant here

---

1 For a discussion of the pre-Corellian *sonate da camera* see John Daverio, "In Search of the Sonata da Camera before Corelli," *Acta musicologia*, 57/2 (1985): 195–214. Daverio observes that the current spelling "sonata" was never used; instead, "sonate" is indicated on all the title pages of the printed editions ("sonate da camera" or "sonate da [or de] chiesa").

2 In describing Stradella's numerous trio sonatas (mostly composed in the late 1670s), Eleanor F. McCrickard states: "No movement is designated a dance, yet the rhythms from dances of the period permeate the movements. Whereas these rhythms are most often found in the binary movements, they are not limited to those movements." Eleanor F. McCrickard, "Temporal and Tonal Aspects of Alessandro Stradella's Instrumental Music," *Analecta musicologica*, 19 (1979): 186–243.

3 Trans. Pierre Pidoux, in Girolamo Frescobaldi, *Orgel- und Klavierwerke*, ed. Pierre Pidoux, vol. 4 (Kassel, 1963).

is not simply cadence structures which temporarily arrive at diatonic key centers while still deferring to the tonic. Rather, contrapuntal expansions of non-tonic harmonic areas are not yet present within these works. Certainly, applied dominants were becoming known and used from at least the beginning of the seventeenth century, especially in vocal music.[4] But while instances of applied dominant relationships are plentiful, these tend to be localized affairs which do not contrapuntally expand the point of arrival or articulate a non-tonic harmonic area. Instead, they are conceived as subsidiary passing motions within the prevailing tonic.

Monteverdi's *Vespers* of 1610 provides a case in point. The "Laetatus sum" from this impressive work is composed in transposed hypodorian mode on G in *cantus mollis*. However, Monteverdi's adjustments of the original plainsong (the penultimate F♮ is consistently written as F♯) and the harmonic context within which it is set render the mode emphatically G minor.[5] Thus, the first six measures of the movement clearly establish G as G minor,[6] which is presented in the continuo as a complex "walking bass" that is both contrapuntal and harmonic in design. The bass unfolds a complete harmonic progression which supports a statement of the

---

    4   Examples of applied dominants, used within an elementary harmonic context, can already be seen in the monodies of the Florentine cameratas and in the *stile rappresentativo* of early opera. One particularly striking instance, appearing later on in the seventeenth century, occurs in the final chorus of Carissimi's oratorio *Jeptha* (c. 1640), "Plorate filii Israel," where the first half of the chorus, in A minor, moves to G major via an applied dominant before the second ending. The second half of the chorus remains in G, prolonged throughout by its dominant. Further, the A minor of the first half of the chorus can be heard as part of a large-scale progression, II–V–I in G major, the key (or more correctly, the G mixolydian mode) in which the oratorio opens. Carissimi's chorus is unique in that such large-scale harmonic progressions are extremely rare at this time, yet it does portend future developments in tonal prolongation that become standard only during the last quarter of the seventeenth century. See also Beverly Stein, "Carissimi's Tonal System and the Function of Transposition in the Expansion of Tonality," *The Journal of Musicology*, 19/2 (Spring 2002): 264–305.

    5   Significant is the fact that the chant melody is not stated at the outset of the piece; instead, it enters in m. 3 during a prolongation of the relative major, B♭. The chant itself is composed in transposed B♭ hypodorian, which at first seems to contradict the G minor tonic harmony of the piece. Monteverdi's use of the *cantus* melody is thus very different from that of the sixteenth century, where it acted as the structural voice, often determining the shape and harmonic content of the voices around it. Here the harmonic construction of Monteverdi's bass is the governing factor, overriding the transposed B♭ hypodorian mode of the chant melody. The upper voices, as well as the *cantus*, are contingent upon, if not derived from, the triadic implications of the bass. This new approach to counterpoint which is instrumentally conceived – i.e., derived from the continuo bass – will replace the voice-derived counterpoint of the previous century by the middle of the seventeenth century. Monteverdi must be accounted one of the first composers to utilize this new style.

    6   Monteverdi was probably not thinking of G hypodorian (in *cantus mollis*) as G minor in the modern sense of common-practice tonality, but as a "church key" or "tone;" that is, as a fixed transposition a fifth down from D dorian, the first church key. The lower fifth relation, as an exact transposition of D dorian, was thought of as "hypo." For a more complete discussion of church keys and their derivations, see Joel Lester, *Between Modes and Keys: German Theory 1592–1802* (New York, 1989), pp. 77–82.

plainsong chant in tenor 1, upon which the movement is based. The background structure of the bass is g–B♭ (III defined by its dominant, F)–D (V)–G (in this case, major). This tightly organized progression, which ultimately derives from the reordered F hexachord, governs the entire psalm setting, with the opening "walking bass" returning periodically in the manner of a ritornello. Again, one notices the pairing of localized fifth relations, here B♭–F, F–C, and d–G, all hexachordal pitch classes of the *mollis* system.

Typical of ritornello structures of the first half of the seventeenth century, the "theme" is never transposed, but remains in the tonic at each appearance. Thus, while the bass-*cum*-ritornello possesses an extensive internal motion to the relative major (B♭) via an applied dominant, F, the relative major is heard only as a prolongation of the G modal tonic – that is, as part of a larger harmonic progression – and is never established as a separate key in its own right. The thematic material that acts as transition material between each return of the ritornello simply emphasizes the dominant, sometimes with a passing motion to the relative major, as a preparation for the return of the ritornello in the tonic. As a result, the entire movement, of some considerable length (116 measures), does not, in fact, prolong the tonic on a background level, but is organized sectionally. Each section is clearly within the G mode, albeit with a G major triad sometimes substituted at final cadences.

The absence of non-tonic expansions may be one of the few lingering aspects of late modality in Monteverdi, Frescobaldi, and their contemporaries; but, within a few decades, particularly with the music of Corelli, composition will have more of a "modern" sound and begin to include tonally directed harmonic progressions. By this, we mean that a tonally conceived phrase contains certain assumptions and expectations on the level of the phrase that are generally absent – or at least not consistently present – in a modal composition, even one of the late seventeenth century. In a sense, a tonal phrase, with its establishment of a tonic, the contrapuntal expansion of the tonic by means of some kind of subdominant or pre-dominant entity, and its culmination in a cadential figure, creates a tonal hierarchy, a kind of musical "gravitational pull" that is unmistakable. Of course, it is unreasonable to criticize Monteverdi or Frescobaldi for not being Vivaldi, and this certainly should not be inferred! However, we are at a historical juncture where the art of Western musical composition was not just about to change, but, indeed, needed to do so in order for the modern developmental process to become an integral part of a burgeoning tonality.

With Marini, we will see both the last gasps of modality and the birth of a new compositional ideal that will alter the face of composition for the next 200 years.

II. Biagio Marini: Unresolved Modal-Tonal Conflicts and the Possibilities they Pose for Development

The sonatas of Biagio Marini (c. 1587–1663) furnish, within themselves, an excellent illustration of the move from a stagnant tonality, meaning one that still adheres to modal progressions based on localized fifths within the prevailing three-hexachord system, to a nascent tonality; that is, a tonality in which the hexachordal pitches are organized into harmonic progressions that support a background tonic.[7] In general, Marini's sonatas evidence a lack of contrapuntal voice-leading of the sort which would allow for the establishment of non-tonic harmonic expansions. Often, harmonic areas are simply juxtaposed through modal bass motions of a third or a fourth, rather than fulfilling large-scale tonally conceived cadential progressions. In Marini's earliest collection of sonatas (dated 1617), modal constructions clash head-on with attempts to create tonally organized sections. "La Foscarina," from this collection, clearly illustrates the multiplicity of harmonic designs available to composers at this time.

Example 4.2 is taken from one of the many brief sections of this canzona-like piece. At first, it is difficult to determine the overriding "key:" C major seems at first to be the most likely candidate (it was the tonality of the previous section), but from m. 60 the music veers toward F. Instead of completing the cadential progression in that key, the music suddenly shifts again (in m. 63) to A, a completely unprepared third motion. A as a harmonic area is itself never secured by its dominant, either before or after its initial statement, and is further undermined by C♮/C♯ cross relations in mm. 67–9. A dramatic pause follows, in m. 70, in order to prepare for a lengthy passage of *stile concitato* in which A finally reveals itself as the dominant of the dominant of G hypodorian (the second church key), the mode (or "key") of the sonata. Initially, however, A as V/V is not immediately related to D, but is contrapuntally prolonged by B♭ and G as upper and lower neighbors. Only when the bass rises from A at the beginning of the *stile concitato* to B♮ in m. 76, and again to C♯ in m. 77, forming a first-inversion A major triad, do we recognize a contrapuntal line leading up to D. Thus no part of the voice-leading of the first six measures of the passage supports any kind of harmonic direction to the dominant D major triad which appears in m. 79. Taken as a whole, then, the A major passage that bursts upon the scene in m. 63 cannot be heard as part of a large-scale II–V–I cadential motion to G minor since it is neither convincingly motivated nor convincingly prolonged.

---

7   For an overview of Marini's sonatas see Thomas D. Dunn, "The Sonatas of Biagio Marini: Structure and Style," *The Music Review*, 36/3 (August 1975): 161–79.

Example 4.2 Biagio Marini, "La Foscarina, Sonata a 3 con il tremolo" (mm. 50–80)

Admittedly, viewing the above harmonic relations in terms of common-practice tonality would seem to make little sense, but the same relationships do make perfect *modal* sense if one hears the entire movement in terms of the *mollis* 1♭ three-hexachord system. While G is the modal final of the piece, the internal motions to C and A, along with the fifths attached to them, F and D, all contained within the 1♭ system, create a well-balanced symmetry between the subdominant side and the dominant side of the *mollis* hexachord:

B♭	F	C	**g**	d	a
III	VII	iv	i	v	ii

The use of symmetrical fifths surrounding a modal tonic is quite common in music of the first half of the seventeenth century, and is quite unlike the tonal hierarchies inherent in common-practice tonality. Such tonal organization was simply not an issue to composers during the first half of the century as long as the modes remained a vital compositional force. The problem stems from the fact that modes, by definition, are purely linear constructs.[8] When harmonized according to the gamut system that underlies them, they become unstable in a key-defining sense: each tone of their central hexachord theoretically may have either a minor or major triad constructed above it, and this may result in cross-relations and modal progressions: that is, progressions that emphasize minor triads and localized harmonic motions around hexachordal fifths, that prevent any possibility of tonal voice-leading. For tonality to be clearly established, there must be present a major-quality dominant triad which contains the leading tone of the key. Harmonized modes may or may not contain such triads. In addition, the major dominant triad must itself be preceded by a chord progression that defines its function as the penultimate goal of motion, the ultimate goal being, of course, the tonic. Such tonally directed progressions, absent from modal theory, shift the emphasis from the linear to the harmonic, and thereby endanger the very nature of the linear mode they purport to harmonize. During the first half of the seventeenth century, a period in which the confrontation of modality and tonality is at its most extreme, the listener is often presented with modal-tonal passages that constantly fluctuate between minor and major triads and often leave the tonic itself in doubt. By definition, these pieces are limited in scope. Large-scale forms, such as the late Baroque concerto and the Classical symphony, require a fully developed tonal system, one capable of supporting a structural hierarchy. Such a tonal structure is capable of prolonging the tonic through the contrapuntal articulation of large-scale harmonically dissonant areas. These non-tonic harmonic areas become the points of formal division within the composition.

To use voice-leading terminology, modality was never capable of sustaining or supporting a middleground. Therefore, in most instances, the background structure

---

8 In discussing Glarean's *Dodecachordon*, Harold S. Powers states: "... for him [Glarean] as for others the modes were monophonic, and a principle for integrating the voices was needed." See "Mode," in Stanley Sadie and John Tyrrell (eds), *The New Grove Dictionary of Music and Musicians*, 2nd edn (London, 2001), vol. 16, p. 811.

of a modal composition could be viewed as harmonically static, or perhaps even non-existent.[9]

Marini's obscure tonal progressions in the sonatas composed before 1655 illuminate the problem clearly: there is little or no sense of structural hierarchy. As a result, there is a certain amount of confusion as to which is tonic and which is prolonging. For example, Marini's contrapuntal motions toward non-harmonic areas are often not completed, and remain within the tonic orbit. Consequently, phrases are short-winded and often seem to end before their time without defining the key.

Marini's final collection of sonatas (op. 22, 1655) shows the composer attempting a grander design with a concomitant increase in his contrapuntal skill. These works and those of Giovanni Legrenzi (op. 2, 1655 – discussed below) form a direct link to the ensemble sonatas of Stradella and Corelli and deserve closer inspection.

The *Prima parte* and *Seconda parte* ("movement," as a term for a self-contained section of music within a larger piece, was not used until the early eighteenth century) of Marini's Sonata op. 22 no. 1 in D dorian (first church key), in *cantus durus* (*naturalis* three-hexachord system), already show the formal outlines of the *sonate da chiesa* of Corelli. The sonata, scored for violin, string bass obbligato, and continuo, begins with a through-composed movement (see Example 4.3) which attempts to expand upon two thematically contrasting motives stated unaccompanied from the outset in the bass. This flamboyant, fantasia-like movement prepares a fugal second movement equally quixotic in nature. Juxtaposing a through-composed movement, one which contains a certain degree of instability, with a more stable fugue becomes standard in the *da chiesa* sonatas of Corelli. What makes this particular Marini sonata interesting is the expansion of motivic material through the use of elementary contrapuntal *Fortspinnung* techniques (to use the German term) with the express purpose of unifying the movement. These expansion procedures usually entail parallel or conjunct motion between the outer voices and result in sequences such as 5–6 exchanges, parallel sixths or tenths, 5–7 cycles, and so on.

Fortspinnung (or "spinning-out") is a fundamental stylistic feature of the late Baroque and serves two purposes: (1) to prolong given key areas, often through sequences, while providing a sense of directed harmonic motion, and (2) to create bridge material, providing tension and instability, as the music progresses from one harmonic area to another. Owing to the irregular phrasing of Baroque music, *Fortspinnungen* may be applied at any point within the composition, even within its initial thematic statement. However, *Fortspinnungen* become most effective when judged against an established tonic background. Only in this way can the "spinning-out" technique create harmonic dissonance and thus musical drama, the very basis of the late Baroque concerto.

---

9   The question may also be raised whether there is any validity to the use of Schenkerian analytical techniques to explicate pre-tonal music. Schenker assumed the unfolding of a tonic triad, the background harmonic organization, and its middleground and foreground contrapuntal elaborations to be at the heart of a tonal composition. Thus Schenker's theory represents a philosophical unity of harmonic and contrapuntal thinking. If modality was ultimately incapable of rationalizing the horizontal and vertical aspects of composition, then the application of Schenker's theory to such compositions may exemplify musical-theoretical sophistry.

Example 4.3 Marini, Sonata op. 22 no. 1, *Prima parte*

Marini's *Fortspinnung* progression begins in m. 17 as an expanded motion within the dominant (Example 4.3). The particular contrapuntal technique employed here is a series of 5–7, or cycle-of-fifths, sequences (mm. 17–19 and mm. 24–8, plus cadential material) which is directly related to the second motive (*b*) of the movement (mm. 6–7). Thus Marini is developing the second motive and expanding it throughout the second half of the movement. Such a process gives the whole a tight structural unity. Contrasted with this is motive *a* (note that both motives are played at first unaccompanied in the bass), which moves at a decidedly slower harmonic rate. In addition, both motives contrast in function as well as in design: the first motive attempts tonal stability, while the second is harmonically unstable and sequential. Here, Marini anticipates the use of *Fortspinnung* in the later concerto.

In this movement, Marini adumbrates Classical developmental procedures by working out foreground details on deeper structural levels, notably the phrygian cadence which first appears in mm. 4–5. The B♭ upper neighbor to the dominant A complements the opening gesture of the C♯ lower neighbor to the tonic. Since the motive itself is open-ended, it can be used to explore more distant dominant relations, in particular the dominant of the dominant. In mm. 15 and 16, for instance, the phrygian cadence to E, initiating a brief prolongation of the dominant A, occurs naturally as part of a transposition of the opening subject in V (m. 12). Even motive *b* (mm. 6–8) projects the phrygian B♭–A of the first motive as an inner-voice motion in the bass, supported by a cycle of fifths, resulting in a descending contrapuntal line from B♮ in m. 6 to B♭ on the downbeat of m. 7, which then resolves to the A in m. 8. This gesture is repeated in the bass between mm. 24 and 26, where the structural dominant is reached and then restated immediately in the bass at the upper octave as preparation for the final cadence of the movement. (It is significant that the previous motion to the dominant, in m. 21, avoids this inner-voice descent.)

The question remains, then: is Marini's movement tonally conceived (in a manner in which Corelli might have expressed it) or are the harmonic progressions still tied to modal thinking? Marini's harmonic plan for this movement centers on, and remains within, the confines of this eleven-note *naturalis* three-hexachord system where no E♭ or D♯ is present to provoke a modulation of system:

Third degrees present:	A	E	B/B♭	F/F♯	C/C♯	G/G♯
C hexachord pcs:	F –	C –	g –	d –	a –	e
	III	VII	iv/IV	i/I	v/V	ii/II

(B♭ is the allowable flat in this system and used to form its own major triad)

Marini's innovation here is the background harmonic progression from the final of the mode, D, to its dominant, A (m. 12), and then to its dominant E (m. 17: see the brackets in the above diagram), before returning to D via A. This decidedly tonal harmonic plan points to similar tonally conceived background progressions that become standard by the end of the seventeenth century, notably in the works of Arcangelo Corelli.

In this case, the structural harmonic goals of this movement occur in fifths up the hexachord and away from the tonic instead of moving down in the subdominant direction toward g, C, and F (although these hexachordal pitches from the subdominant side of the hexachord often appear together within local sequential progressions, as in mm. 6–7). Likewise, the opening five measures are also progressive in the sense that they constitute a perfectly clear tonal progression within the tonic, i–V6–i–VI–V, that ends on a phrygian half cadence. This kind of tonal progression arpeggiates the structural tonic and fifth of the mode (or "key") with the dominant degree prolonging tonic harmony. In addition, every pitch in the bass is diatonic within the mode, with C♯ as its leading tone and B♭ forming the motivically important phrygian cadence to the dominant. In other words, there are no altered chords that could confuse the progression and obstruct our understanding of the background tonic.

Equally "modern" is Marini's use of *Fortspinnung* sequential progressions (contrapuntal elaborations organized in fifths cycles) to prepare formal cadences or to extend phrases. For example, the sequential *b* motive that serves to complete the opening *a* phrase temporarily suspends the tonic with the purpose of motivating the tonic cadence in m. 10, giving the whole ten-measure period a sense of forward direction. Significantly, the *b* motive is the basis of all the *Fortspinnung* sequences in the movement – a further unifying device.

Similarly, the *b* motive sequence (beginning with the E triad in m. 17, functioning as V/V) directs the progression back to A, the dominant, and culminates in a formal cadence in m. 22. The dominant is then prolonged by two large *b*-motive fifths cycles (the first from m. 24 to m. 26, and the second from m. 26 to m. 30), each terminating in a cadence on the dominant. The first sequence, starting on E, and intensified by a *stretto* imitation between violin and string bass, once again raises B♭ (m. 25) as an upper neighbor to the A in m. 26, just as it did in mm. 7–8. The downbeat A in m. 26 starts the second sequence, a transposition of the previous sequential passage but still incorporating the B♭–A relation. Instead of a formal cadence re-establishing the tonic, the last four measures prepare a contrapuntal 6–8 cadence to the D final, the last triad being D major. In this way, Marini ends the movement on a D triad that is bifocal; meaning that the root D relates to the tonic of the movement, but, as a major triad, it also prepares for the second movement (*Seconda parte*, Allegro), which starts in G hypodorian.

Marini's op. 22 sonata is typical of mid-seventeenth-century compositions of this type in that it evidences modern tonal tendencies as well as more modal, conservative thinking. The first movement clearly adumbrates later tonal organization in that the progress of the movement moves up in fifths away from tonic harmony, only to return to it via its dominant. The second movement of this work (*Seconda parte*) is somewhat more modal in thinking: the movement begins in G hypodorian, the subdominant relation of D dorian, with consistent B♭s, yet its signature is still that of *cantus durus*, and consequently, the *naturalis* three-hexachord system governs the pitch material of the movement; again, Marini uses only the eleven pitch classes of the *naturalis* system without a single instance E♭ or D♯. Halfway through the movement (m. 53), B♮s displace B♭s as the mode turns into G mixolydian (the eighth church key), heard here as the parallel major of G hypodorian, which ends the movement. Marini's harmonic conception here goes against what will become standard in later ensemble sonatas, namely the second fugal movement, perhaps the most developed of all the movements of the work: it is invariably in the tonic, certainly not the subdominant, and the mode is consistently stagnant throughout. However, Marini prolongs both G minor and G major modes with dominant progressions. Of interest is the Bb–A relationship that pervaded the opening movement. During the first half of the second movement, in G hypodorian, the Bb–A relationship is worked out (or "developed" – we use the two terms interchangeably), culminating in the cadence on the dominant in mm. 50–52 that ends the first half of the movement.

The last movement (*Terza parte*, in triple dance meter) has even more modal tendencies. No background tonic, modal or tonal, is established until the end of the movement; rather, the harmonic motion proceeds along the localized fifths of the *naturalis* hexachord (in *cantus durus*), beginning on G, the eighth church mode, and ends on D (the first church key and the modal tonic of the entire piece). The whole movement is entirely in major modes without any modulation out of the *naturalis* gamut system. The subdominant relationship between G and D, worked out intra-movement (and inter-movement), emphasizes the authentic/hypo-modal relationship that characterizes the entire sonata on a background level.

The opening of the third movement moves swiftly in localized fifths, one per measure – G, C, F, Bb – and then reverses the process until a cadence on D is reached in m. 77 (the measure numbering follows the Hortus Musicus edition). The D is not yet expressed as tonic, but as V/G, the tonic being confirmed with an authentic cadence in m. 81. Curiously, Marini now changes the meter to duple in m. 87, and the G tonic now moves up the *naturalis* hexachord to arrive at D in m. 94. From here to the end of the movement, D displaces G as tonic.

Obviously, Marini is trying something quite new compositionally: a semblance of unity and thought that goes beyond individual movements, projecting design elements to higher levels of structure. Following Marini's example, both Stradella and Corelli will extend this process over the course of an entire sonata, sometimes working out details from the first movement in subsequent movements. In this regard, Marini's elementary attempts take on great significance in light of later compositional practice.

III. Giovanni Legrenzi: Nascent Tonality

Giovanni Legrenzi (1626–1690) published his *Sonate a due e tre* op. 2 (Venice, 1655) in the same year as Marini's op. 22.[10] In this unique collection, Legrenzi deliberately set out to compose a series of sonatas in the eight church modes, probably for church services. Here, the conflict between the requirements of modal linear construction and tonal harmonic progression reaches a historic climax. It is significant that no other collection of sonatas was ordered in this manner before or since. Significant, too, is Legrenzi's compositional success or failure within the collection, and this in turn seems to be dependent upon how close a particular mode is to the contemporary

---

10 Giovanni Legrenzi, *Sonate (1655)*, critical edition with introduction, ed. Stephen Bonta (Cambridge, Massachusetts, 1984). For more information on Legrenzi see Stephen Bonta, "The Church Sonatas of Giovanni Legrenzi," 2 vols, Ph.D. dissertation, Harvard University, 1964.

major or minor. The phrygian and hypo-mode settings are the least successful since both modes lack the necessary dominant to establish tonality.

To illustrate the modal-tonal conflict, the second sonata, "La Spilimberga," for two violins and continuo, is most instructive. The sonata was composed in the same year, 1655, and in the same church key (transposed hypodorian, or second church key) as Marini's op. 22 no. 1 discussed above. Almost identical to the opening progression in Marini's sonata, Legrenzi's opening statement clearly prolongs the G modal tonic with the same inverted major dominant, embellished with the same phrygian relationship to V, here, however, as part of iv6 (see Example 4.4, mm. 1–3). Since the linear organization of the hypo mode demands a strong tendency toward the plagal, g hypodorian (or G minor, if one hears the piece tonally) as a "key" center is undermined by lengthy passages in C minor (see mm. 10–21 and mm. 28–35); both passages together take up a significant portion of the music, that is, almost half the movement.

Between these two subdominant passages, G minor is regained (mm. 22–8), prolonged once more by both G and A♭, its dominant and submediant. At the end of the progression (mm. 26–7), Legrenzi moves the continuo bass up in half-steps to the structural dominant: C (♭II6)–C♯(07)–D(V); this is a gesture that becomes motivic throughout the rest of the opening movement. For example, the second subdominant passage in C minor (m. 28) is an exact transposition of the previous G minor passage, complete with the same ascending continuo bass motive to the V/iv (here, F–F♯–G). When G minor is regained in m. 36, the chromatic trichord in its original state returns as well, in fact, twice, both times affirming the G as the modal tonic of the movement (see mm. 48–50 and mm. 53–4). As in Marini, the same phrygian relation to the dominant is iterated several times, both gestures, the chromatic trichord and the submediant, acting as unifying devices, controlling the middleground harmonic progressions of the movement.

The very brief last movement, of only nine measures (Example 4.4b), functions as a coda to the whole sonata. It mostly comprises a long subdominant pedal on C, supporting C minor in the upper voices, which finally "resolves" to a G major triad at the end. In this respect, the movement is not unlike the last movement of Marini's op. 22 no. 1. Both movements seem more intent on following the fifths of their respective central hexachords than on establishing an overriding modal tonic. The G major triad which ends Legrenzi's sonata thus sounds very much like a dominant of C minor and not a plagal cadence in hypodorian.

Example 4.4a **Legrenzi, Sonata op. 2 no. 2, "La Spilimberga," first movement**

Example 4.4b   Legrenzi, Sonata op. 2 no. 2, last movement

It is interesting to note that both Legrenzi and Marini emphasize the phrygian relationship to the dominant within their opening phrases. They incorporate this gesture as a contrapuntal embellishment of the dominant triad, which, in turn, completes its harmonic implications with a return to the tonic. Marini artfully expands, and thus delays, the harmonic resolution of his B♭–A phrygian motion right into the entrance of the theme in the top voice through the use of the *Fortspinnung* motive *b*. However, Legrenzi's opening phrase is remarkable in quite a different manner. Though he uses the same phrygian gesture, Legrenzi effectively combines a strong tonal motion on the background level with middleground references to the hypodorian mode. The bass descent from G to C within the opening five measures adheres to the plagal requirements of the mode, but Legrenzi also interprets the C as a lower neighbor prolonging the dominant, D, which resolves to G at the end of the phrase.

The emphasis on the subdominant within the first phrase prepares for the extensive C minor passages that follow, a working-out of the applied dominant G–C of mm. 4 and 5. Legrenzi, like Marini in the op. 22 sonata, is able to project foreground details into a deeper level of structure. In fact, two characteristic gestures contained within the opening phrase are simultaneously worked out over the course of the entire sonata: the subdominant relation and the phrygian to V. In order to strengthen our perception of these two issues, Legrenzi incorporates both relationships in the final cadence of the initial phrase (see mm. 8–9), where E♭ descends to the dominant D via the lower neighbor C as an embellishing tone. The chord of arrival in m. 10 is not the expected G minor triad, but its parallel major, forcing the music into the subdominant. The expected arrival of C minor in m. 15 is likewise deflected by a turn to the parallel major, initiating a similar motion to the subdominant of the subdominant. Interestingly, the actual confirmation of C minor in m. 21 is prepared by a dominant 6/4–5/3 cadential motion which utilizes the sixth degree in the upper voice, thereby raising once again the E♭–D relationship of the opening phrase. (This cadence first appears in m. 14 with the upper voices inverted.) Note also that the bass in mm. 19 and 20 replicates the bass of the cadence at mm. 8 and 9, now transposed to the subdominant.

The opening of the second movement is outstanding. It centers on the relative major, B♭. The first measure begins with an E♭ triad which descends to a first-inversion B♭ chord in m. 2 with D in the bass, once again emphasizing the E♭–D relationship. Plagal relationships abound in this movement, prepared by the contrapuntal descent in the bass of the E♭–B♭ tetrachord in the first four measures.

Legrenzi's sonata also forecasts compositional procedures associated with later Baroque composers. The Presto of the second movement, for example, initiates a cyclic progression of fourths: D minor, G minor, C minor, and F as the dominant of B♭ (notice again the plagal relationships within and among these keys). Toward the end of the cycle (mm. 69–72), the phrasing accelerates and breaks into a *Fortspinnung* cycle of sequences that acts as a bridge to the return of the tonic, B♭.

In addition, both the first and second movements derive their thematic and rhythmic material from their opening gestures. In the case of the second movement, the opening of the Presto is an artfully disguised variation of m. 1 of the Adagio. Even though a change of rhythmic pattern occurs at the Presto, both sections are thematically and motivically unified within themselves. Such motivic unity is characteristic of all of Legrenzi's sonatas from this period on.

Along with rhythmic unity, Legrenzi's phrase structure tends to be balanced more evenly than Marini's. Legrenzi's symmetrical phrases throw his *Fortspinnung* passages (see those in the second movement) into stark relief and further differentiate stable thematic material from unstable, harmonically dissonant, material. As a result, Legrenzi achieves a dramatic thrust in his late sonatas that foreshadows a new direction in Baroque composition.

In summary, Legrenzi's chamber sonatas represent a substantial increase in artistic compositional development over that of many of his predecessors and contemporaries. In the areas of (a) development of foreground details on deeper levels of structure, (b) local harmonic organization, and (c) motivic/thematic unity, Legrenzi stands at the gateway of the late Baroque. However, even in his late sonatas (for example, op. 10, published in Venice in 1673), partly because of the lingering influence of modality, Legrenzi finds it difficult to prolong the tonic convincingly over the course of an entire movement. As with his predecessors, modulation from the tonic to tonal areas that are diatonically related, and yet are heard as non-tonic harmonic areas, remains, with few exceptions, elusive. It is evident from these works that a system of contrapuntal tonal voice-leading, supported by harmonically directed tonality and free of modal influence, had not yet been formulated.

IV. An Incipient Historical Development: Tonal Structure and Early Ritornello Design in the Instrumental and Vocal Works of Alessandro Stradella

From a historical perspective, evidence suggests that the aria forms in Italian opera of the 1670s and 1680s, rather than the contemporary ensemble sonata, provided the musical context for one of the first major attempts to move from harmonically distended modality toward a more concise harmonic system based on a clear hierarchy of tonal function. Such a musical reorganization meant that every harmonic motion within the aria would relate all structural layers to a background tonic. In particular, the "key" of the piece still operates within the three-hexachord system of its *cantus* signature, but now defines the tonic through its relationship to closely related harmonic areas, areas whose roots are still associated with the central hexachord of that system. As yet, these motions cannot be considered modulations in the eighteenth-century sense of the term, since there is no real departure from the tonic; composers do not even attempt to displace the tonic locally with another large-scale harmonic area. Harmonically progressive, however, is the fact that the motions which prolong the tonic are themselves reinforced with localized or subsidiary progressions. However, this does set the stage for modulations to autonomous key areas, an essential ingredient of the late Baroque concerto.

At this stage, arias tend to be brief. This helps to consolidate their tonal cohesiveness and also to restrict their modulatory capabilities. They are written in any number of forms, including binary (*A B*), strophic (usually two stanzas without variation), ostinato (passacaglia and chaconne, with and without modulatory basses), and the new *da capo* aria forms which began to flourish in the Italian opera in Rome and Venice.[11]

Arias, during this period, are tightly controlled by forms which need harmonic coherence and direction in order to articulate their internal divisions. For example, the popular strophic form is usually constructed in two strophes and has to reach tonic closure at the end of the first strophe. In order to provide harmonic contrast, the midpoint of the strophe tonicizes a closely related harmonic area, often the dominant or the relative. This motion, then, necessitates a clear return to the tonic. The brevity of the strophes makes it unlikely that elaborate sequential or motivic expansions may be exploited, while its texture remains predominantly homophonic – except for opening or closing ritornellos, which often contain some imitative counterpoint.

Other aria types are equally concise in their tonal organization, particularly those based on dance rhythms. And herein lies the major difference between the aria and the through-composed sonata movement: composers of sonata movements had to create their own forms as they proceeded without the benefits of preconceived structures based on poetic schemes. To obtain thematic coherence, not to mention length, composers relied on imitative procedures and *Fortspinnung* techniques. Since musical

---

11 See Carolyn M. Gianturco, "Evidence for a Late Roman School of Opera," *Music and Letters*, 56 (1975): 4–17. For a more lengthy discussion of aria forms during the 1670s and 1680s, see Carolyn M. Gianturco, "Caratteri stilistici delle opere teatrali di Stradella," *Rivista italiana di musicologia*, 6 (1971): 236–45.

form depends upon repetition for its comprehensibility, these techniques provided necessary thematic repetition without the aid of a text. Further, the polyphonic texture which resulted was admirably suited for the church. But, as we have seen, it was this very method of contrapuntal elaboration, often avoided in contemporary arias, that caused problems for the composers of these works: contrapuntal working-out, supported by tonally directed harmonic progressions, had not yet congealed sufficiently to express the tonic convincingly. Non-directed motion in the opera aria was circumvented, at least in part, by the temporal limitations imposed on it by the text, thus avoiding the tonal ambiguity inherent in the through-composed forms of contemporary instrumental music.

Composers of instrumental music, many of whom (such as Stradella and Legrenzi) also wrote operas, could well have been encouraged to apply the procedures of tonal direction found in the aria to that of the instrumental sonata, combining contrapuntal technique with a harmonic motion whose direction was strengthened by large-scale harmonic progressions. The most elaborate aria form, which may well have been a primary influence in this regard, was the *da capo* aria in all its variant formations.

Unlike other aria forms common at the time, the *da capo* aria often had a distinct middle section that was clearly set apart harmonically from the surrounding tonic. However, at this early stage in its development, the middle section, *B*, was not always harmonically articulated as an autonomous entity. This characteristic feature is found with greater regularity in operas composed at the end of the seventeenth century, where the *B* section was made harmonically distinct by its motion into a distant harmonic area, usually the relative major or minor. Rather, the opening tonic statement, comprising the orchestral ritornello and first vocal entrance, was just as likely to be open-ended, eliding into closely related tonalities. In these early, variant forms of the *da capo* aria, the return of the *A* section was often limited to just a restatement of the opening ritornello. In this abbreviated form, the ritornello was the only section of the aria with a complete period in the tonic since the first vocal entrance, instead of stabilizing the tonic within an extended period, often provided the signal for rapid motion into other harmonic areas.

A particularly fine example of a background tonic prolonged through motion to subsidiary harmonic areas arrived at via dominant preparations can be found in Alessandro Stradella's late opera *Moro per amore*, probably composed c. 1680.[12] The aria "T'intendo, si t'intendo" is sung by Lucinda in the second act and is accompanied throughout by a string ensemble of two violins and basso continuo (Example 4.5).

12 Alessandro Stradella, *Moro per amore*, facsimile edn reproduced from Vienna, Öesterreichische Nationalbibliothek, Cod 18708 (New York and London, 1979). The date of c. 1680 is suggested by Carolyn M. Gianturco, "Music for a Genoese Wedding of 1681," *Music and Letters*, 63/1–2 (1982): 43. For a fuller discussion of Stradella's operas, see Gianturco, "The Operas of Alessandro Stradella," D.Phil. dissertation, Oxford University, 1970.

Example 4.5 Stradella, *Moro per amore*, Act II, Lucinda's aria "T'intendo, si t'intendo"

Example 4.5 Stradella, *Moro per amore*, Act II, Lucinda's aria "T'intendo, si t'intendo" continued

Looks are enough
for a poor soul in love.
Yes, I know what your looks mean to me.

Blind god, you have no mercy on
Lucinda, I am condemned to despair.
I see that for my unlucky fate
I'll be faithful in vain.

Structurally, this aria (like many similar ones composed by Stradella and others) is in a loosely constructed *da capo* form in that the opening material returns, varied, with the return of the tonic near the close of the aria (mm. 39ff.), complete with a direct restatement of the opening theme as a closing ritornello in the tonic. However, there is no articulated *B* section set off in a contrasting harmonic area typical of the standard *da capo* form. Instead, it is constructed in a type of embryonic ritornello form which adumbrates the later ritornello concerto structure employed by Torelli and Albinoni at the end of the century.[13] The opening ritornello in F major returns, modified, in D minor (mm. 15–19) and in G minor in back-to-back statements, (mm. 27–9, and more completely in mm. 30–34). Similarly, the tonic also reappears in back-to-back ritornello statements at the end of the aria. The first is abbreviated, but is significant since it regains tonic harmony, while the second forms a complete closing statement in the tonic (mm. 45–9). Thus the aria assumes *da capo* character only in that there are two complete tonic ritornello statements: at the beginning and at the end. All the thematic material in between is related directly to either the ritornello (indicated as *a* in Example 4.5) or to a motive (*b*) found in the second vocal entrance (upbeat to mm. 8 and 9); there are no other contrasting motives of any significance. The voice enters in the manner of a *devise*; that is, it restates the opening motive of the ritornello in the tonic.[14] After a short instrumental interruption of one measure, the voice again restates the opening figure and continues with a slightly different motive characterized by four repeated eighth notes. The two motives are thereafter associated with either the orchestra (motive *a*) or the soloist (motive *b*). This characteristic differentiation of material between orchestra and soloist becomes standard in concertos after 1700.

Even more important is Stradella's sophisticated harmonic plan for this aria. Every harmonic motion in this short aria can be understood as a product of tonal voice-leading; *there is no trace of modality*. Each new harmonic area is convincingly arrived at and secured before proceeding to the next harmonic area; in addition, every auxiliary cadence and tonal digression relates to F major, the tonic of the aria.

If the plan of the aria is represented according to an F hexachord in *cantus mollis*, Stradella's harmonic plan becomes apparent:

B♭–	F –	C –	g –	d –	a
IV	I	V	ii	vi	iii

Harmonically, the aria's first harmonic motion is from F to C (m. 11) although the dominant is not articulated with its own ritornello. Moving along the *mollis* hexachord, the next harmonic area is vi (D minor), supported by a six-measure ritornello statement. Following a relatively lengthy area in vi, the next motion is to ii (G minor), which area is also prolonged, this time by two ritornello statements as described above. Stradella then simply reverses the harmonic progression and moves back to the tonic in a fifths progression from g to C (m. 39) as dominant preparation, and to F in m. 40. Thus, the whole aria simply moves around the central fifths of the F hexachord: F–C–g–d, without any modulation of system, there being exactly eleven pitch classes, with A♭/G♯ missing from the 1♭ system of the aria.

---

13 Stradella's ritornello aria form thus anticipates J.S. Bach's ritornello *da capo* forms in his cantatas and passions ("Erbame dich" from the *St Matthew Passion* is just one of numerous examples that can be cited).

14 Albinoni often favored the *devise* technique of the aria in his oboe concertos – the solo oboe being treated as though it were a voice (see John E. Solie, "Aria Structure and Ritornello Form in the Music of Albinoni," *The Musical Quarterly*, 63/1 [1977]: 31–47).

Significantly, Stradella anticipates the instrumental harmonic construction of the late Baroque in this aria.[15] In chamber music, as well as concerti grossi (at least by the time of Corelli's first publications, in which the procedure seems to have been standardized), the relative minor (vi) invariably *follows* the dominant as the next important point of harmonic articulation. In fact, the dominant is often used as a springboard to move away from the tonic toward other harmonic areas, often following the rotated fifths of the central hexachord within which the piece operates.

In Stradella's aria, the first structural area after the tonic is D minor (vi), emphasized by an orchestral ritornello (mm. 15–18). In this case, the dominant is not first articulated as a separate harmonic area, but remains only within the sphere of the tonic up to the dominant cadence in m. 11 (refer to Example 4.5). At this point, the bass, C, jumps up an octave and descends contrapuntally through B♭ to A, the dominant of D minor (m. 13). Concurrently, the upper voice, in contrary motion, ascends from F (m. 12 in the voice) to G (m. 13, second violin) to A (m. 14, first violin). The imitative texture staggers the arrival points among the voices (while the inner voice moves up in half steps from m. 11: E–C♯–D), creating a constant flow of motion. Each harmonic area within the aria is carefully prepared by a dominant progression. The second point of articulation is G minor (the aria progresses from the D minor ritornello in m. 15 through a cycle of fourths: D minor, G minor, C as structural dominant, and F). The motion away from D minor is accomplished through B♭ as a pivot (mm. 19–22). The B♭ is interpreted, by m. 22, as the relative major of G minor (ii), and leads naturally to a dominant cadence (m. 23). From m. 23 to m. 27, D is confirmed as V/ii through upper neighbor E♭s, all this in preparation for the ritornello in ii beginning with the upbeat to m. 28. The ritornello itself (mm. 28–30) stabilizes G minor with a brief cadential progression, I–V–I–IV–V–I, which is further articulated by a "walking bass."[16] It seems that Stradella was intent on an unusually long prolongation of the G minor area since the whole procedure is repeated, in invertible counterpoint, in mm. 30–34, as another ritornello statement in the same key.

---

15 In operatic music of the 1670s and 1680s, the text, owing to its single "affect," often precludes a middle section that is set off from the main body of the aria, and in which there is a large-scale motion to the relative minor (in major-key arias), though examples do exist of smaller passing motions in the relative minor if a phrase in the text will allow for it (see "Ti lascio l'alma in pegno" from Legrenzi's *Il Giustino*, 1683, repr. in Giovanni Legrenzi, *The Opera I*, ed. Hellmuth Christian Wolff [Cologne, 1971]. In Stradella's aria the background harmonic plan is A [as tonic], –E, –b, f♯, [vi]A).

The situation changes toward the end of the century, when poets deliberately design lyrical poetry to accommodate such a move by incorporating two or four lines of differing "affect." In this way, the *B* section of the *da capo* aria becomes articulated as a separate section in mood, key, and orchestration. In Stradella's *Moro per amore* major-key arias with auxiliary cadences in the relative minor are rare. "T'intendo, si t'intendo" is, therefore, unique in this regard.

16 Characteristic of late Baroque style is the more or less continuous "walking bass" of even quarter or eighth notes. This operates on several levels: it outlines the triads of the harmonic progression; the bass line contains numerous leaps of fourths and fifths, clearly demarcating cadential periods as well as providing a firm harmonic support to the progressions that lead up to these cadences; and, lastly, the bass often assumes the character of a contrapuntal voice moving against the upper parts.

The returning dominant, C, is thus already in a position to assume its structural role though a simple modal exchange whereby G minor is transformed into a G major triad as B♭ yields to B♮. After the G minor cadence which concludes the repeated ritornello (m. 34), C major appears, but is not secured until m. 36 with the arrival of the dominant G major triad. Interestingly, the high B♭ in violin 1 (m. 33), which forms the minor third, descending contrapuntally to G in m. 34, ascends to B♮ in the bass (m. 35), through octave displacement. The bass duplicates the violin descent, now from the major third, B♮. With the return of C, the tonic F major quickly follows, leading to a final and complete statement of the ritornello at the end of the aria.

The quality of the contrapuntal sequence has also changed with Stradella. In the chamber music of the previous generation, it was often difficult to determine the compositional intention of a sequence. What tonality did it prolong? How was it initiated? What direction was it taking? With Stradella, the sequence is harmonically directed: the beginning and ending of each sequence is defined with its harmonic or melodic goal clearly in sight. For example, the melodic sequence in the voice (mm. 12–13) moves C in the inner voice up to C♯, the major third of the dominant triad of D minor. At the same time, the imitative sequence that accompanies the voice in the strings completes the ascending contrapuntal motion initiated by the voice from F to A.

V. Alessandro Stradella: Tonality and the Emerging Concertino/Concerto Grosso Technique

Aria forms in Stradella's operas clearly foreshadow the tonal organization of the late Baroque. However, not one of the arias in his operas uses concerto grosso instrumentation; rather, those arias that contain instrumental accompaniment are entirely restricted to first and second violins with continuo. This relatively simple orchestration was most probably one of economic expediency on the part of the opera managers, who invested the greater portion of their budget on lead singers and set designs. The situation is quite different for sacred but non-liturgical works, such as oratorios and sacred cantatas, for use in the oratory of a church or for private performance in the homes of the aristocracy and the high clergy.

The only examples of concerto grosso instrumentation that survive before Corelli are those composed exclusively by Stradella.[17] Of these nine works, eight are vocal and include one oratorio, two sacred cantatas, and five serenatas (for private performance and for academies). Besides the sinfonias that act as overtures to these works, and which are also composed as concerti grossi, one purely instrumental work included in this group, the *Sinfonia in re maggiore*, is the earliest instrumental concerto grosso known.

Of those works that utilize concerto grosso orchestration, Stradella's sacred cantata *Per il Santissimo Natale, Ah! Troppo è ver*, based on the Christmas story, must be considered his most dramatic. Stradella wrote only five sacred cantatas and

---

17   See Owen Jander, "Concerto Grosso Instrumentation in Rome in the 1660's and 1670's," *Journal of the American Musicological Society*, 21 (1968): 169. Jander comments that "concerto grosso instrumentation was already in regular use in Rome in the late 1660's. This evidence is supplied by records of payments to musicians at the Oratorio of San Marcello" (p. 171).

only two use concerto grosso instrumentation; all the others are secular (161) or moralizing (6).[18] The Christmas cantata is undated, but owing to the nature of the work (that is, its concerto grosso scoring) and its sacred but madrigalistic text (the words are in Italian and the story is not biblical), it was most probably written in Rome (c. 1670s) as an entertainment vehicle for members of the high clergy for performance on Christmas Eve.

Example 4.6a **Stradella, cantata *Ah! Troppo è ver*, sinfonia first movement (mm. 1–13)**

The overture (sinfonia) to the cantata is in the so-called "Italian overture form" of three separate movements, the outer movements fast, and the middle movement in a canzona-like form that fluctuates between diverse tempos, though none is actually indicated in the manuscript. Of primary interest is the spectacular opening movement,

---

18 For an overall discussion of Stradella's vocal music, including a catalogue of his complete works, see Carolyn Gianturco, *Alessandro Stradella (1639–1682): His Life and Music* (Oxford, 1994).

in an embryonic ritornello form (Example 4.6a) but with highly sophisticated musical content. The orchestra is subdivided into concertino and *concerto grosso di viole* groups, each, presumably, with its own basso continuo (the manuscript is unfigured, but each group is supported by an instrumental bass) so that they could be spatially divided – on opposite sides of either a stage or an altar – if the work were performed in the oratory of a church. Stradella's concertino group in the first movement is basically that of a trio sonata for strings with two solo violins and string bass, with additional lute or keyboard to fill out the remaining harmonies. The larger group, the *concerto grosso di viole*, from which the name of the genre is derived, is in the typical Roman scoring of the period, that is, violins in unison, viola 1 in alto clef and viola 2 in tenor clef, cellos, and double basses and continuo.

Stradella's sinfonia to his Christmas cantata is innovatory to say the least. In fact, he seems to have had no interest in creating a formal structure for his concerti grossi, since no two are exactly alike in their formal construction. Instead, they show a wide variety of emotion and thematic development, perhaps reflecting the composer's own wayward and certainly gregarious personality: Stradella was murdered in Genoa because of his penchant for having illicit love affairs with women of high social status. The ritornello statement in this first movement anticipates the more formalized segmented ritornello designs of the next generation of composers; most notably Torelli, Albinoni, and Vivaldi. Stradella's theme, announced by the concerto grosso, comprises two contrasting segments, an initial statement *a* (mm. 1–5) that defines the tonic D major (as a transposed ionian mode)[19] through its dominant, and a cadential segment *b* (upbeat to mm. 5–6), which ends on a half cadence. The theme is dance-like, cheerful, and totally diatonic, and may have been meant by Stradella to represent the joy of Christ's birth. This theme returns only three times in the movement, twice at the beginning (in D and then in G) and once at the end in a concluding tonic statement. Within the body of the movement, Stradella introduces a secondary ritornello idea (Example 4.6b) that is anything but cheerful. This theme is characterized by a slithering chromaticism – Lucifer as the snake in the Garden of Eden comes to mind here – that obscures the background D major tonality by moving, so to speak, "in the wrong direction," away from the "good" major mode of the tonic and toward the "evil" of Lucifer's eventual E minor tonality, the key of his first aria. By illustrating the reordered tonic hexachord of this movement (D major being a 2♯ system), it is easy to see how Stradella's key relationships can reflect this harmonic interpretation of the concerto's programmatic conception:

---

19 Stradella's conception of "key" was most probably based on the theoretical writings of Giovanni Maria Bononcini and his *Musica prattico* (Bologna, 1673, rev. 1688). Bononcini believed that the twelve modes of Zarlino and Glarean could be reduced to four, two major (mixolydian and ionian) and two minor (dorian and aeolian). All the rest were simply transpositions of these four. Therefore, Stradella's sinfonia was actually thought of as a transposition of ionian (the eleventh mode), a step up. See Stein, "Carissimi's Tonal System," pp. 292–5.

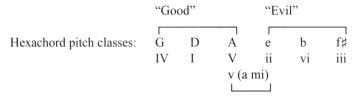

The major-mode ritornellos in I and IV oppose Lucifer's secondary ritornellos in minor keys (E minor and A minor). The minor dominant is more than just a member of the "evil" tonalities of the movement: its destructive force against the tonic occasions the only system modulation in the piece, moving the 2♯ system of the tonic into that of 1♭, the system of the parallel minor.

Example 4.6b   **Stradella, cantata *Ah! Troppo è ver*, sinfonia, first movement, secondary ritornello (upbeat to m. 24 – m. 28)**

We now come to the all-important question of tonality vs. modality in the music of the 1670s. The opening movement of Stradella's Christmas cantata can no longer be convincingly analyzed according to earlier modal principles; indeed, the sinfonia is *clearly* within the confines of a D major tonality that controls all the harmonic functions within the movement. In modal composition, cadences on non-final degrees of the mode do not necessarily relate to a background final; instead, they often interact locally with other chords built on various degrees of the central hexachord, often organized by fifths relationships or by contrapuntally articulated 5–6 exchanges. In addition, modal inflection creates degree inflection: a triad within a modal framework may be either major or minor with the only provisos that (1) the root of the triad is part of the central hexachord, and (2) the missing pitch is not introduced, thus causing a system modulation. With the extreme flexibility of chord quality, *modally* conceived works often lack a sense of *tonal* direction, with their internal cadence points not necessarily directing the ear toward the tonic or even away from it.

Tonality, in its own way, is just as rich in its harmonic resources as modality. But so long as every harmonic event within the piece is heard as part of a larger tonic unfolding, the piece is said to be "tonal." Thus the opening movement of Stradella's sinfonia must be understood as tonal in that the various harmonic digressions from tonic harmony are understood to be contrapuntally related to a background tonic, here D major. Stradella often favors the subdominant as a goal of motion after asserting the tonic; and ordinarily, such a gesture would indicate some kind of hypo-modal thinking. But Stradella's motions to G major within the body of the movement do not seem to displace the tonic; that is, the opening D major progression is not eventually heard, or misunderstood, as a dominant of G, or V/IV. On the contrary, G major is distinctly heard as a contrapuntally related subdominant, awaiting that moment when it is displaced by V (m. 45) before the return of the D major tonic in m. 46; this is accomplished by a short fifths cycle: G (IV)–D–A (V)–D (I).[20] The "evil" minor-mode harmonic areas, in E minor and A minor respectively, only intensify the urgency to resolve this motion into the tonic. Thus, the entire movement has a directed flow in which the tonic is firmly established at the beginning, after which ever more distant harmonic areas (all related to the background D major tonality) displace it, only to be resolved with a final ritornello in pure D major harmony at the end of the movement.

If one considers Stradella's D major tonic to be tonally expressed, how does this effect the single system modulation that occurs in the first movement? Unlike modality, where the signature of the *cantus*, whether natural, sharp, or flat, could theoretically accommodate each of its gamut transpositions up to twelve modes, a tonal or "key" signature collapses the total number to two; namely, a major-mode tonic and its relative. Thus, a 2♯ signature encompasses both D major and B minor, and it is up to the composer to determine the rotation of its eleven notes and to determine which of these notes will function as the tonic. In either case, the 2♯ system that governs both keys still maintains eleven-pitch-class integrity as it did in the older modal system, with the same missing pitch being the minor third or augmented second above the tonic of the system. As also in modal practice, tonal hexachord systems can be conceived only as major, the minor mode being understood as a rotation of its relative major; therefore, a piece written in minor will follow the hexachord of its relative major.[21] For example, the key structure of B minor is based

---

20 Typical of most Baroque music composed before the development of sonata form, beginning some time in the late 1730s, the return to the tonic is unarticulated, often appearing within a larger sequential progression or, as in the case of the fugue, as an answer to a subdominant subject entrance. The reason for this is simply that the tonic is never actually displaced, but is prolonged by a series of auxiliary cadential areas, which may or may not be further prolonged within themselves. These cadential or harmonic areas invariably follow along the course of the system hexachord of the piece.

21 In modal thinking, the minor-mode octave of dorian and all of its transpositions would start on *re*, the second pitch class of the natural hexachord. In tonal thinking, as expressed by Rameau in the supplement to chapter 25 of the first edition of his *Traité de l'harmonie* (1722), all minor-mode octaves begin on *la*, implying that Rameau considered the minor mode to be a rotation of the pitch classes of the relative major. Rameau discusses in detail the hexachordal

on a D 2♯ system. The chord relationships will change position within the same hexachord as follows:

		2♯ system generated from D				
Hexachord pcs:	G –	D –	A –	e –	b –	f♯
Chord function in D major:	IV	I	V	ii	vi	iii
Chord function in B minor:	VI	III	VII	iv	i	v

In either case, F♮ or E♯ would still be the missing pitch and would effectively transpose the initial 2♯ system either up or down, depending on the spelling of the missing pitch.

We now come to a crucial distinction between the function of the missing pitch in modality and its new function within tonality. In modality, the missing pitch, if spelled as a flat (or minor third) would have been recognized as *fa* within a subdominant hexachord. Thus, within a C gamut system, E♭ would be *fa* of a B♭ hexachord, the subdominant hexachord of a transposed *mollis* or 1♭ gamut system. In tonality, the minor third is now recognized as initiating *its own* gamut system, the minor third pitch being sung as *do*! The rationale for this assumption is this: the minor third above the tonic of any major mode is derived from the pitch content of its parallel minor. In reference to the 2♯ system of Stradella's sinfonia, the appearance of an F♮ within the context of the prevailing D major tonic would imply the parallel minor, D minor. Consequently, its system must be that of 1♭, an eleven-pitch-class system three key signatures down (meaning in a subdominant direction) from that of the tonic major. On the other hand, had F♮ been introduced into a *modal* piece with a 2♯ signature, the F♮ could be accounted for only within a C hexachord (F♮ being sung as *fa*) belonging to the subdominant hexachord of a 1♯ system, that is, a three-hexachord eleven-note system a fifth below the prevailing 2♯ system of the piece.

In the first movement of the sinfonia of Stradella's Christmas cantata, there is only one instance where F♮ effects a system shift into the complementary mode (mm. 37–8, Example 4.6c). In this instance, the F♮ appears within the context of an A minor expanse, the dominant minor, during a repeat of the movement's secondary ritornello (refer to Example 4.6b for its first occurrence in E minor). The A minor relates to the tonic D minor and therefore the system shift implies a modulation to a 1♭ system. Since the D minor octave is understood as *la* within the larger context of its relative major, F, the system to which D minor belongs is that of the F three-hexachord system. It bears repeating that all hexachord systems, whether modal or tonal, are major, there being no such thing as an A minor hexachord.

---

differences (in terms of solmization) of both modal and tonal octaves in his treatise (*Treatise on Harmony*, trans. Philip Gossett [New York, 1971], pp. 172–4).

Example 4.6c   **Stradella, cantata *Ah! Troppo è ver*, sinfonia, first movement, secondary ritornello (mm. 35–9)**

Once the system shift to 1♭ occurs, displacing the prevailing 2♯ system, all the music composed from the point of the shift remains in that eleven-pitch-class system *until the missing pitch of the 1♭ system is introduced to redress the modulation.* Consequently, the new governing 1♭ system will need to shift up three signatures if the piece is to end in its original 2♯ system. The minor third of a 1♭ system on F would be A♭, but this pitch, if introduced, would only throw the system down another three notches in the subdominant direction. What is required, instead, is to respell the missing pitch of the 1♭ system as a sharp, in other words, as an augmented second instead of a minor third, reversing the operation in the sharp direction. In this case, the missing pitch would have to be spelled as a G♯ (used locally as a leading tone to the dominant) to move the 1♭ system back up to the original tonic 2♯ system. Dramatically, Stradella delays the entry of G♯ until the very end of the movement (mm. 59–63); when he does so, however, G♯ is reiterated several times in succession, confirming the move back to the original 2♯ tonic system.

The lengthy middle movement (also in D) is a movement complex in canzona style with more technically complex sections for the concertino (here the unusual combination of two violins, solo lute, and cembalo, the last with elaborate solo passages as well) alternating with a pastoral refrain in a slower tempo for the concerto grosso. However, it is the last movement that is dramatically most daring. Here the full string orchestra plays throughout in a binary dance form in 3/8 (again in the tonic, D major). At the very end of the second half, Stradella starts to modulate out of the tonic toward E minor, the key associated with Lucifer. It is as though Lucifer, interrupting the merry dance of the shepherds in the fields, drags the proceedings into his own key in an effort to destroy the joy of the faithful. The last movement of the sinfonia, therefore, does not end in the tonic of D major, but moves directly, without stop, into Lucifer's *arioso*, whose opening text, "Ah! Troppo è ver," gives the cantata its name. The *arioso* in E minor, featuring elaborate coloratura that brings Lucifer's bass range down to a low E!, and formally cadences in that key before moving into Lucifer's first aria (also in E minor), is an elaborate movement in concerto/ritornello form.

Stradella's inventiveness in utilizing his various instrumental and vocal groupings reaches new heights in this aria, a work unique in his vocal output. In effect, the aria pits the concerto grosso's motives against that of the concertino (two violins with violoncello, the same orchestration as in the first movement of the sinfonia) as they swirl around Lucifer's vocal line, whose melodic formation is actually a decoration of the concertino bass. Without going into overly burdensome detail, it should be noted that some characteristics of the aria directly relate to the state of tonality at the time of the work's conception in the 1670s. The ritornello theme itself is divided into two contrasting motives, *a* and *b*, the first (*a*) a cadential motive for the concerto grosso and the second (*b*) an open-ended scalar motive for the concertino (see Example 4.7a).

Example 4.7a   Stradella, cantata, *Ah! Troppo è ver*, Lucifer's aria "Ah! Troppo è ver," opening ritornello (mm. 1–5)

$$\left(\begin{array}{l}\textit{And there will be one of you who prepares}\\\textit{My followers, to take revenge.}\end{array}\right)$$

Stradella's use of ritornello form in his arias adumbrates the ritornello construction of the late Baroque concerto: complete tonic instrumental statements of the ritornello theme frame the aria; internal statements, which often include secondary ritornello formations, often articulate non-tonic harmonic areas, setting off text phrases. However, Stradella's harmonic constructions are still tied to certain modal inflections and functional ambiguities that for the most part disappear in the early stages of common-practice tonality. For instance, segment *a* of the opening ritornello begins with an incomplete progression in E minor: v–i6–iv–V–i. The lowered third of the opening dominant triad is modally inflected to a major dominant before resolving to the tonic. The concertino continues this phrase with the second ritornello segment (*b*) moving from the tonic back to v (m. 2, second beat). The pattern is repeated, but this time Lucifer enters just as the concertino begins its segment again. Once more, the phrase ends on the minor dominant and again the pattern seems to repeat itself: segment *a* returns in the concerto grosso with the same opening progression, but this time the concertino's *b* segment modulates to the relative major via its own dominant, the relative, which in common-practice tonality is a standard goal of motion of the minor mode. What is innovative, and, it must be said, unique within Stradella's own *oeuvre*, is that not only is the relative major convincingly achieved, but it is prolonged at length. In fact, G major takes up the entire middle portion of the aria. In a manner similar to later ritornello practice, the new harmonic area is at first stabilized by a ritornello statement, in this case the cadential segment *a*, extended by two measures. In the subsequent passage, G major is prolonged by its dominant, D. Unlike composers of later ritornello structures, however, Stradella goes an extra step by implanting a secondary ritornello formation, segment *c*, within the larger G major prolongation (Example 4.7b).

Example 4.7b   **Stradella, cantata *Ah! Troppo è ver*, Lucifer's aria "Ah! Troppo è ver," secondary ritornello, segment c (mm. 14–18)**

The first time segment *c* appears, it encircles V/III (mm. 13–14). Soon after this statement, it reappears transposed into E minor seemingly as vi/III (mm. 17–18). We say "seemingly" because the passage that precedes the second statement of segment *c* moves to a B major triad (mm. 16–17) as if Stradella were planning a move to V in order to regain the tonic. Instead, he returns to G major harmony within the next passage, capping off the passage with a formal cadence in the relative (m. 21). How then is one supposed to interpret the cadence on B major followed by the transposed ritornello *c* segment in E minor? E minor cannot really be heard as tonic since it is rhythmically in a weak position, and the segment is too short to establish a harmonic area; instead, the E minor segment initiates a motion back to III. The cadence on B major is strong (it is prepared by its dominant, and could even be heard as III♯/III, although this interpretation would be a highly unusual one since such a harmonic goal within the relative would be most unlikely). As it happens, ritornello segment *a* returns immediately after the cadence on G in m. 21. But instead of establishing the tonic, it initiates an inverted fifths progression: E–A–D–G–C, followed by A minor (iv) and B major (V). Again, segment *c* returns in E minor (m. 24), but this time the B triad really does function as V/i, and the subsequent ritornello *c* segment is heard as tonic. All this is confirmed a few measures later with a closing ritornello in the tonic, E minor, here reversing the order of the segments: segment *b* in the concertino is followed by segment *a* in the concerto grosso. Stradella ends this remarkable aria with a short four-measure coda.

Stradella's sometimes quixotic harmonic language in this aria (as well as in the sinfonia before it) ultimately derives from the wide variety of chordal vocabulary which was inherent in the harmonized modal system of the seventeenth century, and which was still a viable choice for composers. Although Stradella had begun to create progressions that were progressive in their tonal clarity, his creative spirit also required the coloristic chromatic ambiguities of a dying harmonized modality with its degree inflections and liberties of harmonic relationships. Only in the work of Stradella's successor, Arcangelo Corelli, along with that of some of his contemporaries, was the tonal system codified into a fixed hierarchy of chord function, and it is to the ensemble sonatas of Corelli that we now turn.

VI. Corelli and the Advent of Common-Practice Tonality

Arcangelo Corelli (1653–1713) was undoubtedly one of the most respected and influential composers of his age. Not only did he teach his technique of violin-playing to numerous pupils, many of whom became important composers in their own right, but his compositions were studied as models of perfection in terms of their harmonically conceived counterpoint, arresting thematic content, part-writing, overall form, and emotional expressiveness.[22] We are less concerned here with Corelli as violinist than with Corelli as composer. It is a well-known fact that Corelli never discussed his theoretical approach in any written form (after all, how many great composers do this?), but the consistency of his style in his six published opuses allows us to draw an accurate picture of how Corelli conceived a tonal system capable of expressing his ideas. Since Corelli's chamber sonatas form the bulk of his *oeuvre*, and show the most consistency in his harmonic language, we may look at a few examples to determine Corelli's unique achievement.

We believe that the clearest way to interpret Corelli's innovative conception of tonal organization is to compare Corelli's middleground harmonic plan to that of three-hexachord systems. At least by the 1670s, composers understood that the root pitch classes of the reordered central hexachord of earlier modal systems were capable of projecting a background tonic (see our discussion of Stradella above). However, there was no consistency in the relationship of hexachordal root pitches to the tonic background; harmonic and contrapuntal progressions were just as likely

---

22 For a general examination of Corelli's life and works, see Peter Allsop, *Arcangelo Corelli: "New Orpheus of Our Times"* (Oxford, 1999). See also the important reviews of Allsop's book by Michael Talbot, *Journal of the American Musicological Association*, 55/3 (2002): 532–8; and Gregory Barnett, *Journal of Seventeenth-Century Music*, 6/2 (2000) at www.sscm-jscm.org/jscm/v6/no2/Barnett.html.

to support a tonic as not to do so. The very fact that Stradella in his chamber music (as well as some of his sinfonias to his larger works) often chose to move to the subdominant as a first goal of motion would indicate that he still thought, to some extent, modally, but within a larger tonal context (thus our term "nascent tonality"). The fact that Corelli never moves to the subdominant as a first goal would seem to support the notion that Corelli was seeking a more concise tonal system, one that had more direction.

For an illustration, look at Example 4.8a, the opening movement of Corelli's *Sonate da chiesa* op. 3 no. 2 in D major. The reordered 2♯ central hexachord of this sonata is as follows (again, lower case indicates minor):

Quality of third	B	F♯	C♯	G/G♯	D/D♯	A/A♯
Hexachord pitch classes	G –	D –	A –	e –	b –	[f♯]
	IV	I	V	ii	vi	[iii]
				II♯	V/ii	V/vi

The first observation that one makes is that on a foreground level, hexachord roots are now fixed in relation to their position within the tonal hierarchy, as indicated by the Roman numerals placed underneath each hexachord root. Thus, major triads remain major, and minor triads remain minor (in this movement Corelli omits iii altogether). Degree inflection occurs only when the minor triads in the hexachord are raised to major in order to form leading tones, temporarily tonicizing hexachordal pitches as auxiliary cadences on the middleground (see the more detailed discussion of Corelli's middleground harmonic plan below). Degree inflections in these cases serve to strengthen harmonic goals that help define the background tonic, rather than weaken it as certain modal progressions would tend to do. In modality, the fifths relate to each other, not necessarily to a background *finalis*.

What is also significant is that system and key have now merged so that a key has now become its own gamut system, governing two keys, the tonic and its relative, instead of the eight or twelve of the older modal gamut. Further, since we are now dealing with a hierarchal system of chord function related to a background tonic, whenever the system hexachord is illustrated, the Roman numeral under each hexachord pitch class will now refer to its exact harmonic position relative to the tonic of the key (and, consequently, its system as well). Corelli's achievement was now to standardize the ordering of harmonic events within any given movement; in other words, its direction (hence the term "directed tonality"), as the music progresses from one hexachordal pitch to another in the form of auxiliary cadences. With Corelli, the modal construct of localized fifths within the central hexachord, without relation to the background tonic, ends.

Example 4.8a   Corelli, Sonata op. 3 no. 2, first movement

The *Grave* of Corelli's op. 3 no. 2 begins with a four-measure phrase that clearly moves from the tonic, D major, to a half cadence on its dominant, A. Against the background of a "walking bass" that clearly articulates the underlying harmonic progression in even eighth notes, the two violins (in the same range) form fourth-species suspensions that drive the phrase to its first structural cadence. Corelli now repeats the opening progression, transposed, on the dominant, and it likewise culminates on a half cadence on E. What is significant about this progression is that Corelli is deliberately moving up the 2♯ hexachord away from D to A and then to E in order to create harmonic tension. After the opening parallel period, with its two emphatic cadences on A and E respectively, Corelli now moves to the next hexachordal fifth, B (m. 12), the furthest point away from the tonic within the 2♯ hexachord that Corelli tonicizes. B minor, vi, is therefore heard as a point of highest tension, it being the only auxiliary cadence in minor, as well as the terminus of the middleground harmonic progression that unfolds over the course of the movement. Each one of these cadential points is prepared by its respective applied dominant, highlighting their structural significance as goals of motion. However, Corelli's fifths progression upwards from the tonic avoids cadencing on the last fifth of the hexachord, f♯, since this would force a modulation out of the prevailing 2♯ system into a 5♯ one! (That is, E♯, the leading tone of F♯ minor, and the missing pitch of the 2♯ system, would divide a B major octave, and would, consequently, imply a 5♯ system.) Corelli may have resisted a shift of system simply because that action might have been too intense for so short a movement. In fact, in most of Corelli's trio sonatas in major mode, those movements that are in major tend to restrict themselves to eleven pitch classes, omitting each time the same pitch – the minor third or augmented second above the tonic – in order to remain within the work's tonic three-hexachord system. As a result, Corelli's background harmonic plan in his trio sonatas rarely if ever goes beyond a tonicization of the submediant (the situation is somewhat different in his op. 5 violin sonatas). In order, therefore, to create the necessary applied dominants to both the fifth and sixth degrees of the reordered hexachord, Corelli must inflect the minor thirds of the ii and iii chords of the tonic hexachord to major in order to get the necessary leading tones to form the cadence. One hastens to add that the raising of the third degree in this instance does not at all have the same effect as the older technique of modal degree inflection, with its direct chromaticism (minor v, major V, resolution). On the contrary, the applied dominant to either the fifth or the sixth degree is heard within the context of the harmonic goal and not as a distortion of the background tonic.

To return to Corelli's first movement, after Corelli has reached the last cadence on vi, he now retraces his harmonic steps, as it were, and returns to tonic harmony, almost unobtrusively; the B minor chord is simply interpreted as a contrapuntal upper neighbor to V in m. 13 which resolves to I on the third beat of the same measure. After the tonic has been firmly regained, Corelli needs only to extend the tonic progression in order to stabilize the return as well as to provide enough tonic harmony to balance the final progression with the rest of the movement. That is why these pieces often end with a coda-like tag of three or four measures that anchors the tonic for the last time.

By systematically moving in a single directed harmonic motion upward from the tonic fifth of the hexachord, only to reverse direction in order to regain the tonic, Corelli has provided a game plan, as it were, for large-scale tonal direction in which every point of arrival along the hexachordal plain relates to the background tonic. One can see this more clearly, perhaps, in the second movements of Corelli's church sonatas, those in fugal style. It is the second movements (always allegro) that are the most extensive in the church sonatas, and therefore it is these movements that provide Corelli with enough musical expanse to explore and develop his innovative harmonic scheme.

The second movement of op. 3 no. 2 is a case in point (see Example 4.8b). The first goal of motion in Corelli is always going to be the dominant, which cadence is formally achieved on the downbeat of m. 13. The dominant arrival is prepared by its own dominant (downbeat of m. 12), and a look at how Corelli activates the V/V now gives us a chance to discuss tonal direction in music in terms of a specific ordering of chord progression that begins contrapuntally and ends harmonically at the cadential arrival. It is this type of progression ordering that will inform the progress of tonality for the next 200 years.

Example 4.8b   Corelli, Sonata op. 3 no. 2, second movement (mm. 1–17)

Within the harmonic structure of the 2♯ hexachord, ii (E minor) occupies a special position in that its inflection to a major triad – II♯ – signals the arrival at V, invariably the first goal of motion in any Corelli sonata movement, at least those that are in major mode. In effect, the motion to V is accomplished through a contrapuntal stepwise ascent in the bass, in this case from D to E. This contrapuntal progression to II♯ now must be confirmed by a cadential harmonic V–I progression in order to anchor the arrival at V. In the second movement from Corelli's op. 3 no. 2, the tonic D in the bass (m. 10) moves first up to ii on the downbeat of m. 11 (see Example 4.8b) and then up to II♯ on the downbeat of m. 12. The E major triad now acts as V/V and resolves to A in a formal authentic cadence, the bass arpeggiating the harmonic fifth, E–A, on the upbeat to the downbeat of m. 13. Corelli's next goal of motion is vi, B minor, the cadence of which is articulated by its own harmonic authentic cadence on the downbeat of m. 17.

The return to tonic harmony, after vi has been achieved, often involves another contrapuntal motion. In the trio sonatas Corelli uses several different approaches to regain the tonic. The simplest, and the one that was discussed in relation to the opening movement of this sonata, is to treat vi as a contrapuntal neighbor to V, and then move the V to I. In the second movement of this sonata, Corelli's return to the tonic is a bit more sophisticated, but is essentially an expansion of the same contrapuntal motion. In this instance, instead of immediately resolving to V, the bass pitch b of the vi triad is first reinterpreted as V7/II♯ six measures later (m. 22), initiating a short fifths progression.that reaches the tonic in the middle of m. 26:

B (V7/II♯)–E (II♯)–A (V)–D (I).
└_____┘

Here the E triad interposes itself between the B and the A, disguising the actual contrapuntal motion between the latter two triads. Once the tonic is regained, Corelli adds his usual four measures of tonic coda.

Corelli's slow movements are usually the only ones in a key related to the tonic, usually the relative minor. The third movement of op. 3 no. 2, in B minor, will now give us a chance to examine the hexachordal nature of such minor-mode movements, in this case, in relation to the tonic 2♯ hexachord governing the sonata. The following indicates the Roman-numeral positioning in both the tonic D major and the relative B minor keys:

	2♯ three-hexachord system					
Hexachordal pitch classes:	G –	D –	A –	e –	b –	f♯
Chord function D major:	IV	I	V	ii	vi	iii
Chord function B minor:	VI	III	VII	iv	i	v

One notices that D and b lie at opposite ends of the 2♯ hexachord and while both share the same three-hexachord system, the chord functions within their respective tonal hierarchies are opposite in function as well – that is, major and minor chord qualities are reversed. More importantly, however, B minor as tonic lies at the far end of the hexachord, succeeded only by its dominant pitch class, f♯, the last pitch class of the 2♯ hexachord system. One more fifth beyond f♯, that is, C♯, would invite the missing pitch of the system, E♯ as leading tone to V. Consequently, every time V is tonicized within the minor mode, there will also be a shift out of system to one that is three signatures higher, a 5 one, the system of the parallel major (E♯ divides the B octave symmetrically in half). Below is a comparison of the 2♯ system hexachord with that of the parallel major.

							Out of system
B minor 2♯ system:	G –	D –	A –	e –	b –	f♯ ‖	C♯
Chord function:	VI	III	VII	iv	i	v	V/V

B major 5♯ system:	E –	B –	F♯–	c♯–	g♯–	d♯
Chord function:	IV	I	V	ii	vi	iii	V/V

The C♯ triad that was out of system with the 2♯ hexachord now finds its rightful place as either ii or V/V of the 5♯ B major system. Once shifted into the system of the parallel major, the only way back to the original 2♯ system would be to invert the process; that is, spell the missing pitch of the 5♯ system as a minor third: minor thirds are system roots; augmented seconds form tritones with system roots. Thus, the minor third of B major would be D, the root pitch of a 2♯ system and three signatures *down* (meaning, in the subdominant direction) from a 5♯ system.

Example 4.8c gives the first 22 measures of the third movement of op. 3 no. 2, which is composed in the style of the opera aria of the period, in a slow 3/2 meter. Corelli's opening progression first firmly establishes the tonic, B minor, with a seven-measure phrase that ends on an authentic cadence. From here, Corelli now prepares a motion to his first significant non-tonic harmonic area, that of the relative, D. Baroque modulation schemes now rely more and more on the cycle of fifths to drive the music from one goal of motion to another. Corelli's progression to III begins with an A triad (m. 8), leading to D (m. 9) and then to G (m. 10). In order to articulate this progression, all these foreground events are on downbeats, the last one, G, being interpreted as subdominant of the relative. D itself is thus prepared by a progression in that "key" that culminates in an authentic cadence in m. 13. After the relative, the next non-tonic goal is that of the minor dominant. Here is the only instance of a system shift in the sonata: the dominant, F♯ minor, is tonicized with its dominant, C♯, introducing E♯, the missing pitch of the 2♯ system. When first introduced (m. 19), the E♯ is prevented from shifting the system up to 5♯ since its missing pitch, D♮, is played against it in the first violin. The two missing pitches of both systems, E♯ of the 2♯ system and D♮ of the 5♯ system, thus effectively cancel each other out. However, E♯ returns at the end of m. 19, in the bass. This time there is no D♮ to interfere with the new system shift. The new 5♯ system does not last, for D♮ returns in the first violin on the last beat of m. 22 as part of a III6 chord, reverting the system to the 2♯ one. The rest of the movement remains within the 2♯ system, moving first back to III before regaining the tonic. As usual, the tonic is then anchored by a seven-measure coda. Typical of Corelli's slow movements, a phrygian cadence is placed right after the final tonic cadence. Such phrygian cadences act both to summarize the outer parameters of the tonic hexachord, here G and F♯, and to act as a transition into the final fast movement. But before we briefly discuss the final movement, we should remark on the unstable nature of the minor mode.

Example 4.8c   Corelli, Sonata op. 3 no. 2, third movement (mm. 1–22)

The relative minor is, in fact, a rotation of the tonic scale, starting on *la*. As such, it seeks to move to its own relative major in order to create stability; a stability conditioned by the fact that the major mode has a major dominant, and a tonic major triad with a major third. Thus the major mode vibrates, one might say, in harmony with the overtone series. Also, a tonic with a minor third in its triad is relatively unstable, the interval of the minor wanting to close in on itself into a unison: for example, C and its minor third Eb will tend toward D as a tone of resolution. But no matter how you explain it, the minor mode, because of its various inconsistencies, will tend to move toward more stable major-mode areas within its harmonic borders, as it were. Thus, the relative major sounds almost as a release of tension when it arrives. In the case of Corelli's B minor movement, the relative major is the tonic D major itself, and achieving it as a structural goal allows the rotated B minor scale to revert to its prime state as a D major scale. D is also the root pitch of the 2♯ system, another reason for its stability within B minor. Significantly, in Corelli's slow movement the relative major occurs both after the unstable tonic and again after the unstable minor dominant.

Emotionally, all the instability of the minor mode now needs to dissipate into the major tonic of the final movement, whose form is often some form of dance. Dance forms allow for periodic phrasing, lively dance meters in triple or compound duple, and large-scale repetitions in binary movements. Corelli's binary movements follow the same harmonic middleground as all the other major-mode movements in his sonatas; however, the harmonic plan is now couched within the symmetrical phrasing of the dance. Invariably the opening half of the movement moves from the tonic into the area of the dominant, via II♯, at the double bar. The polarity of tonic against dominant adumbrates the formal tonic/dominant polarity of the sonata form of the Classical sonata. After the double bar, the dominant modulates to the next harmonic area, usually vi. In the last movement of Corelli's op. 3 no. 2, the B minor area initiates a typical inverted fifths cycle, moving first to E minor (immediately converted to II♯), then to V (A) and finally to I, all three harmonies falling on downbeats and all prepared by their dominants. A three-measure coda in tonic harmony ends the movement.

What of those major-mode movements in Corelli's *oeuvre* that actually contain a modulation out of system? Corelli's op. 5 solo violin sonatas contain numerous examples of complex system shifts that reflect the more sophisticated nature of these sonatas in comparison to Corelli's own simpler, more accessible trio sonatas. Most extraordinary is the first sonata of op. 5 in D major, a work in five movements. The first movement of this sonata is a movement complex that alternates several short slow and fast passages without any change of system, the movement centering primarily on tonic and dominant harmonic areas. But the next three movements all contain system shifts that are of considerable compositional interest. While it would be unfeasible to analyze the entire work, it would be worth our while to look briefly at the second and third allegro movements.

Second movements in Corelli's *sonate da chiesa* are usually stylistically fugal or imitative. The op. 5 violin sonatas loosely follow the *da chiesa* format, with its freely formed movements in alternate slow and fast tempos. The second movement of op. 5 no. 1 is therefore typical in its canonic imitations between the solo violin and the continuo bass. These imitative movements also show off Corelli's considerable double stopping technique, albeit within the lower positions on the violin. The double and triple stopping is not just confined to chordal arpeggiations, but also includes numerous examples of two-part counterpoint complete with fourth-species suspensions that must have influenced J.S. Bach's own spectacular solo violin sonatas and partitas.

Corelli's elaborate contrapuntal display at the opening of the second movement disguises the lack of harmonic motion – the first 62 measures remain firmly in the tonic, articulated by frequent cadences in the home key. After arriving at a complete tonic authentic cadence on the third beat of m. 62, Corelli now moves rapidly to vi,

B minor, prolonging that harmonic area for a total of eight measures. Instead of now backtracking, Corelli moves up to the final fifth of the 2♯ hexachord and tonicizes iii (F♯ minor), causing a system shift up to a 5♯ system. From this point on (the violin sonatas were published in 1700), composers will frequently move to tonicize the last fifth of the tonic hexachord as a point of climax within the overall structure of the movement. Regaining the tonic system is simple since the missing pitch of any mediant minor system is the tonic itself! Therefore, an immediate return to tonic harmonic after iii has been tonicized would immediately correct the system back to that of the tonic. This is why so many Baroque concertos move to a climactic ritornello in iii only to revert to the tonic in the very next measure, often without a prepatory dominant. However, Corelli, in his second movement, follows his usual path in returning to the tonic via an inverted fifths cycle: f♯ (iii)–B–e–A (V)–D (I). All this takes place within four measures, the end of which, culminating on tonic harmony, reverts the 5♯ system to the 2♯ system. A lengthy tonic prolongation now ensues for ten measures, at the end of which another motion to iii occurs. Again E♯ is introduced, throwing the systems up to five sharps, only for them to revert to the tonic 2♯ system three measures later.

Corelli's harmonic ground plan for this movement is typical: after each tonic prolongation, there is a move to a more distant non-tonic area, vi or iii, or both, which in the case of the latter invokes the missing pitch and a shift of system. After each of these harmonic excursions, the tonic returns, rondo-like, to re-establish tonic harmony and tonic system. Thus every shift of harmonic system up to five sharps in this movement is counteracted by the systematic return of tonic harmony soon after, consequently reverting the system to two sharps. For example, the last E♯ in the movement (m. 84) is soon corrected by a D♮ in m. 86, in the bass, which also signals the return of the tonic. However, Corelli goes one step further; the ending of the movement moves, without preparation, into the parallel minor (introduced by a single g♯o7 chord). The switch into minor is dramatized by a sudden change in tempo to Adagio along with a drastic slowing-down of harmonic rhythm, the bass accompanying the cadenza-like arpeggiations of the solo violin (see Example 4.9). With the introduction of F♮, the flat enharmonic of E♯, the system now shifts down three signatures to 1♭, the implied signature of D minor, the parallel minor. It is as though Corelli was almost consciously trying to balance the system shifts so that the previous sharp modulations along the dominant side of the cycle of fifths were now needed to be reinterpreted in the opposite direction along the subdominant side of the same cycle.

The 1♭ system remains in effect right into the D major opening of the last allegro movement until G♯ is introduced in the second measure to shift the 1♭ system back up to a 2♯ system.

Example 4.9 Corelli, Sonata op. 5 no. 1, end of second movement to opening of third movement

To summarize, Corelli is the first major composer to create a hierarchy of function between the fifths of the central hexachord of a key and the background tonic. In major mode, Corelli's background harmonic progression, over the course of any given movement, invariably moves along the hexachord from the tonic of that movement to its fifth as the first goal of motion. From the dominant, the submediant is the next goal (it is understood that each of these goals is articulated by an authentic cadence in that harmonic area). If the submediant is the furthest point away from the tonic, as it usually is, the next harmonic event will be to regain the tonic, often via a passing motion through the subdominant, or at least harmonies that have a subdominant function (that is, they precede the structural dominant) such as ii or even iii. After the tonic is achieved (often rhythmically attenuated), a coda-like passage anchors the tonic before the final cadence. In minor mode, after the tonic is expressed in an opening phrase, the next goal is usually the relative major, eventually passing on to the dominant in order to return to tonic harmony. In between

III and V, there may be passing motions to iv or VI before the structural dominant is reached. An alternative progression is to achieve V (immediately after III) and then to extend the passage through iv or VI before reaching the tonic. In either case, Corelli will conclude the movement with a short coda anchoring the tonic. In terms of the hexachord and its hierarchal functions, the minor mode inverts the operations of that of the major; that is, the harmonic progression from one hexachordal pitch to another, away from the starting tonic pitch, is toward the major side of the system hexachord rather than toward the minor: major moves toward vi and minor moves toward III before reversing the process back toward the tonic. Both vi and III may be extended with motions further away before the music begins its tonic return. Thus, in major, vi may move further away to iii, the last pitch of the system hexachord, necessitating a system shift. In minor, III may move to VII or V, in the latter case also causing a system shift. After the movement has progressed to its furthest harmonic area, supported by system shifts into complementary systems, the return to tonic harmony will most often restore the tonic system as well. However, the opposite is also possible: movements may end in their complementary systems in order to prepare for the next movement whose key is harmonically related to the new system, a process that will be explored in subsequent chapters.

Remarkably, Corelli's systematic approach to tonal organization will remain in effect until the latter part of the nineteenth century, especially in absolute music forms, which depend upon tonal clarity on a background level. It now remains for us to see how Corelli's basic harmonic plan was extended in larger compositions, notably the concerto, in the music of the late Baroque period.

VII. Common-Practice Tonality and the Late Baroque Concerto: Torelli, Vivaldi, and J.S. Bach

The advantage of a tonal system capable of establishing non-tonic harmonic areas was to allow composers the ability to create forms that were at once longer and yet unified in tempo, meter, rhythm, and motive. Before this, composers had to rely on fugal or imitative techniques that created length by the sheer number of fugal entrances and subjects, but were limited in harmonic scope or were conditioned by the older canzona technique of short contrasting sections of differing meter, tempo, and thematic material, all basically in the same mode or "key." Once Corelli had established a method of tonal direction whereby the tonic was left in favor of auxiliary cadences in non-tonic areas, the next step would logically be to stabilize each of these non-tonic harmonic areas with full periods. The first attempts to achieve just such a structure must be attributed to Giuseppe Torelli (1658–1709) of Bologna. It was Torelli, following in the footsteps of Stradella, who realized that one could both rhythmically and thematically unify and lengthen an entire concerto movement by simply transposing its opening theme to various hexachordal degrees. What was once just an auxiliary cadence in a Corelli ensemble sonata could now appear as a complete and stabilized period in a non-tonic area. Torelli had thus discovered a systematic approach to ritornello form, a form devised by Alessandro Stradella, who had employed it in only a rudimentary manner.

Torelli had begun to experiment with elementary ritornello structures in his op. 6 church concertos (1698), but it was not until his op. 8, published posthumously by his brother Felice in 1709, that it crystallized into its modern standardized design. Torelli's ritornello structure takes Corelli's harmonically directed tonal background as a point of departure, and expands it by broadening simple cadential arrivals into complete harmonic progressions that stabilize non-tonic areas through transposition of the ritornello statement. For instance, an initial goal of V is achieved with an authentic cadence, as it would be in Corelli, but also *by transposing the opening ritornello statement into V*; thus a stable and complete harmonic period in that "key" is attained. The solo episode that follows contains technically difficult figurative music that differs from the thematic material of the ritornello theme in its inclusion of virtuosic material for the soloist or soloists.[23] Just as important is the character of the solo episode, which provides a bridge or transition into the next non-tonic harmonic area – usually IV, vi, or III, depending on the mode of the movement – which is similarly achieved by a transposition of the ritornello theme and an authentic cadence. After a new and more elaborate solo episode, a final ritornello statement in the tonic ends the movement. Naturally, composers such as Torelli have a wide choice of ritornello transpositions, with solo episodes occurring between each ritornello statement: some movements contain three or four statements in non-tonic areas, while others may contain fewer. The ordering of solo and full orchestra (referred to as ripieno or tutti) is not yet standardized, with some concerto movements beginning with the soloists *followed by the ripieno* (op. 8 no. 2 in A minor is an example). While Torelli establishes a three-movement design in which the outer movements are invariably fast, the middle movement is still in canzona form in the style of Stradella; therefore, the middle movement is subdivided into smaller sections that alternate tempos and thematic material. These middle movements do, however, contain elements of ritornello form since thematic material does return, at least at the open and close of the movement, but it is not subjected to the same rigorous harmonic discourse or thematic complexity as it would in the outer movements.

The design of the ritornello theme also conditions the suitability of transpositions and how much of the ritornello theme is required to establish a harmonic area. Torelli employs two types of ritornello themes: the first, and by far the more popular, is a fugal one based on an imitative subject. Torelli may have leaned toward imitative subjects because many of these concertos were played during celebratory masses at Bologna's famous basilica, San Petronio, where he was a member of the orchestra. These non-sectional subjects clearly establish the tonic through alternating tonic and dominant harmonies, but cannot be segmented; that is, the entire subject must return as a ritornello statement with or without its fugal imitations. Torelli's op. 8 no. 3 in E major for two solo violins and strings begins with this type of theme (Example 4.10).

---

23 Since the concertos of Stradella and Corelli do not follow a standardized ritornello format, there are no solo episodes. Instead, either the thematic material is shared between concertino and concerto grosso, or both groups have very similar melodic material. In either case, either the two groups alternate short phrases or the larger group sometimes doubles the concertino for dramatic emphasis.

Example 4.10   Torelli, Concerto in E for two solo violins and strings op. 8 no. 3, first movement (mm. 1–18)

Torelli's ritornello fugue subject is accompanied by the basses and basso continuo, a procedure similar to that used by Corelli in the fugal movements of his ensemble sonatas. Therefore, the bass does not participate in stating the subject, the fugal entrances being limited to the upper three voices (violin 1, violin 2, and viola). The opening fugal ritornello statement in the tonic is unusually large, covering 18 measures and including a tonic fugal counter-exposition of the opening subject entrances. The key signature still reflects modal thinking since Torelli conceives of E major as a "tonal" mixolydian; meaning that the signature is modal, but all the Ds in the manuscript are sharped. Modal signatures are not at all uncommon during this period; indeed, both Vivaldi and J.S. Bach still use them on occasion (see our discussion below of Vivaldi for a fuller examination of the problem of interpreting modal signatures in the eighteenth century). Diagram 4.1 is a form graph of all three movements of the concerto. The diagram outlines the background harmonic structure of each movement, showing the placement of ritornello statements and solo episodes. The reader should refer to this graph during the following analytical discussion.

The harmonic scheme of the outer two movements indicates an overwhelming emphasis on the subdominant; both movements avoid the dominant as separate harmonic areas in favor of the subdominant articulated by ritornello restatements in both movements. Indeed, the last movement's only non-tonic area is the subdominant. One might conclude, therefore, that Torelli was thinking of a subdominant bias because he thought of his E mode as mixolydian, perhaps even hypomixolydian, a mode which traditionally emphasized the subdominant as recital tone (or *repercussio*). Further, the internal harmonic areas that Torelli chooses to stabilize with ritornello statements are subdominant-harmony constituents: A (IV) and c♯ (vi). The choice of the subdominant as the first goal of motion, however, is not sufficient proof that Torelli's conception was modal.

The same question of modality vs tonality applies to Stradella's works; we have seen that in the sinfonia of the Christmas cantata, Stradella's motion to IV was related to a larger prolongation of the tonic. Similarly, Torelli's subdominant bias not only *supports* the background tonic, but does so with even more forcefulness. Because of the extreme length of Torelli's opening fugal ritornello, with its reiterated dominant subject entries, there is no need to create a separate dominant ritornello statement. The central episode (see Diagram 4.1) begins with a lengthy prolongation of the dominant (most ritornello movements include a "central episode" which usually occurs just before the closing ritornello statement in the tonic). It is the most lengthy and complex of all the solo episodes, and it is here that the virtuosic material written for the solo(ists) reaches its greatest intensity. Therefore, it is no surprise then that Torelli chooses this moment to incorporate the only instance of the missing pitch in this movement. A G♮ is introduced as the episode turns from the dominant to a short prolongation of the subdominant, effectively shifting the prevailing 4♯ system down to 1♯. The G♮ forms part of an A7 chord temporarily tonicizing D, the subdominant of the subdominant. After this, the music turns back toward the tonic for the final ritornello. However, the 1♯ system remains in effect right through the closing ritornello and does not revert to a 4♯ system until A♯ finally appears as a leading tone to V, six measures before the end of the movement.

Vivace

Ritornello 1

Fugal exposition (3 voices) & counterexposition — Cadence

Subject & Answer

I – V – I   V – I – V   I

E
I

1st Solo Episode (solo violins)	Rit. 2 Ripieno Subject only	2nd Solo Episode	Rit. 3 Ripieno Subject & Answer
E	c#m	c#m ----- A	A ----- E
I	vi	moves to IV	IV I
			unarticulated return to I

3rd Solo Episode

(Central and most involved)

Remains within the area of the tonic

B–   F#–   B–   E–   A–   B →   E

V–   V/V–   V–   I–   IV–   V →   I

Rit. 4 (Closing)

Fugal exposition only

Movement II (subdivided into two large sections)

Part I

Largo

Ritornello 1 (one motive, 4 mm.)	Solo Episode	Rit.2
A major	-----moves to E	E
I		V

Part II

Allegro (soloists)	2nd Solo Episode	Rit. 3 (Closing)	Adagio — Rit. 3 (Closing): abbreviated
E -----	moves back to E	E – solo interruption	A
V		V pedal	I

Movement III

Allegro

Ritornello 1 (fugal)	1st Solo Episode — Cycle of fifths	Rit. 2	2nd Solo Episode	Rit. 3 (Closing)	Coda (Ripieno)
E	B — E	A	moves back to E	confirms E – solo interruption	E
I – V – I	V — I	IV		I V pedal	I

Diagram 4.1 Torelli, Concerto in E major for two solo violins and strings op. 8 no. 3, movements 1–3

Torelli's internal ritornello statements in the first movement of the E major concerto limit their thematic material to either a single-subject entrance, as in the second ritornello in vi, or a subject and answer, as in the third ritornello in A. Having a subject on IV followed by its answer on V/IV becomes almost cliché in concerto movements utilizing a fugal ritornello, since it provides a simple way to return to tonic harmony at the end of the movement without articulating the event with a preparatory dominant. Thus a return to the tonic is effected by reinterpreting V/IV as I, preparing for the central episode, which prolongs the tonic with dominant and subdominant harmonies.

The other type of ritornello theme, and the more innovative of the two, is designed as a series of interlocking but separate motives, each with its own separate harmonic function. This is the type of ritornello statement that is far more often than not utilized by Vivaldi and J.S. Bach.[24] Anticipated by Stradella, and carried on in embryonic fashion by Torelli, this type of segmented theme rarely occurs in Torelli's early works, being confined almost exclusively to the later concertos of the first decade of the eighteenth century. One cannot rule out Vivaldi's possible influence on Torelli's later works, since many of Vivaldi's op. 3 concertos circulated in manuscript form around 1700, that is, before Torelli completed his own op. 8. Torelli, in turn, may have been of some influence on J.S. Bach, who reshaped the subject of the last movement of Torelli's op. 8 no. 8 concerto into the subject of an organ fugue (BWV 537).

Example 4.11 gives the opening ritornello of Torelli's Concerto op. 8 no. 8 in C minor. The entire ritornello theme is 17 measures long and is subdivided into three distinct motives. To use the terminology first devised by Wilhelm Fischer in his seminal 1915 article on the evolution of Classical style,[25] the opening segment of the theme (mm. 1–10) is a fugal *Vordersatz*, that is, a segment which has both subject and answer in the tonic and dominant respectively, and which consequently clearly defines the tonic, C minor, with root-position tonic and dominant harmonies. This segment is tonally closed, ending with an authentic cadence on the tonic. Clearly separated from the *Vordersatz* is the next segment (mm. 11–14), called the *Fortspinnung* by Fischer, which is sequential and follows either a diatonic or a harmonic sequential pattern. In this case, Torelli's *Fortspinnung* segment is a harmonic cycle of fifths that modulates to the dominant. The final segment (mm. 15–17) – Fischer used the term *Epilog* – is cadential. In this case, the *Epilog* reinforces the minor dominant, G minor, with a cadential progression ending with an authentic cadence in that harmony.[26]

---

24 For a detailed discussion of Vivaldi's ritornello themes and their influence on Bach, see Laurence Dreyfus, "J.S. Bach's Concerto Ritornellos and the Question of Invention," *The Musical Quarterly*, 71/3 (1985): 327–58.

25 Wilhelm Fischer, "Zur Entwicklungsgeschichte des Wiener klassischen Stils," *Studien zur Musikwissenschaft*, 3 (1915): 24–84. Fischer's terminology is discussed fully in Dreyfus, "J.S. Bach's Concerto Ritornellos." When discussing the segmentation of the ritornello theme in this and all subsequent analyses, we will adopt Fischer's terminology.

26 Not all ritornello themes end on the tonic, though the majority tend to do so. Whether concluding on tonic or dominant harmony, it is the purpose of the *Epilog* to affirm one or other harmonic area.

Example 4.11   Torelli, Concerto in C minor for solo violin and strings op. 8 no. 8, last movement (mm. 1–17)

The harmonic plan for this movement is given in Diagram 4.2 below. Since the opening ritornello cadenced on v, and since the first solo episode begins in G minor before moving to the relative major (again, it is the function of the solo episodes to act as transitions to the next harmonic goal), there is no need for a separate ritornello statement of the minor dominant. In ritornello 2, Torelli transposes the first two segments of the theme (motives *a* and *b*) into the relative major; however, since segment *b* is a *Fortspinnung* harmonic sequence, he is able to use this segment to move into subdominant harmony. The second solo episode therefore begins in iv and modulates back to the tonic via the dominant. At first, the dominant, G minor, is actually prolonged by its own dominant, beginning in m. 37. In order to turn the dominant area into a progression preparing for the tonic, Torelli simply adds a seventh to the dominant chord in m. 43. This, with the subsequent measures leading up the final ritornello in the tonic, forms what will later be called a "retransition passage" in modern sonata-form analysis: a phrase that centers on the dominant at the end of the development section in preparation for the recapitulation.

By drawing the 3♭ central hexachord of this movement, one can easily understand the underlying harmonic progression:

Harmonic ordering:		2		3	1	4
Hexachord pitch classes:	A♭–	**E♭–**	B♭–	f–	c–	g
Harmonic function:	VI	**III**	VII	iv	**i**	v

The Arabic numbers above the hexachord pitch classes show the ordering of harmonic areas, only two of which are given ritornello statements: i and III. From the tonic, C minor, Torelli first proceeds to the relative major, E♭. In this diagram, the relative is the furthest point away from the tonic that Torelli chooses to explore. He then moves back along the hexachord toward the tonic by first moving through the subdominant and then to the dominant, all within the second solo episode. A full ritornello statement in the tonic concludes the movement.

As Dreyfus states in his article (previously cited), a structural ritornello statement (he calls it "marked") is one that contains enough of one or more segments of the ritornello theme to stabilize a harmonic area. Since motive *a* (the *Vordersatz*) forms a complete harmonic progression in itself, that is all that is required to make that ritornello statement structurally stable. The following sequential segment, *b*, is therefore free to "modulate" into the next solo episode. What we learn from Torelli's treatment of ritornello form is the almost limitless possibilities the form can take, since the segments of a ritornello statement can be re-composed for any number of harmonic considerations. Ritornellos may act as agents of modulation as solo episodes can, provided that the harmonic areas in which they occur are stabilized. This is why Handel, in the later development of the concerto in England, could be so free with his ritornello forms that he was able to stabilize a non-tonic harmonic area with a structural ritornello statement consisting solely of the *Fortspinnung* segment, a condition that Dreyfus insists is impossible since *Fortspinnung* sequences "suspend" tonic harmony and cannot be restated without some other harmony-defining segment.[27]

The minor mode is always volatile when it comes to system shifts since the dominant's leading tone is very frequently present as part of an applied chord to V. In a 3♭ system, either F♯ or G♭ will be the missing pitch; however, in Torelli's movement, only F♯ is introduced as leading tone to the dominant pitch class. Every time F♯ is invoked, it implies a system shift to the parallel major – C major is three key signatures up from E♭, and, in addition, F♯ divides the major octave symmetrically in half – and since the leading tone to the dominant is an ever-recurring pitch class in the minor mode, system shifts are a frequent occurrence. However, these tend to be short-lived since the correcting pitch, E♭ (the missing pitch of the C system), most often follows every F♯, negating the previous shift. Only in cases where the opposite missing pitch, G♭, is introduced is there any sustained motion within the complementary system.

The next stage of concerto development brings us from Bologna to Venice and to the work of Antonio Vivaldi (1678–1741). It is generally acknowledged that Vivaldi brought the Italian concerto to its height; his numerous and inventive concertos display practically every conceivable permutation of the ritornello form that he helped to establish. Diagram 4.3 is a form graph of the first movement of Vivaldi's op. 9 no. 2 in A major for solo violin and strings. The movement displays a number of stylistic features typical of Vivaldi's ritornello structures, both in terms of the segmentation of the ritornello theme itself and in terms of the harmonic plan of the movement, including notable eleven-pitch-class system shifts.

---

27 The organization of the first movement of Handel's Concerto Grosso in C, "Alexander's Feast," refutes Dreyfus's assertion. For example, the *Fortspinnung* segment of Handel's opening ritornello theme (mm. 5–8) clearly moves, via a series of sequential chromatic 5–6 exchanges, from the tonic to the dominant at the end of the passage. This segment returns, abbreviated, as the second ritornello in mm. 23–4. In fact, most of the internal ritornello statements in this movement contain nothing but this segment, complete, abbreviated, or varied, and all capable of stabilizing a non-tonic harmonic area.

Rit. I (Ripieno) ——————————— | **Solo episode 1 (Violin solo)** | **Rit. 2 (Ripieno)**

a (*Vordersatz*) - b (*Fortspinnug*) - c (*Epilog*) | New material | a - b (the Fortspinnung motive winds up in iv)
Imitative 5ths Cycle sequence Cadential | (only the basso continuo accompanies the soloist)

C minor	modulates to ----	g m	g m - moves via a 5th cycle to Eb	→ fm (iv)
i	→	v	v →	III

Solo episode 2 | **Closing Rit. 3 (Ripieno)**
starts in fm | a - b- c + 3-measure Coda

	Cm
	i

iv → moves back to cm via G

Diagram 4.2 Torelli, Concerto in C minor for solo violin and strings op. 8 no. 8, last movement (features a modulatory ritornello theme that ends in the dominant)

Ritornello 1
Allegro (Ripieno, unison statement throughout)

mm. 1 – 6	mm. 7 – 9	mm. 10 – 11	m. 12
Vordersatz	Fortspinnung	Pianoidée	Epilog
	Diatonic sequence over a V pedal	C♮ ↘ "0" system	"0" system holds through
A Major			A Major
I →			V – I

Solo Episode 1

mm. 13 –	m. 22	mm. 23 –	m. 24
Strings accompany the soloist			Harmonic seq.
			D♯↘3♯s
			F♯ → B —
A —	E	E	
I	V	V (prolonged by V/V)	

a minor: arpeggiates a B♭–G♯ aug. 6
i

Rit. 2

mm. 29 – 33	mm. 34 – 35	mm. 36 – 37	m. 38
Vord.	Fort.	Pianoidée	Ep.
		e minor	
E		v	E
V	V/V pedal		V

Solo Episode 2

mm. 38 – 43	mm. 44 – 45	m. 46	m. 48	m. 50
Soloist with b.c. only	Harmonic seq.	B♯↗6♯	A♮↘3♯	B♯↗6♯
	—	G♯ → c♯		G♯
	F♯ → B —			V/iii
E				
V				

PCA beings here:

mm. 44 – 45	m. 46
A♮ – A♯ – B♯ – C♯	B♯ – C♯
0 1 2 3	3 4 (pc 4 is prolonged)

Rit. 3 (modulatory)

mm. 53 – 56	m. 56 –	m. 57 –	m. 58	mm. 59 –	m. 60
Vord.	Fort.	A♮↘3♯	B♯↗6♯	No Epilog, but cadential in function	A♮↘3♯
	Harmonic seq.				
c♯ minor	→ F♯ →			b minor ————————	
iii	V/ii			ii	
(PCA):C♯					(D♮)
4					(5)

Diagram 4.3 Vivaldi, Concerto in A major for solo violin and strings, and op. 9 no. 2 first movement

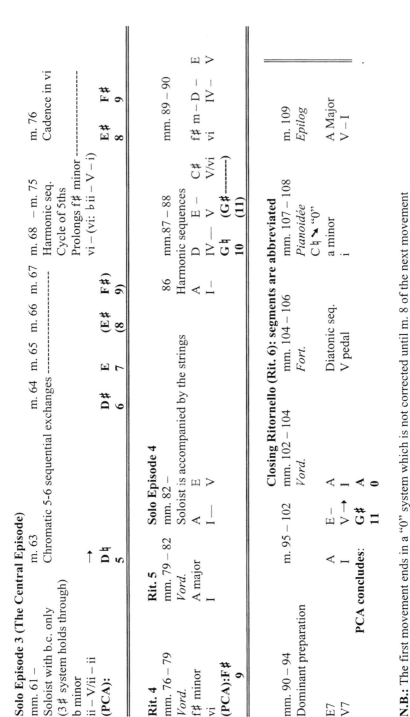

N.B.: The first movement ends in a "0" system which is not corrected until m. 8 of the next movement

Diagram 4.3 Vivaldi, Concerto in A major for solo violin and strings, and op. 9 no. 2 first movement continued

Vivaldi's opening ritornello is orchestrated for unison strings, in a typical opening gambit of many Venetian concertos of the early eighteenth century (Example 4.12). Measures 1–6 comprise the *Vordersatz* segment of the theme, which ends on a half cadence. The function of the *Vordersatz* is to establish tonic harmony clearly with root-position tonic and dominant triads; in this case the realization of the basso continuo would fill in the missing triadic pitch classes implied by the arpeggiations in the unison melody. Since so much of early eighteenth-century music relies upon variety of rhythmic pattern rather than on melodic profile, at least in the fast movements of concertos, it is no surprise that Vivaldi's *Vordersatz* segment should contain at least three different rhythmic patterns within it: an opening tonic arpeggio in quarters and eighths, a sixteenth-note neighbor figure, and a concluding syncopated arpeggiated motive. Following the *Vordersatz*, the *Fortspinnung* segment, a diatonic sequential progression covering three measures, continues with the sixteenth-note neighbor figure of the opening, thus maintaining continuity as well as rhythmic momentum. Vivaldi's innovation is the segment that follows the *Fortspinnung*. Labeled by some the *pianoidée*,[28] this segment appears in a selected number of Vivaldi concertos; it is not a regular feature of his ritornello themes. By definition, the *pianoidée* is a passage that shifts the tonic major mode into its parallel minor, usually accompanied by a lower dynamic level and reduced scoring. This segment, when it appears, disrupts the mode by injecting a disorienting chromatic element into it. In this case, the missing pitch of the prevailing 3♯ system, C♮, enters. The resulting system shift down to a "0" or C system also allows for another chromatic pitch to enter the diatonic pitch field, the B♭ in m. 11, the allowable added flat of the "0" system.

---

28 It was Walther Krüger who first coined this term in his *Das Concerto Grosso in Deutschland* (Wolfenbüttel and Berlin, 1932), p. 26. Pippa Drummond, referring to Krüger, also adopts this term in her *The German Concerto: Five Eighteenth-Century Studies* (Oxford, 1980), pp. 71–2 n. 98. See also Bella Brover Lubovsky, "'Die schwarze Gredel,' or the Parallel Minor Key in Vivaldi's Instrumental Music," *Studi Vivaldiani*, 3 (2003): 105–31, who discusses Vivaldi's minor-mode shifts in his ritornello themes, but without using the term *pianoidée*. To us, the term *pianoidée* aptly fits the nature of this segment, and although somewhat anachronistic, is still a useful designation.

Example 4.12   Vivaldi, Concerto in A major for solo violin and strings op. 9 no. 2, first movement (mm. 1–12)

At this point, it would be beneficial to draw the system matrix of this movement in order to clarify how the system changes incurred by the shift into the parallel minor affect the compositional design of the movement. Figure 4.1 represents the matrix of a 3♯ gamut system that is conceived within the tonality of the common-practice period (see also Figure 2.2 for another representation and discussion of this matrix, but from the complementary "0" system).

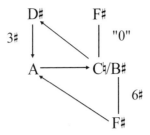

Figure 4.1   3♯ system matrix

Starting from the left-hand side of the figure, the tritone A–D♯ represents the defining interval of a 3♯ eleven-pitch-class collection whose root is A and whose chromatic octave is symmetrically divided by D♯. In the first movement of Vivaldi's op. 9 no. 2, this collection is centered on A major, the tonic of the piece (it could just as well have referred to F♯ minor since both keys share the same 3♯ system as well as hexachord). The arrow pointing to the right, emanating from the A in the figure, shows what happens if the missing pitch of the 3♯ system, C♮, is introduced. When Vivaldi switches mode to a local A minor tonality in the *pianoidée* segment of his ritornello theme, the new eleven-pitch-class system that results is one whose root is C and whose tritone divider is F♯. The complementary system will remain in effect until the missing pitch of that system is introduced, to move either down another three systems if the pitch is spelled E♭, or up three systems if the pitch is spelled D♯. In the latter case, as here, the D♯ that enters in m. 30 would bring us back to the original 3♯ system as indicated by the arrow shooting up diagonally from C♮ to D♯ in the figure.

Alternatively, when Vivaldi moves into C♯ minor, the missing pitch spelled as B♯ (instead of C♮) is introduced. The new eleven-pitch-class system is one whose root is F♯, B♯ being the symmetrical divider of an F♯ chromatic octave. The missing pitch of this 6♯ system that would return us to the A major tonic would be the tonic pitch itself, A. What is important to note here is that C♯ minor is a subset, as it were, of the larger 6♯ system and does not comprise a separate 4♯ system lying outside the prevailing matrix of the movement. Only one matrix can exist at any one time, and all harmonic events are subsumed within the tritone axes of the tonic eleven-pitch-class system.

An important compositional question arises when we consider the relationship between any two opposing pitch classes that comprise the complementary systems of the matrix. For instance, if the relationship between the chromatics D♯ and C♮ is important in motivating system shifts within the original 3♯ system of the movement, do these same pitches play a larger developmental role in the movement as well? In view of the system modulatory potential of D♯, it is no wonder that Vivaldi articulates this pitch as *the only chromatic* within the first two segments of the ritornello theme. It first occurs at the onset of the *Fortspinnung* in m. 7 (refer to Example 4.12) as a leading-tone embellishment of the dominant. The D♯ is then displaced by its diatonic equivalent, D♮, in the next measure, thus forming a dyad conflict between the raised and lowered fourth degree of the A major scale. Dyad conflicts between chromatic inflections of pitch classes with the same family name (here D♯ and D♮) may also become a source of development along with *system* dyad conflicts (in this case, C♮ and D♯). Such relationships as these can only be ascertained, however, by further examination of the movement.

The note D♯ becomes more and more prominent as we move into the area of the dominant, eventually reaching the goal of the second ritornello statement in m. 29. Now D♯ becomes an essential pitch, displacing the diatonic D♮ of the tonic scale. Vivaldi keeps the D♯ active as he moves into the area of iii, C♯ minor. The D♯ becomes a controlling pitch or motivator in the sense that it now governs the progression of eleven-pitch-class harmonic areas. Both the dominant and the minor mediant relate to each other in that C♯ minor can also be understood as the dominant's submediant, the one following the other as ritornello statements. They therefore theoretically share the same key signature of four sharps, understanding them as keys instead of harmonic areas. Thus, the D♯ which articulated the dominant also motivates its "parallel," the mediant. The brackets in the following diagram of the system hexachord of the movement show which hexachordal pitches share the same implied key signatures:

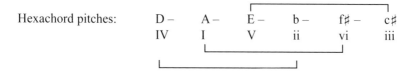

Hexachord pitches:

D –	A –	E –	b –	f♯ –	c♯
IV	I	V	ii	vi	iii

Thus each pitch class from one side of the hexachord links up with its opposite member from the other side of the hexachord: E and C♯ minor, A and F♯ minor, D and B minor. The composer may use a particular chromatic pitch class to unite the movement between one harmonic area within the hexachord and another, thus binding the relationship between the two, as is the case here with D♯ binding both the dominant, E, and the mediant, C♯ minor. Eventually, the D♯ will have to yield its position to its diatonic counterpart if the composer ever intends to return to the tonic of the movement.

The expansion of C♯ minor allows the next pair of system conflicts to present itself: namely, B♯ (a respelling of C♮) and its conflicting pitch, A♮ (see the above system matrix). These two pitch classes now govern the system shifts of the second solo episode leading up to and throughout the third ritornello, which is in the mediant. The A♮ finally "wins out" in m. 60, returning the previous 6♯ system temporarily to a 3♯ system.

What is most unusual about this movement is that Vivaldi reverses the usual order of harmonic events by placing a ritornello statement in the minor mediant, C♯ minor, *before* a ritornello in the submediant, F♯ minor. In the vast number of concertos composed in the major mode during this period (including Vivaldi's own works), the penultimate ritornello statement before the return of the tonic was often the minor mediant. In terms of sheer dramatic intensity, composers would naturally choose iii as a climactic event, since iii is the furthest pitch class away from the tonic within the reordered hexachord of the key. In addition, the tonicization of the minor mediant automatically entails a system shift up three signatures, which would then be immediately corrected with the return of tonic harmony, usually as the final or penultimate ritornello of the movement. (Some concerto movements end with two tonic ritornello statements to strengthen the home key, having passed through so many intervening subsidiary harmonic areas.) Instead, Vivaldi prefers a smoother approach to the return of the tonic by inserting another ritornello (ritornello 4) in F♯ minor (mm. 76ff). F♯ minor (vi) is closely related to the tonic (see the above hexachord diagram) since the two are relatives of each other. Ritornello 4 states only the *Vordersatz* segment of the ritornello theme and it is immediately succeeded by ritornello 5 in the tonic, also with only a *Vordersatz* segment. The return of tonic harmony results from a simple diatonic 5–6 exchange between F♯ minor and A major.

But, in the meantime, what has happened to the D♯? This pitch was put into play early in the movement when Vivaldi moved into the dominant, and continued to be active right into the C♯ minor harmonic area. Maintaining D♯ through two tonal centers, and thus further dramatizing (and, in a sense, "developing") the relationship of the background dyad conflict between D♯ and D♮, could be a possible reason why Vivaldi chose to move directly from the dominant to the minor mediant, bypassing, albeit temporarily, the submediant.

To refer again to Diagram 4.3, the third ritornello was modulatory, moving from C♯ minor at its beginning to B minor (ii) at its end. In the process, the previous D♯s that controlled the harmonic direction of the middle of the movement now resolve to their diatonic counterparts as D♮s. But this is not yet the end of the story: D♯ returns once more in m. 64 as part of a larger chromatic unfolding that runs over the course of the movement. A desire to fill out the chromatic octave, in whole or in part, is nothing new in music, as was discussed in the previous chapter. This inclination can be seen as early as the 1530s, when chromaticism was first investigated as a compositional dialectic along with the diatonic. In the eighteenth century, the filling-out of the chromatic octave, starting on the tonic pitch of the key, becomes an increasingly important compositional tool that often coincides with the harmonic background. The term we have adopted for this procedure, "Primary Chromatic Array" (PCA), was mentioned in the previous chapter in terms of chromatic modality, and now we can observe its unfolding within a purely tonal construct.

No matter at which point it begins to unfold, the PCA always begins on the tonic pitch (pc 0) and continues to ascend, unfolding each chromatic pitch class in successive order until the octave is completed.[29] The PCA often interacts with other significant pitch classes, ones that form either dyad conflicts or system conflicts, or both, depending upon the piece and the whim of the composer. The rate at which the PCA unfolds – how many chromatic pitch classes are introduced at any one time – may also create tension and expectancy. In Vivaldi's op. 9 no 2,

---

29 The PCA does not always have to include every pitch class of the chromatic tonic octave. For example, many Renaissance vocal pieces begin on pc 0, the final of the mode, but then skip to pc 3 before continuing in ascending chromatic order. Chapter 5 will discuss in detail the variable constructs allowable within the PCA in terms of eighteenth-century sonata-form movements.

after tonic harmony is established in m. 1 (pc 0), the first movement's PCA does not begin to ascend with pc 1 until m. 43 (see Diagram 4.3 for the exact placement of the PCA), as part of a dramatic diversion to C♯ minor. At this point, Vivaldi unfolds the first five pitches of the PCA in quick succession: A (pc 0) – A♯ (pc 1) – B (pc 2) – B♯ (pc 3 as leading tone) – C♯ (pc 4). This last pitch, the goal of the first part of the PCA, now achieves structural significance as the harmonic area of the third ritornello. The C♯ (pc 4) is not displaced until D♮ (pc 5) displaces it in m. 60. The PCA's arrival on pc 5 is part of a developmental process that highlights the dyadic conflict between D♯ and D♮. Only now does the D♯ finally resolve as part of the rising PCA chromatic octave. Dramatically, Vivaldi delays the resolution of D♯ to E♮ by breaking into the third solo episode in m. 61, leaving the D♮ "hanging," as it were, before the line continues upward in m. 64: D♯ (pc 6) passes to E (pc 7), which, in turn, moves up to E♯ (m. 66) before reaching the next structurally significant goal of F♯ minor in m. 67. The move of the D♮ upward to D♯ is not the actual resolution of the dyad conflict; that must wait until the very end of the movement. Meanwhile, the F♯ (pc 9) now becomes a harmonic area in its own right, articulated by its own ritornello passage. Thus both C♯ (pc 4) and F♯ (pc 9), as rising pitch classes within the PCA, are compositional determinants that help to fashion the movement's unique emotional harmonic character when they are fleshed out as harmonic areas in their own right! It is no wonder, then, that Vivaldi chose to insert the F♯ minor ritornello where he did since the placement of F♯ is so crucial to our understanding of the rising chromatic octave at that moment of the movement. Pc 10, G♮, is introduced in m. 86 within an area of subdominant harmony; there is even a trill on it to give added significance to this pitch. The subdominant, D major, forms part of a tonic progression that reinforces tonic harmony in ritornello 5. Only the leading tone, G♯, is needed now to complete the PCA; this occurs immediately in m. 88 as part of dominant harmony. The G♯ occurs again, with more structural significance, as part of the penultimate tonic cadence to the closing ritornello in m. 102. Thus, the last two pitch classes of the PCA (pc 11 as leading tone and pc 0 as tonic) are reiterated at the end of the movement as a final gesture, completing the chromatic octave. The last abbreviated ritornello statement (ritornello 6) in the tonic finally resolves the D♯/D♮ dyad conflict. Vivaldi has planned the opening ritornello in such a way that the reappearance of D♯/D♮ within the closing ritornello becomes the last chromatic gesture in the movement, automatically resolving the conflict into tonic harmony, a compositional lesson not lost on J.S. Bach.[30] Since the rising PCA has already reached completion, mm. 7 and 8 of the opening ritornello now return in mm. 105 and 106 to resolve the D♯ *down* to its diatonic counterpart, D♮, instead of up to E♮ (the issue of "resolution" is discussed below). Both conditions are now fulfilled: the PCA has reached its conclusion, meaning that D♯ has moved up to E♮, and the dyad conflict between D♯ and D♮ has been settled.

---

30 See, for example, Bach's Brandenburg Concerto no. 1 in F, first movement. The opening ritornello is completely diatonic except for B♮. By the time Bach reaches the closing ritornello, he has shifted into a 4♭ system which can be corrected only by introducing B♮. Thus at one and the same time, the final ritornello in the tonic both redresses the system to 1♭ and resolves the B♮ back into its diatonic counterpart, B♭.

It should be noted that the term "resolution" is not only used here in the traditional voice-leading sense of the term, meaning that sharps move up to the next chromatic pitch class and flats move down in the same fashion, but also to mean the resolution of inflected non-diatonic tones into their diatonic counterparts. One of the basic precepts of our theory is that chromatic issues are raised from adjacent pairs with pitch classes of the same "family name," the chromatically inflected pc being, therefore, dissonant against its diatonic neighbor. Ultimately, for the tonic to reign supreme at the close of the movement, the chromatic neighbor must return, in other words "resolve," into the pitch class from which it was originally inflected. Therefore, while D♯ is understood to resolve locally to E♮, in a more comprehensive manner, the D♯ chromatic variant is now restored to its D♮ diatonic form.

But what about the C♮ component of the *pianoidée*? This segment returns as well, also abbreviated, bringing along with it the missing pitch of the 3♯ system, C♮. As it happens, there is no correcting D♯ – since D♯ has already resolved to D♮ – to bring the system back up to three sharps. In this way, Vivaldi has made certain not to resolve all the issues of the opening movement, but has managed to keep the tension at a high level even at its close. The subsequent two movements, both in the tonic A major, revisit the same dyad conflicts, the second movement temporarily resolving the system back to a 3♯ system by introducing D♯ in m. 8 as the leading tone of a dominant prolongation. The D♯ in the second movement is thus worked into the larger system conflict with C♮ that runs throughout the concerto; besides, its introduction again raises the D♯/D♮ conflict from the first movement. Only in the last movement are all these issues finally resolved.[31]

As a coda to this chapter, we would like to discuss briefly J.S. Bach's approach to ritornello form in terms of system analysis, an approach remarkably similar to that of Vivaldi and his Italian contemporaries, all of whom exerted a notable influence. Bach became absorbed in the current Italian style in Weimar, where he was court organist and vice-*Kapellmeister* (1708–17). It was here that he transcribed a number of Italian concertos for harpsichord and organ for his pupil Prince Johann Ernst, a distant cousin of his employer, Duke Wilhelm Ernst. Bach knew, for instance, many of Vivaldi's op. 3 concertos in manuscript copies before they were published since the Prince collected Italian concertos on his various sojourns, many in manuscript, for the purpose of study: he had Bach transcribe them for keyboard. Prince Johann Ernst was a composer himself and must have been an excellent organist since Bach's transcriptions for organ of Vivaldi's op. 3 concertos could only have been played by someone of exceptional capabilities.

---

31 There are interesting cases where whole compositions end in their complementary systems: for example, Beethoven's Fifth Symphony in C minor, whose last movement in C major ends in a 3♭ system, as well as his Piano Sonata in D major op. 10 no. 3, whose last movement ends in a 1♭ system. These pieces often have some sort of emotional or extra-musical reason for their system endings; the Fifth Symphony is particularly apt in this regard (see Owen Jander, "Let Your Deafness No Longer Be a Secret – Even in Art": Self-Portraiture and the Third Movement of the C-Minor Symphony," *Beethoven Forum*, 8 (2000): 25–70). In the D major sonata, the opposition of D major and D minor is a significant ploy permeating the entire composition.

Bach's own concertos follow Vivaldi's ritornello harmonic plan and motivic segmentation, but with several important stylistic distinctions: Bach's whole conception is far more polyphonic than that of his Italian contemporaries; the solo and ripieno groups (most likely played one to a part) are so closely intertwined that it is often difficult to know where a ritornello ends and a solo episode begins. Even in the segmentation of the opening ritornello theme, it is often difficult to determine precisely where the segments begin and end. For instance, Bach was particularly sensitive to the *Fortspinnung* segment of the ritornello theme, being always careful to disguise its obvious redundancy.[32] Yet, given the conspicuous stylistic differences between Bach and his Italian contemporaries, Bach's approaches to systems and hexachordal unfoldings are remarkably similar. Take, for example, the first movement of Bach's Brandenburg Concerto no. 2 in F major, whose 1♭-system central hexachord may be presented in the following way:[33]

Hexachordal pitch class:	B♭	F	C	g	d	a
Harmonic function:	IV	I	V	ii	vi	iii

The missing pitch of the 1♭ system that governs this piece is either A♭, the minor third of the root F, or its enharmonic equivalent, G♯, the augmented second of the root F as well as the leading tone of the mediant. Bach explores the entire harmonic spectrum of the 1♭ hexachord, beginning with the tonic and dominant, F and C. In fact, the first 24 measures of the opening movement do nothing other than articulate the motion from the tonic to the dominant; this is done within a most elaborate solo episode in which each member of the concertino is introduced separately in between fragmented, non-structural ritornello segments by the ripieno. Only in m. 25 does the movement "take off" with the second ritornello in the dominant.

The next harmonic goal is D minor in m. 31, the first ritornello in the minor mode. The motion to vi, which enters after a ritornello in the dominant, is not unusual in itself, since a submediant harmonic area usually signals the imminent return of tonic harmony (see the analysis of the first movement of Vivaldi's concerto op. 9 no. 2 above). In fact, Bach does return to the tonic in m. 45 with a ritornello in F, but the return to the tonic midway in the movement acts as a movement divider in which the tonic now signals a change in harmonic direction away from the dominant and back toward the tonic, a procedure common to all genres of Bach's *oeuvre* from fugues to concertos. Specifically the return to I halfway through the movement prepares for a movement into the subdominant, where I is reinterpreted as V/IV, redirecting the harmonic path back toward the tonic. The subdominant thus forms the beginning of a larger tonic progression that achieves its goal with the final tonic ritornello of the movement. The redirection of the tonal scheme from the tonic as V/IV can ultimately

---

32 In many of Vivaldi's concertos the *Fortspinnung* segment is basically a cycle of fifths with a repeated rhythmic motive that leaves off from the tonic, but ultimately returns to it in the final *Epilog* segment. Bach's *Fortspinnung* segments disguise their sequential nature, through subtle rhythmic variations and asymmetrical phrase patterns.

33 Dreyfus, "J.S. Bach's Concerto Ritornellos," analyzes the same Bach concerto but does not address the concept of system shifts that we present in our analysis of Bach.

be traced back to Corelli's background harmonic progressions in his trio sonatas (see above), only now the individual movements are altogether much longer and harmonic areas are prolonged over greater time spans. Interestingly, the same use of the tonic as a subdominant preparation will become a staple of later eighteenth-century sonata-form movements, particularly at the opening of their development sections.

Of particular interest to us is what happens in the first movement of Bach's concerto after the subdominant is reached in m. 55. From here, Bach's ritornello statements, sometimes extended into overlapping episodes, climb up the full extent of the F hexachord by fifths: B♭–F–c–g–d–a. The dominant in this progression is deliberately kept minor in order not to return prematurely to the tonic: C minor becomes just another member in a contrapuntally conceived fifths cycle, without structural significance. Bach's penultimate ritornello (ritornello 8) prolongs the mediant, A minor, via its dominant, E, forcing a system shift into the complementary 2♯ system – G♯, the major third of the E major dominant triad, is the missing pitch of the 1♭ system of F and therefore modulates the 1♭ system up three signatures to a 2♯ system, G♯ being the octave divider of the D chromatic octave.

Immediately, the last ritornello returns directly to tonic harmony, not only restoring the F major tonic, but also correcting the previous system shift back down to 1♭ (F♮ is the missing pitch of the 2♯ system). Having a penultimate ritornello in the minor mediant is a common Baroque procedure and appears as well in countless Vivaldi concertos. What is significant about this construct is the fact that early eighteenth-century composers felt no need to precede the final tonic ritornello with a preparatory dominant or retransition of any kind, especially when the penultimate ritornello was in the minor mediant; the introduction of the tonic pitch class, and its "automatic" correction of system, must have been heard as a sufficient preparation for the return to tonic harmony. Besides, once the tonic was regained, it would automatically be defined by its dominant during the concluding ritornello. It is no wonder, then, that the early symphonists adopted this harmonic organization, centered on the reintroduction of the missing pitch of the complementary system before the return of tonic harmony, as an important design feature. The next chapter traces the development of this device over the course of the eighteenth century, especially in the newly burgeoning sonata form of the Classical symphony.

Chapter Five

Tonality and Systems in the Mid- to Late-Eighteenth Century: The Classical Ideal

I. The Development of the Early Symphony: Vivaldi and the Ripieno Concerto, G.B. Sammartini

We now turn to a discussion of the development of sonata form, perhaps the most important form, or, more accurately, compositional procedure, of the entire eighteenth century. Its flexibility of design allowed for the greatest variety of expression, second only to the multiplicity of ritornello designs in the concertos of the first decades of the century. Our present concerns are the ways in which the system hexachord, the eleven pitch-class areas, and the *Primary Chromatic Array* (PCA) inform sonata procedure. Perhaps the best way to start would be to investigate first the derivation of the early symphony from its immediate predecessor, the ritornello form of the late Baroque concerto.

The symphony evolved from both the early eighteenth-century concerto in ritornello form and the opera overture, the latter called *sinfonia*. Both of these genres were invariably composed in a three-movement format that alternated fast and slow movements, and especially in the opera sinfonia the last movement tended to be dance-like in character. Regarding the concerto, there were two different types that were influential on the early symphony. These included the concerto grosso proper, characterized by a separate solo group, or *concertino*, set against or accompanied by a fuller group, or *ripieno*; and the so-called ripieno concerto (or *concerto a quattro*) for strings alone, in which there was no separate concertino group, the full orchestra playing both ritornello statements and episodic material throughout the course of the movement. This latter type of concerto was a specialty of Antonio Vivaldi, who often used these pieces as overtures to his numerous operas.[1] Owing to the orchestral nature

---

1   Marc Pincherle seems to have been the first modern musicologist to recognize the importance of Vivaldi as an early symphonist. Pincherle quotes from a letter by Charles de Brosses, who gives a vivid eye-witness account of the music played by the girls at the Ospedale della Pietà in Venice, where Vivaldi worked on and off as the *maestro di concerto*: "It [referring to the *Pietà*] is also the first as regards the perfecting of symphonies ... They have here a type of music that we do not know in France and that appears to me to be more appropriate than any other for the Jardin de Bourbonne. These are the large concertos in which there is no solo violin." Marc Pincherle, *Vivaldi*, trans. Christopher Hatch (New York, 1962), p. 169. For a fuller discussion of Charles de Brosses's Italian tour of 1739–40 and his *Lettres familières* see Michael Talbot, *Vivaldi* (New York, 1992). Talbot also describes

of the ripieno concerto – that is, the entire string group acts as a body projecting all the thematic material – one can easily see its influence on the emerging symphony. What also makes several of these ripieno concertos of interest to us is the frequent use of the parallel minor, either in the form of a *pianoidée* segment (see Chapter 4 for an explanation of this term) within the opening ritornello tonic statement (RV 158 in A major, first movement) or in alternating major/minor periods (RV 159 in A major, third movement), either option necessitating three-hexachord system modulations.

The opening ritornello of the first movement of RV 158 in A major is an example of an elaborate multi-segmented theme whose importance lies in the placement of the *pianoidée* right before a series of modulatory *Epilog* segments (see Example 5.1). In this particular example, the switch into the parallel minor, with its consequent shift into a "0" system, signals a structurally significant event within the form: *a harmonic shift* toward the dominant. In effect, the *pianoidée* prepares for a bridge passage,[2] the function of which is allotted to the three *Epilog* segments that follow. The first *Epilog* (mm. 13–14) acts as a jumping-off point by initiating tonic harmony (V–I), but the final sixteenth-note A in the bass of m. 14 moves contrapuntally up a step to B in m. 15 at the start of the second *Epilog* (mm. 15–16). The B at the downbeat of m. 15 is sustained as a bass pedal which supports a D♯, at once correcting the previous "0" system to a 3♯ system, and at the same time acts as V/V, the dominant itself now being anchored by the third *Epilog* (mm. 17–18) constituting the formal cadence in E major. A second ritornello follows immediately in V, strengthening the arrival and extending it into a lengthy harmonic area in its own right. The entire passage, from the *pianoidée* through to the second ritornello statement, foreshadows similar harmonic progressions to the dominant that characterize later sonata-form movements.

Early symphonists often used the introduction of the minor third degree in the major mode to signal a shift of system, and, consequently, a motion into a new harmonic area, even using the modal shift to displace the more usual dominant preparation. Consequently, the switch of mode from the tonic major triad to its parallel minor within the first period of the movement must have been heard as a dissonant harmonic motion requiring at least a temporary resolution, either restoring the original mode of the tonic (as in Vivaldi's non-modulatory ritornello themes that include a *pianoidée*, but still close off in the tonic) or propelling the music on to another harmonic goal, acting as a bridge of some sort.[3] In this manner, a diatonic

---

Vivaldi's ripieno concertos (pp. 127–8), but his musical discussion is limited to only a few stylistic observations.

2   We use the term "bridge," as opposed to "transition," to mean a passage that connects the first harmonic area to that of the second within the exposition of a sonata-form movement. The term "transition" is reserved for connecting passages that link major subdivisions *within* the second key area, such as that occurring between the opening period of the second harmonic area and the closing period.

3   A possible reason for hearing the minor third degree as dissonant within the major mode may lie in the nature of the tonal system itself and its application to acoustical theory. Scalar systems are based, deliberately or otherwise, in the reordering of the harmonic partials of the overtone series. A characteristic property of the overtone series is the fact that a compound interval based on a minor third between the fundamental and the fifth partial does not exist; indeed, this chromatic pitch class and its enharmonic equivalent are among the

Example 5.1 Vivaldi, Concerto Ripieno in A major RV 158, first movement (mm. 1–10)

passage could be dramatically extended; however, the juxtaposition of major and parallel minor triads raised so strong a conflict between the tonic system and its "foreign interloper" (or "schwarze Gredel" [black Margaret], as Joseph Riepel humorously labels the move into the parallel minor[4]) that its use had to be carefully

---

furthest chromatic partials in the series, and are located so far up among the higher partials as to be rendered impractical. Within a purely diatonic passage in the major mode, the introduction of the flat third degree is heard as unsettling since it implies another mode and/or harmonic series, and thereby creates a conflict with the major third degree of the tonic key.

4   Joseph Riepel, *Grundregeln zur Tonordnung insgemein* (Frankfurt and Leipzig, 1755), quoted in Leonard G. Ratner, *Classic Music: Expression, Form, and Style* (New York, 1980), p. 50.

planned by the composer to avoid mitigating its effect, or to avoid reducing the gesture to a mere cliché.

Several examples exist in the early symphonic literature of bridge material that prepares the second key via the parallel minor, most notably in the works of Giovanni Battista Sammartini (1701–1775), a recognized composer of his day who worked in Milan as "maestro di capella to more than half the churches in that city, for which he furnished masses upon all the great festivals."[5] Milan, during the first decades of the eighteenth century, was a major center of orchestral production, predating Mannheim's famous court orchestra later in the century. Austria's control over Lombardy from 1708 to 1796, and her concomitant encouragement of the musical arts, opera included, was probably the main cultural reason why Milan cultivated an appreciation for orchestral music to the extent that it did.[6] Both first movements of Sammartini's symphonies nos 1 in C (c. 1720s) and 3 in D (c. 1730s)[7] switch to the parallel minor before the dominant arrival; and, interestingly, the forms of these first movements are radically different in construction. In the earlier C major symphony, the form is closely related to the ritornello form of the Baroque concerto, much in the manner of a concerto ripieno for strings by Vivaldi or Albinoni. Thus the "second harmonic area" turns out to be a repetition of the ritornello theme transposed to the dominant (not unlike that of the Vivaldi ripieno concerto discussed above). In place of a solo episode leading to the second ritornello statement, the opening ritornello, which clearly cadences on the tonic in m. 16, is extended by four extra measures of alternating minor tonic and major dominant harmony, the last three measures of which are heard over a dominant pedal in the violas (see Example 5.2). This passage leads directly into the second ritornello statement in the dominant, the purely melodic F♯ of the previous measures now acting officially as the leading tone into the new key, even though no V/V harmony supports this pitch.

5   Charles Burney, *A General History of Music*, vol. 2 (1789), repr. edn (New York, 1957), p. 454.

6   Giovanni Battista Sammartini, *Ten Symphonies*, ed. Bathia Churgin, in Barry Brook (editor-in-chief), *The Symphony: 1720–1840*, ser. A, vol. 2 (New York, 1984), pp. xiv–xv. In her introduction, Churgin states that "The city [Milan] had a strong preference for instrumental music. It boasted many good string players and numerous composers, who provided a rich musical environment for Sammartini's creative efforts. It is no wonder that Milan was the home of the earliest symphonic school in Europe, brilliantly led by Sammartini" (p. xv). See also John Spitzer and Neal Zaslaw, *The Birth of the Orchestra: History of an Institution, 1650–1815* (Oxford, 2004), pp. 166–9.

7   For the approximate dates of Sammartini's early symphonies, see G.B. Sammartini, *The Symphonies of G.B. Sammartini*, vol. 1, ed. Bathia Churgin (Cambridge, Massachutetts, 1968), pp. 10–11.

Example 5.2a   Sammartini, Sinfonia in C, first movement (mm. 1–20)

What makes this transitional passage so very interesting within the context of the present theory is that E♭, the pitch class that would normally indicate a transposition of systems *down* three fifths to that of C minor, is immediately corrected upward by the F♯, the missing pitch of a 3♭ system. The alternation of these two system-shift motivators ends finally (m. 19) with the uncontested F♯ since no E♭ follows to shift the system down again.

In effect, the final F♯ leaves the prevailing "0" system intact despite the temporary juxtaposition of the minor tonic. For the moment, Sammartini introduces the missing pitch, E♭, only to prepare for a larger harmonic motion to V, not to modulate systems for any extended period. He chooses to do this via E♭, not D♯ (the alternate choice); in fact, most composers throughout the century opt for the flat pitch to indicate the first harmonic move away from the tonic since the enharmonic respelling would create harmonic difficulties that would, in effect, move the harmony in another direction. If Sammartini had chosen D♯ instead of E♭ he would have implied a motion to iii, E minor, since D♯ has no voice-leading function that would support the dominant. As in previous concertos discussed in Chapter 4, the move to iii is a distant one in relation to the tonic, the third degree being the last note of the tonic hexachord. Usually, the tonicization of iii would act as a climax of the whole movement and would be reserved for a penultimate ritornello. In Sammartini's C major symphony, introducing D♯ too early would have undercut his eventual motion to iii, a harmonic area of great significance within the movement (see Diagram 5.1). After the second ritornello in V (now complete with an *Epilog* missing from the opening ritornello), the music suddenly swings into E minor, articulated by a contrasting, more lyrical idea constructed in four-measure phrase units. In fact, Sammartini's phrasing from the beginning has been in even four-measure units (subdivided 2 + 2), which have a rhythmic consistency quite unlike Vivaldi's (not to say J.S. Bach's) asymmetrical phrase units within his ritornello themes.

Sammartini's style leans much more to the symmetrical phrasing of the emerging *style galant* of the 1730s and 1740s, a style that derived from the even phrasing of the dance and which found its way both into comic opera (Pcrgolesi's *La serva padrona* of 1733 is a famous example of its early use in opera) and into the Italian keyboard sonata with its close ties to contemporary binary dance forms. Characteristic of the phrasing of the *style galant* is that the second measure of each two-measure phrase unit replicates the first on the same pitch level, automatically forming even two-measure hypermeasures. Sammartini's four-measure phrase groupings remain consistent throughout the movement, lending the contrasting E minor middle section of the movement a lyricism that is almost operatic in its intensity.

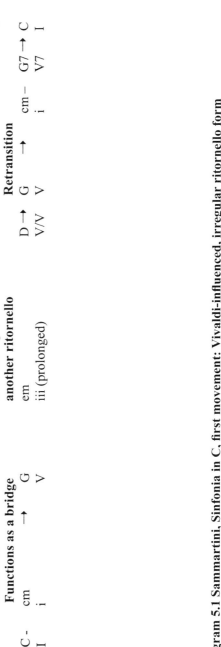

Rit. 1		Rit. 2			Rit. 3 (last 4 mm)
		Pianoidée			
		Functions as a bridge		contrasting idea instead of another ritornello	
					Retransition
C -	cm →	G	em	D → G → cm –	G7 → C
I	i	V	iii (prolonged)	V/V V i	V7 I

Diagram 5.1 Sammartini, Sinfonia in C, first movement: Vivaldi-influenced, irregular ritornello form

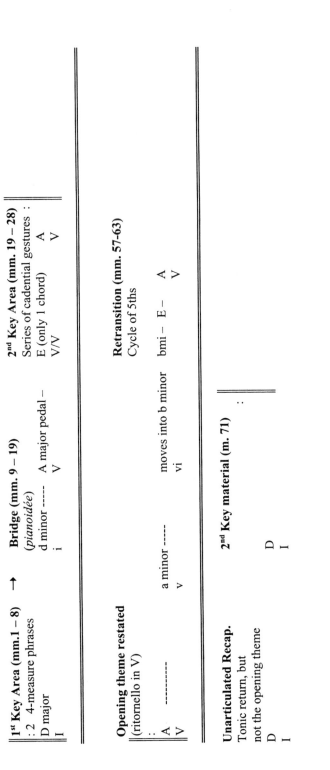

1ˢᵗ Key Area (mm.1 – 8)   →   **Bridge (mm. 9 – 19)**   **2ⁿᵈ Key Area (mm. 19 – 28)**
:2 4-measure phrases   (*pianoidée*)   Series of cadential gestures :
D major   d minor ----- A major pedal –   E (only 1 chord)   A
I   i   V   V/V   V

Opening theme restated   **Retransition (mm. 57-63)**
(ritornello in V)   Cycle of 5ths
:.   moves into b minor   bmi – E – A
A --------   a minor -----   vi   V   V
V   v

Unarticulated Recap.   **2ⁿᵈ Key material (m. 71)**   :.
Tonic return, but
not the opening theme
D   D
I   I

Diagram 5.2 Sammartini, Sinfonia in D, first movement: simple binary sonata form based on Italian keyboard models

Once the E minor harmonic area has been achieved, all the previous E♭s now become D♯s, shifting the system up three signatures from "0" to a 3♯ system. From m. 49 to m. 79, D♯ continuously conflicts with its system complement C♮, throwing the systems back and forth from 3♯ to "0" in a manner not unlike that of a development section from a later eighteenth-century sonata-form movement. Only in m. 79 is C♮ left uncontested, the "0" system remaining intact until the surprise restatement of the E minor lyrical theme in the tonic minor in m. 98 (see Example 5.2b). The previous D♯s now revert to E♭s, shifting the system down once again to a 3♭ system. Sammartini brings back the E minor lyrical theme in order to resolve it into the tonic minor and, simultaneously, resolve the E♭ that generated the harmonic motion into the dominant in the first place. The E♭ first locally resolves down to D at the end of m. 101, but then returns in the next measure, where it finally resolves into its diatonic complement, E♮. Lastly, the 3♭ system itself moves up to the tonic "0" system with the introduction of F♯ on the second beat of m. 103 as part of an Italian A♭ augmented sixth. Thus the minor tonic itself is resolved into its parallel major at the end of the movement, which concludes with a short four-measure ritornello in the tonic major. Sammartini has created a perfectly balanced structure whereby the dissonant gestures – the tonic minor, the E♭ and D♯ system complements, and the lyrical theme in a "remote" harmonic area – are all restated and then resolved into tonic harmony at the end of the movement. In effect, Sammartini has anticipated Classical developmental techniques by four decades!

Example 5.2b   Sammartini, Symphony in C, first movement (mm. 98–112)

The first movement of Sammartini's D major Symphony no. 3 is much less convoluted in form and much simpler in harmonic design than that of the symphony in C major (see Diagram 5.2), yet the movement is more sophisticated in the management of its transposed systems. Binary in form, the D major movement shares with its earlier companion a strikingly similar approach to system modulation, albeit couched within a new musical aesthetic: that of the *style galant* of the 1730s and 1740s, with its dance-influenced rhythmic patterns, symmetrical phrase groupings, and overall diatonic tonal harmonic framework. After an opening eight-measure period (divided into 4 + 4 antecedent–consequent phrases) which ends with an authentic cadence in the tonic, a bridge or transitional passage follows which immediately introduces F♮, which pitch class throws the D major 2♯ system down to a 1♭ system, the key of the parallel minor. The same thrust into the parallel minor that initiated the modulation to the dominant in the earlier symphony is again seen here, but with a radical difference. In the earlier symphony Sammartini was deliberately working within a loosely formed ritornello structure, in which the role of the dominant as a harmonic area existed only as a middleground expression of the tonic, equal in harmonic significance and weight to the extended middle section in E minor. However, in the later work, the binary form of the contemporary Italian keyboard sonata that Sammartini adopts implements a new harmonic background design, based on hierarchal relationships, in which the dominant now becomes a focal point that occupies a deeper level of structure and *outweighs* any other harmonic area within the movement, excepting, of course, the tonic itself. In fact, no other harmonic area, other than the tonic, is granted such prominence. Therefore the arrival at the structural dominant must be sufficiently prepared, both harmonically and rhythmically, for it to have the requisite dramatic strength to sustain it. (In minor-mode sonata forms, the relative major plays the same role as that of the dominant, but lacks the inherent dissonant intensity of the latter, a condition often rectified compositionally by later eighteenth-century composers with intense chromaticism, rhythmic displacement, accelerated phrase rhythm, etc.)

As we have seen, within major-mode movements, one method of achieving tonal disruption as a dramatic preparation for the arrival of the second key is to switch to the parallel minor before actually setting up II♯ as the V/V. In Sammartini's Symphony no. 3, the switch into a 1♭ system at the start of the bridge (see Example 5.3, m. 9), followed by a dominant pedal on A, precedes the structural cadence to V in m. 18. Significantly, the prevailing 1♭ system dramatically shifts back to a 2♯ system with the introduction of the leading tone to V, G♯, on the first beat of m. 17. Thus the correction of the flat system to that of sharps coincides with the emphatic arrival at the dominant supported by an authentic cadence in that "key" in m. 18. The final ten measures anchor the dominant in a series of cadential phrases before the entire first section is repeated. Even within this relatively short "exposition," Sammartini attempts a balanced periodic structure: all three internal subdivisions of the first half of the movement are almost equally subdivided. The opening statement is eight measures long, the bridge is ten measures, and the final dominant period is also ten measures in length. The relationship of bridge and second key to that of the opening tonic statement is 1:3, a proportion maintained in all sonata-form movements from Domenico Scarlatti to Beethoven. In order for the dominant to be heard as a deeper-level harmonic area, it needs several periods to be established as such. This is why, in eighteenth-century sonata-form movements, the dominant area is usually subdivided into several periods, each with its own cadential articulation, a compositional procedure that will be discussed in greater detail later in this chapter.

Example 5.3 Sammartini, Symphony in D, first movement (mm. 1–28)

Sammartini opens the second half of his symphony movement – later inappropriately referred to as "the development" – with a restatement of the opening thematic material in the dominant, perhaps a holdover from ritornello form with its second ritornello in the dominant; this procedure closely follows the Italian binary keyboard forms of the day. He then duplicates the order of events first presented in the first half of the movement; that is, the dominant statement that begins the second half now shifts into its parallel minor, a transposition of the "exposition" bridge passage. The transposed bridge, however, veers toward vi (B minor), and the pedal that was originally on A (V) in the first half is now on B as part of a longer prolongation of the submediant. As it happens, the motion to vi initiates a fifths cycle that follows the D major hexachord in retrograde, b–e–A–D, as a method of returning to the tonic, unarticulated, in m. 63. Typical of keyboard sonata forms during this period, only the exposition bridge material and closing cadential statements are now recapitulated in the tonic, concluding the movement; the opening statement does not reappear in the tonic since it already has been stated in the dominant at the start of the second half of the movement. What is interesting about the second half of Sammartini's movement is that all eleven pitch classes are present except for F♮, the missing pitch of the 2♯ system. It would seem, therefore, that Sammartini was particularly careful to maintain the prevailing 2♯ system throughout the second half in order to avoid raising too much dissonance, a condition that would necessitate a much longer recapitulation, one that would resolve all the dissonances raised in both the first and second halves of the movement. The symphony had not yet grown sufficiently in importance for composers to spend much time on purely developmental procedures since the genre was still considered an introduction, an overture, to the more important work that followed – usually an extended vocal work, either secular or sacred. Only when the symphony came to be regarded as an autonomous genre, toward the middle of the century, do we find composers interested in working out (developing) chromatic ideas that would inform the very depths of the compositional process. To that end we must now turn to selected Austrian composers working in the 1740s, 1750s, and 1760s who, along with their German contemporaries in Mannheim, raised the symphony to the next level of artistic integrity.

II. Viennese Symphonists of the Mid-Eighteenth Century: G.C. Wagenseil and G.M. Monn

Georg Christoph Wagenseil (1715–1777) spent his entire career in Vienna, where he was active as the Viennese court composer (*Kapellmeister*) from 1739 until his death;[8] he studied with the eminent theorist and organist J.J. Fux (himself imperial *Kapellmeister* from 1698), who recommended him for the position. Under the artistic leadership of both Fux and Antonio Caldara (from 1714, imperial chamber composer at the court of Charles VI, as well as assistant *Kapellmeister* to Fux)

---

8 For biographical information on Wagenseil, see John Kucaba and Bertil H. Van Boer, "Wagenseil, Georg Christoph," in Stanley Sadie and John Tyrrell (eds), *The New Grove Dictionary of Music and Musicians*, 2nd edn (London, 2001), vol. 26, pp. 928–30.

the Viennese Habsburgs were notoriously conservative in their musical tastes, for instance, preferring High Baroque *opera seria* to more modern comic opera forms and, wherever possible, fugal, and/or imitative writing in chamber music, as well as in organ music, where such writing was traditional. It is no wonder, then, that, according to Charles Burney, who met the composer in 1772, Wagenseil was a great admirer of Handel. Consequently, Wagenseil favored an approach to sonata form that still had strong conceptual ties to earlier eighteenth-century binary dance forms. Yet even with his conservative tendencies, Wagenseil was equally progressive as a practitioner of the *style galant* in Vienna, and his more modern approach to key-centered tonality and its incorporation of chromatic voice-leading certainly had an influence on later composers, most notably Haydn and the young Mozart. Wagenseil's influence reached indirectly to Beethoven, who received lessons in Fuxian counterpoint from Wagenseil's student Johann Schenk.

The relevance of Wagenseil's style to our previous discussion of Sammartini lies in the manner in which the modulation from the first harmonic area to the structural dominant is accomplished. In Wagenseil's symphonies, the first hint of dominant harmony, introduced within the bridge, is succeeded only by a cadence toward the end of the second harmonic area; specifically, at the point of the codetta, the final cadential passage formally ending the exposition. As a result, there is usually no extended area prolonging the new harmony; rather, the bridge cadence and succeeding codetta are the only confirmations of the new area. Here, one can easily see the historical connection between the first period of a binary dance form from the early decades of the eighteenth century, where tonic harmony is prolonged up to the double bar – the dominant being reduced to a large-scale half cadence concluding the first half of the form – and its later transformation into a rudimentary sonata exposition.

The first movement of the Sinfonia in E WV 393 (1760) is typical of Wagenseil's approach to sonata form (Example 5.4 shows the complete exposition of this movement).[9] A 13-measure dance-like opening statement, subdivided into three four-measure phrases, is followed by an extensive 32-measure bridge (mm. 13ff.) that is articulated by a change in thematic design. The first half of the bridge introduces an A♯ (the leading tone of the dominant), and the second half, articulated by another design change which effectively divides the bridge in half, moves to II♯ (m. 25). In m. 31 a B major chord (V) is presented which allows for the dominant area to take shape gradually during the remainder of the exposition. This is succeeded in the next measure by an augmented sixth chord on G♮, the missing pitch of the prevailing 4♯ system of the movement.

---

9   In addition to a number of symphonies by Wagenseil published in the Diletto Musicale series (Vienna and Munich, 1975), Wagenseil's symphonies can also be found in an edition by Karl Horwitz and Karl Riedal, in *Denkmäler der Tonkunst in Österreich*, xxxi, Jahrgang xv/2 (Graz, 1908); and a selection in Georg Christoph Wagenseil, *Fifteen Symphonies*, ed. John Kucaba, in Barry Brook (editor-in-chief), *The Symphony 1720–1840*, ser. B, vol. 3 (New York, 1981).

Example 5.4 Wagenseil, *Sinfonia* in E WV 393, first movement, exposition

Wagenseil has thus anticipated Haydn's use of the augmented sixth in his own symphonies, most notably the expositions of the Paris set (nos 82–7, discussed below). Historically significant is the fact that Wagenseil's use of the augmented sixth on the flat third degree of the major mode is a direct outgrowth of those *pianoidée* passages in the parallel minor employed by Sammartini (and Vivaldi before him) to signal the arrival of the dominant area.[10] What was once an entire phrase in the parallel minor has here been reduced to a single sonority whose root is the missing pitch of the tonic system. By using the missing pitch in this way, Wagenseil has successfully avoided the harmonic jolt caused by having an entire phrase in the parallel minor. There is an added benefit in that the augmented sixth, instead of occupying the position of a melodic phrase, has a non-melodic, contrapuntal/voice-leading function as part of a harmonic progression that dramatically drops to the V/V. In the present instance, the G♮ augmented sixth resolves to II 7/♯ (now heard unequivocally as V7/V) and then to V. Measure 35 is the first decisive gesture that anticipates the new harmonic area; it is still within the realm of the bridge and is not marked off by a formal cadence, what Hepokoski calls an "unachieved medial caesura."[11] This area, however, denotes the beginning of an auxiliary cadence that will not be fulfilled until m. 45, the beginning of a five-measure codetta and the first anchoring of the second harmonic area. Until the codetta, there has been no formal division within the exposition; however, we might hear m. 35 as a line of demarcation between "trying to leave the tonic" and "trying to arrive at the dominant." The unceasing rhythmic drive is almost consistently governed by four-measure hypermeasures and associated extensions.

The procedure is very similar to that outlined by Koch in his *Versuch einer Anleitung zur Composition* of 1782–93.[12] Koch's description of the form of a sonata exposition is germane, as Koch is one of the few Classical-era theorists to analyze this section as a single period, or to discuss an entire movement as a succession of periods. Koch's description of the exposition simply states that "the first period establishes the tonic and then shifts to the fifth, cadencing there," and thus provides us with a harmonically construed analysis of form, one that makes no "rules" for the position of the second harmonic area.[13] Koch provides a model for the creation of a sonata exposition based on the expansion of a relatively short melody that cadences

---

10 This is not to say that the switch into the parallel minor in Sammartini's works is endemic; far from it, since only a few symphonies actually create bridges to the dominant in this manner, the motion into the parallel minor being too overpowering a gesture. However, the very fact that the shift into the parallel minor was used at all, albeit infrequently, as a bridge to the dominant area, indicates that its function as a possible substitute for, or as an adjunct to, a dominant preparation was a viable alternative.

11 According to Hepokoski, an unachieved medial caesura is an attempted cadence that is not anchored by a complete harmonic progression in the new harmonic area; rather, the music is continuous until a formal cadence is finally achieved. See James Hepokoksi and Warren Darcy, "The Medial Caesura and its Role in the Eighteenth-Century Sonata Exposition," *Music Theory Spectrum*, 19/2 (Fall 1997): 115–54.

12 See Joel Lester, *Compositional Theory in the Eighteenth Century* (Cambridge, Massachusetts, 1992), pp. 284–99, and Heinrich Christoph Koch, *Introductory Essay on Composition*, trans. Nancy Baker, partial trans. of the *Versuch* (New Haven, 1983).

13 Lester, *Compositional Theory*, p. 294.

on the dominant. In his example, a five-measure G major opening statement is augmented by a five-measure extension ending with a half cadence in m. 10. The bridge begins with the upbeat to m. 11, immediately introducing C♯, the leading tone of D major. Later, D major will be secured as the structural dominant. The bridge is expanded over the course of most of the exposition and is not completed until the first note of m. 31. The material that is the remainder of m. 31 and all of m. 32 comprises a codetta, the concluding cadential phrase in the new harmonic area.

Two issues are important here: first, harmonically speaking, the structural dominant is not fully secured until the arrival of the codetta. Second, thematic contrast is simply not an issue in the organization of the form since the second harmonic area is not articulated thematically. Koch's models were Haydn's sonata-form movements (ultimately derived from Wagenseil and his contemporaries in Vienna), and this therefore may be the reason why his descriptions of the process are so generalized: the compositional variety of sonata-form movements composed in Vienna in the middle of the eighteenth century, including those of Wagenseil and Haydn (Koch also cites examples by C.P.E. Bach and other contemporary composers in his treatise) necessitates an inclusive approach rather than a systematic model. Koch's descriptions of principal ideas and subsidiary ideas did not *necessitate* the use of contrasting or lyrical thematic entities, and it was not an integral facet of Haydn's style. In fact, many of Koch's notions about the "Allegro," as he calls it, are found to be completely accurate when examining music by Haydn and his contemporaries. In Haydn's works, we will find that the issue of thematic contrast plays much less of a role than it does in the works of Mozart or Beethoven. Haydn was more inclined toward the use of innovative expansive procedures, which deliberately denied cadential fulfillment, to prolong tonic harmony, much after the manner of Wagenseil, and which often avoided thematic contrast altogether. However, Haydn's monothematic exposition designs did allow for intermediary cadences to set off sizable areas within what Koch defines as the "first period" (meaning the exposition) but contained little thematic contrast, at least by the standards of later nineteenth-century textbook models of sonata form. The lack of such contrast precludes the prevalent use of "themes" as a viable analytic strategy since all new material is essentially an extension, or variation, of previous material.

A notable exception to Wagenseil's general procedure occurs in the first movement of his C major Symphony WV 361 from 1757. In this work, Wagenseil's approach to the subdivision of the exposition may be compared to that of J.C. Bach's tripartite expositions, specifically, one period in the tonic and at least two in the dominant or relative major – a division that is also characteristic of the sonata expositions of Mozart and Beethoven. However, unlike those of J.C. Bach and his later contemporaries, Wagenseil's subdivisions of the second harmonic area are never emphatic; none of the formal periods are set off with articulated cadences, nor are the periods characterized by differing "topics," namely, characteristic figures that formed the bases of melody types associated with various feelings and affections and used in music discourse, in both vocal and instrumental forms, throughout the eighteenth century.[14] Thus Wagenseil still remains true to the basic style of thematic

---

14 See Ratner, *Classic Music*, pp. 9–30.

unity and continuity of period structure of his Baroque-era predecessors: one period simply moves into the other without a break in the rhythmic momentum. This often makes analytical judgments difficult as to where musical periods begin and end, a situation we will encounter again with Haydn's expositions, based, as they are, on Wagenseil's model.

In those of Wagenseil's expositions in which there is a discernable tripartite division of the second harmonic area, the beginning of each subarea is usually defined with a cadence on its dominant (albeit within continuous phrasing), and by an ever more emphatic metrical downbeat. The first period in the new harmonic area appears as a metrically weak period; in the first movement of the C major symphony it occurs in m. 22 (Example 5.5 shows the bridge and second key area of the exposition) and is articulated by a *forte* dynamic and an increased harmonic rhythm. This four-measure period reaches closure with an authentic cadence on the downbeat of m. 26 (thus, the medial caesura, although not set apart formally by a rest, is still one that has been successfully achieved). A transition passage follows, raising V/V (D pedal, mm. 30–33) and achieving another, stronger cadence in m. 34, again without a formal break achieved by a rest to articulate the new period. Here begins the eight-measure closing period, which, in turn, again raises the V/V in m. 40 in preparation for the final period, or codetta, of the exposition (mm. 41–5). Even though the dynamic marking is at first *piano* and then *forte*, the codetta occupies the strongest metrical position of the exposition. Throughout, the texture has been continuous; only changes in harmonic rhythm and thematic design, although rather slight, signal the start of new periods.

In terms of chromaticism, the entire exposition of this movement contains only two chromatic pitch classes, F♯ and G♯, and thus no modulation of system; Wagenseil saves the rest of the chromatic spectrum for the development, which begins in the usual manner for works of this period, with a restatement of the opening theme in the dominant. What is most interesting about Wagenseil's development is its harmonic scheme after the initial dominant. The G (V) simply moves up to A in m. 51 in preparation for a motion into ii, D minor, during which both C♯ and B♭ are introduced. After this, the next harmonic area is IV (F), usually the first goal of motion in a development section since IV serves to neutralize the previous dominant harmonic area and to prepare a return to tonic harmony at the end of the development (D minor, in this case, serves the same purpose since both D minor and F are subdominant functions). What happens next is surprising: the dominant of F, C major, turns into an Italian augmented sixth (m. 67), which drops down to B major as V/iii, forming the climactic point of the development as the whole harmonic progression switches violently into the minor mediant. In fact, E minor ends the development without any preparatory retransition on the dominant. The next formal gesture is the recapitulation in the tonic.

Example 5.5 Wagenseil, Symphony in C WV 361, first movement, bridge and second harmonic area (mm. 11–45)

**Example 5.5 Wagenseil, Symphony in C WV 361, first movement, bridge and
second harmonic area (mm. 11–45) continued**

Thus, Wagenseil has created a harmonic plan that stems directly from late Baroque concertos in which the penultimate ritornello was in iii (e.g., Bach's Brandenburg Concerto no. 2 has a similar organization; see the discussion in Chapter 4), the extreme point of the tonic hexachord, which necessitated a system shift up three signatures in the dominant direction. In Wagenseil's C major symphony, the switch into E minor introduces the sharp missing pitch of the "0" system, D♯, as leading tone. The cadence in iii (m. 74) upholds the 3♯ system, but the recapitulation in the next measure in the tonic, C, immediately redresses the system to "0." The importance of this gesture cannot be overestimated for it demonstrates how close in conception the symphony of the mid-eighteenth century was to the ritornello structures of its late Baroque predecessors. Perhaps even more importantly, this very gesture will recur at the ends of several first movements of Haydn's late symphonies, where the development climaxes on III (or iii) of the key only for it to be redressed at the start of the recapitulation.[15]

The works of Georg Matthias Monn (1717–1750) are also relevant to this study; Monn, too, was born and died in Vienna, where he was organist of the Karlskirche.[16] Just as Johann Stamitz was considered to be the leading musical figure in Mannheim, Wagenseil and Monn were deemed Stamitz's Viennese counterparts. Monn uses a sonata procedure that is, in some ways, more sophisticated than Wagenseil's, and yet still maintains some common features with his contemporary. The first movement of Monn's D major Symphony of 1740 is representative of his general stylistic traits.[17] In a small, 19-measure exposition (see Example 5.6), Monn establishes D major with a three-and-a-half-measure opening statement. The bridge, beginning in the middle of m. 4, begins to modulate in m. 6 with the introduction of G♯ and cadences on II♯ at the opening of m. 10. Monn's arrival at the second harmonic area is achieved differently from Wagenseil's since Wagenseil does not really anchor the new harmonic area until the codetta, and even that is metrically weak. Monn, however, cadences at the end of the bridge (on II♯) and begins a thematically contrasting harmonic area halfway through the exposition. It is a procedure that he uses in most of his other symphonies as well. Yet, m. 10 does not firmly define the new harmonic area since it is in the *minor dominant*. Initiation of the second harmonic area in the minor dominant is not an unusual occurrence in Viennese symphonies of this period; even Haydn was known to use this device in his early symphonies (for example, the expositions of the first movements of Haydn's symphonies nos 1, 2, and 4), and certainly Beethoven has numerous examples in his first-period works as well (for example, the first movement of his Piano Sonata in C major op. 2 no. 3 has a second harmonic area that begins in G minor).

---

15 See Channan Willner, "Chromaticism and the Mediant in Four Late Haydn Works," *Theory and Practice*, 13 (1988): 79–114. Willner's discussion is primarily analytical in the Schenkerian sense and does not conceive of Haydn's motion to III in any historical context. Therefore, the author does not connect Haydn's motion to the mediant to the late Baroque concerto, where the practice of placing the penultimate ritornello in iii is most common.

16 For biographical information on Monn, see Judith Leah Schwartz, "Monn, Matthias Georg," in Sadie and Tyrrell (eds), *The New Grove Dictionary of Music and Musicians*, 2nd edn, vol. 16, pp. 945–6.

17 Monn's symphonies can be found in an edition by Wilhelm Fischer, in *Denkmäler der Tonkunst in Österreich*, xxxix, Jahrgang xix/2 (Graz, 1912); also, a selection of Monn's symphonies are in *Five Monn Symphonies*, ed. Kenneth E. Rudolf, in Brook (editor-in-chief), *The Symphony 1720–1840*, ser. B, vol. 1 (New York, 1981).

Example 5.6 Monn, Symphony in D, first movement, exposition

Example 5.6 Monn, Symphony in D, first movement, exposition continued

It is quite possible that Domenico Scarlatti's keyboard sonatas of the 1730s and 1740s were influential with regard to the use of the minor dominant within a major-mode piece, since his works were well known throughout Europe in numerous editions. Scarlatti is famous for his musical portrayals of Spanish gypsy music in these one-movement sonatas, several of which have the initial period of their second harmonic area in the minor dominant (one of the most famous of these is his Sonata in D major K. 96). Invariably, the closing areas articulate the major dominant as in Viennese symphonies and other works later in the century.[18]

Historically, a composer's choice to begin the second harmonic area in the minor dominant can be seen as a further evolution of the older *pianoidée* technique to destabilize the first harmonic area in the tonic through the parallel minor, the modal switch initiating the bridge into the second harmonic area. But using the parallel minor to achieve tension also creates an instability so jolting that it can easily compromise the hegemony of the major tonic. (Incidentally, this may occur in both major and minor modes; for example, see Gluck's overture to his reform opera *Alceste* in D minor, with a second harmonic area in A minor and in 6/4 position (!), not to mention the most famous example, the minor relative area of the opening movement of Beethoven's Piano Sonata in C minor op. 13, "the Pathétique".)

Composers found that they could accomplish the same destabilizing effect of switching into the minor tonic as in a *pianoidée* by operating against the dominant, a harmony of lesser structural weight than the tonic. At the same time, the motion into the minor dominant invited a concomitant shift of system down three signatures, similar to the previous motion into the parallel tonic minor. The minor dominant, and its implication of flats, could easily introduce the missing pitch of the tonic system, the flat third degree. Even so, the motion into the minor dominant for the purpose of creating harmonic tension, with its subsequent release into the closing periods in the parallel major (along with the correction of system back to that of the tonic), had its own dramatic drawbacks, especially if the composer was looking to have the movement's climax occur in the development section. Perhaps even more importantly, the effect of moving into the parallel tonic or parallel dominant minor for an extended period could easily have become clichéd by sheer repetition from one piece to another. (Even Vivaldi's use of the *pianoidée*, though historically significant, does not appear very common when one considers his entire *oeuvre*.) Wagenseil's solution – introducing the flat third degree as an augmented sixth as a single verticality rather than as an extended melodic period to announce, as it were, the arrival of the structural dominant – was much more practical and definitely more contrapuntally convincing.

As indicated previously, the minor dominant period that initiates the second harmonic area in the first movement of Monn's D major symphony effectively delays

---

18 Not only keyboard sonatas of the 1730s use this device, but Italian *opera buffa* as well. One of the most popular and influential operas in the entire eighteenth century was Pergolesi's *La serva padrona* (1733), an intermezzo in two acts. The finale of Act I (a duet) features a move into the minor dominant (this is later recapitulated in the tonic minor); however, the passage in this instance appears *after* the major dominant has been achieved.

confirmation of the major dominant until the second half of m. 16, and is not fully secured with a root-position triad until m. 19, the last measure of the exposition. Thus the structural dominant occurs just before the double bar, a reminder of early eighteenth-century binary dance forms, which were still influential on sonata-form movements by Viennese composers well past the middle of the century.

Monn's Symphony in B major is atypical in some respects, yet is an excellent example of a piece that could have had a considerable impact on Haydn. In some respects, the procedure of delaying the dominant arrival is closer to Wagenseil's than that used by Monn in his own D major symphony. Aside from its use of an atypical tonic key, this symphony is also in triple meter, which was somewhat unusual but not unknown in early Viennese symphonies (although not so unusual in the first movements of symphonies by Haydn). Monn begins with a four-measure statement, which is answered by a four-measure counterstatement and followed by an eight-measure expansion of tonic harmony. A bridge begins in m. 16 and continues for another twelve measures, without securing the dominant cadence in F♯ major until m. 28, which coincides with the beginning of a four-measure codetta.

In summary, both Wagenseil and Monn delay any strong emphasis of the second harmonic area until the codetta of the exposition. In Wagenseil's symphonic works, such a scheme is accomplished either by avoiding a strong articulation of the dominant in first period or by delaying its arrival in the new harmonic area altogether through the expansion of the bridge; there is hardly a break in the texture of the exposition. Such a seamless quality allows one to hear the arrival of the second harmonic area as structurally delayed through an auxiliary cadence. Often in Monn's works, the dominant is presented in the minor mode initially (a possible influence from Scarlatti as mentioned above), usually with a concurrent thinning of the orchestration to a trio texture, not unlike the thinning of the texture typical of Vivaldi's *pianoidée* ritornello segments. However, in Monn's works, the initiation of the auxiliary cadence is sometimes announced by a bridge cadence and a rest before the harmonic change, a stylistic convention used by both Johann Stamitz in Mannheim and J.C. Bach in London, as well as by Leopold and Wolfgang Mozart in Salzburg. Both Wagenseil's and Monn's works are still very much in the earlier style of the slightly expanded binary form. Lastly, no matter how the missing pitch of the tonic system is introduced, either as a complete thematic statement in the minor dominant or as an augmented sixth to V, its introduction is always a dramatic event of some harmonic significance.

III. Joseph Haydn and the Sonata Form: Definitions and Compositional Design Elements[19]

With the multiplicity of design forms and analytical perspectives in what we call "sonata form," no standardized terminology has ever been established to describe it.

---

19 Some of the following discussion on sonata form is adapted or directly quoted from Roy Nitzberg, "Voice-Leading and Chromatic Techniques in Expositions of Selected Symphonies by Joseph Haydn, Introducing a New Theory of Chromatic Analysis," Ph.D. dissertation, City University of New York, 1999, ch. 3.

Composers and theorists of the eighteenth century never imposed labels on what is actually a procedure rather than a form; their conception usually dealt with harmonic periods, phrase extensions, and contrasting topics.[20] Our own approach to sonata form is basically harmonic, since form generally relies upon the construction of harmonic periods whose thematic content may or may not be of structural significance. After all, not every period is distinguished by a distinct melodic profile; many periods, including opening statements, contain motivic material that is more rhythmically than melodically active. Consequently, sonata analyses based on design elements (that is, analyses based solely upon formal areas governed by "themes") often conflict with sonata analyses based on harmonic areas, thus creating ambiguities and disagreements. For instance, in the symphonies of Wagenseil and Monn discussed previously, if one were to view the expositions of these works in purely melodic terms ("theme 1" and "theme 2" or "first and second theme groups", etc.), one would be hard pressed to find the second theme altogether. In fact, the only way in which one can make sense of the internal organization of such works is through an understanding of their harmonic periods articulated by cadential terminations, no matter how rhythmically weak they may be. The same holds true for Haydn, whose many sonata expositions often have little contrasting melodic material and whose phrase structure tends to be continuous.

Ambiguity of structure based on thematic organization is not limited to sonata expositions. Often, entire thematic areas in the recapitulation may be missing, as in any number of recapitulation areas in Haydn's monothematic compositions. Mozart, too, sometimes so "confuses" the placement of his thematic material in his development and recapitulations that harmonic-area examination is the only effective means to navigate analytically through these areas. The first movement of the Piano Sonata in D major K. 311/284c provides one of his most convoluted examples of a recapitulation in which the rotation of thematic events goes beyond the simple reverse recapitulations of the Mannheimers, the obvious influence for this sonata.[21] To fully understand a recapitulation of this kind, exclusively tracing thematic events could lead to a misinterpretation of the underlying form of the movement. Rather, a knowledge of where the large-scale harmonic periods are located within the recapitulation (along with their chromatic content and the resolution of dyad conflicts into tonic harmony) would yield the greatest degree of insight into

---

20 For an approach similar to ours that is more historically based, see Ratner, *Classic Music*. In addition, we acknowledge the writings of James Hepokoski in this area, particularly Hepokoski and Darcy, "The Medial Caesura," and Hepokoski, "Beyond the Sonata Principle," *Journal of the American Musicological Society*, 55/1 (2002): 91–154. For a comprehensive survey of contemporary eighteenth-century theory that includes material on the sonata, see Lester, *Compositional Theory*.

21 Reverse recapitulations are also common in J. C. Bach, who was also influenced by the Mannheim composers, and who in turn was influential upon Mozart's early work. J.C. Bach's Sinfonia op. 9 no. 2, for example, features a first-movement recapitulation that eliminates entire thematic sections of the exposition. See Eugene Wolf's seminal study *The Symphonies of Johan Stamitz: A Study in the Formation of the Classical Style* (Utrecht, Antwerp, The Hague, and Boston, 1981). Wolf includes detailed discussions of the early Classical style, the reverse recapitulation, and other relevant issues.

Mozart's reasoning for his thematic permutations. (See the analysis of this movement below.)

Of course, conflicts between thematic design and the structural harmonic background are not limited to the recapitulation. For example, an exposition's second harmonic area need not be initiated by the tonic of the new harmonic area as long as it cadences in that new area (that is, as long as is achieves a medial caesura). One often finds a second harmonic area beginning on the dominant of that new area, the first movement of Mozart's G minor Symphony K. 550 being a prime example: here, after a measure of silence (m. 43), the second harmonic area begins with an incomplete progression implying a cadential 6/4 moving to a fully realized V7/III (m. 45), the harmony of which is then extended until m. 51, where the cadential arrival to the relative major is finally achieved. A pedal on the V/V begins the second harmonic area in the first movement of Beethoven's Piano Sonata in F minor op. 2 no. 1; and an even more drastic example is the first movement of Beethoven's "Pathétique" Sonata in C minor op. 13, which has a second harmonic area that begins in E♭ minor, and on a 6/4 chord to boot. The major mediant (the expected harmony of the secondary area) is not firmly secured until the closing period is reached. C.P.E. Bach, whose symphonies are noted for their idiosyncratic harmonic schemes (thematic analysis will get you nowhere with these works!) goes so far as to start the second harmonic area of the first movement of his Symphony no. 1 in D major on the subdominant of the dominant! The main point is this: one of the consequences of so flexible a procedure such as this is that the rhythmic strength of the opening of the second harmonic area may be considerably weakened, causing the rhythmic downbeat of the secondary area to occur much later in the exposition.

In many situations, design analysis and structural analysis will differ as to their exact location of major compositional events, perhaps even more so in Haydn's expositions than in anyone else's. Composers probably enjoyed the compositional consequences of that kind of ambiguity, as, one hopes, did their audiences. Generally, the present authors will use terminology that is related to harmonic areas, for example, "first harmonic area" and "second harmonic area," as opposed to nomenclature that labels "themes" or even "groups." Diagram 5.3 gives a detailed plan of a "typical" sonata-form movement, complete with the terminology employed throughout this text. Each aspect of the form will then be explained in turn.

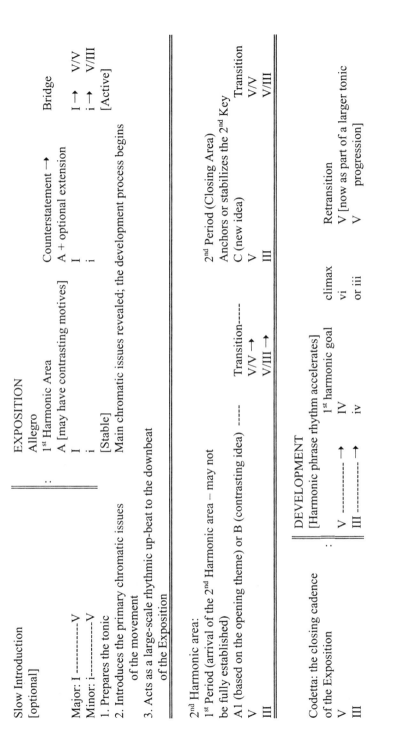

Diagram 5.3 Plan for the sonata allegro

RECAPITULATION [has the job of raising all the chromatic issues of the movement in order to resolve them into tonic harmony]

1st Harmonic Area	Bridge	2nd Harmonic Area (1st Period)	---- Transition ----	2nd Period (Closing)
A	veers towards	A1 or B		C
I	IV → V7	I	Subdominant side →V7	I (now anchors the tonic)
i	iv → V7	i or I		i or I

Transition ----→	Codetta	CODA [resolves all the chromatic issues of the movement into tonic harmony for the last time]
V	I	I
V	i or I	i or I

Diagram 5.3 Plan for the sonata allegro continued

The slow introduction embodies elements that the composer will use to launch a developmental and evolutionary course throughout the rest of the movement; usually, these tend to be rhythmic motives, chromatic conflicts, and/or striking harmonic relationships. Often, the issues created from these elements figure in other movements as well; in fact, the most notable gestures usually find no satisfactory resolution until the close of the last movement. Slow introductions, more often than not, will cadence on the dominant; in some cases, the slow introduction may end on a sonority directed toward the dominant, such as an augmented sixth or diminished seventh chord. The slow introduction of Haydn's Symphony no. 92, the "Oxford," ends on an augmented sixth chord that resolves – in a rather untraditional manner – to a dominant seventh chord, which opens the G major Allegro.

A slow introduction permits a *piano* dynamic level for the opening of the exposition because the slow introduction often begins with a tonic unison or chord played *forte*. When the introduction itself begins *piano*, there is invariably a *forte* climax at some point within the introduction, supported by dissonant harmony. The dissonant tension raised within the introduction now allows for the dissonance to carry over into the exposition as composers attempt to blur the boundaries between the two sections. A *piano* start to the exposition has the effect of maintaining the previous dissonance, the lower dynamic militating against any sense of an emphatic downbeat resolution. The "Oxford" Symphony, for example, has an internal *forte* climax within the slow introduction that is supported by an extremely dissonant build-up, which is maintained into the *piano* opening of the exposition. Historically, the slow introduction replaces the standard *forte* fanfare that usually initiates the Allegro in a symphony without a slow introduction. Beethoven's "Eroica" compresses both events: introduction and fanfare are conflated into a single two-chord gesture.

Following the slow introduction, assuming that one exists, the exposition proper begins. The opening statement may take different forms; but, no matter how it is arranged, it establishes and stabilizes the tonic. The first harmonic area contains all the material in the tonic up to the beginning of the bridge (bridge elements are defined below). Two major categories of eighteenth-century exposition types determine the nature of the opening statement: one is derived from the symmetrical and periodic phrase structure typical of the *style galant*, while the other is based on the motivic segmentation of the late Baroque concerto.

The first kind of opening statement, one that uses an antecedent–consequent construction or a variant of it,[22] is derived from the periodic phrasing of the *style galant*, itself heavily indebted to the dance; these types are characterized by one or more four-measure phrases (often coalescing into eight-measure periods) that may or may not have rhythmic extensions. This type of opening statement is conceived

---

22 The formal definition of an antecedent–consequent eight-measure period is one that is subdivided into two four-measure subphrases, where the first moves to the dominant and the second "answers" the first by completing its harmonic progression through a return to the tonic. Naturally, there are many variants of this, including consequent phrases that do not end on the tonic, but on the dominant or a dominant-related harmony. In this study, we are concerned only with the fact that this melody type is constructed of even phrases as opposed to the separated motives of ritornello-derived melodic types that are unequal in phrase length.

as rhythmically stable. The Allegro of Haydn's Symphony no. 73 (all references to works in this section are to first movements, unless specified otherwise) opens with such a statement: a four-measure phrase is succeeded by another four-measure phrase whose motivic content is totally dependent upon the first phrase. The ninth measure of the Allegro initiates a new subsection. Mozart's Symphony no. 29 in A major is also of this type, but the use of phrase extensions and insertions creates idiosyncratic measure groupings. However, they, too, are ultimately derived from a fundamental eight-measure regularity. Beethoven's Symphony no. 1 in C is similar to the Mozart example: a six-measure phrase, derived from a basic four-measure unit, is succeeded by another six-measure phrase, also an extension of four-measure regularity.

The second kind of opening statement tends toward asymmetrical phrase grouping and is derived from the typical tripartite structure of the ritornello theme of a Baroque concerto (*Vordersatz, Fortspinnung, Epilog*). The three parts contrast both motivically and in harmonic function and are rhythmically irregular, that is, they each have different numbers of measures. Very often, the Classical variant of the opening phrase (a historical product of the *Vordersatz*) has a short, fanfare-like quality. This phrase is generally succeeded either by a lengthier, more lyrical phrase, played *piano*, or one which tends to contain a crescendo (often over a static pedal bass, in the style of the Mannheim symphonists) that connects the opening motivic material to the cadential *Epilog*; either way, this intermediary phrase is further differentiated from the first phrase by various thematic or motivic material that remains within tonic harmony. In this way, the second phrase differs from the harmonically active and sequential Baroque-era ritornello *Fortspinnung*. The last phrase, like the *Epilog* of the ritornello, is relatively short and secures the cadence, either full or half, dramatizing the event with a full orchestra *forte* – often referred to as an "orchestral tutti." An orchestral tutti can also cap off, or punctuate, an opening statement that is antecedent–consequent in design, especially if the theme is played *piano* throughout. Such is the case with Mozart's Symphony no. 39 in E♭ K. 543: the Allegro opening theme begins with an eight-measure period divided into two four-measure antecedent–consequent phrases ending on tonic harmony (last beat of m. 33). The period is extended for a further seven measures before the entire theme is repeated in a varied counterstatement, which too closes on tonic harmony in m. 54. All the while the dynamic has remained *piano*, and only now, in m. 54, does the full orchestra enter with an orchestral tutti played *forte*. This extensive passage, characteristic of all orchestral tuttis, prolongs tonic harmony with contrasting material until the perfect authentic cadence on the tonic (the last of the opening tonic periods) in m. 71 initiates the formal bridge to the second harmonic area. Both orchestral tutti and bridge maintain the *forte* dynamic throughout.

From the above discussion, one could conclude that the placement of orchestral tuttis varies from piece to piece and makes it impossible to fashion a general statement about the relationship between orchestral texture and form. However, upon a closer examination of any number of Classical sonata-form expositions, it would seem that the majority of orchestral tuttis are used to cap, or rather, cadentially close off in the manner of a ritornello *Epilog*, opening *piano* statements that are themselves based on the contrasting melodic/rhythmic segments inherent in ritornello thematic designs;

such is the case in Haydn's Symphony no. 92. It is interesting, nonetheless, that the Symphonies no. 83 and no. 87 in Haydn's Paris set both extend their opening tonic statements as orchestral tuttis, in one unbroken period, right into their respective bridges. Symphony no. 83 maintains an orchestral tutti until the dominant of the new harmonic area is reached in m. 41. Here, only the strings continue, creating a strong contrast between the two large periods of the exposition and paralleling the contrasting harmonic areas. Symphony no. 87 maintains the orchestral tutti until m. 25, which is already within the bridge.

The opening statement of the first movement of Haydn's Symphony no. 87 is an example of the segmented theme type: an opening fanfare-like five-measure phrase is followed by four measures that connect directly to a three-measure close on the tonic. The last measure of the third group is elided to a four-measure phrase and another three-measure phrase afterwards; together, they repeat the second two phrases of the opening statement. The first movements of Mozart's Symphonies no. 39 and no. 41 ("the Jupiter") and Beethoven's Symphony no. 5 are also of this type.

After the opening statement, whether periodic or motivic/segmented, will follow a counterstatement or counterstatement/bridge; that is, a bridge that is initiated by a functional counterstatement. A counterstatement begins as a restatement of the opening theme (the amount of restatement is, of course, up to the composer, but the gamut runs from a simple restatement of the opening measure of the initial statement to a full restatement). Most often, the counterstatement will be open-ended, consisting only of a partial statement of the opening theme, and will, consequently, elide directly into the bridge period. If a symphony opens with an antecedent–consequent construction, in which the consequent phrase ends on tonic harmony and there is no extension that leads to a dominant, no counterstatement is likely to follow and a bridge will begin after the cadence of the opening statement. It should be noted that a counterstatement is a frequent though not indispensable part of an exposition: for example, Haydn's Symphonies no. 86 and no. 87 have expositions with extended opening statements that move directly into bridges without counterstatements.

The frequent use of a slow introduction in Haydn's Paris and London symphonies virtually mandates a *piano* opening for the Allegro and therefore obviates the use of the ritornello opening statement as a feasible option. In Haydn's Paris symphonies, four are of the ritornello-type (nos 82, 83, 87, and 89), and none begins with a slow introduction. The presence or absence of a slow introduction, then, affects the phrase rhythm of the entire movement.

If the security of even phrasing at the opening of a dance-type allegro is necessary to balance the often erratic rhythmic organization of the slow introduction, then succeeding portions of the exposition will abandon regularity to maintain a high level of rhythmic interest. This brings us once more to the counterstatement. As mentioned before, this formal element, if it exists in the movement, repeats the material of the opening statement. This time, the material is presented not to anchor the tonic, but to provide a springboard away from it. The counterstatement may be an autonomous restatement, as it is in Haydn's symphonies nos 84, 85, and 88, or it may appear *to start* as a restatement of the opening material, functionally becoming the bridge, as it does in the first movement of Mozart's Symphony no. 40. In that case, tonic harmony is soon destabilized and developmental material is introduced that no longer parallels the opening statement; this is usually accomplished chromatically. If the latter occurs, as it does in Haydn's Symphony no. 92, then the counterstatement is transformed into the bridge period, the next formal area of the exposition. In a recapitulation, where the movement's exposition contains both a statement and a counterstatement, one often finds that either the counterstatement is deleted altogether or the recapitulation *begins* at the counterstatement (a favorite device of both Beethoven and Brahms); both designs result in a deliberate tightening of the phrase rhythm.

Either the bridge is initiated by the counterstatement (as discussed above) or it begins with an orchestral tutti. In either case, the bridge forms a complete period of its own: it begins on tonic harmony and cadences at the arrival of the second harmonic area, the next significant exposition event. Thus the bridge serves to connect the material of the opening tonic to that of the second harmonic area. There are no rules governing the organization of a bridge other than that its departure is typically within the realm of tonic harmony. Many bridges conclude with back-relating dominants in the manner of Domenico Scarlatti's keyboard sonatas; the symphonies of both J.C. and C.P.E. Bach are of this type. These have been referred to as "bifocal close" bridges and act as simple extension devices; they are also quite common in both Mozart's and Haydn's piano sonatas.[23] Examples include *all* Mozart's early piano sonatas from 1774–55 (K. 279–81/186d–f and K. 283/189e and 284/205b) plus the formally unusual C major Sonata K. 545, with its subdominant recapitulation in the first movement, and the F major Sonata K. a136/547a, both from 1788. Mozart's late-period monothematic Piano Sonata in D major K. 576, from 1789, also employs a bifocal close of the bridge. An example of Haydn's use of a bridge with a bifocal close in a piano sonata is the well-known Sonata in D major Hob. XVI/37 from around 1780 (or earlier); on the whole, a good proportion of Haydn's piano sonatas from the 1760s, those in sonata form (some are Scarlatti-style binary-form first movements), use the bifocal close.

Historically, as bridges became more elaborate and extensive, their function was to destabilize tonic harmony rather than to extend it (notable exceptions in the nineteenth century are several important works of Schubert in which the bridge is an extension of tonic harmonic; see Chapter 6). Although a destabilizing bridge may also cadence on the dominant, that kind of dominant, preceded by its own dominant (II♯–V), is a preparation for the second harmonic area. The cadential goal of a destabilizing bridge points forwards toward the new area, not backwards. Therefore, a destabilizing bridge may cadence on V or II♯ (in major mode); in the first case, it will be preceded by its own dominant, which differentiates it from the bifocal close. Even elaborate expositions, however, will occasion back-relating bridges; this happens in Haydn's atypical Symphony no. 91 in E♭, which, incidentally, is the only

---

23 A back-relating dominant is one whose structural allegiance is to the preceding harmonic material, not to that which follows. For example, in Mozart's Symphony no. 25 in G minor, the second harmonic area is in B♭ major. This is preceded by a D major triad at the end of the bridge, a sonority that "back-relates" to the opening tonic. See Robert Winter, "The Bifocal Close and the Evolution of the Viennese Classical Style," *Journal of the American Musicological Society*, 42 (1989): 275–337.

one in the Paris group to have an opening statement that is a textbook example of an antecedent–consequent period.

A bridge may be framed by a substantial auxiliary cadence; that is, the auxiliary cadence begins with the establishment of tonic harmony and continues to the augmented sixth chord and its resolution, thus "framing" the bridge. Since an auxiliary cadence is often initiated by rhythmically weak and harmonically unstable material that precedes it, especially if the movement begins with a slow introduction, the process of its unfolding and eventual resolution creates increasing tonal stability over its course as it moves, little by little, toward the harmonic security of the second harmonic area. As a result, bridges tend to be "dominant-heavy." At the point where the exposition reaches II♯, the preparation for the second harmonic area has already begun; this cadence will signal the end of the bridge. Therefore, bridges that gradually undermine the stability of the tonic must concurrently rationalize motion toward a secondary tonal area. During this process, the tonic appears to exist in a state of flux while the center of tonal gravity gradually shifts away from the tonic and toward a new tonal center, an area of stabilized dissonance.

Through irregular phrase rhythm and expansive/developmental thematic devices, Haydn is unique among his contemporaries for frequently creating expectations of reaching the new harmonic area while very often undermining those expectations through the continuation of bridge material (for example, the first movements of Haydn's String Quartet op. 33 no. 2 and Symphony no. 92). In this way, the attempt to create a stable environment for the new harmonic area is, itself, continually destabilized, and even temporarily derailed. Therefore, extensive tonic-destabilizing bridges are a cornerstone of Haydn's style.

All bridges are not created equal: whereas an exposition bridge generally destabilizes tonic harmony, a recapitulation bridge is calculated initially to destabilize, but ultimately to secure tonic harmony upon its arrival at the recapitulation of the exposition's second harmonic area. A recapitulation bridge will generally cadence on the dominant, and the succeeding music that parallels the opening statement of the second harmonic area in the exposition will be restated in the tonic. The material before this bridge cadence often moves toward the subdominant to avoid motion into a new harmonic area and, of course, to allow the possibility for the bridge to use the same melodic material as it did for the earlier bridge in the exposition. Therefore, the cadence on V is clearly understood within the context of the reiterated tonic.

Although it is possible for an exposition bridge to fuse with the structural dominant (as discussed below), it is more common for the bridge to cadence on the dominant of the dominant, or the dominant of the mediant in a minor-key first movement, as in Mozart's Symphony no. 40 in G minor.[24]

---

24 As mentioned above, in Mozart's other G minor symphony, no. 25 from 1773, the exposition bridge relates back to the opening tonic, cadencing on the dominant. This is typical of *Sturm und Drang* works where the mediant enters immediately and almost unceremoniously after the bridge cadence. Haydn's Symphony no. 39 in G minor of 1770 uses the same chordal organization. Both symphonies in G minor are scored for oboes, bassoons, four horns, and strings.

If one considers the first harmonic area and its opening statement to be the first stable period of the exposition, the second harmonic area begins with the next stable period, though this is less harmonically stable than the first. As indicated above, the second harmonic area is generally preceded by a bridge cadence. The opening statement of the second harmonic area may or may not have an *obvious* thematic relationship to material within the opening statement, but some kind of relationship generally exists. That relationship may be rhythmic, intervallic/melodic, or harmonic, even when thematic contrast is prominent. By the end of the Classical era, the material of the second harmonic area was often characterized by conspicuous thematic contrast with the material of the first harmonic area, even though strong thematic differentiation was never an obligatory aspect of sonata construction. For example, Haydn's monothematic expositions contributed more than anyone else's to this very legitimate strategy, while Mozart's thematic multiplicity, ultimately operatic in conception, undoubtedly influenced the trend toward more thematic contrast between structural harmonic areas. It was not until the nineteenth century that thematic contrast became a formulaic imperative, no doubt under the overwhelming influence of Beethoven, who adopted Mozart's use of thematic contrast in his expositions.

Since Haydn often assigns the strongest rhythmic underpinning to the closing period or even to the codetta, one may not hear the initial statement of the second harmonic area as a strongly articulated event. In fact, the variety of structural types in symphonic second harmonic areas is at least as abundant as the variety of bridge types. It is common for Mozart and Beethoven to have three periods subsumed under the region of a prolonged dominant period (or mediant period in a minor-mode symphony). The first period initiates the new harmonic area with its own statement. The second period within the second key is the closing period (see Diagram 5.3). Very often, the new harmony is stabilized and rhythmically anchored at this point.[25] The third period, the codetta, is usually quite a bit shorter than the first two. Like the *Epilog* of a ritornello theme, it has the purpose of furnishing a stable area for the articulation of the final cadence of the exposition. If no closing period exists, then the codetta will assume the function of anchoring, instead of confirming, the second harmonic area. Each of these three periods must contain a complete harmonic progression that is autonomous and concludes with a full cadence, in order to validate its autonomy.

Haydn, however, sometimes creates a two-period second harmonic area by omitting a closing period. For example, his Symphony no. 89 in F has an opening statement complete with an autonomous counterstatement followed by a bridge

---

25 Sometimes one may find multiple closings ending the exposition, a characteristic of Mozart's sonata-form movements as well as of those of many nineteenth-century composers. The number of closing periods depends on the number of formal cadences that are arrived at after the second harmonic area has been achieved and before the exposition formally ends with a codetta (in later nineteenth-century sonata-form movements, for instance in the works of Brahms, an actual authentic cadence is not always necessary, nor even desired). Even with a formal authentic cadence the period that follows must be harmonically complete, or else the cadence is nullified and the entire passage is still perceived as part of a larger transition.

period, which cadences on V/V. The second harmonic area begins normally enough with a complete progression in the dominant, C major, followed by a counterstatement leading into an unstable transitional passage which cadences three measures before the end of the exposition. These last three measures form a short codetta without any intervening closing period. Symphony no. 83 is similar: after the arrival in B♭ major (the relative major of the tonic, G minor) there is a statement followed by an autonomous counterstatement elided to a five-measure transition before a five-measure codetta ends the exposition. Again, as in Symphony no. 89, there is no closing period.

Sonata procedure does not require a specific amount of thematic material or a specific number of periods to elaborate the second harmonic area: as long as the structural dominant is articulated by at least a codetta, that is sufficient to secure the new harmonic area. Haydn's Symphony no. 73 is a drastic example of a bridge period moving directly into a codetta, a three-measure *Epilog*, which is the only elaboration of the secured structural dominant. Haydn's curtailment of the second harmonic area by eliminating one or more periods creates a heretofore unrecognized category of monothematicism, not previously discussed in the literature, where only one strand of thematic material is employed in the continuous unfolding of the exposition up to the codetta. We have already seen an analogous but far more rudimentary procedure used by Wagenseil, whose approach to sonata was still very much affected by the tradition of Baroque binary form. When the structural dominant is reached – after a relatively extensive bridge designed to continually raise the specter of dominant harmony – it is elaborated only by a short codetta, and the exposition ends.

By contrast, if we examine Mozart's Piano Sonata in B♭ major K. 333/315c (whose chromaticism is analyzed below), we find a rather extensive second harmonic area articulated by four periods. Here, the opening statement of the dominant is succeeded by a full counterstatement and cadence. The second full period of the second harmonic area is the closing period. The closing period enters in m. 38 and is itself two subperiods long; the first cadences in m. 50 and is succeeded by another with "new" thematic material that cadences in m. 59. Therefore, this sonata has a two-part closing period; in larger pieces, there may be multiple closing periods. For example, Mozart's "Paris" Symphony in D major, no. 31 (K. 297/300a), doubles each structural event of the exposition.

If a recapitulation closely emulates the exposition, those areas which parallel the formal demarcations of the exposition, using the same thematic content, but now transposed into the tonic, are called by the same name (see Diagram 5.3); thus, a recapitulation may also have a closing period (or periods) and even a codetta. It is not essential to the form that a sonata movement include a coda. In fact, the codetta itself may be omitted in the recapitulation if the coda displaces the former's rhythmic position. The main purpose of the recapitulation, as we will see in the detailed analyses that follow, is to resolve the main issues (often chromatic issues) of the movement into tonic harmony. These chromatic events, whether dyad conflicts or trichords, or both, which have been developed from the beginning of the movement, now need to resolve to their respective diatonic neighbors within progressions that cadence on tonic harmony. This is the primary reason, we believe, why composers need not recapitulate all the material from the respective expositions; however, as we will see, the thematic content of the exposition often embeds within it the seeds of these resolutions, which become apparent only when recapitulated in the tonic at the end of the movement. Aspects of the "development section" will be dealt with separately as we investigate individual compositions in the next section.

Lastly, perhaps the most important issue to keep in mind when addressing these design concepts is this: Classical-era composers did not follow any rule books, nor did they have any formalized procedural guidelines to follow. Whatever procedures were adopted were reported later by Classical-era theorists, such as Koch and Kollmann, who utilized Haydn's symphonies as paradigms for discussions about composition in their treatises. These discussions were based on very general descriptions of large periods and the harmonic rationale of cadence points. The ontological problem with finely detailed labels is that composers were probably not thinking about these forms with these minute categories. Today, however, we usually consider analysis that involves extensive descriptions of formal divisions and subdivisions to be essential for a complete understanding of a musical work and of its stylistic context.

IV. Joseph Haydn and the Developmental Process: Selected Compositions

Without a doubt, Haydn's string quartets, next to his late symphonies, represent his most important contribution to the mature Classical style of the late eighteenth century. For the purpose of our discussion, Haydn's op. 33 quartets contain practically every idiosyncracy of his compositional technique and, therefore, a discussion of these works would be most profitable. Haydn himself realized the importance of these quartets since he advertised the op. 33 set as "brand-new quartets ... written in a new and special way, for I have not composed any for ten years." A particularly significant aspect of the sonata-form movements of these works is Haydn's proclivity toward monothematicism. That is, an entire movement is based on a single idea, although some contrasting thematic material may appear on a more superficial level. Haydn constructs two types of monothematic movement (see Diagram 5.4): the first (type A) is characterized by a continuous bridge that does not cadence in the new key until the last minute. In this type of monothematic construction, the bridge extends a single motivic idea that is first presented in the opening tonic statement, but now within an unstable harmonic context, and delays the arrival at the second harmonic area through elaboration and development of this idea until a full cadence is reached – usually at the codetta or short closing period (where some secondary thematic material may be found). The second type (type B) is the one we usually associate with the term "monothematic;" that is, the second harmonic area is arrived at with a medial caesura and further articulated with a rest, but the thematic material is a transposition of the opening statement now in the dominant.

Type A: characterized by a continuous bridge that does not cadence in the new key until the last minute

1st Harmonic Area	Bridge →	[2nd Harmonic Area]
Counterstatement	continues past its normal point of arrival	Short Closing + Codetta
A ------- A + extension -----cadences in I (i)	[V or III is raised but not confirmed]	
I		V V
i		III III

Type B: characterized by a normal arrival to the second key area, but without a contrasting theme to articulate it

1st Harmonic Area	Bridge	2nd Harmonic Area		
Counterstatement		(1st period)		(2nd period)
A ------- A + extension -----cadences in I (i)		A or A¹	transition →	Closing − trans. − Codetta
I	I → V/V	V	V/V	V V
i	I → V/III	III	V/III	III III

Diagram 5.4 Monothematic exposition types

Haydn's String Quartet in E♭ op. 33 no. 2 (the "Joke") is an example of a type-A monothematic exposition (see Example 5.7) in which there is a feigned medial caesura, but the bridge cadence is not achieved until the codetta, four measures before the end. Since the entire first movement of this quartet will be analyzed, several diagrams need to be constructed in order to comprehend fully the interesting development of its pitch material. The first to be drawn is the E♭ system hexachord of the quartet, which can help clarify the important relationship between the tonic, E♭, and C minor, the submediant (the two harmonies are symmetrically related). In addition is the role of A♭, which also supports C as a pitch class:

A♭–	E♭–	B♭–	f –	c –	g	F♯ (shifts the system up to "0")
IV	I	V	ii	vi	iii	D
						V/iii

The seminal relationship of E♭ and C, both as harmony and as individual pitch classes, is already revealed in the opening measures of the quartet (mm. 3–4), where C becomes the focal point of a linear trichord: B♭–B♮–C (the C is first heard within the context of the subdominant, A♭, before being reinterpreted as a root in its own right). This trichord becomes motivic in the sense that this configuration of pitch classes informs the entire movement. As such, this particular trichord becomes the source of a complex developmental process that involves the relationship of the individual pitch classes of the trichord to one another against varying harmonic backgrounds, their transpositions, and, finally, as a harmonic progression leading to C minor. In this way, what initially is heard as a foreground chromatic melodic event in the first violin seeps ever deeper into the harmonic fabric of the movement, controlling its large-scale harmonic direction, especially in the development section, where vi becomes the primary goal of motion, the "development key" – a term referring to the primary harmonic area of a development section (not all developments have "development keys").

The B♭–B♮–C trichord occupies a specific position within the chromatic tonic octave of E♭ as pcs 7, 8 and 9 of the PCA. This is the entire PCA with the seminal trichord shown in boldface:

E♭	E♮→ F	**F♯/G♭**	G	A♭	A♮→ **B♭**	**B♮**	**C**	C♯	D
0	1	**2**	**3**	4	5	6	**7**	**8**	**9**	10	11
I					V		vi		

Likewise in boldface is pc 3, in both enharmonic spellings, since both pitch classes will play important roles in the chromatic development of the movement whenever they are introduced. In addition, the above diagram shows the partitioning of the PCA into trichordal segments, each supporting the background harmonic structure of the movement, although these trichords may support middleground harmonic progressions as well.

Example 5.7 Haydn, String Quartet in E♭ op. 33 no. 2, first movement, exposition

Example 5.7 Haydn, String Quartet in E♭ op. 33 no. 2, first movement, exposition continued

Diagram 5.5 gives an overview of the design of the first movement of op. 33 no. 2. What is of significance to us is how Haydn has extrapolated a chromatic segment from the PCA, namely, pcs 7, 8, and 9, as a primary source of development. At first the trichord is presented as an unassuming chromatic inflection in the first violin (mm. 2–3), Haydn preferring to concentrate instead on expanding, over the course of the opening eight-measure period, the sixteenth-note upbeat figure that begins the first phrase (see Example 5.8). The intensification of this figure in m. 7 propels the phrase into its counterstatement in m. 9, at which point the trichord re-enters and begins to assume an ever more dominating role as the bridge period progresses.

The manner in which the trichord is embedded within the contrapuntal texture as the bridge moves into vi (C minor) is most interesting. Beginning with the upbeat to m. 13, the first violin initiates the phrase with a sixteenth-note B♭ that ultimately moves to B♮ on the last eighth note in m. 13 and which, in turn, moves to C on the downbeat of m. 14 as part of C minor harmony. At the same time, the second violin in m. 13 starts its phrase with a downbeat B♭, which proceeds to B♮ on the second beat of the measure. The two violins now duplicate the motion from B♮ to C as a unison on the downbeat of the next measure, effectively collapsing their contrapuntal duet into heterophony (the imitative texture in the viola and cello disguises the parallelism) and thus punctuating the linear progress of the trichord over these measures. The motion to C minor in the bridge now prepares for the same gesture, which becomes the climax of the development section.

Type A Monothematic Exposition

1st Harmonic Area

Opening statement is an 8-measure period (4 + 4) which introduces the main trichord
issue of the quartet: **Bb – Bh – C**

Eb (1st 4 mm. form a complete tonic progression) ---   Eb (2nd 4 mm. extend the 1st 4 mm.)

I   -----   IV   -----   V   I   I ----------------------------V

Counterstatement leads into a Bridge   Attempted Medial caesura (remains unachieved) --
                                                      becomes an extension of the bridge

[Bb – Bh –   C]

Eb — Bh o7 —   cm — F   Bb

I   vi   II#   V (the dominant cadence is harmonically and rhythmically weak)

Codetta

1st violin plays **Bb – Bh – C** over
the final cadential progression

Finally achieves
cadential closure

F   Bb (1st full progression in V)

V/V   V

Restarts the progression
--------------V 6/4

Development   **Real Recapitulation**
                                                1st Harmonic Area ----

   1st goal   False recap.

                    [**Bb** ---- **Bh** — **C** — **Bh** — **Bb**]

:Bb —   Ab   fm — Ab aug.6→G cm   Bb   Eb

V   IV   ii   vi   V   I

                              Codetta

Bridge is greatly extended
Bb — Bh — C trichord is now resolved into tonic harmony

          Eb

          I

Diagram 5.5 Haydn, String Quartet in Eb op. 33 no. 2, first movement

To refer to Diagram 5.5 above, the entrance into the dominant in m. 21 is undercut as no complete period in V follows; instead, Haydn continuously avoids closure through a number of evasive harmonic gestures until the medial caesura is finally achieved in m. 28; this secures the dominant and initiates a four-measure codetta ending the exposition. The entire passage leading up to the codetta (mm. 21–8) is intensified by the start of the PCA, whose ascending chromatic pitch classes steadily climb up to pc 7 (B♭) at the arrival of the dominant cadence. Significantly, Haydn ends the exposition with a dramatic restatement of the trichord in the first violin (mm. 30–32). The B♭ appears on the third beat of m. 30 and is sustained until the very end of m. 31, where it ascends to B♮ and C, the latter pitch being an anticipation of its formal arrival on the downbeat of m. 32. Since the exposition must cadence on the dominant, B♮ reverts to B♭ at the end of the period. Only now, when the exposition is repeated, do we realize the importance of this trichord, heard again embedded within the opening theme! We also realize that the upbeat figure of two sixteenths and an eighth that pervades the entire exposition from the opening statement of the movement, and is now restated as the thematic material of the codetta, governs the monothematic design of the exposition: the codetta has the function of linking the end of the exposition to its beginning. After examining the details of Classical-period works, we may safely draw the conclusion that most – if not all – Classically designed expositions that conclude with a repeat sign are "circular" in the sense that the end of the exposition connects, either rhythmically or through chromatic issues, or both, to the opening tonic statement: thus the end of the exposition often defines the seminal elements presented at the beginning of the movement. For this reason alone, repeats must be taken in this repertory in order for the listener (as well as the performer, incidentally) to understand fully the internal developmental process.

Using Haydn's quartet as exemplar, it may now be beneficial to review the primary characteristics of the PCA, particularly in relation to sonata-form movements. In most music that is based on an octave species and that centers on a tonic, be it a modal final or a concluding tonic triad, composers have sought to define their tonal compositions through the interaction of the diatonic with that of the chromatic; that is, they have sought to unfold both the diatonic and chromatic octaves over the course of the movement. These octaves are purely linear and are therefore contrapuntal in nature: the pitch classes of the diatonic octave (which we have labeled the *Primary Diatonic Array*, or PDA) descend from the tonic pitch, from *do* down to *re,* and the pitch classes of the chromatic octave (the PCA) tend to ascend from *do* to *ti.* These two descending and ascending octaves coincide at structurally significant harmonically constructed cadence points within the movement. For example, in sonata form, a form driven harmonically, the pitch classes of both the PCA and the PDA are partitioned over each subdivision of the form. In the major mode, the rise of PCA pcs 0–7 articulates the motion from the tonic to the dominant, with each arrival to the next structural cadence within the dominant area – the first period in the second harmonic area, the second or closing period, and the codetta (not all of these sections need be present within any given sonata movement) – replicating the same 0–7 ascent. In addition, the first PCA unfolding from pc 0 to pc 7 will often have pitch classes missing, which are then filled in with successive restatements within the second harmonic area.

In the first movement of Haydn's op. 33 no. 2 quartet discussed above, the first PCA ascent begins in m. 15 with the first violin's E♭ at the end of the measure as pc 0. In the same melodic line, E♭ climbs up to E♮ (pc 1) on the third beat of m. 16 and then to F (pc 2) on the downbeat of the next measure. By initiating this first PCA rise as he does, Haydn cleverly instills the expectation that the linear chromatic ascent to pc 7 will coincide with the arrival of the first period of the second harmonic area somewhere in the middle of the exposition. Pcs 2, 3, and 4 (it is unnecessary to unfold pc 5, A♭, at this point since it is a diatonic pitch class that has been unequivocally stated and has already been displaced by pc 6, A♮) are presented in short order in m. 19. The "attempted" medial caesura in mm. 21–2 brings in the last two pitch classes of the initial rise, 6 (A♮) and 7 (B♭), and this is intensified by the permutations of the seminal trichord in the inner parts in these same measures. But all this elaborate display is simply a ruse, for the dominant arrival is not confirmed at all; instead, Haydn moves off the dominant triad, and raises a cadential 6/4 on the downbeat of m. 25 in preparation for the true structural dominant.

A second PCA rise ensues, this one the more structurally significant of the two, since it dramatizes the progression to the structural dominant in m. 28. This second ascent begins in m. 22, again in the first violin, with pc 0 (E♭); this yields its place to pc 1 (E♮) in m. 23, which naturally moves up to pc 2 (F♮) on the last beat of m. 23. Measure 24 has pcs 3 (F♯) and 4 (G), and temporarily moves up to pcs 6 (A♮) and 7 (B♭), but these last two pitch classes are not yet structurally significant since the cadence has not yet been reached or confirmed. Haydn further intensifies this second, more significant ascent by replicating pcs 0–2 in the cello in mm. 24–5, in counterpoint with the unfolding of pcs 3 and 4 in the first violin (m. 24) above it. These same pcs (0–2) are then inverted in the first violin in m. 26, giving greater weight to this second rise of the PCA (composers will often manipulate or develop segments of the PCA as individual trichords before moving to the next pitch classes in the series). The first violin restates F♯ (pc 3) at the end of the measure as well as pc 4 (G) on the downbeat of m. 27. Again, there is no pc 5 (A♭) since this is a diatonic pitch and is redundant in our understanding of the rising chromatic unfolding. Pcs 6 (A♮) and 7 (B♭) now reach completion in the second violin at the cadence on the third beat of m. 28. Note that above the second violin's completion of this segment of the PCA, the first violin has the last pitch classes of the PDA (C, with a trill, moving down to B♭).

Once the dominant arrival has been confirmed, the PCA may be reiterated from pc 0. Within a sonata exposition, the second harmonic area defines the limits of the first segment of both PCA and PDA. Thus in major mode, if the second harmonic area is in the dominant, then the PCA will go no further than pc 7. In minor, the relative major is the goal and the PCA will go no further than pc 3. The remainder of the series (pcs 8–11) will find their completion in the development, with pc 0 returning at the point of recapitulation. In Haydn's E♭ major quartet, the codetta is so short that only a partial restatement of the line to pc 7 is possible, a not uncommon occurrence in this music. However, it is notable that A♭, pc 5, missing from the first rise of the PCA, is now present: the viola's pc 4 (G) in m. 31 ascends, in the same measure, to pc 5 (A♭) in the second violin, and in the same register. Pcs 6 and 7 round off the first segment of the PCA for the last time at the final cadence of the exposition. It should be noted that whenever a pitch is missing from one rise of the PCA, it is usually found in another rise; thus, in more sophisticated sonata movements, the entire segment of pitch classes from 0 to 7 will have been eventually presented over the course of the exposition.

From the above discussion of Haydn's expositions, one becomes aware that the developmental process, of both rhythmic motives and chromatic issues, begins right in the opening statement of the movement, a truism that pertains to all composers, of any period, who are concerned with the exploration of the fullest range of rhythmic and harmonic manipulation. The exposition of a sonata-form movement "exposes" these issues against the background of first and second harmonic areas; for example, the pitch classes of the seminal trichord will have different functions, consonant or dissonant, according to whether they are projected against the background of the tonic or of the second harmonic area. The same goes for the various ascents of the PCA. However, it is in the development section that these same issues can be explored against other harmonic terrains. Thus, while C minor, the goal of the seminal trichord B♭–B♮–C, is first introduced as a simple passing motion to vi in the bridge of the exposition, C can now be harmonically developed as a goal of motion, that is, as a fully extended harmonic area in its own right within the subsequent development section.

Haydn's development section begins by reiterating dominant harmony, a common procedure in later eighteenth-century sonata-form movements. But even here, the second violin (m. 33) presents the initial trichord in transposed inversion, B♭–A♮–A♭, against the all-pervading sixteenth-note upbeat motive in the cello. After the second violin, the cello, in m. 43, continues with a transposition of this inverted motive, now E♭–D♮–D♭. All this leads to the first harmonic goal of the development, the subdominant, in m. 36. While this is not absolutely necessary, developments often move quickly into the subdominant area (a move from IV to vi is one of several standard subdominant progressions) in order to begin the process of returning to the tonic at the point of recapitulation. The subdominant not only negates the previous dominant as a harmonic area, but also forms the beginning of a large-scale tonic progression supporting the latter segment of the PCA, which must continue to pc 11 just at the beginning or during the retransition. In this particular case, the next three pitch classes of the PCA are also those of the seminal trichord of the movement. Finally these three pitch classes (7, 8, and 9), whose first appearance in the exposition was totally outside the PCA rise, now find their rightful place within the concluding half of the PCA that unfolds, beginning where it left off at the end of the exposition with pc 7, over the course of the development section. Pitch class 7 is maintained in the upper voice from m. 39 to m. 43, where it is displaced by pc 8 – here spelled as C♭ – also in the same register. Pc 8 moves into the second violin in m. 45 and is in turn displaced by pc 9 (C♮) in the same voice in m. 46, which pitch rises immediately, as part of the sixteenth-note upbeat motive, to pc 10, D♭. Although D♮s follow, D♭ returns in m. 50. Quite often within the PCA rise, the next pitch in the series serves first to embellish its immediate predecessor before displacing it. Thus D♮ embellishes the more locally significant D♭, and succeeds it in the series only in m. 54 (still in the same voice). At the same time, Haydn has moved the harmonic area to vi (C minor) via an A♭ augmented sixth chord in m. 52.

Neither pc 11 (D♮) nor C minor is yet structural; these measures serve only to prepare the actual arrival of these events several measures later. The motion into C minor is part of a large-scale development of the seminal trichord (B♭–B♮→c). On a local level the high B♭ in the first violin (m. 50) descends a diminished octave to B♮ in m. 54, the B♮ resolving locally to C in the same measure as part of C minor harmony. However, on a background level, that same diminished octave descent of B♭ to B♮ finds its true goal only in m. 58, supported by a G major triad. A false recapitulation now ensues in C minor, but Haydn immediately reverses the trichord so that C now *descends* to B♮ in m. 48 (in the first violin) and then to B♭, an augmented octave lower, in m. 62, just in time for the recapitulation (see Example 5.8).

Example 5.8 Haydn, String Quartet in E♭ op. 33 no. 2, first movement, false recapitulation (mm. 58–63)

In counterpoint to the inverted trichord in the first violin, is the accompanying viola (mm. 60–61) whose part also unfolds the trichord in inversion (C–C♭–B♭), but at a different rhythmic rate (notice a similar gesture between the first and second violins in the exposition bridge, mm. 12–14). Finally, m. 62 finally presents pc 11 (D♮), the last pitch class of the PCA, as a structural pitch, the leading tone, within the dominant 6/4/2 chord that leads directly to the tonic in m. 63. With the completion of the PCA and the return of tonic harmony at the recapitulation, we now hear the seminal trichord once more as it was originally stated, within the opening statement of tonic harmony. But its restatement also raises again its dissonant character since the trichord has never resolved up to the tonic; the passage before the recapitulation was inverted. But there is also a further consideration: at this stage of the quartet, Haydn cannot resolve his issues, including the seminal trichord, since the quartet still has three more movements to go! It is only at the very end of the last movement (a rondo) that this trichord is finally and conclusively resolved to the tonic. Even with this, Haydn never fully resolves his rhythmic motives, since the quartet ends up in the air, the final cadence being a restatement of the opening motive of the last movement on a metrically weak measure. This, incidentally, is the "joke" (and only one of many) that makes the quartet famous.

In the recapitulation of the first movement, the seminal trichord resolves locally into tonic harmony in mm. 76–8 (first violin), but is then raised again in mm. 79–80, within subdominant harmony, the same harmony that initially introduced the trichord at the start of the movement. By repeating the trichord within the subdominant, after it has already been "resolved," Haydn has effectively postponed its ultimate resolution until the last movement, whose rondo theme significantly embeds the trichord motive within its second phrase.

Also characteristic of the recapitulation is the final repeat of the PCA, but now totally within tonic harmony. The repetition allows the full chromatic octave to resolve into tonic harmony and thus to fulfill its nature in defining the tonic key of the movement along with its partner, the descending diatonic octave, their individual pitch classes now heard directly in relation to the background tonic without motion to other harmonic areas. Quite often in sonata form the PCA will be repeated several times during the course of the recapitulation, depending on the number of formal cadences one finds. Just as there was a rise to the dominant in the exposition, with secondary rises dependent on the number of periods within the second harmonic area, so there may be full octave rises (pcs 0–11) of the PCA within each period of the recapitulation; the tonic itself is now the sole goal of motion. However, not every composition follows this scenario exactly; the extent of chromatic unfolding is entirely contingent upon compositional imperatives imposed by the composer. We cannot stress strongly enough that our theory tries to account for *what is in the music*; it is not designed to impose a theoretical construct *upon the music*.

In Haydn's E♭ quartet, for example, the PCA begins in m. 72 during a transposed restatement of the analogous bridge passage from the exposition: pcs 0, 1, and 2 are first introduced in the first violin, over a B♭ dominant pedal. These first three pitch classes then chromatically ascend to pc 7 (B♭) – with pcs 5 (A♭), 6 (A♮), and 7 (B♭) in the cello in m. 85 – and clearly accentuate the dominant in preparation for the tonic cadence at the codetta. In this case, Haydn jumps over pcs 8, 9, and 10 and concludes the PCA rise with pcs 11 (D) and 0 (E♭) at the cadence. Haydn's purpose in not presenting the entire PCA may have to do with the fact that the entire development and recapitulation are to be repeated. Thus, the B♭ which ends the chromatic rise in the recapitulation could conceivably be linked back to pc 7 at the start of the development, whence the PCA reaches completion at the recapitulation. Since the final segment of the PCA of the development section operates within a background tonic progression, Haydn may have hesitated to reiterate the complete series in the recapitulation, regarding this as redundant. Alternatively, Haydn may have deliberately avoided unfolding the full series in the recapitulation of the first movement for the same reason that he did not emphatically resolve the seminal trichord: he wanted the first movement to sound open-ended, and the real completion of the PCA within tonic harmony to be effected only in the last movement; and it is: the rondo movement is entirely tonic-oriented since the opening theme keeps returning in E♭. In this way, the rondo acts as a large-scale recapitulation of the entire string quartet since it never leaves tonic harmony. What is unusual, however, is that Haydn continually leaves out pc 8 (B♮) from each PCA rise (all the other pcs are accounted for), only to dramatize this very pitch class at the end of the movement when the seminal trichord is finally resolved, the B♭ rising to C♮.[26]

While Haydn's quartets reflect practically every aspect of the composer's compositional traits, they are still geared to the medium of chamber music, a genre in which minute details of phraseology and pitch relationship may be savored within an intimate performance setting. The symphony, however, was a genre that played to the crowd, as it were, and for most of its history within the first half of the eighteenth century did not aspire to the sophisticated development objectives inherent in chamber music. Remember that the symphony was conceived as an overture to a more important event, usually a vocal one. However, beginning in the 1770s the symphony began to show signs of a sophistication in composition that would eventually rival that of the string quartet, especially in the hands of Haydn and Mozart, and later, of course, Beethoven. Haydn's Paris symphonies (the first six composed in 1785–86, and a later three in 1788–89) are about as compositionally elitist as the most advanced string quartets of the same period, having been commissioned by Claude-François-Marie Rigoley, Comte d'Ogny, for performance at both the Concert de la Loge Olympique and the Concert Spirituel. These concerts, especially those sponsored by the Masonic Loge et Société Olympique, were meant to be of professional status: "the principal aim of which was to 'cultivate music, and to give excellent concerts to replace those of amateurs', that is, the famous earlier Concert des amateurs, disbanded in January 1781 for financial reasons."[27] Thus the audiences for these highly popular works were expecting, and received, the very best this composer could produce. Haydn was, after all, the most performed composer at these concerts in the entire eighteenth century! – not an inconsiderable achievement.

Of the first set, Symphony no. 84 in E♭ major (composed in 1786) is perhaps the most intriguing, the exposition of its first movement posing any number of design questions as to its construction. We will focus on the importance of systems integration within the first movement as a primary source of development, a knowledge of which may reveal the reason behind Haydn's seemingly erratic compositional choices.

Symphony no. 84 begins with a slow introduction, a device Haydn often uses to prepare the listener for the developmental process to follow. The introduction introduces all of the main dyad conflicts that will be explored throughout the symphony. In order of appearance they are: D♭/D♮, B♭/B♮, A♭/A♮, and, finally, G♭/G♮. If one draws the PCA of the E♭ chromatic octave, one immediately sees the logic in Haydn's ordering of dyad conflicts, as they are introduced in retrograde along the PCA starting from pcs 10 and 11 (the Arabic numerals over the brackets indicate the ordering):

---

26 Considerations of space do not allow us to examine the elaborate system shifts in this quartet since much of the discussion has concentrated on the unfolding of the PCA. Our discussion of the Haydn symphony that follows will focus on system shifts and their importance within the totality of the work.

27 Quoted in Bernard Harrison, *Haydn: The "Paris" Symphonies*, Cambridge Music Handbooks (Cambridge, 1998), p. 1.

		mm.16–17		m.9		m.8			mm.3–4		
		4	←	3	←	2		←	1		

0	1	2	3	4	5	6	7	8	9	10	11	0
E♭	E♮	F	G♭	G♮	A♭	A♮	B♭	B♮	C	D♭	D♮	E♭
I					IV		V					

These various dyad conflicts, once introduced, play a continual role in the thematic unfolding. Thus once A♭/A♮ comes into play in the basses in m. 9, Haydn continues to develop the linear and harmonic potential of this dyad within the middle and upper registers over the course of the next five measures. For example, any one of these dyad conflicts can and does become trichords; in this case, A♭/ A♮ is expanded to A♭–A♮–B♭ in m. 13 as part of dominant harmony and is then immediately further extended to a G–A♭–A♮–B♭ tetrachord in the next measure, an octave lower, in the second violin. Of overriding significance, however, is the fact that Haydn leaves the G♭/G♮ dyad conflict until last, introducing it at the close of the introduction. Notice too that Haydn deliberately avoids introducing the E♭/E♮ dyad conflict within the confines of the introduction, it being the last dyad conflict in the chromatic series. In fact, the pitch class E♮ is omitted altogether, and is the only chromatic omitted in the introduction. The E♭/E♮ dyad conflict does not appear until the opening statement of the following Allegro; its appearance any time earlier, as the last conflict to be unfolded, would potentially diminish the effect of the G♭/ G♮ conflict at the close of the introduction. Thus the first dyad conflict between D♭ and D♮ finally generates G♭ and G♮ as the last unfolded conflict in the introduction. As a consequence, Haydn has saved the missing pitch of the 3♭ system, G♭, for the last chromatic of the introduction, placing on this pitch a special emphasis that will become increasingly focused and will also become a major component of the developmental process over the course of the movement. Figure 5.1 illustrates the movement's 3♭ matrix system.

Figure 5.1   Haydn, Symphony no. 84, first movement, 3♭ matrix system

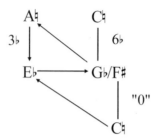

In observing the matrix, one notices that the missing pitch of a G♭ system is A♮. When both pitches occur simultaneously, a diminished harmony results that prevents the 6♭ system from displacing the prevailing 3♭ system. This is exactly what occurs at the end of the slow introduction, in mm. 16–20. Here a dominant pedal supports an A♮ diminished harmony in the upper voices, which pits G♭ and A♮ against each other without causing a system shift. The pitches G♭ and A♮ then become a "system dyad conflict" as opposed to a neighbor-note dyad conflict in which the same pitch name is presented as both diatonic and chromatic inflections. A system dyad conflict occurs on a much deeper level than a neighbor conflict, since system conflicts involve the pitch-class relationships of the complementary tritones that underlie the tonic itself. As we will see, the tension created by the system dyad conflict between G♭ and A♮, the former trying to establish a 6♭ system and the latter pitch class trying to negate it, will govern the compositional process of the latter half of the exposition.

Similar to many of Haydn's slow introductions and their subsequent allegros, with their contrasting meters and dynamics, the E♭ symphony's introduction is in triple meter and starts on an incomplete E♭ triad with a *forte* dynamic while the Allegro switches into cut time (2/2) with an opening eight-measure statement played *piano*. The exposition itself is a type-A monothematic exposition with an articulated second harmonic area, complete with an achieved medial caesura, whose thematic content replicates the opening thematic material transposed into the dominant.

By a happy coincidence, saving the last dyad conflict, E♭/E♮, for the opening statement of the Allegro allows Haydn to articulate the first trichord of the PCA (pcs 0, 1, and 2). Thus there is an interesting correlation between the presentation of dyad conflicts, which runs in retrograde along the PCA from pcs 10 and 11 in the introduction, and the prime statement of the PCA now beginning to unfold with pcs 0, 1, and 2 (viola, m. 25) at the start of the exposition. The preceding may provide a more compelling reason for Haydn's decision to omit the E♭/E♮ dyad conflict from the introduction than just undercutting the significance of the G♭/G♮ dyad (see above).

After the initial eight-measure period of the Allegro, a five-measure orchestral tutti follows. An almost autonomous counterstatement follows in m. 33, but the orchestral tutti turns into a formal bridge, once more reiterating pcs 0, 1, and 2 of the PCA as the bridge period prepares for the dominant via a V/V pedal (mm. 53–7). As Haydn unfolds the next pitch classes of the PCA (pcs 3 and 4, mm. 62ff.), no fewer than three dyad conflicts, E♭/E♮, A♭/A♮, and D♭/D♮, return, supported by a succession of diminished harmonies. Pc 3 is here spelled as F♯ and forms, with E♭, the system dyad conflict complementary to that of G♭/A♮ (see the above matrix). Here is an instance of why a composer chooses a particular spelling of a missing pitch over another. If Haydn wishes to explore the E♭/E♮ dyad conflict at this point, he has no choice but to spell the missing pitch (pc 3) as F♯ in order to avoid a system shift, a shift Haydn is saving for the climax of the exposition later in the movement. The diminished harmonies that form what seems to be the climax of the bridge now coalesce into the dominant preparation for the arrival of the second key. Indeed, pcs 6 and 7 (Haydn skips over pc 5, a diatonic pitch and the one that is most often omitted at this juncture) duly inaugurate a full authentic cadence on the dominant, B♭, in m. 73, complete with three beats of rest.

In several of Haydn's Paris symphonies, for example, nos 84, 85, and 87, the augmented sixth chord (in its function as a flat sixth relation to dominant) appears to secure the structural dominant at the close of the bridge period, a compositional trait that Haydn may have acquired from Wagenseil (see the discussion of Wagenseil's symphonies above).[28] A high-level contrapuntal structure, the augmented sixth chord often creates a rather sizable chromatic voice exchange between the opening tonic and the harmonic progression into the second harmonic area, and therefore becomes a significant center of attention in the exposition.[29] Therefore all material between the tonic of the opening statement and the augmented sixth chord at the end of the bridge is subsumed under the background tonic. As it happens, the unusual aspect of the first movement of Haydn's Symphony no. 84 involves the placement of a "misspelled" augmented sixth chord – and, therefore, the voice exchange – that contradicts our assumptions about the formal location of the second harmonic area. Although the second harmonic area appears to begin in m. 74, the voice exchange that typically initiates that area does not occur until m. 88 (the G♭ augmented sixth chord has F♭ instead of E♮). In addition, the medial caesura that is attempted in m. 73 is not achieved since no fully realized progression in the dominant occurs until the authentic cadence is reached at the codetta in m. 104. Therefore, the second area is not fully secured until the codetta, and we are left with the inevitable conclusion that the arrival of what appeared as the second harmonic area in m. 74 must still be ultimately subsumed under tonic harmony![30] Adding to the ambiguity of the design

---

28 A prominent augmented sixth chord appears just before the recapitulation of Symphony no. 83 in G minor; in Symphony no. 88 in G major, a prominent augmented sixth chord appears in the second harmonic area, applied to V/V. In Symphony no. 89 in F major, much in the style of G.M. Monn, the augmented sixth sonority is horizontalized so that it does not appear as a single vertical sonority but is spread out over several beats; since the outer voices are in such close proximity, however, the augmented sixth applied to II♯ still creates a long-range voice exchange with the tonic.

29 See Roger Kamien and Naphtali Wagner, "Bridge Themes within a Chromaticized Voice Exchange in Mozart Expositions," *Music Theory Spectrum*, 19/1 (Spring 1997): 1–12.

30 Much of the discussion and analysis of the exposition of this symphony appears in Nitzberg, "Voice-Leading and Chromatic Techniques," pp. 130–41. The present analysis updates our thinking on this topic and appends extensive new material related to the topics of fixed dyads and the unfolding PCA within the exposition and the remainder of the movement.

of the exposition is the fact that Haydn introduces second-harmonic-area material where we would normally expect to find it, but then contradicts our previous expectations by shifting the exposition's center of gravity toward the double bar by placing the augmented sixth chord in a position that appears halfway through *the second harmonic area*, instead of at the close of the bridge period. Therefore, a conflict between melodic and harmonic elements, not to mention a conflict of purely harmonic elements, creates a strong rhythmic shift toward the double bar.

Haydn's false second harmonic area (mm. 74 ff.), with its open-ended restatement of the first theme in the dominant, thus turns out to be part of an extraordinarily lengthy bridge period. This period is so extensive that Haydn actually repeats the first eight pitch classes (pcs 0–7) of the PCA in this passage. In mm. 74–80, Haydn manipulates, almost in the manner of a curtain-raiser, the first three pitch classes of the series (E♭, E♮, F) before the "entrance" of the most crucial pitch, G♭ (pc 3, in m. 81), the missing pitch of the 3♭ system. At first G♭ appears within the minor dominant. Switching into the minor dominant (or the minor relative in minor-mode pieces) either before the arrival of the second harmonic area or as an intensification of it after its arrival, in the form of an unstable transition, has a long historical precedent going back to the keyboard sonatas of Domenico Scarlatti. In Vienna, both Monn and Gluck used this technique, as did Haydn himself in his very earliest symphonies, as well as later ones (see for example the first movement of Haydn's Symphony no. 92 in G, the "Oxford"). In the case of Symphony no. 84, the shift into the minor dominant not only emphasizes pc 3, G♭, but within the rising PCA, the minor dominant also raises the D♭/D♮ dyad conflict, and, in addition, the system conflict of G♭ against A♮ (see the above matrix). However, G♭ "wins out" temporarily in m. 85, becoming the root of its own, brief, harmonic area, which simultaneously shifts the 3♭ system down to a 6♭ system. At this intense, climactic point, Haydn now adds the final dyad conflicts of the PCA chromatic octave; namely, C♭/C♮ (mm. 86–7) and F♭/F♮ (mm. 88–95). Perhaps Haydn deliberately misspelled the G♭ augmented sixth chord in m. 88, with an F♭ in place of an E♮, for this very reason – to complete the chromatic dyad pairings of the tonic chromatic octave. More than that, the spelling of the G♭ augmented sixth as a G♭7 chord implies a motion into C♭! This feint into "the wrong key" was soon to be copied by Beethoven at the climax of the development in the first movement of his Piano Trio op. 1 no. 3 in C minor, where an unassuming A♭ harmony turns unexpectedly into an A♭7 chord, implying a motion to D♭, only to be converted into an augmented sixth resolving to the dominant of the tonic C minor.

Pc 3 (G♭), which is the most difficult of the chromatics to unfold persuasively in the major mode, is given a great deal of prominence not only within the augmented sixth chord, but also during its resolution. In m. 93, G♭ is first transformed into G♮ before it resolves to F, pc 5, in m. 94. The resolution of G♭ to G♮ is more *chromatically* significant as it occurs on a higher level of structure than the more local resolution of G♭ to F. The note F now has to pull the tonal center strongly back to B♭, the dominant. This is accomplished by balancing the augmented sixth chord with a lengthy pedal point on F, beginning in m. 94 and continuing until m. 100. Pc 3 is again raised, this time written as F♯, a chromatic passing tone that resolves to G (pc 4) in m. 101. Pc 5, A♭, is skipped, as it often is at the point where local dominant harmony displaces the tonic, and the PCA culminates at the cadence before the codetta (m. 104) with pcs 6 (A♮) and 7 (B♭), restoring tonal stability. The coordination of the PCA in its second rise (from m. 74), especially with its emphasis on pc 3, and the arrival to the structural dominant help to shift the rhythmic weight of the exposition further toward the double bar. In a sense, the first PCA statement is a "dry run" for the more heavily emphasized second PCA statement (pc 3 as F♯ within the first PCA rise is not nearly as dramatic as pc 3 as G♭ in the second).

Haydn's complex development section to Symphony no. 84 works out all of the primary dyad conflicts introduced in the exposition, often tying a conflict into elaborate system modulations. The actual harmonic background of the development is really quite straightforward, following as it does the fifths of the reordered tonic hexachord as illustrated below:

Reordered E♭ hexachord

A♭	E♭	B♭	f/F	c	g
IV	I	V	ii/II♮	vi	iii

Development harmonic plan

	Initiates a fifths cycle			False recapitulation			Recapitulation
B♭ ---	c	[A♭ – D♭]→	C→	F –	[c – D♭]→	B♭→	E♭
V	vi	IV		II♮	♭VII	V	I

If one counts back from C minor in the reordered tonic hexachord, one can clearly see that Haydn is simply following the fifths of the hexachord in retrograde from C minor to E♭. The crux of the development section falls on F major (II♮) as a false recapitulation.

By following the system modulations in the development, one can posit a plausible reason why Haydn had to have an F major section where he planned it, instead of using the diatonic, and more commonplace alternative, F minor. At the beginning of the development the 3♭ system carries over from the end of the exposition, extending the previous dominant harmony. As the above harmonic plan shows, C minor is the first goal of motion in the development, prepared by an A♭ augmented sixth chord on the last beat of m. 114. The augmented sixth carries both F♯ and E♭, both pitch classes being system dyad complements that effectively cancel each other's potential for a system shift (F♯ and E♭ negate each other's potential again in m. 122). At the same time, pcs 8 (B♮) and 9 (C) of the PCA are unfolded in m. 115, pc 9 now gaining structural significance as a harmonic area in its own right. The next PCA pitch, D♭ (pc 10), is actually "worked out" – this pitch and its neighbor, pc 11, D♮, form one of the important dyad conflicts in the movement. Pc 10 is sustained over a very long harmonic area that culminates in the F major false recapitulation in m. 148. From m. 128, where it is first introduced, D♭ motivates a motion into subdominant harmony, A♭; D♭ itself is kept active by becoming the root of its own harmony, functioning as ♭VI/F. The motion into D♭ now raises G♭, the other important pitch class that framed the slow introduction, which here functions as the flat seventh of an A♭7 chord (mm. 130ff.). Both D♭ and G♭ are now worked out simultaneously, the G♭ as a system-shift motivator which causes a system shift down to a 6♭ system. What started out as an F♯/E♭ system dyad conflict at the opening of the development has now turned into its system complement, G♭/A♮, although the persistent G♭s prevent the A♮s from shifting the system back up to a 3♭ system (see mm. 140–41 with A♮ as a pedal in the bass against the G♭s in the first violin). With the motion into A♭, followed by the G♭/A♮ dyad system conflict, Haydn has also raised the third primary dyad conflict of the movement, that between A♭ and A♮, which is now worked out as part of the background system conflict. Only at the false recapitulation in m. 148, with the introduction of F major along with its major third degree, A♮, can the system now revert to a 3♭ system! Haydn could not have canceled the previous 6♭ system if he had gone into F minor instead of F major. He obviously thought the move into F major important enough to dramatize the event with a false recapitulation.

Once the 3♭ system has been restored, Haydn reverses direction by introducing F♯ as a system-shift motivator (m. 152), shifting the system up to "0." Since E♭ is now necessary to bring the system down again, Haydn has once again developed a primal dyad conflict, here E♭/E♮, as part of a larger system conflict. Eventually E♭ returns in m. 161, returning the system to a 3♭ system (any F♯s introduced after this are effectively canceled by prevailing E♭s). C minor (vi) returns as a harmonic area, linking it with the previous C minor at the start of the development, but instead of moving contrapuntally to V, C shifts up to D♭ in m. 181 as ♭VII. Our D♭ has returned with a vengeance, and now forms the climax of the entire development! The D♭ again motivates G♭, which pitch plunges the system down once more to a 6♭ system. (Incidentally, D♭ as pc 10 has not yet been displaced by D♮, pc 11.) During the ensuing intensely chromatic passage (mm. 182–92), the dyad pairs actually pile up on top of each other, causing a number of rapid system shifts. Eventually, A♮ "wins out" – note the chromatic climb up to B♭ in mm. 191–2 – as it conflicts with its chromatic neighbor A♭, causing the system to return to a 3♭ system.

The retransition starts on dominant harmony in m. 192. Before this, D♭ has finally been displaced by D♮, a pitch that now becomes the leading tone of the dominant retransition. But Haydn has yet another trick up his sleeve in the measure immediately preceding the recapitulation. In m. 201, F♯ returns on the third beat of the measure, causing a system shift up to "0," but the return of tonic harmony at the point of recapitulation, in the very next measure, cancels the system shift, leaving the 3♭ system intact.

The recapitulation itself is refashioned to allow all the basic issues of the movement to be raised against the background of tonic harmony. While there is certainly at least a momentary sense of resolution at the end of the movement, the recapitulation is harmonically so disturbing that any conclusive sense of resolution will have to wait until the end of the last movement. Thus all the primary dyad conflicts are restated in due course beginning with D♭ as flat seventh in an E♭7 chord (m. 214) as the recapitulation bridge veers into subdominant harmony. The A♭/A♮ dyad conflict soon follows in m. 216, both dyad conflicts being restated against the start of the final rise of the PCA in the second violin with pcs 0, 1, and 2. The PCA continues in order with pcs 3, 4, 5, 6, and 7 unfolded in mm. 225–31, leading up to the restatement of second-harmonic-area thematic material, now transposed into tonic harmony in

m. 237. Instead of lessening the tension as the movement reaches its conclusion, Haydn increases it dramatically by plunging the major tonic into its parallel minor at the start of the transition (m. 244), which leads to the codetta in m. 260. As a result, G♭, the missing pitch and the system-shift motivator of the 3♭ system, is once more introduced, shifting the system down to a 6♭ system. The swing into the parallel minor generates diminished harmony based on the pitch classes of the tonic system matrix, but with G♭ instead of F♯ (mm. 248–9). During this passage, A♮ is pitted against G♭, effectively preventing a system shift back to a 3♭ system. Pcs 7, 8, and 9 are now unfolded before the arrival of the codetta. Within the codetta itself (m. 260), D♭ as pc 10 (in the bass) now resolves up to D♮, pc 11 (in the second violin), in preparation for the final authentic cadence of the movement. With the resolution of the primal D♭/D♮ conflict with which the symphony began, the movement ends. However, Haydn does not correct the 6♭ system; no A♮s appear to effect the change back into a 3♭ system. Only in the final movement are both dyad conflicts fully resolved: D♭ becomes significant again during a false recapitulation in A♭ major and is not fully resolved until the retransition in m. 189. The G♭ is finally resolved to G♮ in m. 269, just before the coda beginning in m. 271. At the end of the last movement when G♭ is introduced, an A♮ appears against it, preventing the G♭ from shifting the prevailing 3♭ system down – just the opposite of what occurred at the end of the first movement!

V. Alternative Design Elements in Sonata-Form Movements: J.C. Bach and W.A. Mozart

Just as Wagenseil and Monn set the scene for Haydn's approach to sonata form in Vienna during the middle of the eighteenth century, so Johann Christian Bach (1735–1782) did much the same for the young Mozart, especially during Bach's later career in London. In 1754 Bach moved to Italy, where he studied counterpoint with the famous Padre Martini of Bologna. While in Italy he began to compose *opera seria* and became the organist of Milan Cathedral in 1760, a post that required Bach to convert to Catholicism. Bach's tenure in Italy brought him into contact with the leading *style galant* composers of the day, including G.B. Sammartini. Bach's love of the Italian *style galant* was undoubtedly a major influence on his symphonic music (including keyboard concertos) and chamber music, most of which was composed in London, the city in which Bach spent most of his later career. He moved there in 1762 to become music master to Queen Charlotte, and in 1764, the year Bach met the Mozarts in London, he and Carl Friedrich Abel teamed up to create a popular concert series which featured Bach playing the fortepiano in public for the first time.

The period of Bach's London symphonic production still saw the symphony as an overture to some "higher" artistic entertainment, either vocal (opera or oratorio) or instrumental (as an introduction to an evening's concert). Bach therefore wrote symphonies (actually named "Overtures" in the printed scores) in batches, each opus usually containing six such works. This does not mean that Bach did not expend considerable creative energy on these symphonies; if they had been simply tossed off, the young Mozart would never have taken an interest in them. On the contrary, many of Bach's symphonies display a sure compositional technique that features both rhythmic vitality and melodic expressiveness, especially in the slow movements. Bach's approach to the partitioning of subdivisions within sonata-form movements must surely have influenced Mozart, as well as his controlled handling of chromatic events. Unlike the expositions of his Viennese contemporaries, where continuity of musical periods, avoiding rhythmically articulated cadences, seems to have been an overriding factor, the expositions of J.C. Bach have clearly defined subsections, usually subdivided into four parts: the first part establishes the tonic with a stable period. A formal bridge passage then leads to the arrival of the second harmonic area (invariably the dominant in major keys and the relative major in minor keys), which is itself divided into three stable periods, each set off by a formal cadence that serves to define the tonic of the second harmonic area: the opening period which establishes the area, a closing or second period, and a final cadential period, or codetta. The subdivisions within the second harmonic area are clearly separated by transitions that motivate the cadence initiating the next stable period ("closing," "codetta," etc.). Each division of this quadripartite exposition is thematically differentiated with contrasting topics, and each is prepared by rhythmically defined downbeat authentic cadences, complete with rests. Unlike Mozart, however, Bach prefers expositions that are not repeated, a feature typical of overture-style sonata form. Perhaps most importantly, in all of J.C. Bach's compositions, tonal motion is centered on the cadence; in fact, most of the movement consists of establishing, moving away from, or approaching a cadential goal. While for the most part Mozart agreed with the validity of this approach in terms of its ability to provide formal clarity, he was rarely as obvious in its realization.

The Sinfonia in E♭ op. 9 no. 2 (1773) is a typical example of J.C. Bach's symphonic style (see Diagram 5.6, which details the form of the first movement), and is composed as an overture-sinfonia in three movements. The first movement begins with a tonic statement divided into two contrasting subperiods (Bach avoids antecedent–consequent period structure in the opening statements of his fast movements): the first is a "Mannheim crescendo topic" constructed entirely of two-measure phrases over a tonic pedal (Bach was quite familiar with the Mannheim symphonists, having sojourned at Mannheim in 1772 to produce his *opera seria Temistocle*). The second subperiod (mm. 13ff.) serves to cap the preceding crescendo with an orchestral tutti whose phrasing changes from the preceding 2 + 2 to 3 + 3, accompanied by a change in harmonic rhythm. The second subperiod ends with a cadence on tonic harmony, which now elides into a bridge beginning in m. 19. The bridge period itself is constructed as a series of harmonic sequences in four-measure phrases that never leaves the tonic (see Figure 5.6), even with its feint toward the dominant in m. 33 with a V6/5 of B♭. Bach's prevarication between moving toward the dominant and then away from it functions to introduce the main dyad conflict of the movement, A♮/A♭ (A♮ as leading tone to V and A♭ as flat seventh of the dominant seventh chord). In fact, the A♮/A♭ dyad is the only chromatic event unfolded with the tonic statement. The bridge ends with a bifocal close, and the arrival at the dominant triad is back-relating; that is, it relates to the previous tonic. As an aside, it is interesting to note that in their symphonies both J.C. and C.P.E. Bach prefer non-modulatory bridges that maintain tonic harmony; however, the accelerated harmonic rhythm, while not actually preparing the next harmonic area, does give a sense of forward momentum that at least sets up the new harmonic area.

Main Issue: A♭/A♮ dyad conflict
Quadripartite Exposition: 1 harmonic area in the tonic and 3 in the dominant

Allegro 4/4

First Harmonic Area (topics)	Bridge
A (2+2 phrases) ---------- B (3+3 phrases)	Harmonic sequences (*Fortspinnung*)
"Mannheim crescendo" topic "Orchestral Tutti" topic	prolongs I: note change of harmonic rhythm
over E♭ pedal (Cadential motive – Epilog)	[A♭ – A♮ conflict introduced]

E♭ -------   E♭ – B♭ – cm – A♭ – F6/5 → B♭7 →E♭♭6←B♭

I   I   V   vi   IV   V6/5/V V7   I6   V

Second Harmonic Area (1ˢᵗ Period)   Counterstatement – transition →   **Closing Area (2ⁿᵈ Period)**   transition →

"Singing Style" topic (melody in 3rds)   "Military style" topic ----

–simple, unadorned 8 measure phrase   [this area is the most chromatically

Pedal on B♭   intense]

B♭   F   B♭   B♭

V   V/V ---------   V   V

3ʳᵈ Period (Codetta)   **Development**   1ˢᵗ harmonic goal ---- [Bridge material] ----   [2ⁿᵈ area theme]

New idea   E♭→ A♭   cm (climax)   B♭

3 measures of B♭ cadence   B♭ pedal------------   V/IV IV   vi   V

V   V

Recapitulation

Retransition	First Harmonic Area	Bridge [no 2ⁿᵈ Area, 1ˢᵗ period]	Closing Area (2ⁿᵈ Period)
			"Military style" topic – transition →
B♭	E♭	→	E♭ --------
V →	I		I

Codetta

E♭

I

Diagram 5.6 J.C. Bach, Sinfonia in E♭ op. 9 no. 2, first movement

The second harmonic area begins with a "singing allegro" topic with the violins in thirds over a B♭ pedal in the violas. This stable eight-measure period is then repeated in a counterstatement with the winds, accompanied by the horns, taking over the melody and with the same pedal point in the violas (the variation in orchestration upon the repeat was certainly noticed by the young Mozart). On the last measure of the period (m. 54), the counterstatement is elided to an unstable transition centering on the V/V. At the close of the transition (m. 62) the basses, for the first time, introduce a chromatic element so far missing in the exposition; namely, E♭, E♮, and F, the first three pitches of the PCA. Since the cadence to the closing area is fast approaching, Bach has no time to unfold a complete PCA rise to the dominant; instead, he jumps up immediately to pcs 6 and 7 to form the cadence in m. 64. The closing, or second, period within the dominant area presents a third contrasting topic in military style (a march figure), featuring two-measure phrases within an eight-measure period. Again, Bach begins to create a final PCA rise, and here the rise is complete with one unexpected turn. Pc 5 (A♭) appears out of series.[31]

Most often, pc 5 of the PCA ascent is the one pitch class that is omitted. Within the dominant area its presence would imply a subdominant motion; however, Bach seems to have carefully calculated the effect of such a motion since the A♭ would naturally have to move up to A♮, reviving the dyad conflict between these two pitch classes first presented in the exposition bridge. In the earlier bridge passage, A♭ pertained to tonic harmony and was pitted against the attempt of A♮ to effect a cadence to the dominant. Within the closing period A♭ is once again raised within E♭ harmony, but now the E♭ is interpreted as IV/V within a larger dominant progression. At the cadence before the transition to the codetta (m. 72), the A♮ of the F major triad (V/V) displaces the previous A♭, a pitch class that does not reappear until the development section that follows. Approaching this cadence, Bach presents all the pitch classes of the first segment of the PCA ascent, beginning once again with pcs 0, 1, and 2 in mm. 67–8 (basses). Pcs 3 and 4 appear in the upper voices in mm. 71–2, with, as stated before, the A♭ presented out of series in m. 70 in the violins. By isolating A♭ in this way, Bach effectively dramatizes the dyad conflict between A♭ and A♮, a relationship underlying a development process that informs the entire movement. Finally, pcs 6 and 7 end the rise at the cadence that begins the transition. The transition period itself only presents pcs 6 and 7 at the cadence before the codetta in mm. 77–8. The codetta is hardly a period, but a three-measure statement of a single dominant harmony. In summary, up to this point, J.C. Bach's handling of chromatic events is carefully calculated to achieve a climactic close at the end of the exposition. As the later subsections within the dominant area of the exposition unfold, the introduction of chromatic pitch classes increases, coupled with an accelerated harmonic rhythm within the transition leading to the codetta.

---

31 Presenting a pitch out of series is not unknown, and in this case J.C. Bach is closer to Haydn than he is to Mozart. While Haydn often unfolds a pitch (or sometimes reverses two pitch classes) within a PCA rise in the second harmonic area, both Mozart and Beethoven rarely if ever disturb the series by reversing pitch classes or presenting them out of series. However, all these composers do omit pitch classes from one rise but then introduce them in a subsequent rise, as Bach does in this symphony.

Chromatic events become even more prominent in Bach's development section, which begins immediately in m. 81 with yet another idea, this one also a "singing allegro" topic. At this point it might be well to diagram the 3♭ hexachord of this movement:

A♭/A♮ dyad conflict is developed

```
                              A♭/A♮
A♭ —    E♭ —    B♭ —    f/F —       c —     g
IV       I        V        ii V/V      vi      iii
```

Bach's harmonic plan for the development simply follows the hexachordal pitch classes beginning with the dominant, B♭. The B♭ turns into a dominant seventh leading to E♭ (this is a passing harmony and is not heard as a tonic return). The E♭ now gains a seventh and moves to A♭ on the downbeat of m. 99. All this sequential motion around fifth-related harmonic areas naturally raises the A♭/A♮ dyad conflict in its wake, and one can see a dramatic presentation of it in m. 90, where A♮ moves up to B♭ as V/E♭ and is immediately followed on the next beat by A♭ (as flat seventh) descending to G.

Having reached the subdominant on the downbeat of m. 99, Bach moves quickly to explore the minor side of the tonic hexachord, first with F minor on the second beat of m. 99, and then with C minor (vi), a harmonic area that forms the climax of the development. The motion into C minor is made all the more dramatic by reiterating the rhythmically intense thematic material of the exposition bridge. At the same time, pcs 8 (B♮) and 9 (C) are now presented within vi, a structurally significant harmonic area.

Surprisingly, during this time the missing pitch of the 3♭ system, F♯ (G♭ is never introduced), has been heard once, during the PCA rise at the end of the closing period (m. 70). But that pitch was never able to motivate a system change since E♭ canceled the F♯ right on the downbeat of the next measure. However, the F♯ raised in the development section is quite a different matter; it occurs at the most intense moment of the development section as Bach is leaving the area of the submediant. What Bach does now is to reverse course, and, instead of moving directly from C minor to G minor, he moves to the opposite end of the tonic hexachord, interposing A♭ between the harmonies instead (m. 106). The A♭ now swings violently in the other direction toward G minor (the extreme ends of the hexachord are thus juxtaposed), and it is at this climactic moment that F♯, the missing pitch of the 3♭ system, is introduced. Instead of immediately canceling the system shift up to "0," Bach leaves the E as E♮ until the E♭ in m. 110 reverts the system to a 3♭ system, thus maintaining the "0" system for two measures. From G minor, the harmonic ordering follows the root hexachordal pitch classes in reverse order: g, C, f, F (as V6/5 of V), and finally B♭ in m. 111. At the same time, the A♭/A♮ conflict has returned, the A♮ being reintroduced as leading tone to the dominant B♭ in m. 111.

Once the dominant is reached, Bach reintroduces the thematic material of the first period of the second harmonic area; specifically, the counterstatement of the "singing allegro" topic is given to the winds. After the relative instability of the preceding passage, the return of a periodic melody in dominant harmony has a stabilizing effect, but since the dominant has already been preceded by the submediant, it is heard within the context of a larger tonic progression, and not as an autonomous harmonic area. In addition, the return of the dominant at this point also dramatizes the A♭/A♮ conflict: the A♭ is regained in m. 115 along with the anticipation of tonic harmony. However, during the retransition period (mm. 118ff.) on dominant harmony, the violins reintroduce A♮ as a passing tone to B♭, over a dominant pedal.

In the development section, the climax on vi (C minor) allows pc 9 to be articulated as part of the latter PCA segment. In development sections, it is most unusual not to present every note of the rest of the series, but in this case at least, Bach does omit pc 10 (C♯/D♭): either spelling of this pitch would be quite difficult to introduce at this juncture because of harmonic considerations. Normally, C♯ would tonicize D, but Bach's harmonic scheme does not allow for this event to happen; instead, he is more intent on moving rapidly to the dominant, passing through hexachordal root pitch classes along the way. In this instance, D tonicizes G minor in m. 108, G minor being an important fifth within the tonic hexachord. However, the presentation of D (pc 11) within G minor harmony allows that pitch class, and that segment of the PCA, to be extended into the restatement of the second-harmonic-area thematic material in dominant harmony. The D becomes structurally significant at the point of retransition, which begins in m. 118, where the dominant is now clearly related to the tonic of the approaching recapitulation in m. 124.

As in most classically conceived sonata forms, the recapitulation is truncated; here, the "singing allegro" topic is omitted altogether. What is, perhaps, more important is not the presentation of exposition thematic material, but the ultimate resolution of chromatic issues into tonic harmony. The thematic material of the exposition bridge now returns (mm. 142ff.), and along with it, the A♭/A♮ dyad is restated as well (remember that in the exposition bridge there was a motion to the subdominant, A♭); the same motion is now reiterated in the recapitulation, along with the move to the dominant, raising A♮ in the process. With the opening period of the second-harmonic-area material missing, the bridge is redirected toward the closing area, now in the tonic. As it was in the exposition, where the chromaticism became most intense, the thematic material of the codetta, transposed into the tonic, now acts as the final source of resolution for the whole movement. The rising chromatic segment of the PCA in the exposition, E♭, E♮, F, is now transposed into tonic harmony – A♭, A♮, B♭ (mm. 168–9) – conveniently resolving the primary chromatic issue of the movement. After studying any number of sonata-form movements from the late eighteenth century, we have consistently noted that composers seemed to have deliberately planned their movements around seminal chromatic issues, presented at the outset of the exposition, which when transposed into tonic harmony in parallel segments of the recapitulation would "automatically" find themselves resolved.

One can see that J.C. Bach was a sophisticated composer whose compositional methods were certainly influential on his contemporaries as well as composers of the next generation, in particular W.A. Mozart. However, what distinguishes Mozart's work from that of J.C. Bach and his immediate contemporaries is not only the memorability of Mozart's themes and their orchestration, but also his complete mastery of large-scale rhythm, from the smallest phrases to the most extensive hyperperiods – meaning those periods that extend over larger areas of the form, such as the internal subdivisions of the second harmonic area. For us, Mozart's genius also lies in his extraordinary ability to articulate chromatic events through their rhythmic placement within the movement, as illustrated in the following discussion of the first movement of his String Quintet in C major K. 515.

The first movement of Mozart's quintet in C is striking in the manner in which it presents E♭, pc 3. As early as the counterstatement (m. 21), E♭ is introduced within C minor harmony, a most unexpected mode switch (see Diagram 5.7, which details the system shifts as well as the PCA deployment within the first movement). Mozart prepares the dramatic presentation of pc 3 by preceding this pitch class with pcs 0, 1, and 2 in the second viola (mm. 14–15), followed by a complete measure of silence in m. 20. Even the phrase structure of the opening statement is unusual in that it is not divided into the usual duple groupings (4 + 4 or 2 + 2); instead, the opening period divides into two five-measure subphrases (3 + 2) followed by a longer ten-measure phrase (five measures plus an extension of five measures), which includes the one measure of rest that concludes the entire period. The counterstatement provides a necessary downbeat at this point, and this is where Mozart rises above his contemporaries in his sensitivity to large-scale structural rhythm and its relationship to dissonant events. The very downbeat that should have been supported by the major tonic at the counterstatement is here turned dissonant, its harmony suddenly being thrown into the complementary system of the parallel tonic minor.

The presence of E♭ is so strong throughout the period preceding the formal bridge in m. 57 that F♯, the corrective pitch class, can gain little headway (see Example 5.9). In fact, the 3♭ system initiated by E♭ in m. 48, within the context of Neapolitan harmony, refuses to move up to the C system at all, and instead continues to move down with the introduction of G♭ in m. 49. Not even Schubert, in his own C major String Quintet of 1828 (discussed in Chapter 6), will go this far afield at this point – into a 6♭ system! Only with great effort does the music reverse direction by introducing first A♮ (the missing pitch of the 6♭ system) and then an uncontested F♯ in m. 62 within the bridge passage. But Mozart does not stop there: he now reinterprets the E♭ as a D♯ and temporarily shifts the system up to a 3♯ system in m. 64. A C♮ follows in m. 67, finally restoring the original "0" system. (All the system shifts in this remarkable passage are detailed in Diagram 5.7; the arrows indicate shifts either up or down.) Mozart's introduction of E♭ initiates a jumping-off point where the missing pitch of the prevailing "0" system creates dissonance through the parallel minor, propelling the counterstatement into ever-increasing flat-key harmonic areas, only to be rectified, via F♯ and D♯, in the bridge.

Example 5.9 Mozart, String Quintet in C K. 515, first movement, opening tonic statement and bridge (mm. 1–86)

Example 5.9 Mozart, String Quintet in C K. 515, first movement, opening tonic statement and bridge (mm. 1–86) continued

Against all these whirling system shifts is the underlying development of the main dyad conflict of the movement: C/C♭, often extended into a C–C♯–D trichord with the C♯ moving up to D. This configuration is first presented, almost innocently, as the first three pitch classes of the PCA (mm. 14–15, second viola). The conflicting C♯ becomes harmonically significant as the root of a first-inversion C♯ diminished seventh chord in m. 31, the C♯ and its C♮ neighbor moving into deeper structural levels during the development section (see Diagram 5.7).

Exposition

1st Harmonic Area | **Counterstatement + Extension**

Measure:	1	14-15	21	30-31	35	37-38
System Active Pcs:			Eb ↗		F# ↗	
System:	"0"		3 bs		C	
PCA:	C(0)	C(0) – C#(1) – D(2)	Eb(3)			
Harmony:	C / I	[Main trichord issue]	c minor / i	c#o7	V6/5/V	IV

Bridge

M.:	48	49	52-53	53	55–56	57	58	62
System Active Pcs:	Eb ↗	Gb ↗	A♮ ↗					F# ↗
System:	3 bs	6 bs	3 bs	(F#/Eb)	3 bs ———			"0"
PCA:	Db 6/4			Ab		C(0) C#(1)	D(2)	
Harmony:	bII6/4		Ab	Ab aug.6	G6/4– 5/3 / V6/4– 5/3	C / I		

2nd Harmonic Area

M.:	64	65	66	67	68	86	87	89 & 93	95	98
System Active Pcs:	D# ↗			C♮ ↗		G(7)	C(0)			(Eb/F#)
System:	3 #s			"0"		G				
PCA:	D#(3) E(4)	F(5)			F#(6)	G(7)	C(0)	PCA repeats: C#(1) – D(2)	[D(2)]	
Harmony:					D / V/V	G / V ——————				

Transition | | | | **Closing Area** | |

M.:	101– 102	103	105– 106	114	115	116
System Active Pcs:	(D#/C♮)		(D#/C♮)	(Eb/F#)		
System:						
PCA:	D#(3)– E(4)– F♮(5)	[F#(6)]		F#(6)	G(7)	C(0)– C#(1)– D(2) PCA repeats:
Harmony:				D / V/V	G / V	

Diagram 5.7 Mozart, String Quintet in C K. 515, first movement: system/PCA

Block 1

M.:	119–120–121	122	123 (Eb/F#)	130	Codetta 131 132	134 (D#/C)
System Active Pcs:	(D#/C)					
System:						PCA repeats :
PCA:	[C(0)– C#(1)– D(2)]	Eb(3)– E♮(4)		F#(6) G(7) C(0)		
Harmony:				D V/V	G pedal —— V	

Block 2

M.:	135	136 (D#/C)	146–147	148	149 (D#/C)	150–151
System Active Pcs:						:‖:
PCA:	C#(1)– D(2)	D#(3)– E(4)	F♮(5)		F#(6)– G(7)	F#(6)– G(7)
Harmony:	G pedal ——— V					

Development: the C#/C♮ conflict is developed on the background level

M.:	152	156	162 (Eb/F#)	164	169	170	171	174	177 (Eb/F#)	182 185 Eb↘
System Active Pcs:										3 b's (holds until m. 200)
PCA:	["0"] G(7) c#°7		Bb	[G(7)] CM		G#(8) A(9) AM/am		Bb(10) holds through until m. 204 Gm		Cm Fm

Retransition / Recapitulation

M.:	187 (F#/Eb)	188	190–192 (F#–Eb)	193–194 (F#–Eb)	200 F#↗ "0"	204	Recapitulation 205
System Active Pcs:						B♮(11)	C(0)
PCA:		Ab bVI	Ab bVI aug. 6→	G pedal V			C I

Brackets indicate the presence of non-structural pitch classes within the PCA.

Diagram 5.7 Mozart, String Quintet in C K. 515, first movement: system/PCA continued

Mozart further develops this trichord through an enharmonic reinterpretation of C♯ as D♭ which results in a new trichordal configuration: D♮–D♭–C. The now-enharmonically respelled and retrograded trichord, with D♭ at its center, is raised within those harmonic areas controlled by the flat complementary systems of the matrix (3♭ and 6♭), while the primary trichordal configuration with C♯ at its center appears within the context of the "0" and 3♯ systems.

Another extraordinary feature of the opening tonic statement of the exposition is the lengthy period of extension following the abbreviated counterstatement in C minor (see Example 5.9). After a three-measure counterstatement in which the outer voices are inverted (the first violin playing the arpeggiated triad that was first heard in the cello), Mozart now elaborates the arpeggiated figure which features the complex system shifts and dyad conflicts discussed above. Extensions of this sort present Mozart with the opportunity to downplay the development section proper: his developments tend to be much shorter in duration, but no less intense, than those of either Haydn or Beethoven. Mozart prefers to expand his ideas within the exposition and recapitulation sections of the form while both Haydn and Beethoven, who develop their ideas in these sections as well, place more of an emphasis on the development section proper (and, as consequence, the coda), which is, therefore, more pronounced and more protracted.

After the extended period following the counterstatement, the bridge period begins in m. 57. As in all Classical sonata forms, the bridge begins after the last statement of tonic harmony; more specifically, the bridge commences on the tonic, whether as a separate period after an autonomous counterstatement or as an extension of an open-ended counterstatement. Since there is a full authentic cadence on the tonic in m. 57, after which the music veers toward dominant harmony with a II♯ in m. 69, we must conclude that m. 57 initiates the bridge period.

With the start of the bridge period, the reappearance of the C–C♯–D trichord now signals the structural beginning of the PCA within the second harmonic area. Notice that Mozart gives the C–C♯–D trichord prominence by stating it once at the start of the bridge and then restating it a few measures thereafter (mm. 60–61). Now instead of presenting pc 2 (D) rising to pc 3 as E♭, Mozart enharmonically respells this pitch as D♯ in m. 65, causing the system shift up to a 3♯ system that the D♯ occasions (note, also, the scoring in octaves between the two violins), and moves the D♯ to E♮ (pc 4) in the next measure. Pc 5 (F♮) appears in the first viola part on the third beat of m. 66; the F♯s, a consequence of the previous system shift to a 3♯ system, are now displaced by an F♮ in preparation for the C♮ in m. 67, the introduction of which now returns the system to "0." However, the F♮ quickly moves up to F♯ (pc 6) as part of the II♯ chord in m. 69 that formally announces the arrival of the dominant harmonic area.

Mozart clearly presents the second harmonic area in m. 86; a fully achieved and embellished medial caesura prepares the dominant arrival (mm. 81–6). What is notable about the rest of the exposition is Mozart's consistent unfolding of pcs 0–7 within each of the structural periods of the second harmonic area (the opening period, the closing period, and the codetta). The codetta itself is extensive (21 measures) and allows Mozart to unfold an entire 0–7 PCA segment within what is usually a short, diatonic cadential anchoring of the second harmonic area. Mozart is unique among the great three Classical composers in invariably insisting on chromatic completion within each segment and subsegment of the PCA over the course of virtually any sonata-form movement. Diagram 5.7 outlines the details of the various system shifts and PCA rises of the exposition.

Our discussion will now focus on the development section. Mozart's relatively economical development is constructed as one seamless period that begins with the opening five-measure theme of the exposition restated in a series of harmonic sequences based on diminished harmony. This fluid harmonic undertow never coalesces into well-defined harmonic periods, but proceeds in one continuous flow until the G pedal of the retransition in m. 193. The contrapuntal projection of the seminal dyad conflict, C♯/C♮, into deeper realms of structure, motivates the harmonic scheme of the development. Diagram 5.7 shows that the C♯ diminished seventh chord that opens the development relates contrapuntally to C, both as C major in mm. 164–7 and as C minor in mm. 181–2; in keeping with the fluid texture of the development, both harmonies are weakly defined as there are no articulated authentic cadences in either. Until m. 182, the "0" system controls the progress of harmonic reference points, all of which relate to the tonic C major hexachord of the quintet: B♭ (the one allowable flat within the system), C major, A major/A minor, and G minor. Note that Mozart emphasizes the A major/minor juxtaposition in m. 169, momentarily throwing the contrapuntal C♯/C♮ conflict of the bass into an inner voice. Even more, the second violin part in mm. 168–9 presents the complete D–C♯–C♮ trichord.

When C minor enters the picture in m. 182, its E♭ causes a large-scale system shift down to a 3♭ system that is extended to the end of the retransition, where F♯ finally enters to correct the system back up to "0," five measures before the recapitulation in m. 205. Throughout the 3♭ system, F♯s keep recurring (see Diagram 5.7), but they are incapable of invoking a system shift to "0" by the ever-present E♭s that control the area. Further, the system shift down to a 3♭ system now displaces those tonal areas governed by the previous "0" system and, consequently, substitutes harmonic areas associated with the parallel minor system. Consequently, C minor and the new 3♭ system generate F minor and then A♭ major, this last harmony turning into an augmented sixth chord on the very last eighth note of m. 192. Closing the development, the A♭ in the augmented sixth resolves down, in the next measure, to the G pedal that signals the start of the retransition.

In summation, the entire development is governed by the E♭/F♯ dyad system conflict between the tonic "0" system and its complement, the 3♭ system, the same two system conflicts that likewise controlled the C minor counterstatement and its extension within the opening tonic period of the movement. (Interestingly, the E♭/F♯ conflict in the development comes after the extensive codetta with its complementary "sharp" system dyad conflict of D♯/C.) At the same time, the seminal C♯/C♮ dyad operates on a deep contrapuntal level, and occasionally appears in the upper voices (most notably in the second violin passage cited above). However, Mozart has flooded the contrapuntal upper voices with so much chromaticism that this particular conflict becomes only one of many that pervade the development section.

In terms of the completion of the PCA, Mozart unfolds all the pitch classes necessary to complete the chromatic tonic octave from pc 7 to pc 11. What is interesting, however, is that pcs 10 (B♭) and 11 (B♮) conflict from m. 174 right up the point of recapitulation in m. 205. Pc 10 appears within G minor harmony, while pc 11 is introduced as the leading tone of C minor. However, since C minor itself initiates a 3♭ system, B♭ regains control until it is displaced by B♮ in m. 201 as a consequence of the return of the "0" system in the measure before.

While a full analysis of the recapitulation is impossible because of space limitations, it is interesting to note that with the return of tonic harmony, Mozart prefers to spell the missing pitch as D♯, creating a D♯/C♮ dyad system conflict that controls the harmonic motions of the recapitulated exposition up to m. 286, where the material of the second harmonic area turns into a transition leading to the closing period. The emphasis on D♯ displaces what would have been a return to the parallel minor in a counterstatement; instead, Mozart elides the extension material directly into the recapitulation bridge, omitting the exposition's counterstatement altogether. What is significant about this recomposed passage is how it illustrates the almost tortuous progression Mozart goes through to raise D♯ instead of E♭. One of the reasons why composers choose to introduce the flat third degree within a tonic statement is that the minor third degree has voice-leading properties that can easily move it into dominant harmony as, for example, ♭VI of the new harmonic area. Spelled as a sharp, the missing pitch is much harder to justify harmonically. In Mozart's case, raising D♯ results in a passage of enormous complexity in which the G♯ pedal in mm. 232–5 is reinterpreted as an A♭ (m. 239), a harmony which is then converted into a German sixth on the last beat of the measure. The G♯ harmony raises D♯ and thus supports both C♯ major and minor before G♯ is redefined as V6/5 of A minor. The A♮ in the cello in m. 236 forms a localized trichord as it descends to A♭ in m. 239 and then to G in m. 240 as part of a cadential 6/4. The bridge that follows in m. 242 again raises the C♮/C♯ conflict, which is now worked into the background D♯/C♮ system dyad conflict that governs the bridge period. It need only be stated that the C♮/C♯ conflict is resolved in the concluding passage beginning in m. 361, eight measures before the end of the movement. Here the trichord configuration of C♮–C♯–D is reiterated at least four times within this space, scored in octaves between the two violin parts. At the last moment, C♯ descends to C♮ one measure before the end over a C pedal in the cello, thus temporarily resolving the seminal chromatic conflict of the quintet. The reader is urged to look at the last movement of the quintet, an elaborate sonata rondo, where all these issues are raised once more (for example, look at the prominence of the C/C♯ dyad conflict within the opening rondo theme) and then resolved conclusively at the very end of the quintet. Most spectacular for us is the fact that the very last chromatics heard in the last movement, and therefore the quintet, are E♭ against F♯, played simultaneously, within the context of an A♭ German sixth chord 22 measures before the end.

Exactly ten years earlier in 1777, Mozart composed his Piano Sonata K. 309/284b, also in C major. A comparison of the two works is most instructive since both are in the same key and utilize similar chromatic issues. One might be tempted, in fact, to consider the piano sonata a model for the later quintet, albeit with all of the structural events in opposite positions.

Most notable in the piano sonata is the presentation of the C♮/C♯ dyad conflict, the same one that governed the quintet, within the opening statement. In the sonata this statement is divided into two unequal phrases (see Example 5.10); the first is two measures long, *forte*, and triadic, similar to the fanfare motives that begin so many Mannheim symphonies. This is followed by a quieter six-measure phrase that is elided to a counterstatement in m. 8. The emphatic C that opens the movement begins the first PCA rise, followed in short order by pcs 1 (C♯) and 2 (D) in mm. 3 and 4. Before continuing the PCA segment, Mozart manipulates the C♯/C♮ dyad conflict, first by correcting the C♯ in m. 3 to C♮ in m. 5. No sooner has he done this, however, than C♯ is reintroduced in m. 6 as an embellishment of ii6 harmony. With the counterstatement in m. 8, the PCA begins again, and again C♯ embellishes ii6 harmony, but this time the pitch is contained within a diminished chord that now adds the pitch class B♭ to the chromatic pitch field. As it turns out, the ii6 is transformed into the subdominant on the third beat of m. 14. Instead of immediately moving the counterstatement material into a bridge, Mozart now extends the previous subdominant harmony into the beginning of an eight-measure tonic extension (subdivided into two symmetrically related 4 + 4 phrases) that serves as a purely diatonic "orchestral tutti" topic whose purpose is to cap off the opening tonic period. The "orchestral tutti" topic along with the opening "fanfare" topic would seem to indicate that Mozart is deliberately trying to incorporate symphonic elements into a piano sonata, a feature generally associated with the early to middle-period sonatas of Muzio Clementi.

Up to this point only pcs 0–2 of the PCA have been unfolded, along with the quasi-development of the primary C♯/C♮ dyad conflict. With the beginning of the bridge in m. 21, the chromaticism becomes ever more intense, for now D♯ as pc 3 enters the tonal pitch field, with its implication of a 3♯ system. However, the pedal C prevents the D♯ from shifting systems, at least for the present. The D♯ as pc 3 moves directly to E as pc 4 within the same measure. Mozart is able to present D♯ as pc 3 instead of E♭ since the former pitch is here only embellishing, the implication of a potential move into E minor never being actualized since the C pedal mitigates the harmonic potential of pc 4. Instead, Mozart concentrates on the *linear* potential of pc 4 to move to the next pitch within the rising series, pc 5, here spelled as E♯ on the last eighth of m. 25. At this point within the bridge (mm. 25ff.) Mozart is setting up the arrival to the dominant area through the V/V. The sustained harmony of V6/5 of V in m. 25 reduces the function of the E♯ (in the upper voice) to that of a linear lower neighbor of F♯ (as part of the sustained V6/5), the next pitch class in the series. At the medial caesura in m. 32, the F♯ becomes structurally significant as pc 6. Mozart's first PCA rise thus introduces all the pitch classes of the first segment (pcs 0–7) in order, a not uncommon trait in Mozart's works. Haydn, on the other hand, will often omit pc 5 (as well as other pitch classes) from the initial PCA ascent, only to present them in later rises during the second harmonic area of the exposition.

Example 5.10   Mozart, Sonata in C K. 309/284b, first movement, exposition (mm. 1–43)

Mozart's second harmonic area in the dominant begins with a preparatory two-measure introduction on the V/V of the new area (mm. 33–4). Both measures of the preparation feature the primary dyad conflict as an accented dissonance on the downbeat of each measure: C♯ in the first, C♮ in the second. Measure 35 begins the dominant area proper with G in the bass as pc 7. Typical of the more expansive phrasing of opening periods of second harmonic areas, this one is an eight-measure period, here divided into 4 + 4 subphrases, both of which begin on G harmony. Returning to the dominant, G, at the second subphrase allows Mozart to precede that phrase with an arpeggiated V7/V chord with C♮ as flat seventh (see Example 5.10, m. 38). The close of the second subphrase (m. 42) before the transition repeats the same progression, again with C♮. In this way, the C♮/C♯ dyad conflict is maintained throughout the first period of the second harmonic area and, in addition, forms pcs 0, 1, and 2 (C♯ moves up to D as a matter of course), which begin the second PCA rise within dominant harmony. Measure 43 begins a relatively lengthy transitional period to a five-measure codetta (mm. 54–8) which closes the exposition; there is no closing period. The transition itself begins with pc 2 (D) reiterated as an accented half-note downbeat. Curiously, Mozart does not present pc 3, D♯, during the entire second harmonic area! But he does unfold the rest of the segment, continuing with pcs 4 (E) and 5 (F♮) as accented half-note downbeats in mm. 47 and 50 respectively, continuing the contrapuntal rise in the upper voice from the half-note D in m. 43. Pc 5 is then displaced by pc 6 (F♯) in m. 52 before resolving cadentially to pc 7 (G) at the start of the codetta in m. 54.

The gap in the PCA series created by omitting pc 3 actually highlights the primary dyad/trichordal issue of the piece – C♮, C♯, and D. Composers, Haydn especially, often isolate important segments of the PCA chromatic octave by skipping over intervening pitch classes within the series. In addition, the basically diatonic framework of the second harmonic area lets the listener hear the PCA ascent all the more clearly as it ascends to pc 7 at the close of the exposition. Finally, the relative lack of chromatic display in the second harmonic area now presents a startling contrast with the beginning of the development, which, without any preparation, restates the opening theme transposed into the minor dominant!

Typical of Mozart's development sections, this one is short and highly dramatic in its chromatic intensity. Thematically, most of the development section is based on the opening fanfare topic transposed into minor harmonic areas that follow along the minor areas of the reordered tonic hexachord, emanating from the minor dominant up to an extensive prolongation of the submediant, A minor, the "development key:"

Development ----------

F –	C –	G/g –	d –	a –	[e]
IV	I	V/v	ii	vi	[iii]

From the above harmonic scheme, we may then derive a background sketch of the development as follows:

Development			Retransition		Recapitulation
Fanfare topic			Fanfare topic		
m. 59	m. 67	mm. 73–86	m. 86	m. 90	m. 94
g	d	a	a	G	C
v		vi	vi	V	I
└──fifths cycle──┘					

As a consequence of the motion into the minor dominant, E♭, the missing pitch of the background "0" system, forms, for the first time in the movement, a system conflict with F♯ that governs the progress of the first seven measures of the development: the E♭ in m. 61 shifts the prevailing natural system down to a 3♭ system, only to be corrected with the F♯ in m. 65. The natural or "0" system remains in effect until m. 79, where D♯, the missing pitch class that governed the opening tonic statement of the exposition, now combines once more with C to form the opposite system conflict from that of the previous E♭/F♯. The D♯, first introduced in the bass in m. 79 as part of an internal prolongation of the submediant, never does get a chance to effect a system shift since C♮ is consistently pitted against it. All the same, the two system conflicts actually serve to frame the development, the E♭/F♯ conflict emerging from the flat side of the harmonic spectrum (G minor), while the D♯/C conflict is associated with the sharper or neutral side (A minor, C) of the spectrum.

In addition to the organization of system conflicts, the primary dyad conflict of the movement, that between C♮ and C♯, is also worked out in the development, often being tied into the system shifts. At the outset of the development, C♮s appear within the context of G minor harmony (mm. 59–62). As the music moves into the next fifth area, D minor, C♯s displace the previous C♮s (mm. 64–71) only to reach a rhythmic climax of sorts in m. 71, where both C♯ and then C♮ are presented in rapid succession within an eighth-note figure in the right hand. As it happens, C♯ returns in m. 76 within the context of G minor harmony, which functions as a neighbor harmony to the prevailing A minor prolongation. The C♯ in m. 76 (note the high register) is actually a deeper-level contrapuntal neighbor-note embellishment of the C♮ in m. 73, where the prolongation of A minor begins. The completion of the neighbor note comes in m. 77, where C♮, in the same high register, and supported by a C major triad, now displaces the previous C♯. Actually, the ultimate completion of this upper-voice embellishment does not occur until the articulated cadence to A minor in mm. 81–2; however, here the C♮ is heard at the lower octave. From this point until the recapitulation itself in m. 94, C♮s displace the previous C♯s altogether, the former pitch now being needed to counteract the system potential of D♯.

Of interest is how the completion of the PCA in the development motivates harmonic changes. The exposition left off with pc 7 (G), which is now restated at the start of the development in m. 59. The next pitch in the series, pc 8, is G♯, which is presented in mm. 70–72 as part of the dominant progression into the submediant. The harmonic potential of pc 8 as leading tone now makes pc 9 (A) structurally significant with its arrival as vi (A minor) in m. 73. The next pitch to unfold is pc 10, a difficult one to present in either of its enharmonic spellings. Mozart chooses B♭ to represent pc 10, but he must do so within the context of G minor harmony (m. 75). Thus the need to present the next pitch class in the ascending PCA determines the unusual lower-neighbor prolongation of A minor by G minor. The last pitch in the series, pc 11 (B♮), needs little comment since it is the leading tone of the tonic and appears quite naturally enough within the retransition passage (m. 90) that prepares for the recapitulation.

Diagram 5.8 gives the background harmonic plan of the recapitulation. Comparing this diagram of the piano sonata with that of the exposition of the string quintet in Diagram 5.7, one notices some fascinating relationships between the earlier and the later works. In particular, the piano sonata's opening statement at the start of the recapitulation moves most unexpectedly into a counterstatement in the parallel minor, an event completely missing from the exposition, which maintains the tonic major at this point. Perhaps Mozart was thinking of this passage when he composed the string quintet some ten years later; however, instead of a counterstatement in the parallel minor in the recapitulation, as occurred in the piano sonata, in the quintet the passage in the parallel minor is situated within the exposition. Both maneuvers are fully justified in their contexts, the string quintet perhaps being somewhat more startling in its placement of the parallel minor. In the case of the piano sonata, the counterstatement in the parallel minor is in fact prepared by the statement of the opening fanfare topic in the dominant minor at the start of the development section. In addition, the E♭ now raised in the counterstatement dramatically unfolds pc 3 of the recapitulation PCA, the previous pitch classes, C, C♯, and D (pcs 0–2) already having been presented at the start of the recapitulation as a matter of course. As well as being the start of a new PCA ascent, the introduction of pcs 0–2 naturally raises the basic dyad conflict/trichord issue of the movement. With the switch into a 3♭ system occasioned by the sudden move into the parallel minor, the passage from m. 101 to m. 105 is made all the more unstable by the constant fluctuation between 3♭ and "0" systems; F♯ is consistently pitted against the E♭, preventing any long-range system shift into flats. As in the exposition of the later string quintet, D♭ as an enharmonic reinterpretation of C♯ is also notable, but in the piano sonata, the D♭ is raised from an E minor diminished seventh chord and occasions no further motion into flat systems, while in the string quintet, the same D♭ is heard as the root of a ♭II6/4 chord which motivates an even greater dissonant motion into the 6♭ system which follows (see Diagrams 5.7 and 5.8). In the piano sonata, the E minor diminished seventh chord that supports the D♭ is structurally significant in that E♮ is pc 4 within the recapitulation PCA. Pcs 5 (F) and 6 (F♯) quickly follow in mm. 106–7. Mozart then dramatically fills in the rest of the PCA pitch classes in a single rising chromatic line in octaves (m. 109), which leads into the restatement of the "orchestral tutti" topic that closes the opening tonic period.

Recapitulation
1ˢᵗ Harmonic Area

m. 94	m. 101	m. 105	m. 107	m. 108	m. 110
Fanfare topic	Counterstatement				Orchestral Tutti
C – C♯ – D trichord restated	C♯ is now D♭				
	E♭/F♯ systems conflict				
C	c minor	e 07 -	f♯ 07 -	G6	F - C - G
I	i			V6	IV I V

m. 116
Bridge
D♯/C systems conflict (D♯ displaces E♭)   m. 123   **D♯/C is the last systems conflict of the movement**

C	G
I	V

2ⁿᵈ Harmonic Area

m. 127	m. 131	m. 137	mm. 143 –	145	
	C – C♯ – D trichord raised	Transition	C -		
			C6/4 - C♯ -	F	D trichord leads into →
C		C6	I6/4 c♯ 07	IV	d6
I		I6			ii6

Codetta (no Coda)
m. 148   mm. 150-51
Resolution of the C♯ - C♮ dyad conflict into tonic harmony

C
I

Diagram 5.8 Mozart, Piano Sonata in C K. 309/284a, first movement, recapitulation

Since the subsequent bridge passage begins again on tonic harmony, a second PCA rise now unfolds. Within the bridge, the D♯/C system conflict now displaces the previous E♭/F♯ conflict, the former system conflict finally dispelling any further flat-side harmonic motions for the rest of the movement. From pc 0 (C) at the start of the bridge, pcs 1 (C♯) and 2 (D) are again introduced (and thus the primary trichord issue of the movement) in m. 118. Pcs 3 (D♯) and 4 (E) follow in m. 123 with pc 5 (F♮) not entering until the restatement of second harmonic area material (mm. 128ff.). Because of the harmonic design of the recapitulation section (meaning that it remains totally within tonic harmony), the PCA may move *through* internal sections: in many cases, since internal divisions are marked by *tonic* cadences, multiple PCA unfoldings may occur, with all twelve pitch classes unfolded from one tonic cadence to another. However, just as many recapitulations elide their PCA rises so that one rise encompasses two or more internal divisions of the recapitulation, as is the case here. Thus the second harmonic area, now transposed into the tonic, *continues* the previous PCA unfolding instead of beginning a new one. Pc 5 (F♮) in m. 128 now ascends to pcs 6 (F♯) and 7 (G) in m. 132, all within the transposed second harmonic area. Mozart omits pc 8 (A♭/G♯) and continues the PCA ascent to pc 9 (A♮ in m. 143) and to pc 10 (B♭ in m. 144) within the lengthy transition to the codetta. Pc 10 (B♭) is presented within diminished harmony (m. 144) on a C♯ minor diminished seventh chord that again raises the primary dyad conflict of C♯/C♮ with the C♮ in the previous measure. Pc 11 (B♮) completes the PCA rise as part of dominant harmony that prepares for the tonic cadence introducing the codetta in m. 148. Mozart then concludes the movement by finally resolving the C♯/C♮ conflict within a permutation of the trichord, now heard as C♯–D–C♮ in mm. 150–51, the C♯ resolving into its diatonic counterpart, C♮, after first locally moving up to D.

Of course, Mozart resolves the C♯/C♮ conflict conclusively in the final rondo movement of the sonata. It is interesting that the very first chromatic heard in the last movement is, in fact, C♯ (m. 16), played in both hands and as part of the primary trichord of C♮–C♯–D that is unfolded in mm. 16–17. It is also of interest that the last 27 measures of the last movement treat both E♭/F♯ and D♯/C system conflicts as the last chromatic events of the movement, and therefore the whole sonata! After these two conflicts have been resolved into tonic harmony, the rest of the movement (21 measures in all) is completely diatonic except for two B♭s seven measures before the end. These B♭s that occur at the end of the last movement finally resolve the subdominant harmony that first appeared at the start of the "orchestral tutti" in the first movement and which became the tonic of the second movement.

Considering the complexity of composition envisioned by both Haydn and Mozart in terms of the chromatic development of their works, it is no wonder that only one composer could follow in their footsteps. It is to the work of Ludwig van Beethoven that we now turn.

Chapter Six

Nineteenth-Century Approaches to Eleven-Pitch-Class Systems Derived from the Viennese Classical Tradition

I. Beethoven, Sonata Form, the Minor Mode, and Chromatic Development at the Beginning of the Nineteenth Century

With chromatic events already saturating the tonal surface in compositions composed during the last decades of the eighteenth century, especially those of Mozart and Haydn, what more could a composer do to develop chromatic issues before the entire tonal system would collapse? Clarity of thought regarding what constituted a well-defined "tonality" became increasingly blurred as composers sought to expand the tonal spectrum by emphasizing the chromatic over the diatonic in their operas and sonata-form works. Put another way, utilizing the chromatic potential of the *Primary Chromatic Array* (PCA), along with structurally significant system shifts, could allow a composer to challenge the hegemony of the tonic itself by heightening localized chromatic events that related more to each other than to supporting the governing tonic key. Large-scale neighboring and third-related progressions, which increasingly articulate each note of the ascending PCA, now vie in importance, not to say motivic interest, with the diatonic harmonic goals they seem to defy. Chromaticism, as a symmetrical force within a hierarchal tonal system in which all musical events support our understanding of the background tonic, now becomes an end in itself and begins to dominate the musical discourse in much the same way it did in mannerist compositions of the sixteenth and early seventeenth centuries (see Chapter 3).

Of all the composers who followed in the footsteps of Mozart and Haydn, it was undoubtedly Beethoven who was most successful in pushing chromaticism to its limits, yet always within the confines of the tonic background. Beethoven found so many innovative ways of expressing tonic harmony through a greatly extended chromatic surface, which was consistently projected into deeper structural levels, that his compositional methods in this regard became a source of inspiration for most of the composers who followed him over the course of the nineteenth century, consciously and unconsciously.

We have previously discussed, albeit somewhat superficially, Beethoven's compositional methods and their relevance to PCA and system analysis in Chapter 2, using Beethoven's Symphony no. 5 in C minor and his Piano Sonata in C major op. 53 ("Waldstein") as examples. Now that we have had a chance to examine the relevance of this theory in more detail in the works of Haydn and Mozart, a more detailed discussion of Beethoven's approach to chromatic development would seem a logical next step. We have deliberately picked minor-mode works as examples of Beethoven's compositional methods, since the minor mode seems to have had a great attraction for this composer and, in addition, we have not as yet given detailed examples of minor-mode pieces in relation to the present theory.

Beethoven's Piano Sonata in F minor op. 57 ("Appassionata") was composed in 1804–05. The work is notable for its motion into the minor relative of the tonic at the close of the exposition, a harmonic event unprecedented in the literature before this point. In fact, Beethoven had begun to work out the consequences of this gesture as early as 1793 in the first movement of his C minor Piano Trio op. 1 no. 3, where the relative minor in the bridge precedes the major relative as the second harmonic area of the exposition. Beethoven becomes quite a bit more daring in his treatment of the minor relative in the first movement of his Piano Sonata in C minor op. 13 ("Pathétique"), where the second harmonic area itself is in the minor relative before releasing its tension into the major relative at the closing period. Finally, the "Appassionata" is the most extreme in that stage of this evolutionary process since the end of the exposition *is in the minor relative*, an event anticipated in the bridge and then presented in the closing period *after* the major relative has been achieved as the second harmonic area. The expositions of these three works may be illustrated as follows for the sake of comparison (note that the counterstatement in the early C minor trio *beings on the submediant degree*, a most unusual procedure for its time and one not lost on Schumann in the first movement of his Piano Quintet op. 44, whose counterstatement begins on the dominant – see discussion below):

1. Piano Trio in C minor op. 1 no. 3 (1793)

Exposition

First harmonic area	counterstatement/bridge		second harmonic area
c	A♭ --- e♭		E♭
i	VI iii		III

2. Piano Sonata in C minor "Pathétique" op. 13 (1799)

First harmonic area	second harmonic area	closing
c	e♭	E♭
i	iii	III

3. Piano Sonata in F minor "Appassionata" op. 57 (1804–05)

First harmonic area	counterstatement/bridge		second harmonic area	closing
f	f– a♭		A♭	a♭
i	I iii		III	iii

In each case, the turn toward the minor relative causes a shift of the prevailing system into extreme flats. In C minor, the system-shift motivator (that is, a chromatic pitch class that, when introduced, causes a system shift either up or down from the prevailing system, depending on its spelling) would be G♭, shifting the tonic 3♭ system down to a 6♭ system. In both the early piano trio and the "Pathétique," the correcting A♮ returns the system to a 3♭ system before the structurally significant relative major is reached. In the case of the "Appassionata," the shift of system into a 7♭ system, first before the second harmonic area (which is corrected by a D♮ in m. 32) and then at the closing period in m. 51 (here, the C♮ remains uncontested), is so distant a system shift that Beethoven plunges into the development section without repeating the exposition.

Diagram 6.1 gives an overall background harmonic plan for the first movement, which also indicates the PCA rise. The PCA in minor mode operates somewhat differently from that of the major mode since the second harmonic area is usually in the relative major and not in the dominant. If the relative major is the goal of the second harmonic area, as it is in this case, the PCA ascent within the exposition will terminate at pc 3, the root pitch of the relative major, here A♭. In Classical sonata form, there is only one harmonic area other than the tonic in the exposition. Consequently, in a minor-mode exposition, the opening statement and bridge will unfold PCA pitches 0, 1, and 2; pc 3, the tonic of the new harmony, will arrive at the opening of the second harmonic area. Each additional cadential arrival within the second harmonic area, namely, those to the closing period and codetta, will be articulated by a repeat of pcs 0–2, with pc 3 occurring at the formal cadence to these structural events. On the other hand, if VI is the goal of the second harmonic area, as it is in the first movement of Beethoven's Symphony no. 9 in D minor, the PCA rise will terminate at pc 8, replicating the PCA rise of pcs 0–8 at the closing period and codetta. Most importantly, it should be emphasized that it is not necessary to replicate *all* the pitches of the PCA within any particular PCA rise; however, a pitch missing from one rise will usually turn up in a subsequent one. How complete the various rises are within any given section of the form (meaning the extent of the chromatic pitch content) will thus inform the compositional, not to say the emotional, intent of the composer.

EXPOSITION

1ST Harmonic Area	C.S. + Bridge	2ND Harmonic Area (1st period)	Transition	Closing (2nd period)

basic rhythm: ♫ established
main dyad conflicts (expanded to trichords):
G♮ – G♭ (♭II) – F
D♮ – D♭ (VI) – C

Unison theme
f minor

							a♭ minor (relates to
f minor	– a♭ m	A♭		d♭ minor			F♭ major)
i		III		iv/III			iii
	[harmonized]						a♭
PCA: F	F– G♭ –	G♮→A♭					a♭
0	0 1	2 3					3

DEVELOPMENT

Codetta	E major	G♮ ----	G♭	D♭ – G♭ – bm – G6/5 – C – d♭ dim.7 → C7	Retrns.
a♭ minor–B6	I]	e minor	A♭7 →	VI V	C7
iii [V6]	(E is enharmonic F♭)	c minor	G♭ -----	V	V7

PCA: a♭	A♮	B♭	C♭ – C♮	D♭	D♭
3	4	5	6 7	8	8 (sustained through the recap.)

RECAPITULATION

1st H.A. [the melody in m. 138 has D♮]

		C.S. +	Bridge	2ND H.A. (1st period)	Transition
D♭→C (in the bass)	G♭		F Major	D♮ –	D♭ —
i6/4	D♭	C	→	F Major	b♭ minor
	♭II6/4	V		I	iv

					I	

PCA:	D♮	E♭	E♮	F	[D – D♭ – C raised again]
	9	10	11	0	

Diagram 6.1 Beethoven, "Appassionata" Sonata op. 57, first movement: background harmonic plan

CODA

Closing (2nd period)

[D♭] – C   [G♭/G♮ raised again]   [2nd **H.A. theme**]

D♭/D♮

G♭/G♮ conflicts raised again & resolved! [D♮/D♭ conflict resolved]

C   **f minor**   **f minor**   **D♭ – G♭ – C**

V   **i**   **i**   **VI ♭II V6/4 – 7/5/3**

tonic arrival – answers the reason
why a♭ minor as the Closing period
in the Exposition

Adagio [D♭ finally resolved into f minor]   Più Allegro

[**G♭/G♮ resolved** + ¯⁔ .... rhythmic issue]

D♭→ C   **f minor**

V   **i**

(Actual point of resolution)

Unlike the longer PCA ascents in the expositions of major-mode pieces, the PCA rise to III in the expositions of minor-mode works is relatively short. The bulk of the PCA ascent (pcs 4–11) is thus relegated to the development section leading to the recapitulation, at which point the first octave ascent is unfolded and pc 0 is once more regained at the point of recapitulation and the return of tonic harmony. Developments in minor mode tend, for this reason, to be highly chromatic and dramatically intense. In order to balance the emotional content of the development with that of the exposition, in which the stable nature of the relative is the only goal of motion, Classical composers tended to load the second harmonic area with as much passing and structural chromaticism as possible; an excellent example of this is the second harmonic area in the first movement of Mozart's Symphony no. 40 in G minor. One can infer from the above diagram comparing three of Beethoven's minor-mode first movements that the composer must have been concerned that the arrival in the relative major in a minor-mode sonata-form movement would create an expanse that was – curiously – too stable. In fact, if we read into Beethoven's inclination to work through the same problem over and over again (with a variety of creative resolutions), we may suggest that the composer may have been preoccupied with what he perceived as a significant musical problem. The main issue with III as a second harmonic area in minor mode is that the root of the relative major functions as the hexachord system of the key; thus, the unstable first harmonic area seems to resolve at the point where the relative major is reached. This may be the reason why Beethoven was at such pains to destabilize the relative major through juxtaposition with its parallel minor in the examples above.

The destabilizing effect of modal switching, either before or after the arrival of the relative major (or both, as in the case of the "Appassionata"), does not, however, affect the PCA rise itself in the exposition, which still terminates at pc 3 in either case. Notwithstanding so short an initial rise, Beethoven seizes upon the harmonic potential of each pitch class within the PCA to create a tense harmonic atmosphere within an already unstable minor tonic and, subsequently, in the minor relative. Diagram 6.1 charts the course of the PCA up to the recapitulation (see also Example 6.1, which examines the exposition of the first movement through the start of the development section). Notable is the emphasis given to pc 1 (G♭) as the Neapolitan degree within the initial rise. The G♭, which first occurs in m. 5 as part of an arpeggiation of ♭II, itself generates its fifth, D♭, the Neapolitan to the dominant.

Example 6.1 Beethoven, "Appassionata" Sonata op. 57, exposition–development (mm. 1–72)

Example 6.1 Beethoven,"Appassionata"Sonata op. 57,exposition–development (mm. 1–72) continued

Both G♭ and D♭ as individual pitch classes are worked out over the course of the movement, either as controlling pitch classes that inform harmonic areas, as in the very opening of the movement, or at climactic points within the development section. In addition, these same pitch classes are sustained as members of vertical sonorities, often projected as dyad conflicts, that keep them ever present throughout the movement. An example of the former is the motion into D♭ minor as iv/III during the transition between the first and second periods within the second harmonic area, in which the D♭ displaces the previous D♮ that was part of the previous A♭ major harmony. Similarly, the G♭/G♮ dyad conflict becomes a focal point in the unison run which culminates at the end of the transition just before the closing period (mm. 47–50). On a deeper level, the G♭/G♮ conflict permeates the development section, often appearing as chord tones within adjacent harmonies; for instance, G♮ as part of E minor and C minor harmony, followed by G♭ as seventh within the A♭7 chord that leads to D♭ within the climax of the development section. Once D♭ is reached as a goal of motion (m. 109), it is sustained through the passing harmonies of B♭ minor and G♭ major (see Diagram 6.1). After resolving to C in m. 122, D♭ is sustained within diminished harmony up to the point of retransition in m. 132, where it temporarily resolves to the dominant seventh. Lastly, both D♭/D♮ and G♭/G♮ conflicts may be extended into trichords: D♮–D♭–C and G♮–G♭–F respectively. The last member of each trichord acts as a point of temporary resolution.

We may now postulate that pc 1 of the PCA (G♭) becomes a dominating pitch class from the very opening of the movement, and this fact holds true for each subsequent pitch class over the course of the exposition. Continuing with the PCA ascent, the G♭, as pc 1, now progresses to pc 2, G♮, an equally significant pitch since it both is associated with the dominant of the tonic and is the leading tone of the relative major. The G♮ first appears as a PCA pitch class in m. 9 as part of a localized dominant harmony, and continues this way until into the bridge, where its function is transformed to that of leading tone to A♭, the goal of the bridge. With the arrival of the major relative in m. 35, pc 3, the terminating pitch class of the exposition's PCA segment, is reached.

At this point, the first segment of the PCA is repeated, now within the area of the relative. Pc 0 (F) appears at the start of the consequent phrase (m. 37) as the first melodic pitch of a linear arpeggiation of the subdominant triad of the relative (D♭), only to change course suddenly and descend to C as part of an A♭ 6/4 chord in the next measure. The D♭/C relationship is extensively worked out over the course of the entire movement, often articulated by the characteristic rhythm: ♫ ♩. Pcs 1 and 2 (G♭ and G♮ respectively) are, as stated previously, introduced within the unison scalar passage (mm. 47–50) that dramatically leads into the closing section in the minor relative. Interestingly, these two pitch classes are introduced, at first, in reverse order; that is, G♮–G♭. Beethoven thus highlights both the fact that these are the next pitches within the PCA and the fact that they form a seminal dyad conflict within the sonata. Incidentally, from the beginning of the movement pc 1 has been consistently spelled as a flat and not as a sharp. If pc 1 had been spelled as a sharp, F♯, Beethoven would have been forced to move into a dominant direction, a path he chose to avoid.

The closing section of the exposition now unfolds a final PCA rise, but with one necessary adjustment to the array. Since the harmonic area of the closing period plunges into the minor relative, the previously diatonic F♮ (pc 0) is now displaced by F♭, making pc 0 of the PCA quite difficult to present. Therefore, this last PCA rise within the exposition starts with pc 1 (G♭), a pitch which is now diatonic within the area; previously, G♭ was dissonant and G♮ was consonant. Pc 2 (G♮) follows on the downbeat of m. 58 as part of diminished harmony, but becomes activated as a PCA pitch class on the third beat of m. 60, where it is a cadential leading tone within the dominant seventh to the minor relative. Pc 3, A♭, is attained on the downbeat of m. 61, at the start of the codetta, leading directly into the development section.

In minor mode, the bulk of the PCA unfolding takes place within the development section, and ends (usually) at the point of recapitulation and the return of pc 0. Since the development in minor mode must unfold many more pitch classes in its move to complete the tonic chromatic octave than one would find in the major mode, minor-mode developments tend to be relatively lengthy as compared with their major-mode counterparts. However, both major- and minor-mode development sections are compositionally geared to create as much harmonic tension as possible, and therefore both modes tend to emphasize diminished harmony and harmonic areas that stress the minor (vi or iii in major are preferred climactic areas).

In order to avoid being overburdened with unnecessary detail, the reader is directed to Diagram 6.1 for the placement of the remaining pitch classes of the PCA rise within the development section of the "Appassionata." However, it is necessary to point out some salient aspects of the development's PCA unfolding, since this too ties into the developmental process that lies at the heart of the movement. First, and most striking, is the fact that the closing period in A♭ minor relates more to F♭ major than it does to the tonic, F minor. Consequently, the F♭ within the closing harmonic period enharmonically switches into E (m. 65), a pitch class that motivates the E major harmonic area initiating the development section. (As a matter of course, all the previous flats are enharmonically respelled as sharps.) The note A♮, pc 4 within the continuing PCA ascent, is now easily presented within E major harmony. Note how each of the subsequent pitch classes of the PCA reflects the harmonic area in which it is presented. For example, pc 5, B♭, arises out of C minor harmony, and, later pc 8, D♭, is structurally significant as the harmonic goal of the development (VI).

Beyond this is the way in which Beethoven intersects the PCA unfolding with the ongoing development of one of the seminal trichords of the movement, D♮–D♭–C. This trichord, in retrograde (C–D♭–D♮), forms the nucleus of the development section, centered as it is on pc 8 (D♭). Pc 7 (C♮) is presented as leading tone to D♭ (part of a linearized V6/5/VI) in m. 108 (pc 6 immediately precedes it in the same measure). As Diagram 6.1 shows, the D♭, once it is presented as a harmonic area, becomes a controlling pitch; meaning that D♭ determines the harmonic progression surrounding it to the extent that D♭ is sustained right through the recapitulation. On a more foreground level, the D♭ area gives Beethoven a chance to develop the seminal trichord of D♭–D♮–C on different structural levels. For instance, there is the large-scale contrapuntal motion between the D♭ of m. 109 and the C attained in m. 122. Within this area, D♮s enter within B minor harmony (mm. 120ff.), functioning as temporary upper neighbors to the sustained D♭ underneath; this indicates that D♭ has not yet been displaced by D♮ within the rising PCA.

More locally, the d♭07 that pervades the rest of the development section descends to C in its guise as rhythmic motive in m. 132, the C now sustained as an eighth-note pedal into the recapitulation. Since the tonic in root position has not yet been reached, the PCA, in this instance, continues past the expected point of recapitulation: pc 9 (D♮) appears in m. 138 over the C pedal at the end of the melody's first phrase, but D♭ again returns as the harmony veers toward the Neapolitan, the harmony of the melody's second phrase, this time over a D♭ pedal. The G♭ 6/4 harmony brings in pc 10 (E♭) in m. 142, which is then displaced by pc 11 (E♮) in m. 144, the latter pitch now acting as a leading tone of dominant harmony and remaining activated as a note of the array until the counterstatement brings the PCA to its conclusion – and does so in the surprising key of F major (m. 151). Throughout the highly charged passage that began with the recapitulation, D♭ and D♮ are in continuous conflict over the D♭ and C pedals seething underneath. The presence at the opening of the recapitulation of all three trichord pitch classes (D♮, D♭, C) brings the last member of the trichord, D♮, into prominence, as pc 9 of the development section's concluding array.

Once the PCA has been completed at the point of recapitulation (or, in this case, at the counterstatement within the recapitulation), the complete PCA is again unfolded over the course of the recapitulation. In this way, major dyad conflicts and other chromatic issues can now be resolved into tonic harmony since the recapitulation remains entirely in the tonic, whether major or minor, or both. Since the tonic is never actually abandoned, the design of the PCA ascent may take any one of several forms depending on compositional choices. One possible choice would be to reiterate the entire chromatic octave on the way to each point of tonic arrival: specifically, from the bridge to the beginning of the second harmonic area (now transposed into the tonic), from the transition up to the closing period, and, finally, from the transition to the codetta up to the arrival of the restated codetta material at the conclusion of the recapitulation. In addition, another iteration of the PCA ascent may take place in the coda if this section is sufficiently extensive, as it often is in Beethoven. Another possibility, and the one adopted by Beethoven in his "Appassionata" Sonata, is to extend a single PCA unfolding over the course of the entire recapitulation, the chromatic ascent cutting through all the internal divisions of the recapitulation without any repetition. What is interesting in this regard is how the rising PCA actually coincides with, and even conditions, important harmonic events and resolutions.

If we take the recapitulation PCA as starting with pc 0 at the F major counterstatement in m. 152, pc 1, either G♭ or F♯ is the next pitch. Oddly enough, Beethoven elects pc 1 to be F♯ in m. 170 instead of the expected G♭, the Neapolitan pitch class that initiated the PCA rises previously. However, F♯, as part of diminished harmony, soon turns into its enharmonic equivalent, G♭, in m. 181, where the minor subdominant, B♭ minor, presages the return to the minor tonic in time for the closing period (m. 190). G♭ is sustained until the opening phrase of the closing period, where Beethoven moves this pitch up to pc 2, G♮, within the same measure (m. 192, left hand). The rise to G♮ is repeated in m. 196, and G♮ is displaced by A♭, pc 3, in m. 199. This A♭ is now sustained until m. 213, when A♮ appears. Typical of PCA segments, the next passage, mm. 213–22, works out the A♭/A♮ dyad, even to the extent of passing through a prominent G♭ area in m. 218. The A♮ finally resolves to pc 5, B♭, in m. 222, pc 5 remaining active until it becomes structurally significant in m. 227 when the minor subdominant is restated. The next pitch in the sequence, B♮, pc 6, follows in m. 229 as the root of diminished harmony that also, most interestingly, coincides with the final resolution of the D♮/D♭ conflict that has been one of the major dyadic concerns of the movement. The B♮ leads to C, pc 7 (m. 231), as part of a larger 6/4–5/3 cadential motion that coalesces into the dramatic final resolution of the D♭/C motive at the Più Allegro in m. 238. Because of the dramatization of pc 8, D♭, and also since the D♭/D♮ conflict has now been resolved, there is no need for pc 8 to proceed to pc 9, D♮; instead, pc 8 goes directly to pc 10, E♭, in m. 243. This latter pitch is sustained until the formal cadence in mm. 248–9, where pcs 11 and 0 complete the octave. Pcs 11 and 0 are restated in more emphatic form as part of the authentic cadence in m. 257, the actual rhythmic downbeat of the entire movement.

Beethoven's strategy of restating both the counterstatement and the second harmonic area material in F major, rather than in the tonic minor, is part of a larger compositional design to delay the tonic minor until the closing period of the recapitulation, thereby balancing, and even justifying, the unusual A♭ minor close of the exposition. As a general procedure, it should be noted, Mozart, Haydn, and Beethoven often use the expositions of their sonata-form movements to "ask questions" or to "pose problems," which only the recapitulation can "solve," since the recapitulation traditionally provides the locale to resolve these issues within an area of tonic harmony (the coda also has this function, if it is prominent enough). Thus, the two most important dyad conflicts of the movement, D♭/D♮ and G♭/G♮, return in the recapitulation, and are further developed before they finally resolve. Beethoven's motion into the parallel major keeps both D♮ and G♮ "alive," as it were, and the switch back into minor, raising D♭ and G♭, only serves to intensify these conflicts.

After the second harmonic area is recapitulated in the tonic major, the transitional passage that leads back into the original tonic minor becomes a highly dramatized harmonic event (mm. 181–8). In the exposition, this same passage preceded the closing period in the minor relative, with equally dramatic results, but in the recapitulation, the transition now has the added function of leading to the return of the tonic minor!

The coda, beginning in m. 204, restates the rising arpeggios of the opening theme once more before veering off into D♭ (mm. 210ff.) and then to G♭ (mm. 218ff.). Within both of these harmonic areas, D♮s and G♮s continue to raise the dyad conflicts until in m. 229, a d♮^{07} chord, the final expression of D♮, slowly gives way to the D♭–C motive in the bass in m. 235. This motive grinds to a halt on a root-position dominant seventh with the dynamic marking of *pp* along with a fermata and the tempo marking "Adagio" over it, creating one of the most tense moments in all music. With the Più Allegro that follows, the tension is dispersed, and it remains only for the G♭/G♮ conflict to be resolved; this is soon accomplished in mm. 242–3.

Finally, Beethoven resolves the rhythmic tension of the D♭–C rhythmic motive as the eighths of the motive flatten out first into syncopations, and then into even rhythms. The sixteenth notes that have created so much of the rhythmic excitement in the movement are dispersed by slowly sinking five octaves down to the original register of the opening, the sixteenths evaporating into a single held tonic chord in the last measure.

At this point it would be well to illustrate the 4♭ system matrix of the "Appassionata," the diagram of which clearly illustrates the wide-ranging system shifts to extreme flat and sharp systems that govern the course of the first movement (see Figure 6.1).

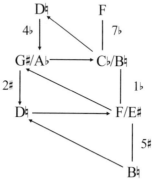

Figure 6.1   Beethoven, "Appassionata" Sonata op. 57, first movement, 4♭ tonic system matrix

How do system shifts inform the progress of this movement? More to the point, how can an understanding of system modulations increase our awareness of the movement's inner structure? Detailing every system shift in the first movement of the "Appassionata" would be an unnecessary labor, but a look at the most important system modulations can be enlightening in the extreme.

In the minor mode, the missing pitch spelled as an augmented second above the tonic of the relative major, in this case B♮, appears consistently, as a matter of course, since this particular pitch class has an important voice-leading function as the leading tone of the dominant: in the 4♭ system of the "Appassionata," B♮ is the leading tone of C, the dominant of the tonic, F minor. When present, the B♮, more often than not, is prevented from shifting the prevailing 4♭ system up to a 1♭ system, since A♭, the missing pitch of the 1♭ system, is ever present. But what happens when the missing pitch, especially in minor-mode compositions, appears as a flat? When presented, this pitch would move the prevailing tonic system down three signatures into a system of extreme flats; and if the tonic is F minor, a 4♭ system, as in the sonata under discussion, the system shift caused by the introduction of C♭ will thrust the prevailing 4♭ system down into a 7♭ system! The resultant move down into the deeper regions of the subdominant cycle of fifths challenges the hegemony of the tonic itself, since distant subdominant motions, whichever flat areas they arrive at, form contrapuntal relationships with their surrounding harmonic areas, but have no direct voice-leading function within the key, unlike harmonic progressions centered on the dominant.

At first, Beethoven is careful not to disrupt the tonic surface with too powerful a harmonic digression, which might obliterate the important move into the relative major at the start of the second harmonic area in m. 35. Instead, he introduces the first C♭ of the movement as a passing motion within the bridge, almost as a seeming afterthought (see mm. 25–31). The system shift down into a 7♭ system that this move occasions is supported by the same A♭ minor harmony that will eventually surface, most dramatically, as the harmonic area of the closing period of the exposition. When Beethoven used this same progression in the first movement of his earlier piano trio op. 1 no. 3 in C minor, the bridge's E♭ minor prepared not for the closing period of the exposition, but for the more acceptable position of the harmonic area opening the development section. Here the extreme shift into the minor relative would not disrupt the structural relationship of the tonic to its relative major. After the arrival of the relative major in m. 35, the transition which follows (starting at m. 41) suddenly veers into the minor subdominant of the relative to prepare for the closing period in A♭ minor. The D♭ harmony moves directly into a cadential 6/4 with E♭ in the bass, the sixth degree of which once more raises C♭, but now has a far greater significance. The concomitant move into the 7♭ system, occasioned by the C♭, forces the closing period into the minor relative, the 7♭ system remaining in effect all the way into the opening period of the development section proper.

The enharmonic switch into E major at the start of the development not only maintains the harmonic tension begun by the unusually dissonant A♭ minor of the closing period, but also compels four system shifts that explode – there is no other term for it – within one measure of music! Each system pitch class is presented simultaneously in m. 71 as part of diminished harmony with each successive missing pitch a minor third away from the previous one; each pitch enharmonically respells part of the *tonic matrix* that governs the entire piece (see Figure 6.1 above). Specifically, m. 71 first introduces D♮, which moves the 7♭ system up to a 4♭ system. Within the same measure, B♮ now shifts the system up again to 1♭. The B♮ yields to G♯, effecting a 2♯ system; and finally, E♯ brings the system in line with the E major harmonic area that initiates the development.

After the 5♯ system has been achieved, Beethoven reverses the process as the harmonic plan of the development moves away from E major toward the next goal, A♭. As it turns out, the system shifts descend quickly from a 2♯ system to a 1♭ system in m. 81. At the moment when A♭ materializes in m. 87, the A♭ shifts the systems back down to a 4♭ system. As the music descends further into the flat direction, so too do the systems associated with it. Thus, in the measure before the D♭ harmonic area (VI is the next harmonic goal) C♭ once more returns, shifting the system further down into a 7♭ system (m. 108). Extreme flat areas follow, B♭ minor and G♭ major in particular, until both D♮ and B♮ enter in m. 120 as the harmony moves into C major. The D♮ raises the system back to a 4♭ system, and is followed immediately by the B♮, which raises the system further to a 1♭ system. This last system transformation is significant because no occurrence of A♭, the note that is required to reactivate the 4♭ tonic system, follows this shift for the next 15 measures, the harmonic rhythm slowing to a crawl on diminished harmony. Only at the exact point of recapitulation (m. 135), with the return of the arpeggiated opening theme, with its third degree, A♭, does the system finally revert to a 4♭ system! Thus systems analysis allows us to see exactly how the various system shifts within the development section prepare for, and perhaps even condition, structural goals. The same is true for all sections of the form.

No sooner does the recapitulation revert the system to a 4♭ system than B♮ (the missing pitch – and thus the controlling pitch! – of the 1♭ system) and A♭ (the controlling pitch of the 4♭ system) collide until B♮ "wins out" in m. 171, raising the system back up to a 1♭ system. The newly regained 1♭ system now prepares for the return of the thematic material of the second harmonic area, now transposed into the tonic major. As the music reverts to the tonic minor, A♭ now "wins out" over B♮ (mm. 182–90) in time for the closing period, now transposed into F minor. From here to the end of the movement, the 4♭ system remains in effect; any B♮s that remain are quickly offset by the surrounding A♭s of the tonic minor.

From this discussion of the "Appassionata" Sonata, one could conclude that C♭, the missing pitch of the tonic 4♭ system, informs the design of the entire first movement, if not the entire sonata. In countless other pieces Beethoven seems to be fascinated with the compositional problems posed by working out the minor third degree, in both major and minor modes. For example, the first movement of Beethoven's Piano Trio in D op. 70 no. 1 (the "Ghost," 1808) is a spectacular example of the potential compositional implications of pc 3. The opening theme of this work (see Example 6.2) climaxes on F♮ (the missing pitch of the prevailing 2♯ system) as early as m. 5! The sudden shift into the 1♭ system is not only shocking, but prolonged: the 1♭ system remains in effect well into the bridge (mm. 21ff.) despite the attempts of G♯ to correct the system, and the continual presence of F♮ prevents any modulation back to the tonic 2♯ system. So strong is pc 3 as a governing pitch from the time when it is first introduced that the bridge itself moves into F major (♭III) as a temporary harmonic area (the entire bridge passage is reproduced in Example 6.3). Only in m. 34, with the introduction of an uncontested G♯ as lower neighbor to A, does the system finally revert to that of the tonic 2♯ system in preparation for the arrival of the second harmonic area in the dominant (m. 43). Interestingly, Beethoven avoids treating F♮ as part of an augmented sixth, which would fall naturally to the V/V, a gesture often found in Haydn's Paris symphonies of the 1780s. Instead, in m. 34 Beethoven moves the F in the bass up to F♯ as part of a D♯ 07, a chord which acts as a leading tone diminished chord to the V/V on the downbeat of m. 35. Beethoven is not just refraining from duplicating a typical Haydnesque progression (see Chapter 5); he is also in the process of working out the seminal F♮/F♯ dyad conflict that is the focal point of the opening phrase of the movement.

Upon a more thorough analysis, it becomes apparent that the F♮/F♯ dyad conflict, along with its concomitant system shifts, controls most of the movement's harmonic events. For example, the development is governed primarily by flat systems, initiated by a lengthy extension of the minor subdominant, G minor, begun in m. 83. As a consequence, F♮, the pitch that informs the developmental process of the entire movement, is raised in m. 87, causing a major system shift down into a 1♭ system. This gesture itself motivates a deeper move into a 4♭ system when A♭, the missing pitch of the 1♭ system, is introduced in m. 94. Thereafter, the development is pulled back and forth between 1♭ and 2♯ systems until finally G♯ in m. 136 confirms the 2♯ system in preparation for the recapitulation in m. 157.

The recapitulation again dramatically raises F♮, this time as part of D minor harmony within the bridge passage that leads to the second harmonic area. Beethoven completely rewrites the bridge so that the opening theme now reappears within D minor harmony (mm. 166ff.). Beethoven's choice of D minor fulfills the modal orientation of the movement's opening phrase, where both F♮ and B♭ were introduced within the context of D major. The recapitulation bridge subsequently plunges further into B♭, which balances the F major section of the bridge in the exposition. Significantly, all this harmonic motion is entirely controlled by pc 3!

Example 6.2 Beethoven, Piano Trio op. 70 no. 1, first movement, opening statement (mm. 1–9)

Example 6.3 Beethoven, Piano Trio op. 70 no. 1, first movement, bridge passage (mm. 21–43)

Among so many of Beethoven's other chamber works that are motivated by the development of their respective system conflicts is Beethoven's Piano Trio in B♭ op. 97 (the "Archduke," 1810–11). This work is equally as impressive as Beethoven's op. 70 no.1, discussed above, in the exploitation of its complementary systems. For instance, the exposition of the first movement of the "Archduke" plays out the conflicting 2♭ and 1♯ systems on a fundamental level: the first harmonic area is in B♭ and the second harmonic area is in G major. The relationship between these two pitch classes is melodically prepared within the opening measures of the movement, where the top line of the piano part falls from B♭ to an accented downbeat G in mm. 4 and 5.

Notably absent, however, is any play of systems within the entire opening statement (mm. 1–33), there being exactly eleven pitch classes, with pc 3, C♯/D♭, omitted. Thus Beethoven has carefully saved this pitch for its dramatic entrance as pc 3 of the exposition's initial PCA ascent of the exposition, at the start of the bridge passage that leads to the second harmonic area (the bridge begins in m. 33 and lasts until m. 51). At first, C♯ is presented as a melodic lower neighbor to D at the outset of the bridge, but it is pitted against B♭ tonic harmony, which prevents a system shift. However, in m. 35 a chromatic 5–6 exchange unexpectedly swings the harmony from B♭ to D major in preparation for the arrival of G major as the second harmonic area. With D major harmony now displacing B♭ harmony, the C♯ is now able to effect a system shift up to a 1♯ system, which remains uncontested until m. 81, well into the closing area. The second harmonic area is so firmly established within the 1♯ system that Beethoven changes the key signature to one sharp eight measures before the arrival of the second harmonic area. Only when the B♭ returns at the end of the exposition, and the system reverts to a 2♭ system, does Beethoven then change the key signature to two flats as well, in preparation for the repeat of the exposition.

Another important aspect of the "Archduke" Trio, in terms of the interplay of its systems, is what transpires in the recapitulation. The second harmonic area returns transposed into B♭ major (thus strengthening the connection between G major and B♭ major), but the closing area surprisingly turns in the direction of the tonic minor! As a result, the C♯ that characterized so much of the exposition has now turned into its enharmonic equivalent, D♭, throwing the prevailing 2♭ system down into a 5♭ system! The amount of time now spent in the 5♭ system balances the equivalent amount of time spent in the 1♯ system in the exposition, since the 5♭ system in the recapitulation is sustained right through both the codetta and the coda. Seven measures before the end of the movement, E♮, melodically enhancing F, the dominant pitch class, finally redresses the system to its original two flats (m. 281). But Beethoven goes one step further. Five measures before the end of the movement, C♯ returns, as if Beethoven felt the need to convert D♭ to the pitch that started it all; and as at the first appearance of C♯ at the start of the exposition bridge, B♭ harmony is pitted against it, allowing the 2♭ system to end the movement. One might even conceive of the final measures as being a systems summary of the whole movement.

Another impressive "systems piece" is Beethoven's earlier String Quintet in C op. 29 (1801), a work not generally discussed in the literature. However, in terms of systems analysis, a look at the general harmonic plan of the exposition of the quintet's first movement is most illuminating:

Exposition		m.17			m.41	
1st Harmonic Area		Bridge			2nd Harmonic Area	
Introduces the main						
trichord motive: C-C♯-D		[C♮			C♯	C♮]
C		C –	am —	E	A —	am
I		I	vi	V/VI♯	VI♯	vi

	m.75			m.91		
	Closing Period			Codetta	1st end.-------	
	[C♯	C♮			C♮]	
E	A ----------	am —		am	C	
V/VI♯	VI♯	vi		vi	III/vi	:

Diagram 6.2 Beethoven, String Quintet op. 29, first movement, exposition

Most obvious in Diagram 6.2 is Beethoven's preoccupation with the major/minor parallel of the submediant and the concomitant working-out of the C♯/C♮ dyad conflict that informs most of the movement. The exposition is further distinguished by the fact that its structural harmonic areas revolve completely around the C matrix, shifting between "0" and 3♯ systems (see Example 6.4). Of interest is the fact that within the opening tonic period Beethoven introduces the missing pitch of the "0" system first as E♭ and not D♯ (not unlike the procedure in the "Waldstein" Sonata, composed several years later and in the same key), the E♭ appearing as a chord tone within an F♯°7 (see mm. 7 and 15). Thereafter in the bridge, the missing pitch is spelled consistently as D♯ as Beethoven moves into A major for his second harmonic area. The preparatory A minor passage within the bridge raises C♮, which conflicts with D♯, the one pitch contradicting the other until D♯ finally "wins out" on the last eighth note of m. 39, just in time for the arrival of the second harmonic area in A major. The rest of the exposition vacillates between A major and A minor, the C♮ and D♯ in constant conflict with each other until C♮ "wins out" within A minor harmony, the A minor area being capped by the codetta at the end of the exposition.

Example 6.4 Beethoven, String Quintet op. 29, first movement (mm. 1–41)

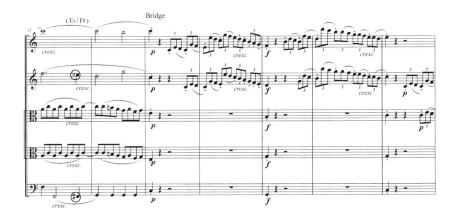

Example 6.4 Beethoven, String Quintet op. 29, first movement (mm. 1–41) continued

Significantly, C major begins the development section, and is quickly turned into V/IV by m. 103. Beethoven then turns the major subdominant into its own parallel minor, F minor, in m. 107, which brings in E♭ and a system shift down to a 3♭ system. F minor becomes the "development key," its associated harmonic areas throwing the 3♭ system further down into a 6♭ system as the music moves into D♭ in m. 111. The D♭ area is actually part of a larger progression that gives harmonic support to the basic trichord of the movement: C–C♯ (here spelled as D♭)–D♮. In fact, D♭ turns into C♯ in m. 117 as part of diminished harmony leading to a G 6/4 with D♮ in the bass (m. 119). Once the G 6/4 is reached, A♮ can shift the 6♭ system up to a 3♭ system, an F♯ in m. 120 further shifting the system back up to "0." From m. 123 and right up to the point of recapitulation in m. 179, E♭ and F♯ conflict continuously, causing any number of harmonic digressions into flat-key areas, including a prominent return into the minor subdominant (mm. 151ff.). The emphasis on pc 3 as E♭ over the course of the development balances the exposition's spelling of this pitch as D♯, now with the opposite effect of flat-side harmonic motions. What is also interesting is how the system shifts become more and more intense during the retransition (mm. 179ff.), the systems changing back and forth practically every two measures! Only in m. 167 does the F♯ finally displace the E♭ altogether, the "0" system remaining in effect in preparation for the recapitulation. Finally, the recapitulation, a virtual summary of the system conflicts of the preceding sections of the movement, transposes into the tonic minor all the areas that were once in the minor submediant within the exposition, thus raising E♭. Similarly, the A major sections of the exposition are now transposed into the tonic major, often necessitating an F♯ in order to cancel the frequent motions into the 3♭ system. While D♯s also appear, the main focus of the recapitulation is centered on the conflict between 3♭ and "0" systems, which serve to balance the 3♯ and "0" systems of the exposition.

The main dyad conflict of the movement, C♮/C♯, often extended to D to form a trichord, now reaches resolution into tonic harmony within the final ascent of the PCA (see Example 6.5, mm. 264ff.), all this taking place during the closing period. This last rise of the PCA ascent is complete with all twelve pitch classes unfolded over the course of 17 measures, from the closing period to the start of the coda. What is of interest is that pc 3 is spelled as D♯, finally displacing E♭ altogether for the rest of the movement. The D♯ itself finds resolution within the first violin, whose part keeps reiterating this pitch class as the PCA unfolds in the cello. The first violin part climbs into the upper octave in m. 276, where D♯ is heard for the last time and finally resolves to E. At the same time, pcs 5–9 of the PCA (F♮–A) are reiterated within the same first violin part (mm. 277–8) in order to highlight the final three pitches of the PCA, A♯–B–C, at the start of the coda (m. 280). From this point until the end of the movement, the pitch field remains totally diatonic, all the issues having been resolved.

Example 6.5 Beethoven, String Quintet op. 29, first movement, recapitulation (mm. 264–80)

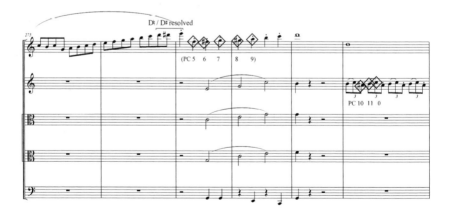

Beethoven's interest in parallel major/minor harmonic areas could well have come from his admiration of the French "rescue" operas of Luigi Cherubini of the 1790s and 1800s. Beethoven modeled his own opera *Leonora/Fidelio* (1804–14), in part, upon Cherubini's *Lodoïska* (1791) and *Les deux journées* (1800). Interestingly, Cherubini's overture to *Lodoïska* has some striking parallels with Beethoven's op. 29 string quintet. Even though the tonic of Cherubini's overture is in D major (as opposed to Beethoven's quintet, which is in C), there is a similar working-out of the C♮–C♯–D trichord, first heard in the slow introduction to the overture. In addition, Cherubini's second harmonic area in the dominant juxtaposes A minor in its first period with A major in its counterstatement (Beethoven *preceded* his second harmonic area in A major with a passage in A minor). In Cherubini's overture, this relationship is reversed in the dominant extension that replaces what normally would have been a development section; here, A major succeeds to A minor. In both instances Cherubini works out the C♮/C♯ dyad conflict that pervades the overture, using a technique similar to that of Beethoven's quintet. Cherubini develops the F♯/F♮ dyad conflict as well, since the tonic major is also juxtaposed with its parallel minor within the recapitulation: the second harmonic area reappears in the tonic minor, with F♮ also appearing within the context of B♭ harmony. Be that as it may, what is significant is that both pieces develop the inherent properties of their complementary tritone systems on a background level.

Besides their increased interest in chromaticism in general, composers of the nineteenth century seem to have been especially interested in exploiting the harmonic potential of the individual pitch classes of the rising PCA chromatic octave as compositional determinants. That is, each chromatic pitch in turn either becomes the focal point of a harmonic area or is treated as a significant voice-leading pitch, either as a leading tone or as a Neapolitan to a structural harmonic area. We have already seen how Neapolitan relationships, often associated with important system conflicts, govern the opening movement of Beethoven's "Appassionata" Sonata, discussed above. But Beethoven goes even further than this in his late quartets, where there are numerous instances of PCA unfoldings which do not support a tonic background. Significantly, these PCA unfoldings justify non-tonic expansions of secondary harmonic areas by providing extra weight to PCA notes that, in earlier works of the period, had often been passed through in an almost unceremonious manner. Just as in seventeenth-century modality, where harmonic relationships were often related by fifths on the local level according to the arrangement of their gamut system hexachords, the immediate pitch classes of the PCA in these late works may lead to local harmonic areas that seem deliberately to avoid tonic definition. A particularly good example of this occurs in Beethoven's String Quartet in A minor op. 132 (1825); the harmonic plan and PCA unfolding of the first movement are given as Diagram 6.3.

EXPOSITION

1st Harmonic Area
(a) Assai sostenuto → (b) Allegro

A minor
i
b07— i6 →

			C.S.	+	Bridge (mm. 30 ff.)			Signature changes to 1 b
	Bb – B♮ – C – E			a	Bb			D minor
	bII				bII (becomes IV/F)			vi/F
	V6/4 – 5/3 → i							
	Bb B♮ C				C (m. 39)	C# (m. 42)		D D#
	1 2 3				3	4		5 6

PCA: A ... 0

[Bridge]	2nd Harmonic Area (1st period)	+ Closing (2nd period)	**DEVELOPMENT**
C7	F	F	Starts in F
V7/F	VI		VI
F			F F# G Ab

PCA: E ... 7   8 (pcs 0-8 repeated)   (pcs 0 - 1 - 2 - 3 - 4 - 5 - [6]-7 repeated →)

8   9   10   11

gm -- cm

[DEVELOPMENT]

Signature changes back to ♮

1st Recapitulation (m. 103): THEMATIC

1st Harmonic Area   Signature changes to 1♯ (m. 111)

C major (becomes bVI/e minor) –   B   E minor (relates to F at the start of the Development)   F
                                   V/v   v   bII/v (becomes IV/C)

PCA: [Ab is sustained until it is enharmonically reinterpreted as G♯ before the 2nd Recap.]
11

2nd Recapitulation (m. 193):
HARMONIC
1st Harmonic Area

Signature changes back to ♮ (m. 138)

Bridge   (mm. 151 ff.)   2nd Harmonic Area (mm. 159 ff.)
D minor –   C   E7 → A minor
vi/C   A minor (F/E)   V7   i
                           vi/C
                           VI/ e minor (e doesn't act like a dominant of a minor) –

PCA: Ab/G♯   A   (pcs 0 -11 repeat)
        11   0

[no bridge]

2nd Harmonic Area (mm. 223 ff.)

A major collapses back into → A minor

E →   A Major   E♯/ F♮ → E resolves (along with all the other important chromatic dyad pairs) ‖
       I   i

Diagram 6.3 Beethoven, String Quartet in A minor op. 132, first movement

Diagram 6.3 is not meant to explore the richness of detail that exists in practically every measure of the movement. However, it does allow us to perceive, at a glance, the most important large-scale harmonic and chromatic relationships that pertain to our discussion. Thus one immediately notices that the second harmonic area is in F, the submediant, and that the exposition closes in that area without any motion to the relative major. In fact, the relative is related more to the submediant as its dominant than to the tonic.

A look at the quartet's "0" system hexachord, with A minor as tonic, allows us to perceive the general *raison d'être* of the harmonic scheme that underlies the movement's exposition:

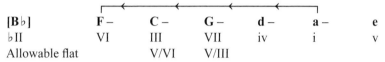

[B♭]	F –	C –	G –	d –	a –	e
♭II	VI	III	VII	iv	i	v
Allowable flat		V/VI	V/III			

Instead of moving three fifths down from the tonic, A minor, to C, the relative, Beethoven moves past C and down one more fifth to F. Through this action, Beethoven's second harmonic area no longer has the same "key signature" as that of the tonic, as it would have if he moved to the relative major. In fact, Beethoven supports this contention himself by changing the signature to one flat during the last segment of the bridge. The reader should note that even though the key signature has changed, *the A minor tonic system matrix still applies*; the tonic continues to function on the deepest structural level. As a result, F major, as a harmonic area, does not displace A minor as a new tonic but remains on a lower structural level; that is, F still functions as VI within the key, no matter how long it is prolonged.

Another consequence of establishing VI as a harmonic area is that the submediant cannot fulfill the function of stability within the key. Remember that the more traditional motion to the relative rotates the scale of the tonic minor so that it now starts on the root of its system, here C. In addition, the harmonic motion to III would have been part of a larger arpeggiation of the tonic triad, *adding to the stability of the tonic*. However, when Beethoven moves to VI, a whole new set of conditions applies: besides the fact that the key signature is now one flat, the F itself, as a hexachordal root, is positioned at the very end of the system, and if this pitch class becomes a prolonged harmonic center, a significant system shift out of the "0" system is virtually a foregone conclusion (see the discussion below). In addition, the submediant cannot take part in the larger unfolding of the tonic triad, further divorcing this area from the support of the tonic background. The move to F, in fact, implies an arpeggiation of the subdominant triad rather than that of the tonic. The above diagram also shows that Beethoven's approach to F follows the harmonic plan of the hexachord, moving down in fifths within a logical sequence: the first move away is toward D minor, then G, as an applied dominant chord to C, followed by the C itself as V/VI, and then finally to F. A moment in B♭ is also included along the way, but is treated as a passing harmony.

The obvious model for a second key in VI within a minor-mode sonata movement is the opening movement of Beethoven's own Symphony no. 9, which was premiered the year before the op. 132 quartet. Similar too, is the way in which the relative major is avoided as a harmonic area in favor of its function as V/VI. However, unlike the Ninth Symphony, in which the submediant area is eventually defined as VI of the tonic key – that is, when B♭ unexpectedly drops to A, the dominant, right before the development section – the quartet avoids this functional relationship by moving directly into the development while still in the subdominant area. So while the contrapuntal relationship of the submediant of the dominant as an adjacent harmonic function is clearly kept separate, Beethoven instead prefers to develop the F/E relationship thematically, as *melodic* pitch classes that operate on a lesser structural level.

Beethoven's preoccupation with dissociating harmonic functions from their traditional relationships, in this case avoiding both C major as relative and the submediant and dominant as neighboring harmonies or harmonic areas, evidences his interest in separating thematic from harmonic events. For example, one notices from the diagram of the first movement (Diagram 6.3) that neither the initial statement of the Allegro *b* motive nor its counterstatement begins on the tonic: the first has diminished harmony and the second is on the dominant triad as part of a 6/4–5/3 cadential progression. Starting the counterstatement on V instead of on I negates its traditional function as initiating the formal bridge period on tonic harmony. Schumann, as we will discover, used this idea in the first movement of his Piano Quintet in E♭ op. 44 where the counterstatement similarly begins on the dominant. However, Beethoven's placement of the recapitulation, or rather, recapitulations, is startling since there seem to be two of them.[1] The first is purely melodic and, like the second, follows the same theme rotation as the exposition, but with the opening statement returning within the minor dominant (m. 103). Within this first recapitulation, the second harmonic area returns in C major as VI/v, maintaining the same relation of i to VI that characterized the exposition. A second recapitulation follows this one (m. 193) – this time the minor tonic returns and the second harmonic area is transposed into the major tonic, balancing the major submediant of the exposition. Thus the return of thematic events, while in the original order, is not always tied to their original harmonic associations.

To return to the exposition of the quartet, of major interest to our discussion is that Beethoven's harmonic path to the submediant not only follows the ordering of hexachordal roots, but articulates every ascending chromatic pitch class of the PCA, leading up to F major as pc 8 (see Example 6.6). Pc 0, A, is first heard in the cello on the second beat of the opening measure. The placement of pc 1, B♭, is most startling since this pitch forms the root of its own harmony, arpeggiated in unison by all the instruments, with a dotted rhythmic motive (mm. 18–19). In contrast with the earlier "Appassionata" Sonata, where ♭II was clearly associated with tonic harmony at the very start of the first movement, the B♭ harmony in op. 132 is unprepared and apparently divorced from tonic harmony; instead, the B♭ arises out of a 5–6

---

1   The unusual phenomenon of a double recapitulation, with each recapitulation in a different key, in the first movement of the op. 132 quartet has been noted in the literature: Basil Lam, *Beethoven String Quartets 2* (Seattle, 1975), pp. 23–4; Harold Truscott, *Beethoven's Late String Quartets* (London, 1968), pp. 73–4; Joseph Kerman, *The Beethoven Quartets* (London, 1967), p. 247.

exchange with the preceding D minor triad which occurs on the downbeat of m. 18. The D minor triad here prepares for its fuller realization during the bridge (mm. 39ff.). After pc 1 has been presented, the B♭ moves up to B♮, pc 2, in the first violin on the last beat of m. 20 in preparation for pc 3, C♮, which arrives at the Adagio on the downbeat of m. 21 as part of a cadential 6/4. Thus, C♮ is absorbed within tonic harmony just at the point where the counterstatement is reached.

The return to tonic harmony now sets the stage for the next significant harmonic motion, the move into D minor, which takes place in the latter part of the bridge. The bridge itself (the entire period covers mm. 30–48) begins in B♭ with a restatement of the dotted rhythm motive that previously preceded the counterstatement at the end of the opening period. Here, however, the B♭ acts as IV within a much larger submediant harmonic progression that moves into C7 as V7/vi (m. 33) and that ultimately reaches D minor, now interpreted as vi of the submediant. Pc 3, C♮, has thus been an active pitch of the array since the Adagio in m. 21 (associated there with A minor), and is now reinterpreted as the root of a dominant seventh applied to F major (see the unfolding PCA in Example 6.6). In order to prepare for the short D minor area that follows, the C♮ becomes displaced by pc 4, C♯, first as a melodic passing or embellishing tone in mm. 37–8 and then, more structurally, as a leading tone in m. 40. Naturally enough, pc 4 now passes to pc 5, D, as we enter into D minor harmony, supported, significantly, by a change to one flat in the signature. Pc 5 is in turn displaced by pc 6, D♯, in the first violin (m. 44). What makes pc 6 particularly noticeable is its sharp dissonance within the preparatory C dominant seventh chord, the D♯ acting as a local half-step lower neighbor to E♮, pc 7. In addition, the D♯ attempts to prompt a system change to a 3♯ system, but is kept in check by the persistent C♮s in both the second violin and cello parts. The E♮ now takes on the function of a leading tone to the submediant (pc 8) at the start of the second harmonic area; the dominant preparation formally concludes at the authentic cadence to vi on the last beat of m. 47 (see Example 6.6). Two other 0–8 PCA rises occur within the second harmonic area of the exposition, one from the opening of the second harmonic period to the closing period in m. 57, and another from the closing period to the start of the development (see Diagram 6.2).

Example 6.6 Beethoven, String Quartet in A minor op. 132, first movement, exposition (mm. 1–48)

There are other important observations to be made about the conclusion of the bridge passage that extends from m. 44 to the end of m. 47. To begin, the first violin part during these measures ascends an almost full chromatic octave from F (m. 44, beat 3) to F (m. 47, beat 3), the only chromatic pitch class absent being D♯, pc 6, the missing pitch! Beethoven is careful not to include D♯ within this Secondary Chromatic Array (SCA) since he has already respelled the PCA pitch D♯ in m. 44 as E♭ in the cello part at the end of m. 45. This time, the missing pitch spelled as E♭ causes a major system shift into a 3♭ system that is sustained through most of the development section! The motion to the 3♭ system at the close of the bridge also prepares for F, a "flat-key" or subdominant area within the overall tonic hexachord of the "0" system. With the switch to the 3♭ system, F major now comes under the control of the complementary E♭–A♮ tritone system, from which it, as well as all other subdominant-related harmonic areas within the movement, is ultimately derived.

Understanding the nature of system shifts also allows us to see why Beethoven would want to maintain pc 8 (F) as a *terminus* that is sustained for so long a period before moving on to the next pitch class in the series: the missing pitch of a 3♭ system is F♯ (pc 9), the next pitch class to be introduced within the ascending PCA. Since Beethoven wishes to prolong submediant harmony until the development section, he is careful not to introduce this pitch at any time within the second harmonic area, since by so doing, he would effect a modulation back to the tonic system of the movement, and, consequently, would have to move out of submediant harmony. Of course, F♯ could have been introduced during the exposition if it had been contested by E♭, preventing a system shift, but then Beethoven would have introduced pc 9 "before its time," as it were, since this F♯ as pc 9 would necessitate a harmonic motion best left to the development section. Referring to Diagram 6.2, we notice that the development starts in F major (in m. 73), the harmonic area that ended the exposition.

The next goal of motion is G minor, which occurs soon afterwards (m. 78ff.), over a dominant pedal. As a leading tone, F♯, pc 9, moves directly to G, pc 10, within G minor harmony. However, the persistent E♭s that surround F♯ prevent the latter from modulating the system up to "0," at least for the present (note that the key signature is still one flat and that the 3♭ system still prevails). C minor follows as the next harmonic goal, allowing the next PCA pitch, pc 11, A♭, to be raised. Interestingly, Beethoven spells pc 11 *not* as a leading tone, but as the *root* of an augmented sixth chord within C minor. Not surprisingly, pc 11 is sustained for an incredibly long period since it does not enharmonically alter its function to a leading tone (G♯) until the structural dominant is reached on the last beat of m. 192, just before the second recapitulation! Thus the first complete rise of the PCA is sustained right through the first thematic recapitulation and does not reach completion with pcs 11 and 0 until the downbeat of the harmonic second recapitulation. While it would be inappropriate to argue the point here, on the basis of the previous PCA analyses, one could make the case that the first thematic recapitulation occupies a "lower structural level" than the second, and could well be considered as part of a much larger development section which has inserted material (in particular, the same thematic ordering as that of the exposition) between the end of the retransition and the start of the second recapitulation, rather similar, in fact, to that of the earlier "Appassionata" Sonata.

But what of pc 9, F♯, and its effect on the system shifts within the development proper? We have seen that F♯, when it was presented as pc 9 at the start of the development, could not effect a system change owing to the E♭s surrounding it. However, at the end of the C minor passage, which introduced A♭ as pc 11, F♯ (the leading tone to G, the V/c) returns, now as a system-shift motivator (m. 91). Here the F♯ is left uncontested and is allowed to shift the previous 3♭ system up to "0", implying a change in mode as well. This last operation is accomplished in the next measure, supported by a change of key signature back to A minor. C major now displaces C minor in preparation for the move into E minor, the harmonic area that begins the thematic first recapitulation in m. 103. Beethoven now balances the lengthy 3♭ system with a move in the opposite direction, to a 3♯ system, brought about by an enharmonic switch of the missing pitch from E♭ to D♯, the latter pitch presented as the leading tone of the dominant minor on the third beat of m. 102.

As the second recapitulation unfolds, Beethoven once again changes key signature, now to one sharp, in the same manner as previously when he moved into F major within the exposition. Again, the reader should note that the change of signature reflects a move to the dominant side of the key, just as the previous change to one flat reflected motion toward the subdominant side. However, the matrix still pertains to the tonic matrix system only: in this case, D♯ has moved the system up to a 3♯ system, the change of signature operating within this background system. The 3♯ system prevails right into the bridge period, which leads to C major as the second harmonic area within the thematic first recapitulation. Consequently, the key signature changes back to A minor immediately before m. 138, where the harmony moves into D minor and then into C minor for a short period; note the return of E♭ and the 3♭ system, if only fleetingly. In turn, C major is first anticipated as a passing harmony mm. 146–8, and it is here that the system finally moves back up to "0": the C♮ dispels the 3♯ system in m. 142, and within the same measure, E♭ brings the system down to a 3♭ system, only to be dispelled in turn by F♯ in m. 145 and the return of the "0" system.

Because of space considerations it is not possible to give a detailed analysis of the rest of the first movement of the op. 132 quartet – for instance, the second harmonic recapitulation has its own complete PCA rise. It is important to note, however, that the entire second recapitulation is governed exclusively by the sharp side of the matrix: that is, either C♮–F♯ or A–D♯, with the two system-shift motivators, D♯ and C♮, continually in conflict with each other in practically every measure. Consequently, there are only minute passages that are entirely in one complementary system or another; at other times the two system-shift motivators operate within very short distances of each other, effectively negating each other's attempts at prolonged system shifts. The conflict continues to the very end of the movement: the D♯ in m. 254 raises the system up to a 3♯ system for a relatively extended period of four measures before C♮, in m. 258, finally reverts the system to "0" for the last time, seven measures before the end of the movement!

Beethoven's legacy was of crucial importance to the evolution of compositional thinking over the course of the entire nineteenth century, especially to composers working in German-speaking territories. We now turn our attention to several prominent German and Austrian composers who were particularly interested in expanding the forms and harmonic language of the Viennese Classicists in new and novel directions. Pertinent to our discussion is how system and PCA analysis can aid our understanding of the compositional process in the work of these composers.

II. Eleven-Pitch-Class Systems in the Music of Nineteenth-Century Romantic Composers: Mode Mixture and System Shifts as Pre-Compositional Determinants in Schubert's String Quintet in C major op. 163

Among Romantic-era composers, Schubert is perhaps most prominent for his unique approach to large-scale mode mixture, specifically in major-mode compositions that simultaneously unfold major and minor modes of the same tonic over the course of a single movement; often this procedure informs an entire multimovement work. Schubert is not alone in this regard. Parallel major/minor juxtapositions are frequent in eighteenth-century and early nineteenth-century works: as we have seen, Vivaldi, D. Scarlatti, G.B. Sammartini, Wagenseil, Gluck, and, most importantly, Beethoven are just a few of the composers whose compositions feature such harmonic parallels. Where Schubert differs from his predecessors is in the extent to which major/minor juxtapositions determine the harmonic plan of the work on the deepest structural level.

The influences upon Schubert for these experiments in tonality come from many sources. Besides the overtures to the operas of Cherubini (see the discussion of Cherubini's overture to *Lodoïska* above), Schubert may also have been influenced by Gasparo Spontini, since Spontini's *La Vestale* (Paris, 1807), an opera known and respected by both Beethoven and Schubert, contains an overture in sonata-overture form (a sonata-form movement with a very short development functioning solely as a retransition). The overture, in D minor/D major, is entirely constructed of major/minor tonic and dominant parallels in both harmonic areas, each area being supported by a change of key signature. It is most striking that each signature change is prepared by the introduction of the missing pitch of the complementary system in the preceding measure.

Schubert's most notable compositions that employ major/minor parallels and juxtapositions include the late String Quartet in G major, the String Quintet in C major, the song "Auf dem Wasser zu singen," and the Impromptu in A♭ op. 90 no. 4 (these last two open in A♭ minor with four flats in the key signature). Since the incorporation of the flat third degree within the major mode implies, if not imposes, a structural modulation between complementary eleven-pitch-class systems, these works provide ideal opportunities to employ system analysis to uncover their symmetrical properties.

The String Quintet in C major op. 163 is outstanding among Schubert's works for its fluid unfolding of the tonic minor triad within the major mode, most notably in the exposition of the first movement (Examples 6.7a, 6.7b). However, unlike the first movement of the composer's G major String Quartet op. 161, with its juxtapositions of tonic and dominant major/minor parallels, the first movement of the C major quintet does not actually move into tonic minor harmony at any point. Rather, the arpeggiation of the minor triad over the course of the exposition, first heard melodically in the first violin at the outset of the movement, is supported by diminished harmony, on a middleground level, and by a motion into ♭III, E♭, on a deeper structural level. Thus Schubert avoids the shock, even the violence, of unprepared major/minor juxtapositions so characteristic of the G major quartet. Yet he still introduces E♭ and its enharmonic equivalent, D♯, as most prominent pitches, controlling large areas of system modulations.

The opening phrase of the first movement immediately presents E♭ within C major harmony. However, every time E♭ appears, it does so against an F♯ as part of an F♯ diminished seventh chord, which prevents the E♭ from becoming an active pitch that would shift the C system down to a 3♭ system (see mm. 4 and 9, for instance).

Example 6.7a   **Schubert, String Quintet in C, first movement, exposition (mm. 1–33)**

As one traces the progress of this one pitch, a narrative emerges involving E♭ in a pitch-class struggle in which it constantly tries to extricate itself from F♯, the missing pitch from its opposite system complement. Along with the main plot with E♭ and F♯ as protagonists in this musical drama, a subsidiary plot simultaneously unfolds involving E♭'s enharmonic equivalent, D♯. By introducing this pitch, Schubert incorporates another eleven-pitch-class tritone system within the original tonic system matrix (Figure 6.2). The missing pitch of the 3♯ system is C, the pitch that will return the system to the tonic eleven-pitch-class system. Thus the potential system-modulatory effects of E♭ are negated by F♯; the same disruptive effects of D♯, in turn, will be neutralized by C♮.

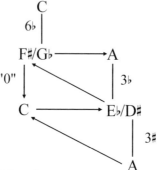

Figure 6.2   Expanded "0" tonic system matrix

The opening phrase continues with a parallel phrase (beginning in m. 11) a whole step higher in D minor. By using this, Schubert can now introduce D♯ as a passing tone to E as part of C major harmony (m. 19). The D♯ is also called into play as part of the thirty-second-note turn in the first violin (m. 23), implying, perhaps, motion to E minor (iii), a motion that is never realized; rather, its dominant, B (m. 24), acts as part of a large-scale arpeggiation in the bass of G, initiated in m. 11 with the opening phrase repeated in D minor. However, no matter what its harmonic significance, D♯ is never given the chance to effect a modulation up to the 3♯ system; it is immediately negated by C♮ (note the second cello part in m. 23) just as E♭ is negated by F♯. Typical of Schubert, the entire first harmonic area never leaves tonic harmony, but is driven by a gradual phrase-rhythmic acceleration that becomes increasingly intense toward the end of the counterstatement, where the D minor phrase is repeated (mm. 40ff.).

Supporting the rhythmic acceleration is the ever-increasing occurrence of implied system modulations in which the two complementary sets of tritone systems that make up the extended tonic system matrix – namely, 3♭ against "0" and 3♯ against "0" – seek to gain control of their respective eleven-pitch-class harmonic areas. At first, the conflicting system-shift motivators, E♭ against F♯ and D♯ against C♮, appear sporadically and simultaneously, canceling each other out (see Diagram 6.4). However, this situation changes drastically as the first harmonic area approaches the intermediate harmonic area, referred to as the "second key" of a "three-key exposition" by some analysts.[2]

---

2   See, for instance, James Webster, "Schubert and Brahms's First Maturity I & II," *19th Century Music*, 2/1 (1978): 18–35; 3/1 (1979): 52–71. Schubert is considered the first

Example 6.7b **Schubert, String Quintet in C, first movement, bridge and beginning of the intermediate harmonic area (mm. 40–60)**

From mm. 49 ff., over a pulsating dominant pedal, E♭/F♯ and D♯/C♮ appear in rapid succession, each pair of system-motivator pitch classes trying to establish their own harmonic territory, but the "correcting" missing pitch of each respective system thwarts any actual system modulation. The process of systematically negating each other's system gambit is repeated twice (mm. 49–52 are identical to mm. 53–6) an octave lower, maintaining the "0" as the governing system throughout the period. The whole passage climaxes on diminished seventh harmony in which the two rival pitch-classes, E♭ and F♯, are brought together once again in the same F♯ diminished seventh chord that began the movement (mm. 56–7).

Only now, with the dominant chord finally resolved, does Schubert make the decisive move to establish E♭, not as a harmonic area (there is no dominant preparation for it, nor is there a full harmonic progression in E♭), but as a prolonged 3♭ eleven-pitch-class area in its own right, without any F♯ to vitiate the motion. Since E♭ is not a self-contained harmonic area, but, on a deeper level, a contrapuntal passing motion to the dominant in m. 100 (not as yet the dominant goal of the exposition, however), one wonders why Schubert dramatized the event by extending the passage with so appealing a melody in the form of a symmetrical double period. As an aside, a similar, but somewhat different, situation is found in the first movement of Brahms's Symphony no. 2 in D, with the introduction of a lengthy and quite beautiful theme in F♯ minor. Like the Schubert theme, it contrapuntally forestalls the eventual move to the dominant by acting as an upper neighbor to the Neapolitan of V/V.[3]

In earlier Classical sonata-form movements, notably those by G.M. Monn, Wagenseil, and Haydn, the introduction of pc 3, spelled as a minor third above the tonic, would have generally signaled the imminent arrival of the structural dominant, the missing pitch of the tonic system, appearing as the bass of an augmented sixth or Neapolitan sonority resolving to the dominant of the new key area (see Chapter 5). Such a progression most often occurs within the bridge passage leading to the new key, and usually as a climax to that passage. What Schubert has done is to take what would have once been a single chord and to extend it into a lengthy lyrical period (in fact, a bridge theme), only to delay its actual resolution by inserting a further transitional period in dominant harmony (mm. 100ff.) that finally resolves the E♭ as part of a harmonically evasive progression, ♭II6 to V, within G, and which does not cadence until m. 138.

3   See Carl Schachter, "The First Movement of Brahms's Second Symphony: The Opening Theme and its Consequences," *Music Analysis*, 2/1 (1983): 55–68.

Throughout this lyrical E♭ period (starting in m. 60), Schubert takes great pains to consistently relate E♭, the root of the complementary system, to C (refer to Figure 6.2 above). Thus, at this point, E♭ refuses to descend to D as V/V, but moves up in the opposite direction to E♮ (see mm. 70–71 and m. 78). The E♭/E♮ relationship that began the movement is further developed here, dramatized by system modulations placed at strategic points within the period. The 3♭ eleven-pitch-class system remains in effect until the end of the first statement of the E♭ bridge theme, veering, significantly, back toward C. Measure 75 once again introduces the F♯ diminished seventh chord, the primary issue of the composition, with E♭ in the bass and F♯ in the top voice. Finally, F♯ returns in m. 80 as the passage cadences on the dominant of C, this time without E♭ to negate its function of returning the E♭ system to "0." The entire period is repeated with the violins restating the original cello theme (mm. 79ff.). Again, the 3♭ system returns (along with the E♭/E♮ conflict) and, again, the E♭ pitch class fails to descend to D and to resolve there as expected.

The measures right before the transitional period to the closing area (see Example 6.7c, mm. 96ff.) are quite revealing when analyzed according to systems: the F♯ diminished seventh chord returns once more, but E♭ descends locally in an inner voice (m. 96, second violin) to D (m. 97) within a first-inversion G chord – not of structural harmonic significance. Rather, E♭ plays a more important function as part of a diatonic contrapuntal line that moves up to E♮ (viola, m. 97) and then to F♯ (same voice, m. 98), the pitch that restores the "0" eleven-pitch-class system despite the passing E♭ (note the E♭/E♮ conflict that results) in the viola in the following measure; the F♯ on the last beat of that measure in the second violin maintains the C system. Only now can G, the dominant, assert itself in the lengthy transitional period that follows at m. 100.

Example 6.7c   Schubert, String Quintet in C, first movement, transition into closing period (mm. 96–142)

The passage from m. 100 to the downbeat of m. 138 (Example 6.7c) is functionally problematic, yet typical of the modular designs of many Romantic sonata-form movements by Schubert, Mendelssohn, Schumann, Brahms, Chaikovsky, and Dvořák, to name only a few. On the one hand, the passage in question prolongs dominant harmony within a self-contained, closed, musical period. Yet, it appears transitional, not really achieving closure until m. 138. The latter interpretation would seem to be more accurate since Schubert does not raise a true dominant preparation until mm. 117ff, and this does not conclusively resolve, either rhythmically or harmonically, until the downbeat of m. 138. Offsetting this otherwise harmonically stagnant passage are dynamic system modulations that further enhance its transitional and contrapuntal nature, and which provide it with a decided magnitude of tension and propulsion.

As is often the case in sonata-form movements, the missing pitch of the tonic system is usually spelled as an augmented second above the tonic if the second harmonic area is within the dominant, or for that matter, in any harmonic area on the sharp side of the circle of fifths (see our discussion of Beethoven's String Quintet op. 29 above and that of his "Waldstein" Piano Sonata in Chapter 2). In Schubert's quintet, the dominant progression that starts in m. 100 naturally raises D♯ (m. 106) within the context of B major harmony (B is interpreted as V/VI of the dominant at this point, a gesture not realized). The D♯ raises the 3♯ system, but C♮, the missing pitch of that system, constantly undermines the former's hegemony. In fact, C♮ in m. 110 manages to displace the 3♯ system altogether (no D♯s follow), creating neutral ground in which E♭ can now make an unexpected appearance.

Up to this point, Schubert has clearly let us understand this transitional period as just that: a passage of music that is kinetic, and which has a deeper purpose, that of establishing the structural dominant. The introduction of D♯ was simply a ploy to prolong the transitional period, since D♯, by itself, is insufficient to initiate a convincing progression to the dominant. In fact, the pitch needed to accomplish the arrival of the structural dominant is E♭, the pitch class that Schubert previously has taken such pains to unfold as a lyrical, but incomplete, harmonic area. Only now does E♭ return to discharge its function of dramatizing V/V as part of a ♭II6/V (Example 6.7c, m. 118) resolving to D as V/V in m. 119. This moment is so crucial in its harmonic import that Schubert repeats the passage verbatim in mm. 122–5.

No matter what the significance of E♭ is in establishing the structural dominant, Schubert could not have introduced this variant of pc 3 without effecting a system change to a 3♭ system. Rather, F♯ appears after each appearance of E♭ to underscore the security of the tonic "0" system. Both E♭ and F♯, however, now take on motivic significance as the primary tones of the original F♯ diminished seventh chord, the development of which is fundamental to the quintet. The diminished seventh chord returns in m. 127 and governs the passage that follows, up to the arrival of the structural dominant on the downbeat of m. 138. What follows can only be interpreted as a closing period with codetta (m. 146). Even here, as Webster correctly points out, Schubert is reluctant to leave C major harmony.[4] Webster attributes Schubert's avoidance of dominant modulations to the fact that "the dominant no longer commanded the power it had for Classical composers."[5] But perhaps this reluctance can be equally attributed to Schubert's awareness that the "0" system, operating continuously in the background, is never really abandoned, no matter which harmonic areas are explored in the middleground. Significantly, only now, after the structural dominant has been reached, does D♯ displace E♭.

Again, as is usually the case with missing pitch classes in expositions, D♯ does not achieve an extended system modulation up to a 3♯ system: at best, only two measures are allowed within the 3♯ system before a C♮ cancels the modulation (see mm. 139–41 and their repetition an octave higher in mm. 143–5).

What we learn from this type of analysis is how only a few pitch classes may have the power to control and to determine large areas of music. In this case, E♭ and F♯ (and their complements, D♯ and C♮) represent far more than just notes in a diminished seventh chord; they control entire eleven-pitch-class areas and act on a motivic level that is the basis of a sophisticated developmental procedure.

Before a discussion of the quintet's development section using system analysis, we need to review the exposition's unfolding PCA, an unfolding that intersects with the structural harmonic goals of the exposition.

Most important to our analysis of the Schubert is how the missing pitch of the "0" system, pc 3 (E♭ or D♯), dramatizes the rise of the PCA as the music progresses toward the goal of the dominant. Notably in the works of nineteenth-century composers, including Beethoven (covering his whole career), the course of an entire movement is quite often constructed around the working-out of pc 3, its rhythmic placement, and its harmonic implications.

To review, the first segment of the PCA occurs in the exposition as the music moves from the tonic to its next structural key, in this case G, the dominant. Most important among the first segment of PCA pitch classes, pc 3 is often highlighted in the music to show its special importance within the line. As the PCA ascends, individual pitch classes may be spelled as enharmonic equivalents, depending on harmonic circumstances. However, because of voice-leading considerations, PCA notes tend to be presented with one spelling more likely than another (as is the case with the Schubert). Thus, in C major, C♯ (pc 1) is far more likely to be found than

---

4   James Webster, "Schubert's Sonata Form and Brahms's First Maturity I," *19th-Century Music*, 2/1 (1978): 28–9.

5   *Ibid.*, 24.

D♭, and in fact, in Schubert's exposition there are no D♭s, only C♯s. Further, each member of the PCA may be dramatized, harmonically and/or rhythmically, treated simply as passing, or even omitted, depending on the desire of the composer and the nature of the composition. (Not all compositions have complete PCA ascents, but the omission of chromatic pitch classes from the PCA says as much about a piece as their presence.) In Schubert's quintet, all pitches of the PCA are present. Further, a trichordal segment is repeated, often within differing harmonic contexts, before the next segment is presented.

Diagram 6.4 gives the PCA unfolding as well as the system changes for the first movement of Schubert's quintet up through the beginning of the recapitulation. Below the first line, indicating measure numbers, is the line showing the "active system pitch classes" ("ASPcs"). These are the missing pitch classes of the prevailing system. If the prevailing system holds through, meaning that a missing pitch is contested immediately, or even simultaneously, by its own symmetrical inversion, then these pitch classes are indicated in parentheses. For example, in mm. 3 and 9 (see the diagram), E♭ motivates a system change from the "0" system to a 3♭ system, but the simultaneous occurrence of F♯, the missing pitch from a 3♭ system, in both measures indicates a move back up to the "0," the two effectively canceling out each other. Thus, the background "0" system has not changed despite the flurry of foreground activity. However, if a pitch class actually accomplishes a system change this is noted in the diagram by an arrow, showing direction, either up or down, without parentheses. Measure 49, for example, shows that E♭ is uncontested by an F♯ and thus shifts the "0" down to a 3♭ system. The measures that follow remain in the new system until the next system change occurs, indicated in this instance in m. 51, where F♯ restores the "0" once again.

One can see in the diagram the extent of system changes at a glance. Note that the system change in m. 81 keeps the music within the orbit of a 3♭ system as far as m. 98 (see Example 6.7c). Similarly, this method of presentation is useful for judging the effect of rapid system fluctuations, such as take place throughout the development section. Here system changes to enharmonic equivalents move the music into quite distant harmonic areas, extending the background tonic diminished system to its absolute limits over a relatively short time span. The third line down on the diagram shows what the underlying system is at any given point, whether "0," 3♭, 3♯, etc. Under this line, highlighted in bold, is the PCA, with both pitch and number listed for each pitch class. Pitches of the array unfold at a gradual pace, always ascending from the tonic of the key (pc 0), and often in irregular groupings. How and when a particular pitch class unfolds play an important function in the harmonic design and structure of the composition, often revolving around the arrival of the missing pitch of the system.

EXPOSITION

1st Harmonic Area

Measure:	1	3 & 9	19	23	26	27———	29	33	35-36
Active System Pcs:		(Eb/F#)	(D#/C)	(D#/C)			(D#/C)		(Eb/F#)
System:	"0"								
PCA:	**C (0)**				**C (0) – C# (1) – D (2)**				
Harmony:	C				G pedal			C pedal	
	I				V			I	

CS + Bridge

Intermediate (or 2nd) Harmonic Area

M.:	48	49	51	52	53	55	56-57	60	75	77
ASPcs:	(Eb/F#)	Eb↗	F#↗ – (D#/C)	(Eb/F#)		Eb↗	F#↗ – (D#/C)	(Eb/F#)	Eb↗	(F#/Eb/Eb)F#↗
System:		3 bs	"0"		3 bs		"0" holds though	3 bs		"0"
PCA:	**[Eb (3)**					**Eb (3)**				
Harmony:		G pedal				Eb				
		V				bIII				

Transitional Period

M.:	81	91	92	93	96	98	100
ASPcs:	Eb↗			**F (5)**	(F#/Eb)	F#↗	
System:	3 bs					"0"	
PCA:	**[Eb (3)]**	**Eb (3) – E♮ (4)**			**F# (6)**		**G (7)**
Harmony:	Eb		C———				D G pedal
	bIII		IV/V				V/V V

M.:	101	105	106	110-111	116-117	118	119-120
ASPcs:			D#↗ – (C/D#)	C↗		Eb↗	F#↗
System:			3#s	"0"		3 bs	"0"
PCA repeats:	**C (0)**	**C (0) – C# (1)**				**D (2)**	
Harmony:			B	C		Ab6	D6/4-5/3
			V/vi/V	IV/V		bII6/V	V6/4-5/4/V

M.:	122	123	124-126	127	128	131	133–136	137
ASPcs:	Eb↗	F#↗	E♮ (4)	(Eb/F#)	(D#/C)	(Eb/F#)		
System:	3 bs	"0"						
PCA:	**[Eb (3)]**				**F (5)**		**[Eb (3)– E♮ (4)– F (5)]**	**F# (6)**
Harmony:	Ab6	D				D		D
	bII6	V/V				V/V		V/V

Diagram 6.4 Schubert, String Quintet in C, first movement: system/PCA

DEVELOPMENT

Closing Period (as 3rd Harmonic Area) — Codetta — DEVELOPMENT

M.:	138	139–140	141	143–144	145	146 (Codetta)	147	149	155	157
ASPcs:		D#↗	C↘	D#↗	C↘		(D#/C)	(D#/C)	G# (8)	[A(9)]
System:		3#s	"0"	3#s	"0"				G#07 →	A
PCA:	**G (7)**					**G (7)**			**G# (8)**	
Harmony:	G / V	B / III#/V	C / IV/V			G pedal / V				

M.:	174	175	177	178	180	181	186	188	198	200	202	250	251
ASPcs:	D#↗		B#↗	A↘	B#↗		B♭♭↘	C↘	A↘	F#↗	D#↗	D#↗	C↘
System:	3#s —		6#s	3#s	6#s		9♭s	6♭s	3♭s	"0"	3#s	3#s	
PCA:	**G# (8) regained**					**A♭ (8)**			**A♮ (9)**				C
Harmony:	G#					A♭			A		em		C

M.:	206	210	218	232–233	236–237	241	242	246	249	RECAPITULATION 267
ASPcs:	C↘		D#↗	B#↗	A↘		C↘	E♭↘	F#↗	
System:	"0"		3#s	6#s	3#s		"0"	3♭s	C	
PCA:	**A# (10)** —			**[A# (10)— B (11)]**		**Bb (10)**			**[B♮ (11)]**	
Harmony:	f#m			bm	dm				em → G	

Retransition — RECAPITULATION

M.:	259	260	261	262	264	266	267
ASPcs:	(E♭/F#)		(E♭/F#)		E♭↗		
System:	A♭ aug.6		A♭ aug.6	G pedal	3♭s ----- holds through the recap.		C(0)
PCA:	**[Bb (10)—**			**B♮ (11)** —	**B♮ (11)**		**C (0)**
Harmony:				V			C / I

M.:	269–270	274	275
ASPcs:	(E♭/F#)	F#↗	(E♭/F#)
System:		"0"	
PCA:		D6	G
Harmony:		V6/V	V

In the Schubert quintet, note that the first three pitch classes of the array unfold at a rapid rate in mm. 26 and 27 – C moves chromatically up to D. The next pitch is the missing pitch of the "0" system, E♭. Note the care taken by Schubert to prolong this pitch over a very long time period, approximately 43 measures! While the pitch itself is introduced at the start of the movement, it does not become part of the rising half-step sequence until after the first three pitch classes have been presented in mm. 26–7. In other words, only after this point does E♭ take its position within the ascending chromatic octave, where it becomes dramatized as an event of some consequence.

In Diagram 6.4, mm. 35–57, the E♭ is shown in parentheses, indicating that it has not yet attained a structural position within the PCA, but is, however, the next note within the series. The E♭ achieves structural status when the intermediate harmonic area is finally attained in m. 60. At this point, E♭ can be shown without parentheses, indicating that this particular pitch class is now operating on a higher structural level than the E♭s that preceded it. The line continues to move up in m. 91 as E♭ moves to E♮ and then to F in m. 93. The F♯ is finally achieved in m. 98 as the leading tone to the dominant pitch, G, in m. 100, completing the first half of the PCA rise.

Next, the ascent of the same PCA pitch classes (0–7) is repeated, culminating in a cadence that inaugurates the closing period in m. 138. In other words, once the dominant is reached in the exposition, there may be one or more additional approaches to the dominant cadence in order to strengthen subsequent cadential arrivals. Each time the music progresses toward the next dominant cadence, the first seven pitch classes of the PCA unfold again from pc 0, affirming the dominant area (or whatever the harmonic area happens to be) as functioning on a lesser structural level than that of the larger tonic background. It should be emphasized that the PCA (as opposed to secondary arrays) fills in only one octave, that of the tonic, and no other, since, ultimately, all harmonic areas within the movement are judged in relation to the underlying tonic, which is never entirely displaced. The Schubert quintet is somewhat problematic only in that the dominant is reached in m. 100, but not anchored. Instead, Schubert creates a passage that is at once in the dominant but that has not achieved full closure in that harmonic area, and, therefore, has more of a transitional function than that of a true arrival. As if in agreement with this perception, Schubert repeats all the pitch classes of the PCA, beginning in m. 101 with C (pc 0), thereby confirming the tonic. When E♭ arrives again, in m. 118, its function is even more dynamic than it was the first time, where it functioned as a contrapuntal extension of the tonic. Now it acts as a harmonic pitch class within the Neapolitan ♭II6 chord, a chord that is pre-cadential in function and which indicates the actual arrival of the structural dominant.

Measures 124–6 show the E♭ rising again to E♮ (pc 4) and to F (pc 5) in m. 131 (the same sequence is repeated in mm. 133–6). The F♯ (pc 6) that enters in m. 137 is significant since it is the leading tone of the structural dominant in m. 138. There are no further repetitions of pcs 0–7 of the PCA in the exposition. The codetta starting in m. 146 simply reaffirms the dominant by reiterating pc 7 (G).

As was previously discussed, the chromatic ascent in sonata-form expositions terminates on the pitch class of the local tonic that defines the second harmonic area and that usually concludes the exposition. (In so-called three-key expositions, the terminus will always be the tonic pitch class of the closing harmonic area; in

Schubert's case, this is invariably the dominant.) According to the theory, octave completion of the PCA is a primary function of the development section. Specifically, the development continues the PCA ascent from where it left off at the end of the exposition, continuing its chromatic rise until the octave is completed with the return of tonic harmony, an event usually coinciding with the start of the recapitulation.

Since it is a chromatic tone, the introduction of pc 8 within the opening period of the development can be quite startling. In eighteenth-century Classical literature, this pitch, spelled as a sharp, often leads the music toward the direction of the subdominant, a procedure utilized by Schubert in the op. 163 quintet. However, Schubert's progression to VI is somewhat shocking, coming as it does after a V7 chord, the last chord of the exposition. (Schubert may have been influenced by Mozart's G minor Symphony K. 550, whose first-movement exposition also ends on a V7 chord; however, unlike the V7 of the quintet, Mozart's V7 is not deceptive in function since the first chord of the development section is the tonic itself.) The immediate juxtaposition of the G7 chord with an inverted G♯ diminished seventh is not only deceptive: it dramatizes the movement of the PCA from pc 7 to pc 8 as an important event within the background chromatic unfolding. Pc 9 (A) follows as a matter of course, but Schubert surprises us again by making the harmony major (m. 157), thereby implying its function as a localized dominant (see mm. 163–4), rather than as submediant.

An important aspect of PCA analytical theory is that chromatic segments within the PCA ascent assume motivic function, and often become involved within a larger developmental process. In development sections, certain PCA pitch classes also serve to control and motivate large harmonic areas before passing on to the next chromatic note or segment. In op. 163, after pcs 8 and 9 have been introduced, Schubert reinterprets their relationship by expanding on their individual harmonic potential, in a sense developing the roles of G♯ and A beyond their conventional voice-leading context. He does this by first reinterpreting G♯ as the root of its own harmony, beginning tentatively in m. 169 as G♯ minor, and then becomes more bold by transforming the chord into its parallel major in m. 175. The G♯ remains the active pitch throughout this entire section (note the G♯ pedal in mm. 179–80), and instead of the pitch being moved immediately upward to A♮, it is enharmonically transformed into A♭ (m. 181; this is indicated in Diagram 6.4). The A♭ (still pc 8, now respelled enharmonically) now has the same function as E♭ had in the exposition: it delays the arrival of the intended goal by expanding a pivot area. In fact, the A♭ controls a large area of music. (By "controls" we mean that a single pitch can determine the harmonic areas of an entire musical period or even multiple periods.) In this case, A♭ throws the music into a flat-key progression that touches on D♭ and G♭, and in which A♭ itself figures prominently. The A♭ as pc 8 is sustained all the way from m. 181 to the last beat of m. 198, where A♮ (pc 9) is finally attained, the next goal within the PCA ascent. The A♮ now becomes the controlling pitch, casting the music into sharp-side harmonic regions.

The next PCA segment, comprising pcs 10 and 11, undergoes a similar developmental process. An A♯ (pc 10) appears in m. 211 as part of an extended harmonic period in sharp-key areas, controlled by sharp-side system changes (see Diagram 6.4). Pc 10 holds through this section as part of F♯ major harmony, which functions locally as the dominant of B minor. Only in m. 241 does B♭ enharmonically displace the As, as the system changes turn the harmony toward flat-key regions. The situation is analogous to what happened with G♯ and A♭ in the first half of the development.

The B♮ (pc 11), the penultimate goal of the PCA, makes a tentative appearance in m. 249 (in the diagram, the pitch is placed in brackets to show that while it is present, B♮ has yet to become a "structural" component of the PCA since it does not yet function as the leading tone of the tonic). In fact, B♭ returns in m. 259 and conflicts with B♮ until m. 262, where B♮ completely displaces B♭ and assumes its function of leading tone, supported by dominant harmony. (In the diagram, the brackets around B♮ are removed in m. 262.) The B♮ can now move up to the last pitch class in the PCA series, C (pc 0), at the recapitulation in m. 267.

A most provocative element of the recapitulation is the fact that it is not in the tonic "0" system, but rather in a 3♭ system, since E♭ was introduced in m. 264 as part of an arpeggiation of C minor harmony over the dominant G pedal. Because no F♯ has appeared to correct the 3♭ system of the minor mode, the recapitulation simply continues within the 3♭ system despite the return of the C major tonic. Only when F♯ is left uncontested in m. 274 does the system shift back to that of "0." Schubert is here intimating that the 3♭ system of the minor mode is perhaps more than just a coloristic alternative to that of the major. The complementary 3♭ system, impinging as it does on the tonic major, may, in fact, be more symmetrically equivalent than we realize. E♭ and its corrective pitch F♯ conflict throughout the first key area of the recapitulation, but the 3♭ system "wins out" yet again at the arrival of the intermediate harmonic area ("bridge theme") in m. 322. Here the lyrical melody first presented in E♭ is transposed into A♭, ♭VI of the C major tonic. Nevertheless, E♭ as a pitch class is still in control (the A♭ harmonic area is a subset of the 3♭ system), so much so that the system change back to C does not take effect until m. 367, where F♯ is finally introduced in the absence of further E♭s.

However, it is the coda (beginning in m. 414, see Example 6.7d) that is most problematic. Here the F♯ diminished chord returns once again, but this time E♭ is isolated from the chord (m. 417) and allowed to control the coda uncontested (if F♯ does appear it is negated each time by the presence of E♭). The arpeggiation of the B diminished chord over the tonic pedal, five measures before the end, with its prominent A♭, is the final remnant of the 3♭ system. Since no F♯ appears to redress the 3♭ system, the movement must be said to end within the complementary system to that of the C major tonic.

Example 6.7d   Schubert, String Quintet in C, first movement, coda (mm. 414–45)

What is perhaps even more remarkable is the conclusion of the last movement. After a series of flat-versus-natural system altercations, F♯ seems to win out at the Più presto (m. 401), deciding the outcome in favor of the tonic "0" system. But then, surprisingly, A♭ returns in m. 421, just nine measures before the end of the movement. A♭, by itself, would not cause a system change, but here the A♭ pitch class prepares for the even more remarkable return of pc 3, E♭, as an upper-neighbor trill to D♭, the root of a French augmented sixth. Without F♯, E♭ by itself would have shifted the "0" system down to a 3♭ system. But the addition of two more flats within the same passage – A♭ and D♭ – firmly fixes the 3♭ system of the tonic minor, and so the entire quintet must be said to end in its complementary 3♭ system. We believe that Schubert has done this deliberately, demonstrating that the tonic major system and that of its minor-mode complement can be treated as equals on the deepest structural level, a compositional procedure that adumbrates the symmetrically conceived works of Béla Bartók in the twentieth century!

Chapter Seven

Eleven-Pitch-Class Systems in the Music of Mid- to Late-Nineteenth-Century Romantic Composers

I. Felix Mendelssohn: Piano Trio in D minor op. 49, First Movement

As we have seen in previous chapters, the tendency on the part of composers to equate complementary systems, in particular the tonic system with its parallel minor, can be said always to have existed, at least since the seventeenth century. Throughout the eighteenth century, with the advent of common-practice tonality, the juxtaposition of parallel major and minor becomes even more striking, especially in operatic overtures (we may add numerous arias and vocal ensembles as well), where the emotional intensity of such parallels acts as a purely sonic preparation for the vocal drama to follow. Mozart, Gluck, and Cherubini are just a few of the most prominent composers to use this device. But it is not until the nineteenth century, especially in the works of Beethoven and Schubert, that composers actually "threaten" the hegemony of the tonic through constant iterations of the parallel mode and, therefore, the complementary system that it engenders.

Nineteenth-century Romantic composers seem to have had a special affinity for the minor mode, not only because it suited their emotional character, whether elegiac or demonic, but also because of the compositional problems inherent in the instability of the mode itself. To review our discussion of this topic in the previous chapter, what underlies the instability is that the missing pitch of the minor mode is the leading tone of the dominant. Therefore, minor-mode compositions easily fluctuate between tonic minor and parallel major systems, creating unsettled eleven-pitch-class tonal fields. For example, in Beethoven's Piano Sonata op. 10 no. 3 in D major, the second movement, in D minor, constantly shifts from its 1♭ tonic system to the 2♯ system of the parallel major each time a G♯ appears. This brings Beethoven's primary chromatic issue in that sonata – the conflict between F♮ (within the 1♭ system) and F♯ (within the 2♯ system) – to the forefront, the use of one or the other pitch class consistently playing the system-consonant tritone (F–B♮) off against its dissonant complement (D–G♯). In the minor mode, therefore, the raising of the parallel major through the use of the sharp fourth scale degree must constantly be deflected by minor tonic harmony. As a result, the conditions that govern minor-mode compositions are inherently more problematic and more difficult to rationalize than those in the major mode: a minor-mode tonic is considerably less stable than its major-mode counterpart. We therefore believe that systems analysis can best explain the reasons for the inherent instability of the minor mode, aside from its physical absence from the overtone series.

Of those Romantic composers who succeeded Schubert, Felix Mendelssohn (1809–1847) was extraordinarily inventive in finding new and creative solutions to the problems posed by the minor mode. The first movement of Mendelssohn's Piano Trio no. 1 in D minor op. 49 is a particularly interesting example for our discussion in view of how closely united its formal structure is with its system modulations. After a lengthy first harmonic area, one would expect the bridge leading to the formal second harmonic area to raise the dominant of the relative major, F. Instead, Mendelssohn opts for a different harmonic direction, moving toward what seems to be A minor, the minor dominant (see Example 7.1a, mm. 91–122). In fact, the relative major plays no part in the structural harmonic unfolding of the movement, a compositional choice no doubt influenced by the first-movement exposition of Beethoven's Ninth Symphony, also in D minor.

In the exposition of the trio, the motion into A minor is confirmed by a harmonic progression in which an F augmented sixth chord resolves to V/V in mm. 989, after which the dominant chord (E major) moves into A minor harmony in the next measure. The progression is repeated twice in mm. 106–11, the ever-present C♮s maintaining minor dominant harmony. Throughout this passage, G♯, the leading tone to the dominant and the missing pitch of the prevailing tonic 1♭ system, is in constant conflict with F♮, its complementary system-shift motivator. As a result, the continued presence of these two pitch classes prevents any long-range system shift away from the 1♭ system to a 2♯ system; the overriding tonic 1♭ system actually supports the motion into the minor, instead of the major, dominant.

Besides the fact that Mendelssohn has chosen to articulate the "wrong dominant," one wonders about the nature of the German augmented sixth chord on F that keeps cropping up within the minor dominant progression leading to the second harmonic area. In contrast with its use in major, where the chord is virtually obtrusive, the augmented sixth makes little if any noticeable effect as a chord supporting the progression into the *minor dominant*, since its root is a diatonic pitch class within the key. As we have seen in previous examples, the augmented sixth in the major mode, formed on the minor third degree of the tonic, also creates a contrapuntal relationship to the opening tonic chord itself (often through a long-range chromatic voice exchange), subsuming all the material from the opening of the movement to the point of the augmented sixth within tonic harmony! However, such a large-scale relationship to the tonic is altogether mitigated if the tonic is minor since the root of the chord within the minor mode is diatonic, and therefore cannot form a chromatic exchange with the tonic. But Mendelssohn has something else in mind, and this chord will loom large later in the composition.

Example 7.1a   **Mendelssohn, Piano Trio in D minor op. 49, first movement, bridge into second harmonic area (mm. 91–122)**

For the moment, events begin to take a different turn as we get closer to the second harmonic area. From mm. 111 on, the focus shifts to the V/V alone, since no dominant chord follows. In fact, the musical texture seems to vaporize in mm. 115–16, where only the piano is left with an isolated E major triad on the first beat of the measure, followed by a simple undulation between E and F♮ in the left hand of the piano part of the next two measures (taken over from the previous cello figure). Up to this point, the presence of F♮ has effectively prevented any G♯s in the area from modulating systems. In m. 117 the bass of the piano moves down to a held dotted half-note D, while the oscillating neighbor-note bass continues in the right-hand, but now with F♯ displacing the previous F♮. This will now allow the next G♯ to activate a system shift up to a 2♯ system. The resultant V 6/4/2 chord acts as a dominant preparation, but the listener still does not know the quality of the dominant that ensues. What makes the shift to F♯ most intriguing is its accentuation; that is, the lower pitch, E, now seems to emphasize the upper neighbor, F♯, with D supporting it. So Mendelssohn has very quietly, and most effectively, projected not just an inverted dominant seventh chord, but also the sound of the major tonic, D major, as preparation for the major dominant as the second harmonic area, beginning with the upbeat to m. 119, along with a concomitant system shift to a 2♯ system. Perhaps Mendelssohn heard A major as a condition of the tonic 2♯ system by actually preceding the second harmonic area with an implied D major sonority in the piano, thus relating the following A major area to the tonic major and not to the tonic minor.

The polarizing of the major dominant and a minor tonic is a most unusual harmonic relationship in a sonata-form exposition since the major dominant as a harmonic area is related to the tonic major, not to the tonic minor, and since the minor mode does not support a major dominant as there is no natural raised fourth degree in minor. Indeed, a large-scale move into the major dominant may well endanger the integrity of the minor mode as a background tonic. This may be the reason why Beethoven avoids minor tonic/major dominant large-scale harmonic relationships in his minor-mode pieces, preferring, instead, third-degree relations (relative or submediant) with the minor tonic. But Mendelssohn, again, has his eyes set on further developments that will justify all his harmonic motions, if not at present, at least through hindsight. One must always keep in mind Mendelssohn's extensive Classical training, and his sensitivity to Classical balance and proportion, especially in his chamber music. An essential component of Classical sonata-form procedure is the relationship between the exposition, which often raises musical ambiguities, and the recapitulation, where these same ambiguities are dealt with and resolved into tonic harmony. In this sense, Mendelssohn is very much a Classical composer.

As soon as the A major second harmonic area begins (C♯ has now displaced C♮), G♯ returns within V/V harmony (m. 122; see Example 7.1a) without any conflicting F♮s to prevent a system move up to a 2♯ system. The 2♯ system remains in effect throughout the A major area until m. 164, where F♮, as part of D minor harmony (iv/V) within the lengthy two-part transition to the closing area, reverts the system to a 1♭ system. D minor, along with its system shift, now prepares for the A major dominant to collapse into its own parallel minor for the closing area – where the opening theme of the movement is repeated – and codetta. Regaining the minor dominant, after it has been displaced by the major dominant at the end of the bridge, is a necessary harmonic gesture at this stage within the exposition if the underlying tonic minor is to retain its hegemony. Beethoven's "Appassionata" Piano Sonata is quite different at this point since Beethoven completely abandons any large-scale reference to the F minor tonic at the end of the exposition (see Chapter 6). Interestingly, neither Mendelssohn nor Beethoven repeats the exposition, but each has a different reason for not doing so. Beethoven's closing is so harmonically intense, and the music has traveled so far away, into A♭ minor, that the end of the exposition has no harmonic relationship to its beginning; meaning that there is no dominant function to motivate a return to tonic harmony. Beethoven's intent here is to thrust the exposition into the development: one dissonant harmonic area follows another without the momentary release of a tonic return. Without a first ending acting as a transition, raising the dominant as a voice-leading chord, a repeat of the exposition would be futile and unconvincing. On the other hand, Mendelssohn's switch to A major at the start of the second key is a powerful gesture that, if left unchecked, would seriously undermine one's understanding of the tonic mode as minor. Once Mendelssohn reverts to the minor dominant, it is pointless to restate the whole process.

Concurrent with the dramatic play of major/minor ambiguity within the second harmonic area is also the dramatic confrontation of complementary systems. Sometimes these system shifts take unexpected turns that only add to the modal uncertainties swirling around them. For instance, one would expect that when D minor re-enters the picture, in the transition to the closing area, not only would the system revert to a 1♭ system, but the tonic system would remain in effect throughout the minor dominant area. Initially, this is exactly what happens (m. 164), but G♯, as leading tone to the dominant, soon returns to challenge the 1♭ system. However, the omnipresent F♮s prevent any modulation out of the 1♭ system. By m. 172, G♯ gains a bit more control, the 2♯ system lasting three measures, before F♮ transforms the system back to a 1♭ system. Measures 183–6 are particularly intense: G♯s and F♮s follow each other relentlessly until F♮ finally remains uncontested right before the closing area begins! Within the closing area itself, G♯ gains greater ground, the 2♯ and 1♭ systems alternating practically every two measures. Again the process accelerates as the music approaches the codetta, but this time it is G♯ that "wins" the conflict, and the codetta, in A minor, actually begins in a 2♯ system. If we draw the three-hexachord system for both one flat and two sharps, we notice that A is a root pitch in both systems – as the dominant minor in D minor and as the dominant major in D major:

1♭ Quality of third:	D	A	E♮/E♭	B♮/B♭	F♮/F♯	C♮/C♯
Hexachord root:	B♭ –	F –	C –	g –	d –	a
Harmonic function:	VI	III	VII	iv	i	v

G♯/A♭ is the missing pitch of the system

2♯ Quality of third:	B♭/B♮	F♯	C♯/C♮	G♮/G♯	D♮/D♯	A♮/A♯
Hexachord root:	G –	D –	A –	e –	b –	f♯
Harmonic function:	IV	I	V	ii	vi	iii

F♮/E♯ is the missing pitch of the system

Likewise, in both systems, the A can support either a major or a minor third, a condition that extends into harmonic areas as well. More precisely, complementary systems within a single matrix system overlap hexachordal roots. For example, in the illustration above, the last three roots of the 1♭ system (g, d, a) overlap with the first three roots of the 2♯ system (G, D, A), creating a certain amount of ambiguity as to the system to which these roots may belong. The same is true in tonal composition in which the composer so weakens a progression that it is sometimes difficult to ascertain what deeper harmonic level it supports. For example, in the Schubert String Quintet op. 163 in C major, discussed in the previous chapter, the E♭ area is ambiguous as to its function: is it a passing harmony to the dominant, an area in its own right, or an extension of tonic harmony? Schubert seems to imply all three. Interestingly, a systems analysis of the first half of the Prelude to Wagner's *Tristan* shows a continual oscillation between an initial "0" system, whose tonic is ambiguous (with no sharps or flats in the signature, A minor, A major, and C major could all vie as possible tonics), and a 3♯ system, while the second half moves back and forth between a "0" system and a 3♭ system. Similarly, Mendelssohn's A major second harmonic area is equally ambiguous as to its background function: is it V of D minor, V of D major, or simply a passing motion that happens to occupy a rhythmically strong position but ultimately leads to a higher structural minor v that ends the exposition? As it happens, the codetta's 2♯ system does revert to a 1♭ system in m. 217, at least temporarily. The G♯ returns, along with the 2♯ system, a few measures later (m. 221), one beat before the start of the development.

After examining the system modulations in the exposition, one is struck by the fact that the entire exposition is governed by only two complementary tritone systems: the tonic 1♭ system of F–B♮, which continually conflicts with its 2♯ tritone complement, D–G♯. Oddly enough, there is not a single instance *in the entire exposition* of A♭ as a pitch class, nor as the root of the complementary 4♭ system of A♭–D, even in passing! Rather, Mendelssohn consistently spells pc 6 as G♯, most likely because of the harmonic design of the exposition and its emphasis on the major dominant. As a result, there is little room, or need, to enter into flat-side harmonic areas. Mendelssohn reserves the exploration of flat-side harmonic areas for the development section which follows.

Like so many Romantic development sections from Schubert on, Mendelssohn's is leisurely, lengthy, and purely melodic, constructed out of material from the exposition which is sequentially repeated in different harmonic areas. The development begins by repeating the thematic material of the codetta (actually, the opening theme of the movement) and, in the same harmonic area, the minor dominant. As in the codetta, A minor is heard within a 2♯ system, but now its function is to initiate an inverted fifths cycle – A minor, D minor, G minor, C minor – where the next fifth after A minor is D minor. Naturally, when the D minor area arrives (m. 230), F♮ returns as well, shifting the system back into a 1♭ system. The 1♭ system is now sustained over the course of the fifths cycle until m. 250, where B♭ (VI) is reached as the primary harmonic goal of the development. The B♭ area, which restates the second theme, is extended by a counterstatement that turns into a fugato, the end of which initiates another fifths cycle: D minor, G minor, C minor, F minor, B♭. It is during the C minor area within the cycle that Mendelssohn finally explores the A♭–D tritone 4♭ system. In mm. 291–315, A♭ is in constant conflict with B♮, the complementary-system pitch-class motivator and the only pitch that can prevent A♭ from sustaining a 4♭ system. Eventually, in m. 315, B♮ displaces A♭ altogether, and the 1♭ system is temporarily restored. We say temporarily, because G♯, along with the 2♯ system, returns in m. 325 as the music moves into the dominant for the lengthy retransition that will lead to the recapitulation (mm. 338ff.) The prolonged dominant of the retransition is heard as relating to tonic harmony primarily because of the B♭ augmented sixth chord that introduces the A major area (m. 337). This same progression will recur in the recapitulation as a structurally significant event (see the discussion below). For the rest of the development, the original complementary tritone systems of F–B♮ and D–G♯ govern the harmonic action, with the 1♭ system finally displacing the previous 2♯ system only in m. 357, ten measures before the recapitulation.

Within the development section, the B♭ area, after being interrupted by the second fifths cycle, returns, now interpreted as a single B♭ augmented sixth chord (m. 327), which then drops to the dominant in the next measure for the start of the retransition. The entire development can thus be reduced to a simple contrapuntal progression: a (v) – B♭ (VI) – B♭ aug. 6 – A (V) – d (i), in which A is continually elaborated by its upper neighbor B♭ throughout.

But our main concern is what happens in the recapitulation, which begins on the upbeat to m. 367. Example 7.1b shows the end of the bridge up through the beginning of the transposed second harmonic area. The bridge itself, not unlike those in Classical treatments of recapitulations, is entirely reworked; however, certain harmonic details remain as significant events transposed from the exposition. For example, we mentioned the effectiveness, or lack of it, of the F augmented sixth chord that occurred at the latter part of the exposition bridge, and that served to prolong the minor dominant area before the major dominant second harmonic area. That same augmented sixth now returns, but this time within the minor tonic, appearing not three times, as it did in the exposition, but only once (see m. 426 in Example 7.1b), and with much greater effect. As a result of the transposition of the augmented sixth chord a fifth down from F to B♭, the chord contains within it the two pitch classes of the primary system conflict of the movement, namely, G♯ and F♮, the two system-shift motivators that have been in continual conflict since the development section's retransition. In fact, this same progression, from the B♭ augmented sixth to the dominant, was anticipated at the point of retransition (see above), with the prolonged dominant supported by a system shift to the 2♯ system. However, in contrast with the retransition passage, the recapitulation's B♭ augmented sixth chord is momentarily prevented from shifting the system to the 2♯ system since both G♯ and F♮ are contained within the same chord. However, the G♯, placed in a prominent register (in the first violin), anticipates the actual system shift that does occur two measures later (m. 428), where an uncontested G♯ is heard an octave lower in the right hand of the piano part. With the restoration of the 2♯ system, we are now prepared for the second harmonic area to return in D major, a transposition down a fifth from the analogous A major area in the exposition. Here the system and the key come together: both are in two sharps, and, perhaps more importantly, the D major in the recapitulation fulfills the implied relationship of A major to the tonic major that we saw in the exposition!

Example 7.1b   Mendelssohn, Piano Trio in D minor op. 49, first movement, recapitulation (mm. 420–38)

The rest of the recapitulation follows the same harmonic structure, transposed into tonic harmony, and thematic ordering as that of the exposition, with the closing area transposed into D minor. As in earlier Classical procedures, the coda summarizes previous events and also resolves system and dyad conflicts, primary issues that have been played out over the course of the movement. With regard to system analysis, the coda's plunge into a prolonged 4♭ system is both fascinating and problematic. In m. 548, an A♭ is introduced as part of a B♭ 6/4/2 chord that acts as an applied dominant to an area in the Neapolitan, E♭, in m. 350. In m. 558, the Neapolitan resolves to D major in 6/4 position when the theme of the second harmonic area is restated. Thus the final major/minor conflict of the movement is now played out on a grand scale between tonic major and tonic minor. However, the move to D major harmony does not effect a concomitant change in systems since no B♮s appear within the passage. Rather, after eight measures of unstable D major harmony, with A in the bass, B♭s enter as part of the minor subdominant, in G minor triads that are sandwiched between inverted D major triads, here functioning as V/iv (mm. 566–7). The G minor subdominant is now extended into one long pre-cadential harmony, delaying the final resolution to the minor tonic until the authentic cadence in mm. 579–80. The entire passage is subsumed under the prevailing 4♭ system, no B♮s appearing to redress the system. Only after the arrival of D minor does B♮ enter the picture (in m. 583) and finally bring the system back up to a 1♭ system.

With the final resolution of D major to D minor, the primary dyad conflict of the movement, F♯/F♮, is resolved as well. Both of these pitch classes interact with the main system conflict of the movement: that between F♯, derived from the D–

G♯ tritone system that supported D major, and F♮, derived from the tonic tritone system of F–B♮ that supported D minor. The constant battle for superiority between the 1♭ and 2♯ systems, with its jostling back and forth between major and minor, maintained both F♯ and F♮ as active pitch classes all the way through the movement. Most sophisticated in this regard is the prolongation of the major dominant that was the focal point of the exposition's second harmonic area. As mentioned previously, the deeper meaning of the A major area was that it presumed the tonic major. Its transposition into the tonic major in the recapitulation lent further support to the contention that the ultimate dyad conflict of the movement was indeed F♯/F♮.

With the emphatic return of D minor in the coda (m. 580), the rest of the movement is free to resolve the last remaining issue: the conflict of the original system motivators, G♯/F♮, each one trying to assert its individual tritone system. The coda, therefore, is systemically quite active throughout its last period, reaching a climax in m. 593, where the tonic matrix G♯ diminished chord appears, supported by a double *forte* in the piano part and a *sforzando* in the strings. Finally, in m. 600, F♮ pre-empts G♯ for the last time, the rest of the movement being totally diatonic except for C♯, the leading tone.

For reasons of space, we cannot go into detail about the PCA unfolding in this work, but this topic will be dealt with more fully in the following discussion of Schumann's Piano Quintet in E♭.

II. Robert Schumann: Piano Quintet in E♭ op. 44, First Movement

Schubert's two other important successors, notably Schumann and Brahms, seem to have been equally fascinated with the compositional problems (or ambiguities) imposed by pitting one system against the other. For instance, Schumann's Piano Quintet in E♭ op. 44 of 1842, a work that seems to have drawn inspiration from both Beethoven's Piano Trio op 70 no. 1 and Schubert's String Quintet op. 163, also arpeggiates the tonic minor triad over the course of the exposition of its first movement. However, Schumann's approach is more dynamic than Schubert's in that the minor third, here G♭, does not create a stabilized period in itself, but appears as part of a larger progression within the bridge, already in *dominant* harmony (Schubert's strategy was to create an expanse for the missing pitch within *tonic* harmony), as ♭VI/V (see Example 7.2). Schumann is obviously following Beethoven's example here in the latter's op. 70 no. 1 (see the discussion above), in an attempt to avoid Schubert's more relaxed exploration of the minor third degree within a highly lyricized intermediate harmonic area. At the same time, Schumann, perhaps trying not to copy Beethoven too closely, differs from Beethoven in that in the trio, the minor third degree leads off from a bridge passage that begins in tonic harmony *on the way to* the dominant, whereas, contrary to common practice, Schumann is already *in dominant harmony* at the start of the bridge.

To continue with Schumann's minor-third unfolding within his bridge passage, the 6♭ system to which G♭ belongs (see Figure 7.1, which illustrates the quintet's extended 3♭ matrix system), is sustained for a full 17 measures as opposed to Schubert's relatively grandiose minor-third intermediate area of 38 measures.

(Compared with those of Schubert and Schumann, Beethoven's parallel minor passage in the bridge of his piano trio is more classically concise, being a paltry seven measures!) Eventually, Schumann's 6♭ system reverts to a 3♭ system with the introduction of A♮ (the missing pitch of the 6♭ system, m. 44) as the music nears its approach to the second harmonic area. Significantly, in the measure immediately preceding, the G♭ harmonic area changes function from ♭VI/V to that of a G♭ augmented sixth, thus intensifying the progression to the dominant. By juxtaposing the G♭ (and its concomitant 6♭ system) with A♮ (as a correcting pitch to reinstate the tonic 3♭ system), Schumann is further working out the relationship of these two complementary system pitch classes, already begun within the opening tonic period, their interaction pervading the movement as a source of development. Schumann's opening statement is designed as a small ternary structure, typical of Schubert's opening periods, in which an unstable middle contrasting phrase is flanked by two more or less identical phrases, the second of which forms the counterstatement. It is in the middle period (mm. 9–16) that Schumann introduces the G♭ in the bass as a passing seventh from A♭ to F.

The F7 on the downbeat of m. 11 contains the A♮, which immediately prevents the previous G♭ from effecting a system shift down to a 6♭ system. The next stage of development occurs within the bridge, where, as previously stated, G♭, along with the 6♭ system, prevails as an internal harmonic area (no A♮ appears to redress the system shift), which has the effect of a parenthetical interruption of the dominant: the G♭ arises from a 5–6 chromatic exchange with B♭ (see Example 7.2, mm. 26–7). Finally, the G♭ becomes structurally significant as an augmented sixth (m. 43) that forms a large-scale voice exchange with the opening E♭ triad and which thus signifies the end of tonic harmony within the exposition. This is why, incidentally, even though the counterstatement begins on dominant harmony, it still pertains to the tonic and cannot yet be considered as initiating the dominant as a harmonic area. Only now does A♮ return to shift the system back up to the 3♭ system.

By using the minor third degree as an augmented sixth chord as preparation for the dominant area, Schumann's exposition, unlike both Beethoven's op. 70 no. 1 and Schubert's op. 163, harks back to the Viennese Classicists of the previous century, especially Haydn, whose works were, by Schumann's own admission, of little interest.[1]

---

1 Schumann, in criticizing Haydn's "Military" Symphony in a concert given in 1840, said, in part: "... He [Haydn] is like a regular house-guest who is always welcome and respectfully received; but he no longer holds any deeper interest for our age." Quoted in James Garratt, "Haydn and Posterity: The Long Nineteenth Century," in Caryl Clark (ed.), *The Cambridge Companion to Haydn* (Cambridge, 2005), p. 232. However, Schumann's disparaging remarks do not necessarily mean that he was not influenced, to some extent at least, by many details of Haydn's compositional methodology.

Example 7.2 Schumann, Piano Quintet op. 44, first movement, counterstatement to bridge (mm. 17–57)

Example 7.2 Schumann, Piano Quintet op. 44, first movement, counterstatement to bridge (mm. 17–57) continued

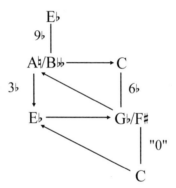

Figure 7.1   **Schumann, Piano Quintet in E♭ op. 44, first movement, 3♭ extended tonic system matrix**

Up to this point, the main system conflict has been between the 3♭ and 6♭ systems, and more specifically, between G♭ and A♮ as system-shift motivators that either raise or negate the systems to which they apply. The relationship between these two pitch classes continues even after A♮ has formally reverted the system to the 3♭ system (see mm. 47–8). However, at the end of the bridge there is a lead-in transitional passage (mm. 51–6) that highlights the arrival of the second harmonic area. During this passage the previous G♭s are temporarily respelled as F♯s, inviting a whole new set of tritone system-related conditions (see Figure 7.1) that are maintained until m. 101, when G♭ is reintroduced, first as part of a seventh chord and then as an augmented sixth. Throughout this lengthy period, the system conflict centers on the 3♭ system and its complementary "0" system. As a result, the previous conflict between system pitches G♭ and A♮ is now temporarily displaced by that between F♯ and E♭.

Of major interest to our discussion is Schumann's sophisticated concept of a development process that is tightly organized around the interaction of tritone system shifts with system-conflict pitch classes, and, as we shall see, PCA rises. We have already seen how G♭ becomes a motivating pitch class that is projected into ever deeper structural levels within the exposition, but how does this pitch class (as well as its enharmonic equivalent, F♯) work into the PCA of the exposition in such a way that both G♭ and its conflicting system pitch class complement, A♮, become a source of development in their own right?

To begin, Schumann's PCA ascents in the exposition are quite active owing to the basically chromatic nature of the thematic material; this procedure will strongly influence Brahms. Diagram 7.1a gives an overview of the PCA rises and system shifts in the exposition of the first movement of the quintet. Unusually, Schumann has two PCA ascents from pc 0 to 7 within the first harmonic area of the movement, the first within the opening statement and the second within the counterstatement and bridge. This is so because the counterstatement itself starts on dominant harmony and Schumann makes it very clear in the music that leads up to it that the arrival to this middleground goal should be dramatized by a complete first segment rise of the PCA (see Diagram 7.1a for exact details). Along the way, pc 3 is spelled first as G♭ (m. 10) and then as F♯ (m. 12), both instances causing temporary system shifts that are corrected by the system's conflicting pitch class, A♮ and E♭ respectively. It is worth noting that pc 3 is the only pitch class within the PCA rise that undergoes an enharmonic respelling. Schumann seems to be preparing for the future possibility that both G♭ and its enharmonic equivalent, F♯, will undergo some kind of developmental manipulation as the movement progresses.

EXPOSITION

First Harmonic Area

Measure:	1	4	5		10	11	12	13	14	15	16
Active System Pcs:					Gb ↗	A♮ ↗	F♯ ↗		E♭ ↗		
System:	3 b s				6 b s	3 b s	"0"		3 b s sustained		G♮ (4) – G♯ (5) – A♮ (6)
PCA:	E♭ (0)	E♮ (1)	F (2) – Gb (3)				F♯ (3) ——— G♮ (4) –	G♮ (4) ———	G♮ (4)		
Harmony:	E♭										
	I										

Counterstatement

M.:	17		19	20		22		27
ASPcs:						(Gb/A♮)		Gb ↗
System:								6 b s
PCA:	B♭ (7) **PCA repeats:**		E♭ (0) – [E♮ (1)]	E♮ (1) – F (2)		G♮ (3) ———		G♮ (3) sustained ———
	[B♭]					Gb		
Harmony:	[V, but not yet structural]					bVI/V		

Lead-in to 2nd Harmonic Area

M.:	43	44	45	46	47	48	51	52
ASPcs:		A♮ ↗			6 b ↗	A♮ ↗		(F♯/E♭)
System:		3 b s			6 b s	3 b s		
PCA:	Gb (3)		G♮ (4) [A♭, pc 5, is omitted] [A♮ (6)]				A♮ (6)]	
	Gb aug. 6 → F				Gb aug. 6 → F		A♮ pedal ———	
Harmony:	V/V prolonged ———						07/V	

Second Harmonic Area

M.:	56	57	58		61	62–64	65	66
ASPcs:			F♯ ↗		E♭ ↗	(F♯/E♭)		
System:			"0"		3 b s			
PCA:	A♮ (6)	**B♭ (7) PCA repeats:**	E♭ (0)					E♮ (1) F (2)
	A♮ pedal	B♭						
Harmony:	Piano arpeggiates a V aug. →	V						

Diagram 7.1a   Schumann, Piano Quintet in E♭ op. 44, first movement, exposition: systems/PCA

Lead-in repeated   **Theme of 2ⁿᵈ HA repeated**   Transition (based on Lead-in)

M.:	73	74	75		79	80–81	83	95	96-97
ASPcs:		(F♯/E♭)			F♯↗		E♭↗		
System:					"0"		3 b s		
PCA:	**F♯ (3)**		**G (4)** sustained			[pcs 2-3-4 repeated]			[pcs 2-3-4 repeated]
Harmony:	A♮ pedal ————		→		B♭			A♮ pedal ————	
	07/V				V				

Codetta: repeats the opening theme — 108

Starts a parenthetical interruption ————

M.:	101-102	102		103	105	106	107
ASPcs: G♭s↗				A♮↗	F♯↗	E♭↗ holds through to the end of the expo.	
System:	6 b s			3 b s	"0"	3 b s	
PCA:		**G (4)** [A♭, pc 5 omitted]		**G (4)** [A♮ (6)]			**A♮ (6)** →
Harmony:	G♭7 - G♭ aug. 6		C6/4/3 (deceptive)	F7	D7		F7 →
							V7/V

107   108

E♭↗ holds through to the end of the expo.	
A♮ (6) →	**B♭ (7)**
F7 →	B♭
V7/V	V

						1ˢᵗ ending————
M.:	109	110	111	113	115	116
ASPcs:	(G♭/A♮)			(G♭/A♮)		
System:						
PCA: **PCA repeats:**	**E♭ (0)**	**E♮ (1) F (2)**		**G♭ (3)**	**G♮ (4) – G♯ (5) – A♮ (6)**	**B♭ (7)**
Harmony:				07		V

:

In the counterstatement, the first segment of the PCA is repeated, but this time pc 3 as G♭, as discussed above, attains much greater prominence within the harmonic unfolding, sustaining a 6♭ system shift over a long period of music. As a consequence, when A♮ is once more attained in m. 44, it too gains in prominence, since only this pitch class can return the system to the 3♭ system. In order to balance the previous G♭ area, A♮, when it reaches its status as pc 6 within the PCA rise to the dominant (beginning in m. 46; see Example 7.2), is dramatized to such an extent that it assumes the function of bass right up to the start of the second harmonic area! Thus the two system pitch-class motivators, G♭ and A♮, seem to control a significant amount of the harmonic motion of the first half of the exposition.

As the second harmonic area gets under way, in the traditional area of the dominant, F♯ replaces G♭, the system conflicts now centering on the "0" and 3♭ systems. As is usual at the start of the second harmonic area, the PCA begins again from pc 0, the E♭ found in the cello part on the second beat of m. 58. Pcs 1 and 2 (E♮ and F♮) are found in mm. 65–6, with pcs 3 and 4 (F♯ and G♮) in mm. 74–5 as the lead-in to the second theme is repeated. During this lyrical, stable period, the 3♭ tonic system prevails, and when F♯ as pc 3 enters, E♭ is pitted against it, preventing a system shift. Events begin to change with the repeat of the second theme itself beginning in m. 80. Here the F♮–F♯–G segment of the PCA is repeated with F♯ left uncontested, therefore allowing a brief shift into the "0" system. What is interesting about this passage is that the PCA never rises beyond pc 4, G♮. An E♭ in m. 83 reverts the system to the 3♭ system, the music once more moving to a repeat of the lead-in material in m. 95. The repeat initiates a dynamic, rhythmically charged transition to the codetta (there is no closing area in this exposition). Along with the repeat of the lead-in material comes the same three pitch classes, 2, 3, and 4, the G♮ still being prevented from proceeding to the next pitch in the series. In fact, it never does! On the contrary, the G♮ first moves down to G♭, which now regains its motivic function as a source of development. Again, the G♭ triad turns into an augmented sixth as it did in the bridge, but instead of immediately resolving it cadentially to the dominant, Schumann interpolates a parenthetical progression (see Diagram 7.1a) constructed from dominant seventh chords. Here the PCA is worked into the system shifts as pc 4, G♮, moves up to pc 6, A♮ (pc 5, A♭, is omitted), in m. 103, temporarily regaining the tonic 3♭ system in the process. Because pc 5 is omitted, the A♮, as part of an F7 chord, is clearly heard against the previous G♭ sonority, reinforcing the G♭/A♮ system dyad conflict that informs so much of the movement's harmonic development.

With the arrival of the dominant at the codetta in m. 108 (note that the thematic material for the codetta is the opening theme, a procedure followed by Mendelssohn in the D minor Piano Trio, discussed above, and ultimately deriving from Beethoven, and most probably from the first movement of his Piano Trio op. 1 no. 3 in C minor), the delayed resolution to the dominant seventh from the previous G♭ augmented sixth is finally accomplished. So too is the PCA rise from pc 6, A♮, to pc 7, B♭. Interestingly, the missing pc 5, A♭, now appears in the first measure of the codetta as part of a V7/IV within the dominant area (the note is doubled with an accent over it in the upper register in both the first violin and piano parts, and with a *forte* dynamic). Since A♭ does not appear within the previous interpolated passage, and is therefore missing from the PCA rise, Schumann seems to have deliberately isolated the A♭ in order to emphasize the A♮, and consequently the G♭/A♮ system dyad, in its place.

Instead of leading into a formal closing period, Schumann's transition jumps right into a quite laconic codetta of only nine measures. The codetta serves a double function of both concluding the exposition with a cadential phrase and rhythmically anchoring the dominant with an emphatic downbeat. In its role as substitute closing period, the opening theme of the movement (itself rhythmically concise) is restated, a device typical of Romantic-era closing periods following in the footsteps of Beethoven, whose chamber music sports numerous such closing periods (for example, the Piano Trio in C minor op. 1 no. 3, first movement). Schumann's codetta thus revives the rhythmic intensity of the opening statement that was attenuated during the extended, lyrical first period of the second harmonic area. Supporting the reinvigorated rhythmic drive, Schumann adds another PCA segment rise from the codetta to the end of the exposition, perhaps once again to emphasize the importance of the G♭/A♮ relationship: G♭ as pc 3 is pitted against A♮ within diminished harmony, the diminished chord containing all the pitch classes of the tonic matrix system. This last PCA rise of the exposition contains all 0–7 pitch classes, which only adds to the chromatic intensity of the passage (see Diagram 7.1a).

Compositionally, perhaps even aesthetically, Romantic composers, Schubert among them, seem to have deliberately switched from the Classical concept of a continuously dynamic development section to that of a more lyrical, less propulsive one that relied more on literal sequential restatement than on thematic reinterpretation. Perhaps this is due to the Romantic conception of what we might call "temporal elasticity," whereby the music ebbs and flows, now dynamic, now placid, the rhythm constantly regenerating itself after a period of repose. Temporal elasticity is characteristic of many Romantically conceived sonata-form expositions where, after a stormy opening, either at the very opening of the movement or at the counterstatement (Schubert's op. 163 String Quintet is an example of the latter) the music relaxes into a lyrical outpouring that is anticipated in the bridge and becomes manifest through the first period of the second harmonic area, only to be "jump-started" again at the closing period.[2]

In retrospect, the slowing-down of the phrase rhythm to allow for a lyrical or "song-like" theme at the start of the second harmonic area can be traced back to the Classical exposition types of the *style galant* composers, including many of the Mannheim composers, J.C. Bach, and Mozart (both father and son), among many others. These "aria-like" melodies were often constructed in rhythmically secure eight-measure periods broken up into 4 + 4 antecedent/consequent phrases. In these works, the phrasing of the subsequent transition that led to the closing area was non-periodic, asymmetrical, rhythmically active, harmonically unstable, and chromatically intensified. The closing period restored the periodic phrase rhythm, but maintained a certain surface rhythmic activity that was often embellished with

---

2   See Gregory Vitercik's insightful remarks on this Romantic tendency in his excellent study of Mendelssohn's early works: *The Early Works of Felix Mendelssohn: A Study in the Romantic Sonata Style* (Amsterdam, 1992), pp. 46 and 307–8.

increased chromaticism. The Romantic composers simply carried this juxtaposition of dynamic versus lyric to extremes, which worked well enough in their sonata-form expositions, where harmonic areas needed to be both stabilized, to establish a background relationship between first and second harmonic areas, and destabilized, to justify cadential arrivals. But when this dichotomy was applied to development sections, it often failed.

The reasons for this lie in the very nature of what a development section was originally intended to do, that is, to connect the end of the exposition with the return of tonic harmony at the point of recapitulation. In order to accomplish this feat successfully, the phrase rhythm of the development accelerates as the music moves quickly through one harmonic area after another, either as part of a larger prolongation of a "development key" (for instance, V or vi) or in a treatment of each area sequentially with more or less equal weight. Perhaps the most important task the composer must face within the development of a major-mode sonata-form movement is to transform the dominant from where it left off at the end of the exposition, as a harmonic area, into a cadential harmony within a larger tonic progression leading into the return of the tonic at the start of recapitulation. At the point of retransition at the close of the development section, the dominant should be heard as preparing the tonic, not as a self-contained and temporarily stable harmonic area. Thus the overall harmonic progression of the development relates to the tonic rather than to the harmonic area that ended the exposition; and, consequently, all the primary harmonic goals of the development form a large-scale tonic progression; for example from IV (as the first goal of motion) to vi (as both a climactic area and neighbor to the V) and, finally, V itself, often carrying a seventh with it in order to directly relate it to the tonic that follows. Naturally, a composer can choose from a wide variety of development progressions, but the essential point is that the listener/performer should perceive the progression, and the best way to accomplish this on the composer's part is through the use of an accelerated phrase rhythm. Consequently, if a harmonic area within the development is ever stabilized to such an extent that it defeats the background acceleration (that is, the stabilization takes the form of a periodic, lyric episode) the rhythmic drive of the development is in danger of collapsing altogether. This is why Mozart, when he does have a lyric theme in his development, usually places it at the very beginning; once the acceleration starts, Mozart rarely, if ever, stops it until he has reached the recapitulation.

Romantic composers, however, lean heavily toward the lyric element in their pieces, a tendency most likely stemming from a deep emotional involvement with vocal music of all types, most especially opera. Lyric phrasing demands both a periodic phrase structure and a slowing of the harmonic rhythm. If it is used within a sonata-form exposition, the result can be highly emotional and deeply satisfying (listen to the theme of any of Schubert's second or middle harmonic areas!), but when applied to a development, the overuse of stable melodic phrases can become tiresome and uninteresting. Of course, the Romantic composer does not feel this way in the slightest. Rather, the Romantic approach to melody and phrase rhythm within the development section is just the opposite: the function of these musical elements is to achieve an almost operatic intensity in which passages of slow, almost non-existent, harmonic motion frame passionate, faster ones that build to dramatic climaxes. The whole concept of temporal elasticity that pervades the Romantic development literally depends upon the ebb and flow of phrase rhythms, which either propel the music forward or retard its momentum. Compared with Beethoven's totally dynamic approach to phrase rhythm, in which the rhythmic propulsion that ends the exposition is further intensified in the development, and without let-up, the Romantic conception, a basically melodic one, appears often to be flaccid, even arbitrary, even though the original intent on the part of the composer may have been the opposite.

That brings us to Schumann's own solution to the problem of phrase rhythm (or the avoidance of it) in the development of his piano quintet. After all the rhythmic build-up at the end of the exposition, it comes as somewhat of a let-down to hear the rhythm slow to a crawl at the opening of the development section. Texturally as well, the interplay between the strings and the piano that characterized the exposition has now evaporated in favor of an overly active piano part that comprises mostly "passage work," during which the string parts are reduced to articulating the harmonic rhythm in whole and half notes.

Further, Schumann's background harmonic plan for the development reminds one of Schubert's large-scale sequential periods that run through numerous harmonic areas lying a fifth apart, and which maintain a single phrase rhythm throughout. A design such as this, one that depends upon sequential repetition, is practically incapable of achieving any sort of cumulative tension or climax. Specifically, Schumann's development centers on two large-scale sequential periods, each one initiating a fifths cycle, the second of which conveniently leads directly into the recapitulation (see Diagram 7.1b). Thematically, each area is introduced by a restatement of the opening motivic theme followed by a steady stream of somewhat characterless eighth-notes in the piano part – the "passage work" mentioned above. At the same time, Schumann's sequential periods maintain a slow harmonic rhythm, which eventually becomes predictable.

These periods, without any lyric content, are unrelated to the melodic/motivic ideas expressed in the exposition. In fact, there is no development of the exposition material at all, except for a constant, unvaried, repetition of the opening theme of the movement, sandwiched in between the two sequential periods.

DEVELOPMENT

Opening motive restated (mm. 128-131)

Measure:	116	123	128	132	138	139	140	142	143
Active System Pcs:		G♭ ↗			A♮ ↗ (Gb/A♮)		G♭ ↗	A♮ ↗	
System:	3 b s	6 b s			3 b s		6 b s	3 b s	
PCA:	**B♭ (7)**			**C♭ (8)**				**C♮ (9)**	**D♭ (10)**
Harmony:	B♭ / V		a♭ m / iv (initiates a 5ths cycle)			e♭ m		b♭ m	sustained for the rest of the development

Opening motive restated
167 –170

M.:	146	150	155	158	159-60	161	162	165
ASPcs:	F♯ ↗		E♭ ↗	F♯ ↗		E♭	G♭ sustained	
System:	"0"		3 b s	"0"		3 b s	6 b s	
PCA:								[Db as pc 10 is kept active within the harmony]
Harmony:		fm / ii	cm		C9 → fm		G♭ / b II/ii	fm / ii

Retransition

M.:	175 – 179	181	183	191	195	196	197
Active System Pcs:	(B♭ b /C♮)			(A♮/G♭)			A♮ ↗
System:	(6 b s holds through ----------)						3 b s
PCA:				[D♮ (11) – not yet structural]		(**D♭**, pc 10 regained)	
Harmony:	g♭ m (initiates a second 5ths cycle)	d♭ m	a♭ m	e♭ m		F9 →	b♭ m

RECAPITULATION

M.:	200	201	203 – 04	206	207	210
ASPcs:	G♭ ↗		(A♮/G♭)			A♮ ↗
System:	6 b s		(6 b s holds though into the recap.)			3 b s
PCA:		**D♮ (11)**		**D♮ (11)**	**E♭ (0)**	
Harmony:	e♭ m (G♭ refuses to relinquish its place			B♭7	E♭	
	i to G♮ within tonic harmony)			V7	I (G♭ is finally displaced by G♮)	

Diagram 7.1b Schumann, Piano Quintet in E♭ op. 44, first movement, development: systems/PCA

The total absence of lyric material is unusual for a Romantically conceived development. Also, the thematic material that is present is sequentially transposed without any manipulation or variation of the melodic surface. However, what is striking, and infinitely more sophisticated, is Schumann's process of working out the seminal "issues" of the movement, hidden beneath all the mundane sequential surface material. At first, we are surprised to find that Schumann's harmonic areas in the development are *entirely in minor*; however, upon further consideration, it becomes clear that these minor-mode areas balance the predominantly major-mode areas of the exposition. Further, these minor-mode areas are not just for "color," but actually support Schumann's underlying developmental process; specifically the working-out of pitch classes G♭ and A♮ as system-shift motivators on the deepest structural level, as well as the further exploration of the harmonic potential inherent in the D♭/D♮ dyad conflict whose presence informed so much of the exposition. As stated previously, the first group of minor-mode sequential phrases begins in m. 128, twelve measures into the development. As Diagram 7.1b illustrates, the opening motive of the movement returns in this measure in the area of A♭ minor. As an aside, we should note that because the fifth cycle starts on A♭ minor, there is an automatic association with this pitch class and its dyad conflict, A♮, which continues the relationship between the two pitch classes from the exposition, but now on an even grander scale. Following this thematic restatement, the harmonies of the subsequent passage-work phrases in the piano move in fifths through E♭ minor and B♭ minor, and finally settle into F minor; F minor is considerably extended by G♭, its Neapolitan. The next cycle begins with a restatement of the movement's opening theme presented in F minor; however, F and G♭ now reverse their roles from the previous period: F functions here as G♭'s lower neighbor.

From the beginning of the development, both G♭ and its complementary system-shift motivator, A♮, play a pivotal role in directing the music into the two large-scale minor-mode fifth cycles upon which the harmonic plan of the development is based. Indeed, the entire development is controlled by continuous oscillations between 3♭ and 6♭ systems (the "0" system occurs rarely), which underlie the lower-level motions into the fifth-related minor mode areas. Diagram 7.1b depicts how G♭ is projected from a system-shift motivator to a pitch class that operates on ever deeper structural levels: eventually the entire development is conditioned by its operations. At the start of the development, G♭ is seen as a system pitch-class motivator that throws the prevailing 3♭ system into a 6♭ system (refer to Diagram 7.1b) while A♮ often thwarts it. Afterwards, G♭ becomes a harmony in itself as the Neapolitan of the F minor harmonic area. Eventually, G♭ expands to become a harmonic area in its own right (m. 175ff.), dividing the development in half by initiating a second fifths cycle that moves back toward tonic harmony. But G♭ invades the tonic itself: when E♭ does arrive as the last harmony within the fifths cycle (first in m. 191 and then, more importantly, in m. 200) the all-pervasive G♭ refuses to relinquish its disruptive status by forcing the tonic triad into its parallel minor seven measures before the recapitulation! This gesture is so powerful that the 6♭ system is not redressed to the tonic 3♭ system until four measures into the recapitulation with the arrival of an uncontested A♮.

Even though the G♭ within the development section is undoubtedly a pitch class of some considerable control, it does not play a part in the continuing unfolding of the PCA. Rather, we now turn to another important dyad conflict, centering on a chromatically inflected D♭ (obviously associated with G♭) and its diatonic neighbor, D♮. The importance of the D♭ can be traced to the very first measure of the opening of the movement, where D♭ is first introduced as a minor seventh above the root of the root, suggesting a functional duality of the E♭ major triad both as a tonic and as a foreground dominant of A♭. The leaning of the development in a subdominant direction is prepared by this opening gesture. The importance of D♭ also lies in the fact that it and D♮ form pcs 10 and 11 of the PCA, which now seeks conclusion to the octave over the course of the development. At the start of the second ending, where the development proper begins, B♭ as pc 7 is reiterated (see Diagram 7.1b for a complete depiction of the development's PCA rise). During the A♭ minor period, C♭ is introduced as pc 8, which is then displaced by C♮, pc 9, in m. 142, where it acts as a passing tone with B♭ minor harmony. The D♭ as pc 10 now enters the picture in the next measure and remains an active PCA pitch class, not being displaced by D♮ until six measures before the recapitulation.

Schumann finds any number of ways of sustaining the D♭ as pc 10 over the course of the development; in fact, one could say that this pitch class is subjected to an intensive development process that is often generated by, and concurrent with, G♭ as a system-shift motivator. For instance, after pc 10 of the PCA is reached in m. 143, D♭ is immediately absorbed into an extended C dominant ninth chord (m. 146) where D♭ appears as the minor ninth. During the subsequent prolongation of F minor, D♭ operates within both the C9 chord and the prolonging G♭ chord, which here acts as the Neapolitan of F minor. The G♭ soon becomes the focus of the next harmonic area, where D♭ now operates as its fifth degree. (The D♭ will again appear as fifth degree at the start of the next fifths cycle generated from G♭ minor in m. 175.) In m. 167 the opening theme of the movement is restated in F minor, with D♭ absorbed into diminished harmony before it emerges as a cadential dominant leading into G♭ minor. Within the fifths cycle itself, D♭ becomes the root of D♭ minor, the next fifth of the sequence after G♭ minor. Only once within the development is D♭ temporarily displaced by D♮. As mentioned previously, the last fifth of the second cycle is E♭ minor, and, naturally enough, the extended dominant, B♭9 – each minor-mode harmonic area is prepared by its dominant ninth – carries within it a D♮ (mm. 187–8). However, D♮ cannot yet be considered structurally significant within the rising PCA since D♮ has not yet become the leading tone of the major tonic. Also, D♭ returns in m. 196 as part of B♭ minor harmony and the last fifth in the sequence. Thus, at least on the level of the PCA, one could think of D♮ as momentarily functioning as a dissonant upper neighbor of D♭. In preparation for D♮ assuming its eventual position as pc 11, and therefore as leading tone to the tonic, Schumann enharmonically respells the D♭ as a lower neighbor, C♯ (mm. 201–2 and 206), stressing the importance of the D♮ in the final measures of the retransition. In summary, at the point of recapitulation in m. 207, the tonic E♭ major is regained, and both D♮ and G♮ finally displace D♭ and G♭, the working-out of these dyads having been a virtual preoccupation of the entire development section.

As so often happens in Romantic sonata-form movements, Schumann's recapitulation is a literal one; that is, all the thematic material of the exposition returns in the same order with little or no change except for the necessary harmonic adjustments needed to transpose all the material into tonic harmony. The recapitulation, then, becomes merely a repetition of past events rather than a rethinking or re-examination of them, a procedure more characteristic of Classical recapitulations. Perhaps the return of the tonic, and its concomitant resolution of pitch-class and system issues, at the beginning of the recapitulation, was too overwhelming, the downbeat too strong, to justify further development within the body of the recapitulation. Even Schumann's counterstatement and G♭ area remain intact, just as they were in the exposition; only the very end of the bridge is redirected toward the transposed second harmonic area in the tonic. As a result of all this literalness, there is not much chance to revive and resolve dyad conflicts and pitch-class issues: one is left with the feeling that all significant compositional issues have already been addressed at the point of recapitulation, leaving nothing to be accomplished afterwards. Such is rarely the case with the music of Johannes Brahms, our next composer.

III. Johannes Brahms: The Sextets, op. 18 in B♭ and op. 36 in G

Johannes Brahms (1833–1897) was lucky enough to appear on the scene after Schubert, Mendelssohn, and Schumann had written all of their major works. He was thus well positioned to learn from these composers, both from their successes and from their mistakes. In addition, Brahms had a thirst for knowledge of music of the past, had an extensive library of original manuscripts, including many by Haydn, and, perhaps most importantly, had an absolute mania for counterpoint, a love for which he may very well have gained from his friendship with Robert Schumann. Brahms's fascination with counterpoint goes a long way in explaining the emphasis on the linear in his music, which is often at the expense of tonal clarity. The nature of his counterpoint also had much to do with Brahms's treatment of chromaticism, along with a unique approach to large-scale harmonic relationships that explored every aspect of the subdominant side of the cycle of fifths. Counterpoint was, for Brahms, a liberating compositional tool, not just a discipline to be learned for its own sake, divorced from current compositional trends. His application of contrapuntal techniques to extend the harmonic possibilities inherent within the tonal spectrum had already been anticipated in the works of Beethoven, a composer Brahms at first feared and then greatly admired.

Brahms excelled in chamber music perhaps more successfully than any of this contemporaries, and his music in this genre exhibits all of his innovative contrapuntal techniques, as well as his reliance upon the composers most meaningful to him from the distant, and not so distant, past. Within this spectacular repertory, Brahms's two sextets for strings offer excellent examples for discussion, not only with regard to our theory, but also for the ways in which these two works successfully build upon and expand the compositional possibilities inherent in sonata form, compositional processes introduced to him through his study of the works of Beethoven, Schubert, and Schumann.

A. String Sextet in B♭ op. 18 (1860), First Movement

We first look at Brahms's earlier B♭ sextet as an example of the composer dealing with the music of his immediate past, most notably the works of Schubert. After completing his Piano Trio in B major op. 8 in 1854, Brahms failed to complete a single chamber work for six years. The String Sextet op. 18, completed in the summer of 1860, became the first of a number of substantial works in this genre to show Brahms's first mastery of the form,[3] which also included the G major String Sextet op. 36, discussed below.

Similar to Brahms's other chamber music works during this period, the thematic material of the B♭ sextet is expansive and lyrical, with an opening statement whose phrase groupings are fashioned along the lines of Schubert's opening gambits. Schubert's initial statements often consisted of a series of well-defined phrases that mirrored the ternary form found in many of his own songs; namely, *a b a¹* (appropriately called "song form"), in which the middle *b* section, coming after an opening phrase establishing tonic harmony, was modulatory and unstable and which therefore necessitated a motion back to the tonic in the form of a counterstatement (*a¹*). This led into a formal bridge passage. A variant of this type, and the one Brahms uses in the B♭ sextet, extends the number of phrases to four, with a division in the middle that yields a closed binary (*a a¹ b c*) structure. In this type, the *b* phrase is harmonically unstable, with the *c* phrase acting as a closing period which ends on the tonic, overlapping with the start of the bridge. As it turns out, this type of tonally closed melodic design was more characteristic of Italian opera arias by Rossini (Rossini's so-called "thematic block": *a a¹*) and later fully realized by Vincenzo Bellini, who extended Rossini's "thematic block" with additional *b* and *c* phrases (Verdi also followed Bellini's thematic design in his early and middle-period operas).[4]

Without a doubt, opera was one of the most important influences on Romantic composition, in all its forms. Even Brahms, the champion of absolute musical forms, fell under the spell of opera (he is known, for instance, to have adored Bizet's *Carmen*); and even though he never wrote one, he certainly admired the genre. It is interesting to note that Bellini's major-mode aria melodies often contained within them a passing harmony that either turned to the Neapolitan or veered elegiacally into distant neighboring minor-mode harmony ("Casta diva" from the first act of Bellini's *Norma* of 1831 is a fine example). Such expressive melodic digressions were quite often heard as climactic areas within the individual phrase, and that is exactly how Brahms treats the distant harmonic inflection that informs the opening phrase of his sextet (Example 7.3a). Brahms's lyrical nine-measure melody (which, incidentally, is similar in contour to that of Beethoven's C major String Quintet op. 29, discussed in Chapter 6), reaches an expressive high point at the end of the first "a" phrase on a G♭ triad (beat 3 of m. 7) that acts as a ♭VI within the progression.

---

3   James Webster, "Schubert and Brahms's First Maturity I & II," *19th Century Music*, 2/1 (1978): 18–35; 3/1 (1979): 52–71.

4   See Scott L. Balthazar, "Rossini and the Development of the Mid-Century Lyric Form," *Journal of the American Musicological Society*, 41 (1988): 102–25; and Robert Moreen, "Integration of Text Forms and Musical Forms in Verdi's Early Operas," Ph.D. dissertation, Princeton University, 1975.

Example 7.3a   Brahms, String Sextet in B♭ op. 18, first movement (mm. 1–9)

In view of the totally diatonic nature of the opening *a* phrase up to the point where G♭ is introduced, the interpolation of ♭VI is heard as something of an event, which, as it turns out, is soon manifested within the complex development of system relationships that governs the course of the movement. Specifically, the G♭ triad introduces D♭, the missing pitch of the 2♭ tonic system (Figure 7.2 illustrates the movement's extended tonic matrix); both of these pitch classes also form important dyad conflicts with their immediate half-step neighbors, G♮ and D♮. In addition, D♭, the missing pitch (or system-shift motivator) of the 2♭ tonic system, is later respelled as C♯; however, in a tonic 2♭ system, C♯ will move the systems clockwise to a 1♯ system, while the missing pitch spelled as D♭ will move the systems counterclockwise to a 5♭ system. Thus the enharmonic respelling of D♭ as C♯ creates a 1♯ system that governs the entire second harmonic area of the exposition.

To return to the opening *a* phrase, it concludes on dominant harmony and is then followed by a linking measure (m. 10), which extends the dominant in preparation for an exact repeat of the *a* phrase, starting again on the tonic and reiterating G♭ harmony at its close. During the statement of the two *a* phrases, D♭ conflicts with its complementary system-shift motivator, E♮, as the harmony moves in and out of G♭. However, within the subsequent *b* phrase, the D♭ now bears both harmonic and system potential by being transferred into the bass, first as part of a B♭ minor sixth chord (m. 21), and then as the root of its own triad (m. 25). As a result of D♭'s prominence, the *c* phrase is governed almost entirely by a 5♭ system, out of which arises the B♭ minor harmony as well as A♭, D♭, and G♭. (Diagram 7.2a shows the system shifts and PCA rises that occur within the exposition.) By the end of the *b* phrase, the G♭ triad has turned into an augmented sixth as part of a cadential motion that overlaps with phrase *c*. As part of the G♭ augmented sixth chord, the E♮ which occurs on the last eighth note of m. 30 has the additional function of returning the system to a 2♭ system, which is sustained into the subsequent bridge period.

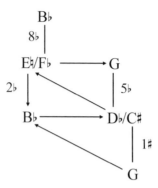

Figure 7.2   Brahms, String Sextet in B♭ op. 18, first movement, extended tonic system matrix

The concluding *c* phrase also has the distinction of beginning the first rise of the exposition's PCA, namely with pcs 0–3, B♭, B♮, and C respectively. As Diagram 7.2a indicates, however, these pitch classes, and a few that follow, only anticipate the PCA rise, which does not formally begin until m. 48, already within the bridge. As so often happens with PCA rises, composers reiterate the opening pitch classes of the PCA several times before the line actually begins to unfold in earnest. In Classical sonata-form movements, a repeat of a particular portion of the PCA usually identifies that segment (most often a chromatic trichord) as a potential source of development. In fact, in a Classical piece, *any* systematic repeat of pitch-class material must be understood as significant within the on-going developmental process of the movement. However, in Brahms, the thematic horizon is often so saturated with chromaticism that all twelve pitch classes of the chromaticized octave are continuously unfolded, and frequently within single periods. Under these circumstances, it is often difficult to determine the significance of individual dyad conflicts and PCA segments, especially when the texture exhibits simultaneous levels of chromatic unfolding. Therefore, both primary and secondary arrays are contrapuntally related to each other. Especially in his early and middle-period works one gets the sense that Brahms's manipulation of specific chromatic issues never extends beyond the surface level; that is, specific chromatic relationships are rarely projected into deeper structural levels. Therefore, when pcs 0–3 are unfolded several times in succession, the B♭–B♮–C trichord does not participate in the developmental process. This is also why G♭ and D♭ are not developed in the same rigorous manner as they are in Haydn's String Quartet op. 20 no. 5. This situation changes dramatically as Brahms matures as a composer, and becomes better able to control Classical developmental procedures, both motivic and harmonic, in the manner of Haydn and, especially, of Beethoven. For example, Brahms's last three symphonies work out seminal chromatic issues on a grand scale where all events are related to a single background chromatic issue.

Main dyad conflicts: G♭/G♮ and D♭/D♮

1st Harmonic Area

	(a)				(a)			(b)			
Measure:	1	7	8	10 –	11	17	18	20	21	25	30
Active System Pcs:		Db↗	E♮↗(E♮/Db)			Db↗	E♮↗(E♮/Db)		Db↗		E♮↗
System:	2♭s	5♭s	2♭s holds through			5♭s	2♭s holds through —		5♭s		2♭s
PCA:	**B♭ (0)**										Aug. 6
Harmony:	B♭	G♭			B♭		07	V	i	b♭m – A – D♭ – G♭ – G♭	
	I	♭VI (implies b♭m)		V→	I						

(c – closing phrase over dominant harmony)

											Bridge
M.:	31	32	33	37	38	39	40	43	47	48	
ASPcs:			(C♯/Bb)		(C♯/Bb)			Db↗		Db↗	
System:	2♭s remains------								5♭s		
PCA:	**[B♭ (0)**	**B♮ (1)**		**C (2)] [B♭ (0) – B♮ (1) –**	**C (2) – C♯ – D –**			**E♭]**		**B♭ (0)**	
Harmony:	F pedal			F				B♭	fm		
	V6/4 –	07 –	V 5/3					I	v		

Intermediate Harmonic Area

	49	50	51	55	59	60	61
M.:	49	50	51	55	59	60	61
ASPcs:		E♮↗					C♯↗
System:		2♭s					1♯
PCA:	**B♮ (1) – C (2)**			**B♭ (0) – B♮ (1) – C (2)**			**C♯ (3) [D (4)]**
	F6/4			C7 implies F major	F6/4		AM (unprepared)
Harmony:	F		cm				III♯/V
	V			V7/V			

Diagram 7.2a   Brahms, String Sextet in B♭ op. 18, first movement, exposition: systems/PCA

Partial Counterstatement   extended into   ——→   **Closing: Part I**

M.:	66	67	68	69	79	80	81	82	83	84	85
ASPcs:		Bb↘		C#↗ Bb↘		C#↗ Bb↘					
System:		2bs		1# 2bs		1#			2bs sustained		
PCA:	D (4)	C7	[D♯ (5)]	E♮ (6)]				E♭ (5)		E♮ (6)	F (7)
Harmony:	dm	C7	F	A6/4	gm6	cm	AM	F7 → Bb		C	F
	vi/V	V7/V	V				III♯/V			IV	V6/4 –7/5/3 V

V

Counterstatement   **Transition**

M.:	90	91	92	94	99	100	101	103
ASPcs:								C#↗
System:								1#
PCA:	[Bb (0)]	B♮ (1)	C (2)]		Bb (0)	B♮ (1)	C (2)	C♯ (3) – D (4) [pcs 5 & 6 missing]
Harmony:	(2bs)			F				B♮ pedal
				V				07 sustained to closing II

Closing: Part II

M.:	107	109	112	119	120	121
ASPcs:					C#↗	Bb↘
System:					1#	2bs remains to the end of the expo.
PCA:	F (7)		[Bb (0)]	Bb (0)	B♮ (1) - C (2) - C♯ (3) - D (4)	[D♯ (5)]
Harmony:	C pedal throughout (lengthy crescendo)				pcs 1-3 are played as a simultaneity	
	F6/4 – C7/5/3					
	V6/4 V7/V					

           Transition back to repeat

M.:	126	127	130	131	137 – 139	140	
PCA:	——| E♭ (5)	E♮ (6) ——	E♮ (6)	F (7)	F (7)		:
Harmony:			C7	F 6/4	F5/3	F7	
			V7/V	V6/4	V5/3	V7	

Diagram 7.2a   Brahms, String Sextet in B♭ op. 18, first movement, exposition: systems/PCA continued

However, in Brahms's B♭ sextet, once the basic issue of the G♭ triad is raised, G♭, as a sonority, plays little part in the larger progress of the movement, its role being confined to more immediate cadential arrivals, where it is turned into an augmented sixth prolonging tonic harmony. Nonetheless, G♭ does play an important role in generating its fifth, D♭, the missing pitch of the tonic system and therefore a significant system pitch-class motivator. As was demonstrated above, Brahms does begin to develop the D♭ in the *b* phrase of his opening statement, but then temporarily leaves off any further discussion of this pitch during the more intensely chromatic closing *c* phrase and the start of the unfolding PCA. Interestingly, Brahms never uses the D♭ as an agent of modulation in the form of an augmented sixth, in the way Schumann composes out the G♭ in his E♭ major Piano Quintet op. 44, discussed above. Nor does the tonic's minor third degree ever participate in any large-scale unfolding of the minor tonic triad, as it does in Schubert's C major String Quintet. In all likelihood, Brahms was deliberately trying to avoid seeming to be overly influenced by his immediate predecessors.

The chromatic unfolding in phrase *c* brings up certain important matters. Diagram 7.2a depicts only those pitch classes associated with the PCA. In fact, Brahms not only unfolds pcs 0–3 but also follows this with pcs 4 and 5; all these pitches are found in the second cello part. Incidentally, what is not shown in the diagram is the simultaneous unfolding of an almost complete secondary chromatic array in the upper voices, missing out only pc 10.) But while pcs 0–5, whether they occur in the bass or in the upper parts, may anticipate the structural rise of the PCA, none of them can as yet be considered structural (that is why they are indicated in brackets in the diagram); in other words, they do not support any large-scale harmonic motion toward the primary and secondary harmonic goals of the exposition: all the music contained within the opening statement is still heard within tonic harmony. Since the function of the bridge, whether or not initiated by a counterstatement, is to modulate to the second or intermediate harmonic area, the chromatic pitch classes of the PCA are now be said to be "activated;" that is, they gain structural significance through their support of motion toward the next large-scale harmonic area.

In the B♭ sextet, the bridge (mm. 43ff.) begins on tonic harmony (see Example 7.3b), reiterating pc 0, B♭. In mm 48–9, the first cello restates B♭ and immediately ascends to B♮ (pc 1) and C (pc 2). Even though the viola part simultaneously presents D♭ (pc 3), which causes a temporary system shift to a 5♭ system in the process, and D♮ (pc 4), the viola's pitch classes are not considered within the formal PCA since they are not a continuation of the series which becomes activated with pc 0 at the start of the bridge, and which then connects to the first cello's ascending line in mm. 48–9. The viola part's D♭ serves another purpose entirely: the resulting 5♭ system conditions motion toward F minor harmony and simultaneously sets up the subsequent series of system shifts leading into the 1♯ system that controls the upcoming A major intermediate harmonic area. At the same time, pcs 3 and 4 in the viola further articulate the dyad conflict between D♭ and D♮, while D♮ also prepares the return to the 2♭ system in m. 50. Diagram 7.2a details all the system shifts in the exposition.

Example 7.3b   Brahms, String Sextet in B♭ op. 18, first movement, bridge to intermediate harmonic area (mm. 43–69)

As so often occurs in sophisticated sonata-form movements, several operations take place concurrently, and on different structural levels. It is often expedient to discuss these various operations together so that the reader may understand how the various levels of chromatic unfolding interact. For example, consider the nature of the A major intermediate harmonic area in terms of simultaneous chromatic operations (refer to Example 7.3b as well as Diagram 7.2a). Within the bridge, pcs 0–2 form a trichord that is repeated three times, each time within a slightly different harmonic context. The first presentation of the trichord discussed above points toward F major, the major dominant, by emphasizing its fifth degree, C. At first, this trichord begins within the area of the minor dominant, controlled by the D♭'s shift into a 5♭ system, but by the end of the trichord's appearance (last beat of m. 49), pc 2, C, is heard within an F major 6/4 chord. The major mode is confirmed by a system shift up to a 2♭ system in m. 50, effected by the E♮ in that measure. The second iteration of this trichord comes at the tail end of a secondary chromatic rise in the second cello (mm. 55–8), answered in stretto by the first cello, also ending with the same trichord a measure later. The second cellos restatement of pcs 0–2 comes out of a progression that begins in C minor, a motion which parallels the previous F minor harmony that initiated the first statement of the trichord, but now continues into an implication of the major dominant, F, via C7, its own dominant seventh. Thus pc 0 (B♭) and pc 2 (C) are chord pitches within the V7/F (see Example 7.3b, m. 59). At the end of the first cellos PCA trichord, the V7/F seemingly resolves to an incomplete F 6/4 chord (last beat of mm. 59–60) with C (pc 2) in both cello parts. The emphasis on pc 2 as a *terminus* prepares for the first significant harmonic event of the exposition, the arrival of an intermediate harmonic area.

Brahms's treatment of A major as an incomplete harmonic area parallels Schubert's treatment of E♭ in the first movement of the latter's C major String Quintet as an intermediate harmonic area that turns out to be a contrapuntal extension of tonic harmony. Specifically, Schubert's C major tonic progressed to a lyric episode in E♭ that was never defined by a dominant progression, but instead wandered almost wistfully back into C major at the conclusion of both its periods. Brahms does exactly the same, but here the A major is quite dissonant against the tonic and is not part of an arpeggiation of tonic harmony (Schubert's exposition unfolds the tonic minor over the course of its exposition). Therefore A major relates not to the tonic, B♭, but, rather, to the dominant, F, as III♯/V. Similar to Schubert in the quintet, Brahms veers the A major harmony away from itself, not back toward the tonic, as happens in the quintet, but toward F, the dominant, via a D minor triad acting as vi/V (see Example 7.3b). After a rather weak cadence on F, the phrase is repeated (as it is in the quintet), but this time it is extended, the progression refusing to resolve to the dominant until m. 85, where a much stronger cadential motion finally anchors the dominant at the start of an extensive two-part closing area.

An analysis of the intermediate harmonic area clearly reveals how the pitches of the PCA intersect with the system shifts that operate on a deeper structural level, and how both these operations control the harmonic unfolding. For example, the PCA rise that centered on the first three pitch classes during the bridge period pointed toward dominant harmony. The octave Cs in the two cello parts at the end of the period now move on to the next pitch in the series, C♯, pc 3, which remains in the bass as part of a first-inversion A major triad. The arrival of pc 3 within the PCA is always a major event, for it is the missing pitch of the tonic tritone system, and therefore invariably causes a harmonic disruption that is supported by a system shift, in this instance up to a 1♯ system. Brahms dramatizes the arrival of C♯ by keeping pc 3 in the bass, doubled at the octave. When pc 3 continues to pc 4, D♮, in m. 66, this pitch too is kept in the bass, forming a D minor harmony that throws the progression toward F major. The dominant seventh that follows raises B♭, the complementary system-shift motivator, to C♯, causing the system to descend into a

2♭ system, which supports the move into F major harmony. The 1♯ system returns in m. 69 as the music moves back into a repeat of the theme, this time starting on an A 6/4 chord. In the approach to the repeat, the D♮ climbs up two half steps, first to D♯ and then to E♮, the bass of the 6/4 harmony (m. 69).

At first glance, these two notes could be mistaken for PCA pitches, but in actuality they play no significant role in directing the music toward its ultimate goal, F major; they simply serve to articulate the repeat of the theme of the intermediate area. The actual continuation of the PCA ascent does not resume until m. 82, where the previous D♯ is enharmonically respelled as an E♭, functioning as the seventh of a V7/IV chord that is in itself part of a larger progression leading straight into the first part of the F major closing area. Because the progression to the dominant begins with subdominant harmony, and, consequently, raises B♭, the system now reverts to the 2♭ system (m. 82) in preparation for the arrival of the dominant. What makes the E♭ more significant as a PCA pitch than the earlier D♯ is that E♭ is presented close to the point of dominant arrival. As a result, when E♭ as pc 5 is displaced by the leading tone, E♮ as pc 6, two measures later, which immediately revolves to F, pc 7, as the chromatic goal of the exposition, the proximity of these pitch classes a half step apart strengthens our aural understanding of a systematic, ordered succession of continuously displaced half steps that act as a *cantus* directing the underlying harmonic progression toward its goal.

In summary, not every grouping of half steps that seems to follow the chromatic ascent of the PCA will have the function of leading the music toward a goal. That is why certain groupings may be "more structural" than others. Sometimes the choice of which chromatic group (dyads, trichords, tetrachords, etc.) is the more significant must be left up to the performer or analyst, just as it often is in other theoretical constructs that deal with complex music.

Similar to Schubert in his C major String Quintet, Brahms, in the B♭ sextet at least, also constructs his exposition as a series of large-scale, self-contained periods, each with its own distinctive thematic profile. Especially within the intermediate and closing areas, each subsection of the form borrows its melodic style from the Austrian *Ländler*, a popular folk dance in triple meter and a favorite *topos* in Brahms's instrumental music. Consequently, the two closing sections are relaxed in feeling and are relatively diatonic, especially when heard after the chromatic intensity of the opening and intermediate harmonic areas.

The progress of the PCA and the various shifts are detailed in Diagram 7.2a; however, we need to comment further on three important points. First, supporting the diatonic, almost folk-like thematic material and expression of the music from the intermediate area to the end of the exposition, the system shifts are confined to 2♭ and 1♯ systems, each system covering a wide expanse of music. One may conclude, therefore, that the more diatonic the music, the less system activity is likely to take place. Second, the first closing area, as in the repetitions of PCA pitch classes within the intermediate harmonic area, replicates the first three pitches of the PCA (see Diagram 7.2a), the second repetition of which is more structurally significant since pcs 3 (C♯) and 4 (D) follow almost immediately within the short transition to the second closing period. But here, too, note that pcs 5 and 6 are missing. We can explain the missing pc 5 as a pitch that is often skipped at this juncture since it is a diatonic pitch and is displaced by the leading tone within the dominant area. But how do we explain the missing E♮, pc 6? As it happens, the second closing area starts inconclusively on 6/4 harmony and more or less stays there, with C in the bass, oscillating between F 6/4 and C7 chords until the very end of the exposition. Melodically, the E♮ does resolve to F *after* the second closing area has started (mm. 110–11, in the second violin part). Therefore, one may conclude that the PCA rise continues through the start of the second closing period because of the unstable nature of the harmonic progression.

The third point involves the final PCA ascent contained within the second closing period. Here, the PCA is complete, reiterating pcs 07; however, at one point Brahms sounds three pitch classes of the series simultaneously. Oddly enough, Haydn often does this, but Mozart and Beethoven rarely, if ever, present PCA pitch classes in this manner. The simultaneity within the PCA rise occurs in m. 120, where pcs 1 (B♮), 2 (C♮), and 3 (C♯) are sounded on the downbeat as a non-chordal dissonant *Klang* in which both C♮ (held as a pedal throughout the closing period) and C♯ are dissonant against B♮, which forms the root of a diminished seventh chord. The C♯ not only is pc 3 of the PCA, but also effects a system shift to a 1♯ system. Within the measure, C♯ continues up to D as pc 4, which is then displaced by D♯, pc 5, in the next measure, where B♭ reverts the system to a 2♭ system. Similar to what occurred in the intermediate harmonic area, D♯ is enharmonically respelled as E♭ in m. 126 (first viola) before rising to E♮, pc 6, in the next measure. Pc 6 is sustained until it resolves to F, pc 7, in measure 131, which completes the exposition's PCA segment.

What makes the development section of this sextet remarkable is the ordered intensity of its systems from a 1♯ system at its commencement to an extreme 8♭ system at its climax (see Diagram 7.2b). This is partly due to an innovative stylistic trait of Brahms that governs the background harmonic plan of many of his developments: that is, approaching the recapitulation through a subdominant cycle rather than through the more traditional dominant. In these cases, Brahms starts the development by moving along the dominant side of the key and then, approximately halfway through the development, switches course to flat-side harmonic areas. A consequence of this procedure is that the arrival at the recapitulation is contrapuntally conceived rather than harmonic, and this weakens the tonic arrival, there being no authentic cadence to prepare for its return. Quite often, with a contrapuntal progression leading up to the tonic, the tonic itself is presented in 6/4 position, as it is here (the first movement of Brahms's op. 34 Piano Quintet also recapitulates the tonic in 6/4 position). Brahms was most probably influenced by Beethoven in this regard (cf. the first movement of the String Quartet op. 59 no. 1), for it was Beethoven who popularized the idea of pushing the tonic resolution further and further into the recapitulation itself. Of course, there are any number of examples by Haydn and Mozart that do something similar, but nineteenth-century Romantic composers were more likely to look to Beethoven for models of compositional design and harmonic innovation.

The first half of the Development follows a dominant cycle of minor-mode harmonic areas

Motivic references to the opening theme

Measure:	141	142	146 – 147	153	158	159	165 – 167	173	177
Active System Pcs:	C#↗		Bb↘				C#↗	Bb↘	
System:	1#		2bs sustained				1#	2bs	
PCA:	F#(8)	G(9)		[G#(10)]	[G#(10 —	A(11)]			G(9)
Harmony:	D6		D7 → gm			am	A6/5 →dm	gm	G7/cm

Climax

M.:	178	182	183	184	185	186	187
ASPcs:	C#↗	Bb↘ ------	Db↘ (Eh/Db)	(Eh/Db)	(Eh/Db)	(Eh/Db)	Eh↗
System:	1#	2bs	5bs holds through ------				2bs
PCA:			Ab (10) sustained but embellished by Ah				
Harmony:	G pedal	Eh o7 →	fm				C
	Relates to cm						V/fm

Second half of the Development follows a subdominant cycle

Intermediate area theme

M.:	192	193	203	204	205	207	209	210	211	212	213
ASPcs:			C#↗	Bb↘		C#↗	Bb↘	Db↘			Eh↗ C#↗
System:			1#		2bs	1#	2bs	5bs			2bs 1#
PCA:	[Ah (11)]							Ab (10) regained		[Ah (11)]	
Harmony:	em prolonged	A7 →	dm prolonged				Eb7 →Ab			Dm 6/4	A7
	(5-6 exchange with C)										

Diagram 7.2b   Brahms, String Sextet in Bb op. 18, first movement, development: systems/PCA

Retransition

M.:	214	218	220	222	223	226	230	231-32	233
ASPcs:	B♭ ↗				D♭ ↗ F♭ ↗				
System:	2 b s				5 b s 8 b s sustained				
PCA:					A♭ (10) regained ————————		A ♮ (11) finally displaces A ♭		
Harmony:	B♭ → E♭ IV	A ♮ 07 →		B♭	G♭7 V7/C♭ (G♭ pedal)	C♭ 6/4		G♭7 →	G♭ aug. 6

V/IV appears under 214.

RECAPITULATION
1ˢᵗ Harmonic Area

M.:	234	235
ASPcs:		G ♮ ↗ E ♮ ↗
System:		5 b s 2 b s
PCA:	B♭ (0)	
Harmony:	I 6/4	

Beethoven may have been innovative in his approach to the sonata recapitulation (see Chapter 6), but Brahms's solution of dividing the development in two, each half moving along a different projectory of the cycle of fifths, is quite definitely his own creation. In the case of the B♭ sextet, the harmonic areas in the first half of the development move up in fifths, mostly in minor mode. The background progression moves from D major to G minor, to C minor, and finally to F minor, with the whole section ending on C, the dominant of that area (see Diagram 7.2b). A change in thematic design, as well as a change in harmony, clearly sets the second half of the development apart from the first, the whole second half being based on a motivic exploration of the theme associated with the intermediate area. Harmonically, the second half begins on E minor harmony (Diagram 7.2b) and proceeds from there into ever more flat-side harmonic areas, from E♭ to A♭, climaxing on C♭, but ends on G♭, the dominant of the area, thus forming a parallel with the previous C major dominant that ended the dominant cycle. As it happens, the G♭7 turns into an augmented sixth, which then resolves to an unstable tonic B♭ chord in 6/4 position at the start of the recapitulation. Thus Brahms, as did Beethoven before him, avoids the usual dominant preparation in favor of purely contrapuntal motion into the recapitulation, which now awaits a more definitive rhythmic and harmonic tonic resolution.

As to the completion of the first PCA ascent in the development (remember that there is a restatement of the entire PCA in the recapitulation), the development begins in D major harmony with F♯ in the bass as pc 8. Incidentally, here is a good example of how a knowledge of the PCA helps us understand a composer's choices: in this case, why Brahms should start the development on an inverted D major triad. Brahms's interest in maintaining a linear chromatic ascent in the bass from the end of the exposition seems to override an overtly harmonic conception, since D major serves no harmonic function with either the dominant, F, or the tonic, B♭. Our perception of a deliberately ordered chromatic ascent is further supported as the F♯ in the bass resolves up to G, pc 9, in that register as the music enters G minor harmony. As Diagram 7.2b shows, despite a move up to pcs 10 and 11 (G♯ and A respectively), first in the upper voices and then replicated in the bass (mm. 158–9), the actual progress of the PCA ascent does not end here (A as the root of A minor harmony cannot yet act as a leading tone to the tonic, B♭); rather, the line more convincingly continues in m. 177, where G, pc 9, is regained in the bass, as the root of a C9 chord, which leads into the climax of the development's first half in F minor harmony. As such, G is displaced not by G♯, as it was previously, albeit temporarily, but by A♭ as pc 10, which conclusively resolves to A♮, pc 11, in mm. 211–12, right before the retransition in m. 214. (Incidentally, all these pitch classes, including those that follow in the development, remain in the same bass register.) At this point, the A♮ temporarily resolves to B♭ and the tonic then immediately turns into a V/IV, the whole harmonic direction of the retransition plunging ever deeper into the subdominant side of the cycle of fifths and reaching its climax in C♭ harmony. During this C♭ passage, A♭ returns, but only as a dissonant lower dyadic neighbor to the A♮, and, more tellingly, only in an upper register; the A♮ finally displaces the former pitch in m. 230.

Throughout the development the PCA rise has remained consistently in the bass register. Brahms maintains this register as A♮, pc 11, resolves up to B♭, pc 0, within 6/4 harmony at the point of tonic return (mm. 233–4). Without a formal authentic cadence to prepare for the recapitulation, A♮ is treated as a dissonance against the G♭ augmented sixth harmony that displaces the normal dominant seventh at this point. In the measures directly preceding the recapitulation, the B♭ tone of resolution is heard, not as tonic, but as part of that same augmented sixth chord, finally revealing itself as tonic at the point of recapitulation, as the G♭ resolves down to F, which remains as pedal for several measures into the recapitulation.

The instability of the tonic in 6/4 position is also mirrored by intense system activity. The recapitulation itself carries over the 8♭ system from the previous C♭ area. Almost immediately, within the second measure of the recapitulation (m. 235), both G♮ and E♮ raise the system back up, first to a 5♭ system and then to a 2♭ one. However, in recapitulating the opening theme, the same plunge into the 5♭ system that was caused by introducing D♭ within G♭ harmony at the end of the first phrase of the melody now recurs in m. 240. The return of both D♭ and G♭ at this point is made all the more effective by coming from a retransition that featured both D♭ as a 5♭ system-shift motivator and G♭ as a harmony operating within an 8♭ system, which culminated in the G♭ as an augmented sixth chord. In this way, Brahms is actually developing the potential of both these pitch classes to control further the harmonic progress of the movement at this juncture within the form.

Following the recapitulation of the *a* phrase, Brahms tightens the phrase rhythm by omitting the second phrase of the melody (*a¹*) and, instead, builds up dominant seventh harmony, which refuses to resolve until an authentic cadence to the tonic is finally achieved at the start of the bridge (mm. 268–9), resolving the previous unstable 6/4 harmony in the process. The conclusion of the bridge is notable for the rapid unfolding of the recapitulation's first PCA rise, whose goal, this time, is pc 8, F♯, as part of D major harmony, the transposition down a fifth of the A major harmony of the intermediate area in the exposition. Brahms again begins the PCA with its opening trichord, pcs 0–2, before repeating the entire series, pcs 0–8, in an upward thrust (notably in the bass register) in mm. 282–7. The arrival to D major is not any more established than A major was in the same spot in the exposition. In this case, no harmonic progression supports D major as an area; rather, the opening phrase of the melody falls to the tonic, B♭, just as A major previously fell to F, the dominant. Incidentally, both areas, the A major and its transposition to D major, are initially governed by a 1♯ system occasioned in each case by C♯. Of course, B♭ as tonic impedes the progress of D major to sustain itself as a harmonic area, and a conflict now ensues between the 1♭ system and its complement, the 2♭ system, the later one "winning out" over the persistent C♯s. Following this, and in a manner similar to its presentation in the exposition, the first closing area is completely diatonic and remains entirely within the 2♭ system until the end of m. 328, where D♭ re-enters the picture.

As a matter of fact, D♭ returns with a vengeance, once and for all displacing its enharmonic equivalent, C♯, which has been maintained as an active system-shift motivator throughout the recapitulation's transposed intermediate harmonic area. As though to signify its importance as a governing pitch class over the course of the movement, D♭ now plays a substantial role in bringing the movement to its conclusion, which also includes the resolution of the D♭ back to its chromatic neighbor, D♮, conclusively resolving one of the movement's two major dyad conflicts. The other is G♭/G♮ and is the last conflict to be resolved. First, D♭, when it is reintroduced in m. 328, causes a major system shift down to a 5♭ system, which, despite the attempts of E♮ to redress the system to two sharps, is sustained over a considerable stretch of music. Only with the onset of the coda in m. 363 does E♮ effect a shift back up to the 2♭ system, in m. 364. From there, the 2♭ system remains in force to the end of the movement, the D♭ returning only twice more and each time pitted against E♮, which prevents any system change back to the 5♭ system. Significantly, the last time D♭ is heard in the first movement (m. 382), not only is it sounded against the E♮, but the two pitches are also linearized in the first cello part as an augmented second, D♭ on the first beat of the measure *followed by* E♮ on the second. By having the E♮ follow the D♭ as a melodic event, thereby negating the ability of D♭ to force a system change in its favor, Brahms dramatizes the end of D♭'s modulatory role in the movement. From that moment on, no further D♭s (or C♯s for that matter) disturb the prevailing 2♭ system. As a final gesture, Brahms now reiterates an almost complete PCA rise, now transferred into the soprano register. With F again serving as a pedal, the first violin part climbs up the chromatic scale from pc 4 to pc 0 (mm. 391–95), spelling pc 8 as F♯, which represents the final resolution of the G♭ into its enharmonic equivalent, no doubt in order to make the chromatic ascent all the more effective.

B. Sextet in B♭: Further Analytical Observations

As in all tonal pieces, no matter how dense the chromaticism, the system operations observed in Brahms's B♭ sextet illustrate another characteristic of system analysis that needs to be clarified at this point, namely, the relationship of harmonic area to system. It is worth repeating that any given system that is in control at any point within the composition *lies at a deeper structural level than the harmonic area being expressed.* We should remember that tritone systems are eleven-note pitch-field gamuts that can be formed into any number of harmonic areas, small or large, including passing and/or prolonging motions (such as one finds within fifths cycles), so long as the missing pitch of the system is not activated. Furthermore, a system that "controls" a harmonic area is defined as one that determines the extent to which that area is sharp- or flat-side oriented. There are cases, however, where a sharp-side harmonic area is short enough that it will not disrupt a flat-side system, simply because the harmonic area does not contain enough pitch material to effect a modulation out of the prevailing system. But in most instances, there seems to be a coincidence between a given system and the harmonic area generated from it. As an illustration, the following chart summarizes the harmonic areas and their underlying systems as they occur in the Brahms sextet:

2♭	1♯	5♭	8♭
e	e	A♭	(B♭)
C	D	f	C♭
a	A	D♭ (only as V/G♭)	
F		G♭	
(b)		b♭	
g			
E♭			
c			

Under each system in the above list, the harmonic areas are arranged in ascending order of sharps and flats, no matter how short or undefined. It is no surprise that the tonic 2♭ system should control the greatest number of harmonic areas and, considering the importance of D♭ as a source of development in this work, it is also not a surprise that its 5♭ system should have the second largest number. As was mentioned previously, a particular harmonic area may be found in more than one system, depending on the extent of its pitch material: an area may contain only a few harmonies, sometimes no more than tonic and dominant, allowing it to be present in systems of more or fewer sharps or flats. Invariably, these areas are of short duration and either quickly revert to a system that more appropriately matches their implied key signatures, or act as brief passing harmonies in more relevant areas within the governing system. For instance, B♭ as a harmonic area (put into parentheses in the above list) is an area, in fact the only one, that appears in more than one system. Its existence within the 2♭ system needs no comment, and we have already discussed its dramatic appearance within the 8♭ system that overlaps the start of the recapitulation. The latter is an instance where the correcting pitch, or pitches in this case, does not arrive to correct, and therefore to coordinate, the system with its harmonic area until one measure after the tonic has been regained.

Another theoretical point, and one that has far-reaching consequences for the future development of the tonal system, concerns Brahms's method of juxtaposing, by means of half-step motion, two or more seemingly distant harmonies or harmonic areas that branch out from the tonic and its fifth. These distant areas represent motions to either the extreme flat side or the extreme sharp side of the tonic and are arrived at either by moving the tonic pitch down a half step or by moving the dominant fifth up a half step, thereby creating a new set of fifths that can then continue to unfold in the same direction either up or down the fifths cycle. Using the B♭ sextet as an example, we notice two such prominent juxtapositions: G♭ major emanating from a half-step motion up from F, the fifth degree from the tonic, and A major emanating down a half step from B♭, the tonic root. The whole operation may be illustrated as follows:

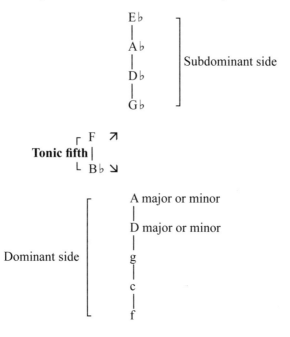

By branching out in this manner, Brahms can cut across the cycle of fifths as an alternative to enharmonic respelling (meaning that Brahms does not have to change the spelling of a particular pitch class to move instantly to harmonic areas that lie on the opposite side of the cycle of fifths), contrapuntally generating unusual harmonic relationships that are not limited solely to the more traditional Neapolitans. These distant harmonies may actually continue in a direction further away from a central point by adding more harmonic areas by an expansion of ever more fifths to explore even more distant relationships to the tonic. Most importantly, they can return along the same path just as quickly to restore tonic harmony. With this realization, we can now find a practical explanation for how Brahms arrived at his intermediate harmonic area in A as simply a half-step motion down from the tonic. The A, in turn, will generate the D below it at the same spot in the recapitulation. By continuing the fifths sequence from D, we can also see how G minor, C minor, and F minor are generated as important areas within the development. On the other side of the cycle, G♭ generated as a half-step motion up from the tonic fifth, F, at the start of the exposition, will itself generate D♭, A♭, and E♭; these areas also play important roles within the development. In fact, every area in the movement can be accounted for as an extension from either the sharp-side or the flat-side fifths cycles that branch out from the primal tonic fifth of the key.

This method of deriving keys from half-step motions emanating from the tonic fifth works hand-in-hand with the theory of systems developed in this book. These distant fifths to tonic harmony, derived from contrapuntally branching outward from the tonic fifth by a half-step motion downwards from the root of the tonic fifth or upwards a half step from its fifth degree, will inevitably cause system shifts in the process of their expansion. This is the case with G♭, whose expansion from its own fifth, D♭, creates a shift into a 5♭ system. Similarly, the A that ultimately derives from B♭'s expansion down a half step is governed by the 1♯ system created by the presence of its third degree, C♯. Therefore, an understanding of the tonic system matrix can be used as a model to demonstrate how the introduction of the missing pitch, in either of its enharmonic variants, can support an unexpected branching from a tonic fifth into distant harmonic relationships that would otherwise be cumbersome, if not difficult to comprehend.

Finally, it is possible not only to juxtapose the tonic fifth temporarily into harmonic areas that quickly revert to tonic or dominant harmony, as is the case in this work, but also to maintain the branching to a point where our understanding of the tonic itself is in jeopardy. Admittedly, Brahms's use of this device in this work is still of an experimental nature, and not that far removed from similar instances in Schubert and Schumann. However, his second sextet, in G major, brings us closer to the world of Debussy and early Schoenberg.

C. String Sextet in G op. 36 (1864), First Movement

In terms of its general design and harmonic structure, the G major sextet is similar to its earlier B♭ contemporary, composed some four years previously. However, the G major sextet is far more motivically dynamic, achieving hair-raising climaxes that the earlier work, infused with an all-pervading, dance-inspired lyricism, cannot match. Of greater importance to our present discussion are Brahms's daring advances in his use of contrapuntally related distant harmonic areas, both implied and realized, through fifths generated a half step from the tonic or dominant fifth. It is this last point with which we will start our discussion.

Example 7.4 gives the opening period up to the counterstatement of phrase *a*. Typical of Romantic opening statements that follow Schubert's model, Brahms's first harmonic period, up to the bridge, is an expansive 95 measures whose phrases divide into the rounded binary pattern of the song form *a a¹ b a* which was so favored by Schubert and his successors and which we have already seen in the earlier B♭ sextet. In general, analysts agree that the opening introductory viola figure, with its oscillating G–F♯ half step, provides the basis for all the motivic material of the movement.[5] But what we find most intriguing is the sudden jump into the neighboring E♭–B♭ fifth that takes place so early in the melody (m. 5), and which is obviously prepared by the half-step viola figure that precedes it. With this sudden shift into flat-side harmonies, Brahms also raises the basic dyad conflicts of the movement, if not the whole sextet: B♭/B♮ and E♭/E♮, the B♭ also playing into the system conflicts that govern the course of the movement.

Right from the start, Brahms opposes the tonic fifth, G–D, with a symmetrical complement that has entirely replaced the usual dominant needed to define a key! This Neapolitan to the fifth degree (melodic, not harmonic) is quite unlike the one we saw previously in the B♭ sextet, where the tonic was fully established *before* the phrase turned toward the ♭VI. Thus, in the earlier sextet, ♭VI functioned as an upper neighbor embellishment to the dominant within a well-defined tonic progression. However, in the G major sextet, at the point where the ♭VI is introduced, the meaning of the progression has yet to be determined! Without a defining dominant, Brahms posits a symmetrical relationship between a G–D fifth and an E♭–B♭ fifth in which the fifths are, at first, of equal weight. Note, also, that B♭, the minor third of the key and its system-shift motivator, arises out of E♭ and is not associated with G as its parallel tonic minor, at least not during the *a* phrase at the start of the exposition. Schubert too avoids connecting the minor third of the key to its parallel minor in the first movement of his C major String Quintet. However, unlike Brahms, who will, in fact, move into the tonic minor at various points within the movement, Schubert keeps the minor third degree from ever being associated with the parallel minor anywhere in the movement. Also, unlike Brahms, Schubert, at the start of his C major exposition, introduces the E♭ as a single pitch class within diminished harmony, and not as the root of a disjunct fifth.

With Brahms, raising a sustained 2♭ system by introducing B♭ into the pitch field supports the symmetry between the two fifths, G–D and E♭–B♭, a polarity which is decided in favor of the tonic, G, only when the E♭–B♭ fifth descends to a cadential 6/4 (m. 9). At this point, E♭ is recognized as ♭VI within the phrase. Yet, even though the tonic is eventually defined by a full progression that includes the dominant, the system remains in two flats until the counterstatement finally presents C♯ (see Diagram 7.3a).

---

5   See, for example, Margaret Notley, "The Chamber Music of Brahms," in Stephen E. Helfing (ed.), *Nineteenth-Century Chamber Music* (London, 2004), p. 253.

Example 7.4 Brahms, String Sextet in G op. 36, first movement (mm. 1–53)

1ˢᵗ Harmonic Area: Bb/B♮ and Eb/E♮ conflicts introduced

	(a)			(a¹)	(b)						
Measure:	3	5	6	17	32	33	38	41	43-44	49	50	51
Active System Pcs:		Bb↘									(C#/Bb)
System:	1#	2 b s sustained									
PCA:	[G (0)]				G (0)		G# (1)	A (2)			[Bb (3)]
Harmony:	G	Eb6/4 5/3	G	G	G	F# – B –	E –	A –	D		G 6/4 gm 6/4 D
	I	bVI ------		I	I	III#		V			cadential 6/4 V

Cycle of 4ths

Counterstatement (a)

							(a¹)			
M.:	52	53	55	59	62	63	67	69	70	71 – 74
ASPcs:	C#↗		Bb↘ C#↗					Bb↗		
System:	1#		2 b s 1#					2 b s		
PCA:	B♮ (4)]		Bb (3) B♮ (4)		C♮ (5)	C# (6) – D (7)		Eb (8)		
Harmony:	D	G	Eb6 D 6/4-5/3					Eb6 F#o7 Eb6 ---		
	V	I	bVI V pedal ------					bVI prolonged---------		

Extension of a¹

				Bridge		
M.:	75	79	84	94	95	99 - 100
ASPcs:	C#↗					(A#/G♮)
System:	1# sustained					
PCA:	D 6/4-5/3	Eb (9) [pc 10 is bypassed]	F# (11)G (0)]		PCA starts:	[G (0) G# (1) – A (2)]
Harmony:	V pedal	climactic build-up on V	G			A7→ D
		V pedal continues, incorporating	I (1ˢᵗ structural downbeat)			V prepared by V/V
		the ½-step motive transposed on V				

Diagram 7.3a   Brahms, String Sextet in G op. 36 first movement, exposition: systems/PCA

Table (measures 108–128)

M.:	108	116	119	120	122	123	124	125	126	127	128
ASPcs:	(A♯/G)						(A♯/G)	A♯↗	G♮↘		(A♯/G)
System:								4♯s	1♯ sustained ------		
PCA:	[A♯ (3) – B (4)]	G (0)		G♯ (1) ——	G♯ (1)	A (2)	A♯ (3)	B (4)	B♯ (5) C♯ (6) ——	Pc 6 sustained	
Harmony:			A · V/V	Cello I rises in ½ steps							

2nd Harmonic Area (measures 134–162)

Transition

M.:	134	135	138	151	153	155	156	158	159	162
ASPcs:					B♭↘	C♯↗	B♭↘	(C♯/B♭)		
System:					2♭s	1♯	2♭s holds through -------			
PCA:	C♯ (6)	D (7) [G (0)]	[G (0)]				G (0) – A♭ (1)	A♮ (2) – B♭ (3)	B♮ (4) – C (5)	
Harmony:	A · V/V	D · V		dm · v			Cello II unfolds a complete ascending secondary chromatic array (SCA) from A' to A (mm. 155-62)			

Closing Period (based on the "Agathe motive") (measures 160–213)

"Agathe motive"

M.:	160	162	190	191	192	212	213
ASPcs:	C♯↗						
System:	1♯ sustained until the end of the expo.					Transition	
PCA:	[C♯ (6) – D (7)]	Incomplete PCA:	G (0)	C♯ (6) D (7)	G♯ (1) – A (2)	C♯ (6)	D (7)
Harmony:	A · V/V		A7 · V7/V	D · V		D	V

1st Ending

M.:	3rd m.	5th m.	7th m.	9th m.	11th m.	13th m.
ASPcs:	(B♭/C♯)	(B♭/C♯)	(B♭/C♯)			
System:						
PCA:	[C♯ (6) – D (7)]					
Harmony:	B♭7 (acts like an aug. 6th to V →			A 6/4 · V6/4	A 7/5/3 · V 7/5/3	G · I

Symmetrical relationships that exist within the hierarchy of a given tonality, in which harmonic areas or adjacent chordal structures are of equal significance (meaning that the one does not define or support the other), become ever more prominent as the nineteenth century draws to a close. Since tonality is inherently a product of hierarchal harmonic relationships that define a given tonic, harmonic symmetry, if introduced on a large enough scale, will ultimately destroy that hierarchy and with it a sense of traditional tonal organization. Of course, Brahms never "destroys" tonality, but he does begin the process of greatly weakening the tonic with symmetrical relationships that begin to undermine the older tonal hierarchy so clearly defined by his predecessors. Perhaps Beethoven first set this in motion when he decided to explore second harmonic areas that did not arpeggiate the tonic triad, but went in other directions instead: the first movements of the Ninth Symphony, the "Archduke" Trio, and the early String Quintet in C are notable examples.

Brahms was already moving in this direction in the B♭ sextet when he unexpectedly arrived in A major as his intermediate harmonic area. At first, A major was heard as a harmony unrelated to B♭, since it had no direct voice-leading connection to the tonic. However, as soon as the A major area began, it moved into dominant harmony, revealing its function as III♯ within that area.

The G major sextet is quite a different matter since it has no intermediate area. Instead, Brahms moves into B major as a harmony symmetrically related to the tonic at the start of the *b* phrase of the opening statement (see Example 7.4). The two symmetrically related major thirds in close proximity that surround the G major tonic, the first, E♭, a major third below the tonic and the second, B♮, a major third above, are both subsumed under a 2♭ system; thus both major thirds oppose the tonic rather than define it. B major remains within the gamut of a 2♭ system because it is never defined by its own dominant triad, and thus no C♯ appears to redress the system. Note, particularly, that both E♭ and B♮ are arrived at through half-step motions branching in half steps from the tonic fifth:

B♭ | E♭] subdominant side

Tonic fifth [D ↗ G ↘

F♯ | B] dominant side

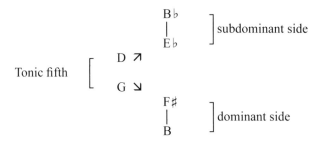

The arrival of B major harmony is a bit more complex than the previous expansion to the E♭–B♭ fifth, since B is not an immediate half-step neighbor to G. Instead, G first descends to F♯ as V/B, with the G reinterpreted as a ♭VI of B major; this reinforces the symmetrical relationship between the two harmonies. Once achieved, B major initiates a fourths cycle that eventually leads back to tonic harmony at the start of the counterstatement in m. 53. With the return of tonic harmony, the hierarchy of the tonic is re-established, and the symmetry is at last resolved into the higher structural level of the tonic key.

Throughout the rest of Brahms's career, adjacent harmonies of equal weight, neither of which are defined by their dominants, abound in his works. Among numerous examples, one may cite the symmetrical relationship of the tonic D major with C major during the opening phrase of the D major Violin Concerto op. 77, as well as that of the F major tonic of the Third Symphony with D♭, also within the opening statement. But no matter how strong the symmetrical relationships, in the end Brahms must revert to tonal hierarchy, no matter how much it is undermined, if the hegemony of the tonic is to be upheld as the ultimate consonant source of resolution.

However, on an even deeper level, the symmetrical relationships that comprise the tritone systems of the tonic matrix *exist as complements*, to the extent that a movement, or even an entire composition, may end in a complementary system to that of the tonic. In fact, the first movement of the Brahms' G major sextet ends in a 2♭ system (see the discussion below). However, the choice of complementary system is of necessity limited in tonal pieces to that of the minor third (the implication being the system of the tonic minor), since any other complementary tritone system within the tonic matrix would imply a harmony whose signature lay outside the realm of the tonic altogether; obviously, atonal works would not be bound by these restrictions. We have already seen examples of tonal pieces that end in tonic harmony, but whose systems end in their complementary minor third complements: the first movement of Vivaldi's Concerto in C for two oboes and two clarinets, and the last movements of Beethoven's Fifth Symphony and Schubert's C major String Quintet. Thus Brahms, and Schubert and Beethoven before him, open the way to the possibility of an ultimate symmetry, one that displaces the tonic hierarchy altogether.

We see the process of tonal hierarchy further challenged by the symmetries of the tritone matrix in pieces like Brahms's G major sextet, where the complementary 2♭ system that displaces the 1♯ tonic system (not unlike the opening gambit of the first movement of Beethoven's Piano Trio in D major op. 70 no. 1, discussed in the previous chapter) conditions the design of both its development and recapitulation sections (see Diagram 7.3b), the 2♭ system acting as the goal in both sections of the movement!

The Development displaces the outward expansion from the tonic G – D fifth with an expansion outward from the dominant fifth, D – A

Thematic material is based entirely on the opening theme

Measure:	217	219	238	240	241	249	253	262	275	291	292
Active System PCs:		(B♭/C♯)	B♭↘			C♯↗					A♯↗
System	1♯		2♭s			1♯					4♯s
PCA:	D (7)							D♯ (8) ————	D♯ (8)		
Harmony:	dm		B♭	F	C	A	c♯m	f♯m	B		

Branches outward harmonically from the D – A fifth

M.:	297	300	301	302	303	305	307	309	311	312	313	Climax 315	317	323
ASPcs:				G♮↗	A♯↗					(G♮/A♯)		G♮↗	B♭↘	C♯↗
System:				1♯	4♯s holds through							1♯	2♭s	1♯
PCA:	E (9)													
Harmony:	B♭ → am		em		bm	f♯m	D	am	em		bm		G9 gm	c♯°7

G – C♯ tritone arpeggiated

Retransition on the tonic minor!

M.:	327	329	330	331	339	341	Recapitulation: 1st Harmonic Area (a) 343	(a¹) 357	(b) 372	373	377
ASPcs	B♭↘(C♯/B♭):										
System:	2♭s holds through into the recapitulation ———										
PCA:	F♯ (10)				F♮ (11)		G (0)	G (0)			G♯ (1)
Harmony:	gm 6/4 i 6/4	G7 V7/iv	gm 6/4 iv		D V		G Major ——— G I I	F♯ – B III♯	E		

Diagram 7.3b Brahms, String Sextet in G op. 36, first movement, development and recapitulation: systems/PCA

Counterstatement (a)   **C.S. (a¹)**   **Bridge**

M.:	381	390	392	393	395-96	399	400	402	403	407	435
ASPcs:		(C#/Bb)	C#↗		Bb↗	C#↗					
System:			1#		2bs	1#					
PCA:	A (2)	[Bb (3)		B♮ (4)]	Bb (3)		B♮(4) C (5)	C# (6) – D (7)			
Harmony:		gm 6/4 / i 6/4	D / V	G / I	Eb6 / bVI	D 6/4 ------ 7/5/3 / V pedal ------				G / I	

Extension

M.:	409	410	411	415	418	424	434	435
ASPcs:	Bb↗	Db↗				E♮↗ C#↗		
System:	2bs	5 bs sustained---------				2bs 1# sustained --------		
PCA:	Eb (8)					E♮ (9) (F♮, pc 10 omitted) F# (11)		G (0)
Harmony:	Eb6 / bVI	Db 6/4/2 / V 6/4/2 / bII	Ab6 / bII6		D 6/4 – 7/5/3 / V pedal			G / I
bass:	G / Db	└System tritone┘						

M.:	439	440	441	442	446	448	450	451	452
ASPcs:	(A#/G)				(Bb/C#)		(Bb/C#)		(Bb/C#)
System:	1# holds through -------------								
PCA:	G (0)		G# (1) A (2)		Bb (3)	B♮ (4) – C♮ (5)		[C# (6) – D (7)]	
Harmony:					C#º7 (the next 9 mm. arpeggiate the tonic system matrix)				

M.:	454	455	456	457	458	459	460	466-67
ASPcs:	(Bb/C#)	Bb↗				C#↗	A#↗	
System:		2bs				1#	4#s	
PCA:	C# (6)	D (7) D# (8)		E (9)	[E# (10)	F# (11)]		E# (10) – F# (11)
Harmony:		Cello I rises in ½ steps -------						

2nd Harmonic Area / Transition

M.:	469 470	471	479 480	485 487 489 490
ASPcs:	G♮↘	(B♭/C♯)		B♭↘ (D♭/E♮)
System:	1♯ holds through ―――――			2♭s holds through ―――――
PCA:	G (0) G♯ (1) – A (2)	B♭ (3)	B♮ (4) C♯ (5)	C♮ (5) – D♭ (6)
Harmony:	G 6/4 / I 6/4 (D pedal)		gm gm / i i	Cello II unfolds a complete secondary array from D' To D (mm. 489-96)

Closing Period

M.:	492	493	494	522	525	540	542
ASPcs:			C♯↗ 1♯	(B♭/C♯)		(B♭/C♯)	(B♭/C♯)
System:							
PCA:	D♮ (7) – E♭ (8)		E♮ (9) – F♮ (10)	F♯ (11) – G (0)			
Harmony:					G / I		

Coda

M.:	547	553 – 54	568 571 572 573	576 579	584 587 591
ASPcs:				Bb↘ 2♭s	C♯↗ 1♯
System:					
PCA:	G (0)		G♯ (1) A (2)	B♭ (3) B♮ (4) C♮ (5) C♯ (6)	D (7)
Harmony:	G / I	B 6/4 – 5/3 / III♮ 6/4 – 5/3 / E♭ is respelled as D♯	Cello II unfolds a secondary array from E♮ to E♭	V6/5/V	V7

E♮/E♭ and B♮/B♭ conflicts resolve into tonic harmony

M.:	596 and 598	601 – 602	603	604	605
ASPcs:	Bb↘				
System:	2♭s holds through to the end; the movement ends in a 2♭ system				
PCA:	E♭ (8) no pcs 9 or 10			F♯ (11)	G (0)
Harmony:	E♭6 – G E♭6		D 6/4 – 5/3	G	
	bVI I bVI		V 6/4 – 5/3	I	

Diagram 7.3b Brahms, String Sextet in G op. 36, first movement, development and recapitulation: systems/PCA continued

By setting up the complementary system as the final goal of motion, at least in terms of its systems, and despite the fact that both recapitulation and coda regain the tonic major, Brahms has, perhaps inadvertently, set himself a compositional problem that goes one step further than the one posed by Haydn in the first movement of his Symphony no. 92 (the "Oxford"), also in G major (see Chapter 5 for a detailed discussion of this work). In Haydn's case, the exposition began "off tonic," on a dominant seventh chord, making a "normal" recapitulation quite impossible since every time the opening theme was restated it began on a dissonant dominant seventh and could therefore not be a goal of resolution. In Brahms's G major sextet, the tonic major in all three of its most significant statements – the opening of the movement, the transition into and including the start of the recapitulation, and the movement's final cadential period – is undermined by flat-side sonorities that support a 2♭ system, a non-tonic, complementary system that militates against a clear statement of the tonic major.

The exposition of the movement has already been discussed in this regard; the working-out of the 2♭ system, and its eventual consequences in motivating the harmonic structure of the development section, are equally, if not more, interesting (see Diagram 7.3b). Unexpectedly, the development begins in the minor dominant, eventually raising B♭ and the 2♭ system by m. 238. The B♭ itself not only shifts the system, but also forms the root of a disjunct fifth, B♭–F, a half step away from that of the dominant, D–A:

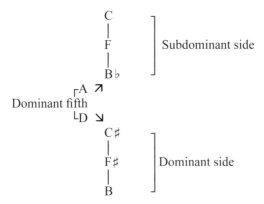

Thus, the development continues the process of outward expansion from a central fifth already exploited in the exposition, but now transposed to the dominant, here displacing the tonic. (The quality of the dominant is of no consequence here, but the root and fifth degree are.) From m. 238 onwards, B♭ initiates a fifths cycle from its lower neighbor A which progresses to F and then to C. It is important to note that B♭ serves a dual function as it simultaneously shifts the system to two sharps and, as a root, begins the expansion outward from the D–A fifth. The other side of the fifths equation soon follows when C♯ enters the pitch field in m. 249, continuing the fifths expansion from D a half step down to C♯ minor, to F♯ minor, and finally to B.

However, our main concern is with how the B♭ as a system-shift motivator controls the harmonic progression of the retransition beginning in m. 327, or rather, what happens a few measures before this point. Before the B♭ regains its function as a system-shift motivator, the passage before its appearance, namely from m. 323 to m. 326, arpeggiates the tonic system tritone of G–C♯ in octaves, all under a 1♯ system. The B♭ that enters the pitch field in the next measure (m. 327) is made all the more effective, suddenly switching the 1♯ system down to a 2♭ system and changing the mode into the tonic minor as well. As it happens, the move into the parallel minor was prepared at the climax of the development (mm. 315ff.), where the G9 chord (under control of a 1♯ system) gave way to a G minor sonority (under a 2♭ system), only to revert to a 1♯ system at the point where the tonic tritone was arpeggiated. However, in contrast to the earlier passage which formed the climax, the switch to tonic minor at the start of the retransition remains in effect up to the point of recapitulation where the tonic is regained. However, as in the exposition, there is no C♯ to return the 2♭ system to a 1♯ system, even when the music once more veers into B major harmony (but note the G minor harmony in m. 390). Only in m. 392, a measure before the counterstatement of phrase *a*, does an uncontested C♯ return the system to the tonic 1♯ system. But even this event is short-lived since the counterstatement brings with it the same plunge into E♭ harmony and its concomitant 2♭ system.

With the restatement of the second *a¹* phrase, the recapitulation, which has been literal up until this point by maintaining the same harmonic progressions as in the exposition, now diverges from the path of the exposition, moving deeper into the flat side of the key, motivated by a system switch from a 2♭ to a 5♭ system. Comparing the passages in Diagrams 7.3a (mm. 69ff.) and 7.3b (mm. 409ff.), we note that the harmony at this point in the exposition, an E♭6 prolonged by an F♯ diminished seventh, has been reworked in the recapitulation, so the progression now veers toward A♭, the F♯ diminished seventh chord here displaced by an E♭ chord in 6/4/2 position functioning as an inverted applied dominant of ♭II with D♭ in the bass. What is of interest to us is the bass motion underlying this progression in mm. 409–10, which actually arpeggiates the G–D♭ tonic system tritone, in its flat-side inversion (C♯ spelled as D♭), as the function of the E♭ chord changes from a ♭VI/I to a V6/4/2 of ♭II. The resultant plunge into the 5♭ system caused by D♭ is sustained for no fewer than 23 measures before first E♮ and then C♯ shift the system back up to a 1♯ system in m. 424.

Arpeggiations of any one of the system tritones that form the tonic matrix, whether confined to the bass register, as the above illustrates, as a unison passage, or as a complete diminished harmony containing all the tritones of the matrix simultaneously, may be found at any point within a given movement, but they occur most often in recapitulations as a result of transpositions, and/or elaborations, of second-and closing-area material in tonic harmony. As a result, the recapitulation becomes a watershed of resolution into tonic harmony, where all important issues of the movement come together, including the matrix that lies behind the tonic key itself. The raising of the G–D♭ tritone in mm. 409–10 of the recapitulation, an event that does not occur at that point in the exposition, is just such an example of how the recapitulation can act as a summary of issues and events, way beyond the simple function it is usually accorded of restating transposed exposition thematic material. In fact, it can be argued that composers deliberately plan important events – dyad conflicts, chromatic issues of various sorts, dissonant harmonic relationships, and so on – in the expositions of their sonata-form movements that, when transposed in the recapitulation into tonic harmony, often as part of a large tonic progression, will automatically transform themselves into the fundamental issues of the movement.

For example, dramatizing the systems of the tonic matrix as a focal point within the recapitulation can be a simple matter of transposing into the tonic an analogous, even innocuous, harmony or progression that first appeared within the dominant area of the exposition. When transposed, this same harmony achieves the status of a major event. For example, at the end of the exposition bridge passage in the G major sextet, there is a moment before the chromatic crescendo that leads into the second harmonic area, which lasts for nine measures and features a G♯ diminished leading-tone chord to the V/V (mm. 114–22). When transposed into tonic harmony at the analogous point in the recapitulation (mm. 446–54), this unassuming diminished chord now becomes a C♯ diminished seventh that contains both complementary tritones of the tonic matrix, including the two system-shift motivators that previously provoked so much of the system activity, and thus the chromatic activity, over the course of most of the movement. More than that, the passage presents both B♭ and C♯ first as a simultaneity and then as motivators of separate system shifts, and, finally, respells B♭ as A♯, causing a sharp-side system shift to a 4♯ system that remains in effect until the recapitulation of the transposed second harmonic area in m. 469 (refer to Diagram 7.3b). Here, G♮ returns the system to a 1♯ system. When originally presented in the exposition, this passage contained only A♯ as an ineffectual system-shift motivator since G♮s had been pitted against it at each one of its appearances, negating its influence to change the prevailing 1♯ system. In the recapitulation, all the tritone systems of the tonic matrix are raised, in various combinations, as though to summarize their role in the developmental process of the movement.

Significantly, the B♭ that is raised in this process once more becomes an effective controlling pitch class whose presence becomes ever more prevalent as the movement draws to its close. At first, B♭ creates a shift into the 2♭ system, supporting the G minor harmony that surrounds the start of the transition leading to the closing area (mm. 485–7). (In view of the important position of B♭ as a pitch class and the source of so much of the developmental processes throughout this movement, it is not surprising that the tonic minor keeps popping up at odd places.) The transition provides another example of how a transposed section from the exposition can play into the continuing developmental process of the movement. Originally, in the exposition, this passage centers on the minor dominant. In its transposed version, the minor dominant becomes the minor tonic, again raising the important issue of B♭, both in terms of its ability to cause system shifts and in its role as a member of one of the movement's most important dyad conflicts, B♭/B♮. One can see this conflict most clearly in mm. 530–42, where the second viola oscillates between the two pitch classes, moving in and out of G major/G minor parallel harmonies at the same time; both the first viola and first cello parts are in quasi-imitation, arpeggiating the same major/minor harmonies.

Both exposition and recapitulation transition periods are chromatically intense, and the second cello part unfolds complete secondary chromatic arrays in both instances. However, in its transposition, the recapitulation transition also unfolds, in counterpoint with the second cello, eight of the PCA's pitch classes in rapid succession in the second violin part. As a general rule, recapitulation sections unfold complete PCA ascents, covering the tonic octave. In fact, there may be any number of such chromatic rises, complete and incomplete, depending on circumstances. The reason for the existence of so many possible repetitions rests on the fact that the harmonic plan of the recapitulation repeatedly goes from tonic to tonic, not just from tonic to dominant (exposition) or from dominant back to tonic (development). Thus, the restatement of the opening harmonic area at the recapitulation leads to a second harmonic area that is often transposed into the tonic as well. This goes additionally for the closing and codetta periods, each of which also composes out tonic harmony. Each time the PCA progresses from one structural area to the next, it invariably returns to the same tonic from which it began, thus encompassing a full PCA ascent each time. (The rhythmic unfolding of each pitch class of the PCA may be as quick or as slow as the composer wishes it to be.) At this point, we should add that Brahms's exposition is exceptional in that the opening period of the exposition and its counterstatements are extraordinarily spacious before the bridge period even begins. Because of its unusual length, Brahms unfolds a complete preparatory tonic PCA, which culminates at the authentic cadence that starts the bridge period (see Diagram 7.3a).

In the recapitulation, the two pitch-class system-shift motivators, B♭ and C♯, more or less have the field to themselves, the one contradicting the system tendencies of the other, that is, until the coda (mm. 547ff.). Here B♭ returns as pc 3 within the final unfolding of an almost complete PCA. The first time B♭ enters the pitch field, the 2♭ system remains in effect for eleven measures before C♯ reverts the system (m. 587). Significantly, the C♯ itself, similar to the B♭ before it, is unfolded as part of the final PCA as pc 6. Pc 7, D, enters in m. 591 as part of dominant harmony, but then the next pitch class in the series, pc 8, E♭ (introduced ten measures before the end of the movement), is the very one that initiated the chromatic expansion at the beginning of the movement. As an inverted ♭VI chord, E♭ generates B♭ as the fifth degree, once more – and for the last time! – shifting the system down to a 2♭ system. The B♭/B♮ dyad conflict is again played out as E♭ and G major triads oscillate, until the first violin swoops up the E♭ arpeggio as the other parts sustain the ♭VI6 sonority underneath. Only now do we realize the full import of that first-inversion sonority. The E♭ triad invariably was presented in first inversion whenever it made an appearance: with G in the bass and E♭ and B♭ above it, we get as close as we can to the opening two fifths, G–D juxtaposed with E♭–B♭, played as a simultaneity. It is, then, only fitting that the movement should end with this sonority as an elaborate subdominant substitute, emphatically resolving into the final V–I cadence of the movement. And if one takes the two adjacent fifths as a single sonority, the conclusion of the movement within the 2♭ system that has always shadowed the tonic is here completely justified.[6]

---

6 Brahms was quite possibly influenced by Schubert's closing passage in the last movement of the latter's C major String Quintet op. 163. There the entire quintet ends in a 3♭ system, with a strikingly similar arpeggiated violin figure, but on the Neapolitan, D♭.

IV. Pyotr Il'yich Chaikovsky: Symphony no. 4 in F minor op. 36, First Movement

Rounding out this chapter is a discussion of Chaikovsky's Fourth Symphony, composed in 1877, the same year as Brahms's Second Symphony. The two works could not be more dissimilar in their general mood, key, approach to sonata form, chromatic issues, and use of systems. Brahms's Second Symphony lies in a direct line stemming from Schubert and his so-called "three-key expositions," including Schubert's tendency to arpeggiate either the major or minor triad over the course of the exposition. In the first movement of Brahms's Second Symphony, an arpeggiated D major triad is responsible for an intermediate area in F♯ minor and a closing one in A. Brahms's symphony is also closer to the Classical developmental tradition, especially Haydn's, in that Brahms works out pc 3, F♮, as the main "issue" throughout the first movement. For example, at the end of the opening statement leading into the extensive bridge period, a unison arpeggiation of the V7 chord ends unexpectedly with an arpeggiation of an incomplete B diminished chord whose last note is F♮. Naturally, the system now shifts into a 1♭ system, which is sustained until a formal tonic cadence, preparing the start of the bridge period itself, raises the G♯ necessary to return to the tonic 2♯ system. What makes this preparatory passage so relevant to our discussion is how the 1♭ system is dramatized by the ominous timpani role following the F♮'s appearance (m. 32 in the score), as if the orchestra itself realizes the seriousness of the situation (the passage is illustrated in Diagram 7.4).

mm. 23-30	m.31	m.32	m.33-35		
2♯ system	F♮⬎1♭ system sustained -------------------		(G♯/F♮) 1♭ holds through		
V7 arpeggiation	B 07 arpeggiated	timpani roll on D (*pp*)	G♯ 07		

					Bridge
m.36	37	38	39	42-	44
---			(G♯/F♮)	G♯⬈2♯ system regained	
timpani roll	gm6	D 6/4	G♯ 07	Cadential motion	
on D (*pp*)	iv6	I 6/4		V7 →	I

Diagram 7.4 Brahms, Symphony no. 2 in D, first movement, exposition: system shifts (mm. 23–35)

As the diagram shows, the entire passage centers on the disrupting influence of F♮ in the harmonic scheme. Immediately after the timpani roll on D, the very next pitch heard is G♯ in the bass (cellos and trombones) as the root of a diminished seventh chord which also includes F♮, which prevents the G♯ from shifting the system back up to a 2♯

The Neapolitan is a sonority that is always associated with the complementary 3♭ system throughout this work. However, with Brahms, the Neapolitan has been shifted to the dominant.

system. The same timpani gesture is heard again, and this time is followed by a minor subdominant chord, a sonority motivated by the prevailing 1♭ system that governs this passage. The G♯ diminished chord returns in m. 39, again with F♮ canceling its potential to redress the system; but this is followed in m. 42 by an uncontested G♯, acting as a leading-tone embellishment to A, finally shifting the system back up to a 2♯ system and thus preparing for the bridge to begin again on tonic harmony.

The passage is itself a preparation for the main event of the exposition; the F♮ at first functions as a ♭VI and then as the root of an augmented sixth chord (mm. 114–17) that subsequently drops to a unison octave E as V/V of the closing period that functions as the "third key." Just as this chord operated in many of Haydn's symphonies as an enormous voice exchange with the opening tonic major tonic triad, the augmented sixth here signals the end of tonic harmony, which in this case includes an entirely melodic intermediate harmonic area in F♯ minor (F♯ and F♮ form the most important dyad conflict of the symphony). It is this kind of developmental detail, with F♮ as a controlling pitch, including the working-out of its large-scale contrapuntal relationship to tonic harmony and its concomitant shifts into the complementary 1♭ system, that ties this work to Brahms's Classical predecessors. Chaikovsky, however, takes a more radical approach to systems in that the basic issue for development in his Fourth Symphony is not confined to the machinations of a single unruly pitch class, but extends to the entire tonic system matrix itself, a tall order indeed.

Our purpose in this study is not to detail Chaikovsky's undoubted emotional symbolism in his Fourth Symphony; which has already been done extensively in the literature,[7] but to explore how Chaikovsky builds an entire sonata-form movement based solely on the tritone symmetries of the tonic system matrix, each pitch class of which is used as root of a structurally significant harmonic area. First we should illustrate the tonic matrix as Chaikovsky uses it in the first movement of the symphony.

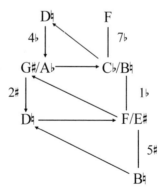

Figure 7.3   Chaikovsky, Symphony no. 4 in F minor, first movement, tonic 4♭ system matrix

---

7   Richard Taruskin's analysis of the hidden symbolism in the first movement of the Fourth Symphony is especially convincing. See his *Defining Russia Musically* (Princeton, 2001), pp. 297–302.

Within the 4♭ system matrix of the symphony, the pitch classes that seem to inform the symphony would most undoubtedly be C♭ and its enharmonic respelling as B♮, the latter enharmonic variant of which forms the harmonic area of the closing period, both pitch classes being tritone relations to the tonic, F. Diagram 7.5 gives the background plan of the sonata form of the first movement with the major system shifts indicated.

The opening slow introduction is of the Romantic type in its operatic, almost overture-like, style: Chaikovsky himself remarked about the operatic nature of this symphony in letters to his friend and patron Nadezhda von Meck. In comparison with more Romantic symphonic slow introductions (the slow introduction to Schumann's First Symphony in B♭ of 1841, the heroic brass fanfares of which served as a model for Chaikovsky's opening, is of much greater length and far more harmonically static), Chaikovsky's introduction is relatively short and harmonically unstable. The instability of the introduction stems from its arpeggiation of the F diminished chord, which also raises the main dyad conflict of the movement, D♭/D♮. This same diminished chord is, in fact, a preparation for the harmonic plan of the movement itself, which arpeggiates the chord in structurally significant areas (see Diagram 7.5): F minor for the first harmonic area, A♭ minor for the second harmonic area, B major for the closing area, and D minor for the transposed first and second harmonic areas of the recapitulation, the whole movement arpeggiating the pitch classes that form the 4♭ matrix of the tonic key.

Such a background harmonic plan begs the question of whether or not the tonic as a background key has any relevance at all; the internal harmonic areas relate only to each other and have no voice-leading function to that of the tonic. Beethoven had previously come close to achieving the same result in the exposition of the first movement of his own "Appassionata" Piano Sonata, a work in the same key (see Chapter 6), and with aspects of design that obviously appealed to Chaikovsky. Most notable in this regard was Beethoven's daring move to have the closing area not in the relative major, the tonality of the second harmonic area, but in the minor of the relative, thereby removing the closing period from any harmonic relation to the tonic. Chaikovsky must also have been influenced by the harmonic design of Beethoven's "Pathétique" Sonata, whereby two structurally significant harmonic areas follow each other in the minor mode: the first area in C minor and the second in E♭ minor, the latter giving way to the "correct" key of the relative major only at the closing period.

Introduction (4♭ system)
Andante sostenuto 3/4 (D♭/D♮ conflict introduced)
Polonaise Brass Motive

A♭ –	D♮ – B♮–	A♭ –	F
B o7	D♭ aug.6 - E6/4	A♭aug.	fm

f minor
i

(B) Very lengthy section:
Consists of variations of the opening theme as well as literal restatements

fm   —   am (opening theme transposed) –   D♭ aug.6 –
i

Exposition: 1st Theme Group (4♭ system)
Moderato con anima 9/8
(A) "Valse Triste"
arpeggiates the F o7 chord

	Counterstatement	Counterstatement → Bridge
		(A)
fm	fm	A♭6/4 – E♭o7 – E♭6/5
I	i	i

V/a♭

2nd Theme Group (7♭ system)
a♭ minor
iii

Lyrical Transition (5♯ system)
B Major (enharmonic C♭)
III/iii

Closing	C.S.
B Major	BM

Codetta
B Major

Development (follows fourth-related sequences that arpeggiate the f diminished chord)

(2♯ system)	(1♭ ——)	(4♭s ——)	(7♭s)			Retransition
						(2♯s) (4♭s) (2♯s)
b minor	em am	gm cm	fm e♭m a♭m [a♭/g♯]			am b♭m– bm – –

Recapitulation (4♭ system)
1st Theme Group (A)
a pedal (fff)

	(1♭ system)	
	Bridge	2nd Theme Group

(4♭s ——————)
D♭aug.6 – B♭ aug.6 –
d minor (completes the minor 3rds cycle) →   d minor

Lyrical Transition
[D♮/D♭ conflict returns]
F Major
I

Codetta
Coda (sectionalized) (begins in a 4♭ system but the movement ends in 7♭s)
Polonaise motive returns
[D♮/D♭ conflict raised for the last time and resolved into F minor]

F Major   f minor
I   i

Diagram 7.5 Chaikovsky, Symphony no. 4 in F minor op. 36, first movement: sonata-form plan

In both Beethoven examples, however, all this seeming harmonic eccentricity is eventually justified and resolved into tonic harmony within the recapitulations, a solution quite unlike the one Chaikovsky has chosen to follow. In the recapitulation of the Fourth Symphony, the transpositions are *at the level of the tritone* as follows:

Harmonic area:	Second harmonic area	Closing area	Codetta
Exposition:	a♭	B major	B major
Recapitulation:	d	omitted	F major

The D minor of the transposed second harmonic area ends the minor-thirds cycle of "keys" and in no way relates to the tonic. Even the raising of F major in the recapitulation, as a tritone transposition of the B major area in the exposition, does not immediately relate to the tonic, F minor, but simply moves, almost by force, into the tonic minor at the coda. Thus, we may deduce that all of Chaikovsky's eccentric harmonic motions are related locally, with each harmonic area a minor third away from the other, and each operating without reference to any specific background tonic. For example, within the exposition, the B major area that comprises the transition, closing area, and codetta is heard, in its enharmonic equivalent as C♭, as the major relative of the A♭ minor area that directly precedes it, and certainly not as ♭V of the tonic, F minor.

Because of the unique harmonic plan of the movement, that is, a diminished-thirds cycle in which every other harmonic area forms a tritone relation – F minor with B major, and A♭ minor with D minor – it is no surprise to find that each harmonic area is governed by a complementary system of the tonic tritone matrix (see Figure 7.3), a situation common enough, albeit to a lesser extent, in all chromatic tonal music. What makes the Fourth Symphony so outstanding is that Chaikovsky employs *five* of the tritone systems of the matrix *in structurally significant areas* (see Diagram 7.5), whereas one most often encounters only two or three of the many possible tritone complements governing these areas: specifically, the primary tritone system, its minor-third flat-side complement, and/or the enharmonic respelling of the minor-third complement as a sharp-side complement.

Every aspect of this movement, encompassing all structural levels, whether harmonic or motivic, is based on the tritone. It has already been pointed out that both the slow introduction and the exposition arpeggiate the tonic diminished chord, but this is also true of the development section (see Diagram 7.5). Within the various fourths cycles that run throughout the development is embedded a large-scale arpeggiation of the F diminished chord, here bounded by B minor and its 2♯ system. Each harmonic area along the tonic matrix projectory is firmly established within its own tritone system. Thus F minor, the first step after the opening B minor area, is subsumed under a 4♭ system, A♭ minor within a 7♭ system, and both B minor areas (at the beginning and at the end) under a 2♯ system. Each tritone system is prepared by the missing pitch of the previous system, and, in addition, each harmonic area within the arpeggiation is given structural support (dynamic, rhythmic, metric placement, etc.) that gives the area a stronger emphasis than the less significant areas surrounding it. For instance, the F minor passage culminates the sequence of fourth-related areas that began with B minor at the beginning of the development section. The change of design initiated by the F minor passage leads, in turn, to the A♭ minor area, which is set apart from the E♭ minor area that precedes it by changing the system from a 4♭ system to a 7♭ one, the most extreme flat-side system shift of the development. In addition, the A♭ minor area is the only one to undergo an enharmonic change, here into G♯ minor, which area sets the stage for a return to the 2♯ system that opened the development. The G♯ minor area (also part of the matrix arpeggiation) is climactic in itself, and the most active in terms of its extreme system shifts, moving rapidly within three measures (mm. 245–7) from 7♭ to 8♯ (C* substitutes for D), 5♯ and then finally 2♯!

The only variable within the unfolding of the matrix systems within the development is the 4♭ system that starts the recapitulation in D minor (see Diagram 7.5), a carry-over from the 4♭ system that supported the previous augmented sixth chords on D♭ and B♭. Ironically, a 4♭ system would naturally occur at this point, since the harmony would have been, under normal circumstances, the tonic, F minor. The D minor of the recapitulation is actually a displacement of the tonic, which harmony is achieved only at the coda, along with its rightful 4♭ system. As it happens, the D minor area does correct itself, system-wise, at the transposition of the second harmonic area, also in D minor. Here, the proper 1♭ system supports not only the harmonic area, but also that of the subsequent F major areas, the transition material and the codetta.

Perhaps the most ironic gesture in this movement characterized by ironic gestures is the way the movement ends. If one had to pick one pitch class that determines the character of any one system matrix, it would have to be the minor third. In the first movement of the Fourth Symphony, C♭ (and its enharmonic, B♮) plays a crucial role in the harmonic design of the exposition. But the pitch may also have had a psychological meaning for Chaikovsky as a symbol of complete despair, a result of fate, or *fatum* as Chaikovsky described it, an element of destruction in his life, preventing any chance of a normal, happy existence.[8] The C♭ in this symphony operates symbolically as it forces, almost as an agent of fate, the harmony to move in all the "wrong" directions. The only period of hope in the movement is the moment during the recapitulation when the prevailing D minor harmony finally gives way to the tonic major in the lyrical transition that leads to and includes the codetta. But the coda that ends the movement smashes this last hope, reverting the harmony to the tonic minor, along with a system shift back into the 4♭ system. The final destruction accompanies the last restatement of the opening theme (a theme associated with Chaikovsky himself), which is stretched out beyond recognition, accepting the polonaise rhythm of the "fate" motive of the introduction. During this final passage (mm. 395ff.), the harmony suddenly moves into D♭ and then into F♭, at which point the C♭ is reintroduced for the last time, but now with telling effect: not only does the C♭ modulate the prevailing 4♭ system into a 7♭ one, but it is left uncontested,

---

8   Chaikovsky wrote about his life and its relationship to "fate" in a famous letter that he wrote concerning this symphony to his benefactress Nadezhda Filaretovna von Meck. Taruskin, *Defining Russia Musically*, discusses the aspect of "fate" in the first movement of the Fourth Symphony in detail. The discussion here is based on Taruskin's perceptive psychological analysis.

as no D♮ appears to redress the system. Thus, although the movement ends in the tonic minor, its system is a7♭ one, making a fittingly symbolic ending for a work so emotionally driven.

Where do composers go from here? Toward the end of the nineteenth century, composers become ever more interested in exploring the potential of symmetrical systems to inform the design aspects of their works, pushing tonal hierarchy ever closer to the outer perimeters of the composition. Led by Franz Liszt, whose latter experiments in symmetrical forms influenced a host of composers coming after him, most notably Claude Debussy and, ultimately, Arnold Schoenberg, the stage was set for the most radical transformation of the tonality yet perceived. It is to these composers that we turn for our last chapter.

Chapter Eight

The Romantic *Avant Garde* and the Rumblings of Modernism

In this chapter, we will discuss some of the works of the Romantic *avant garde* through analyses of Chopin, Liszt, and Debussy and conclude with a hint at some of the consequences their experiments engendered in the works of the Second Viennese School in the years before World War I.

The term *avant garde* is generally applied to those cutting-edge artists who force their craft – whether artistic, philosophical, or cultural – beyond conventional boundaries. Of the composers of the Romantic period we have considered up to this point, all were driven to make their own special contributions to musical composition and, consequently, to the evolution of tonality. Beginning with Beethoven's middle period in the early decades of the nineteenth century, each of these artists, in his own unique fashion, pushed the prevailing tonal language to where a breaking point became a very real possibility. The harmonic, melodic, and, particularly, chromatic innovations of works such as the "Waldstein" or "Appassionata" stimulated contemporary and succeeding generations of Romantic artists to seek further innovation within an already "distended" (as opposed to "disintegrating") chromatic tonality. Oddly enough, the harmonic innovations of nineteenth-century composers, most apparent in Beethoven's works, not only stretched the limits of tonal comprehension, but were, perhaps more significantly, taking place in the very form that was conceived as the epitome of conventional tonal organization, that is, sonata form.

In the works of Schubert, Schumann, Chaikovsky, and Brahms, we have seen not only the increasingly complicated interplay of the diatonic with the chromatic, but also the chromatic itself saturating the diatonic palette in ways that would have been considered unthinkable only a few years before, even though these composers are not generally considered to be *avant garde* – Schoenberg's reference to Brahms as a "progressive" challenged the then-conventional wisdom that still counted him among the ranks of musical conservatives. However, with the arrival of a new group of composers in the early – to mid-nineteenth century, we see the world of diatonically dominated composition plunged into a "crisis" – to borrow an apt term used by Ernst Kurth in reference to Wagner's *Tristan und Isolde* – from which it would never return.[1]

---

1   Ernst Kurth, *Romantische Harmonik und ihre Krise in Wagners "Tristan"* (Berlin, 1923), ed. and trans. in part by Robert Bailey in *Richard Wagner: Prelude and Transfiguration from "Tristan und Isolde,"* Norton Critical Score (New York, 1985), pp. 186–204. Also, see

In Chapters 5 and 7 we analyzed works in sonata form written between approximately 1720 and 1900 utilizing a new theory of chromaticism that examines its influence on the developmental process. However, the composers we will now discuss have a more tenuous connection to that tradition. Although Chopin, Liszt, and Debussy create compositions called "sonatas," these works do not necessarily hail from the *style galant* instrumental tradition with which we have been concerned. Rather, we now see strong influences from vocal genres, particularly those from the world of opera. For example, Chopin's general melodic style is beholden to the *bel canto* tradition of Rossini and Bellini; Liszt's sonatas, tone poems, and concert etudes often have more than just a passing allegiance to the sonata-overtures of the operatic tradition. (A sonata-overture is similar to the sonata form we have discussed except that it lacks an appreciable development section, often having only a few transitional measures between the end of the exposition and the opening of the recapitulation; Mozart's overture to *The Marriage of Figaro* is an example.) Many of Debussy's impressionistic works, such as the *Prélude à l'après-midi d'un faune*, begin to blur the line between traditional sonata procedures and those that are operatically conceived, such as those found in short piano pieces in ternary forms. Consequently, the harmonic-area tensions and delicate balances of phrase structure that comprised the emotional aesthetic of sonata form, as discussed up to this point, no longer operate to the same degree in the works of the *avant garde* composers we will now address.

I. Liszt and Debussy: The Romantic *Avant Garde* and its Manifestation in Impressionism

The works of Franz Liszt (1811–1886) represent an important step in the evolution of nineteenth-century composition, and Liszt himself may be viewed as the vehicle through which early Romanticism helped to create and then influence the *avant garde* of the later nineteenth and early twentieth centuries. Very much affected by the music and physical artistry of Niccolò Paganini, the young Liszt set out to accomplish on the piano what Paganini had accomplished on the violin. Aside from opera's pervasive influence, Liszt's compositional inspirations came most apparently from Schubert and Hector Berlioz, although it is also self-evident that his late-boyhood meeting with Beethoven must have had a profound influence on him, as did his early studies with Salieri and Czerny. Liszt created grandiose piano transcriptions and musical "reminiscences" of modern operas by composers such as Weber, Rossini, and Wagner; he transcribed and played all of Beethoven's symphonies. Although music historians hold his overt showmanship against him as proof of his severe extroversion and wild personal excesses (often while simultaneously congratulating him as the greatest pianist ever), we are more interested here in his contributions to the world of nineteenth-century composition. Liszt invented the symphonic poem (or "tone poem"), a one-movement programmatic work for orchestra based upon a

---

Alfred Lorenz, *Der musikalische Aufbau von Richard Wagners "Tristan und Isolde"* (Berlin, 1926, repr. 1966).

significant personage or philosophical topic, and his developmental style was infused with thematic transformations and transpositions of melodic and harmonic material by equal subdivisions of the octave, particularly major or minor thirds. These compositional techniques were no doubt influenced by works such as Schubert's *Wanderer Fantasy* and appear most evidently in his enormous one-movement Piano Sonata in B minor. In his old age, the consequences of his compositional experiments led him down paths that teetered on the edge of atonality with the use of octatonic scales and whole-tone prolongations. It is quite probable that modern composers like Debussy and Béla Bartók would have moved in very different directions had it not been for the influence of Franz Liszt.

"Un sospiro" is the third of three concert etudes that Liszt composed in 1848. It is typical of Liszt's middle-period piano compositions in terms of its mellifluous arpeggiations, its typical large-scale transpositions by intervals that subdivide the octave equally, and, particularly, its technical difficulty. Our choice for its inclusion in this chapter has to do with the issues of melodic transformation and large-scale transpositions of subsections by major thirds, a consideration that has already been well documented by modern music theory. However, more important is the equal subdivision of the octave into minor thirds: this is the essential interval responsible for the organization of material in the background of the composition. A corollary to the issue of equal subdivision into major or minor thirds are the problems of rampant enharmonicism inherent in any composition that composes out dissonant chordal sonorities on a grand scale. In this etude, the major thirds are composed out in a very obvious manner that we will explore below. On the other hand, the minor thirds are operational on a more subtle level: we will see how the alteration of F♮ to F♭ in m. 18 is the key to understanding a series of questions raised by this simple modal shift from D♭ major to D♭ minor. We will discuss the issues raised by the major thirds first.

"Un sospiro" is only one of many examples in the nineteenth century that illustrates an interest on the part of composers in increasing the level of chromatic density in their compositions. With regard to this etude, the issues of equal subdivision and how it is expressed within the context of the theory of eleven-pitch tonal fields, the missing pitch, and the filling-in of the tonic octave diatonically (through the unfolding Primary Diatonic Array, or PDA) and chromatically (through the unfolding Primary Chromatic Array, or PCA) will inform the following discussion. Liszt still secures his most prominent, structural cadences with dominant–tonic progressions. However, influenced by Beethoven's middle- and late-period compositions (and just about any large-scale work of Schubert's), Liszt's harmonic language incorporates equal subdivisions of the octave, particularly the subdivisions into major or minor thirds. In "Un sospiro," the organizing element of the higher middleground is the major third. While the *A* section establishes and anchors the tonic, D♭, the B^1 section is introduced with a short auxiliary cadence to A major in m. 22 and the B^2 section secures F major between mm. 30 and 34. Therefore, the most stable harmonic areas up to this moment have been D♭ major, A major, and F major, in a descending sequence of major thirds which arpeggiates an augmented triad. Equal subdivision of the octave is one typical characteristic of this period, a characteristic that would be exploited not only by Liszt, but by other *avant garde* composers as well, such as Richard Wagner. Although it is not associated with the music of the more conservative wing of Romanticism, one does not have to look extensively to find this characteristic also in the works of Schubert, Schumann, and Brahms, all of whom have their own *avant garde* sides to their musical personalities. As the century progresses, equal subdivision becomes one of the issues that tears at the very fabric of triadic tonality. Eventually, these symmetrical formations, which in Liszt's early and middle-period works occur in the middleground, will pervade the note-to-note activity of the immediate foreground as well. Later, with Debussy, we will see how chordal symmetries can be harmonically defined and contrapuntally harnessed to a stable background which may or may not exhibit explicit triadic tonality, using "tonality" in the extended Beethoven-era sense of the term. The backdrop to this era of radical departure from more established and more conventional composition, one that culminates in the gradual dissolution of triadic tonality, is the constancy and continued development of procedures for filling in the chromatically ascending tonic octave and the continued organization of surface events with the eleven notes of the tonic system. The shifting of the tonic system to its complements, organized by minor thirds or augmented seconds, and the symmetrical tritone division of the octave to anchor the tonic are still operational, even if the triad no longer has the organizational and, eventually, the structural status it once enjoyed.

The large-scale organization of "Un sospiro" is ternary; all formal divisions are outlined in Diagram 8.1. Notable is the thematic content of the opening period, which shows the influence of *bel canto* opera in its phrase division, *a a b* (3 + 3 + 4 measures respectively), the first two *a* sections constituting a Rossinian "thematic block" (see Chapter 7). Also typical of Romantic thematic organization, the consistent phrase repetitions constitute a formal design element. In addition, Liszt's thematic transformations, in which all the *B* themes of the extensive middle section are simple variations of the opening melody, are typical. Harmonically, the *A* section secures D♭ major with a clear prolongation of the major tonic followed by an embellished counterstatement beginning in m. 12 and ends with the tonic transformed into its parallel minor in m. 18. A transitional phrase (*c*) occurs between m. 19 and m. 22. The most distinct attribute of the etude's *B* section, an extensive area composed of three thematically transformed subsections (labeled B^1, B^2 and B^3), is Liszt's change of key signature: the three sharps in m. 19 uproot the previous five flats, and three sharps are changed to four in m. 38; the D♭ major signature enters again only a measure before the return of tonic harmony in m. 53, which is the opening of the A^1 section. This section is relatively short, simply restating – as well as extending – the opening material, and then appending two codas to it, the first, a restatement of B^3, in m. 62 and the second in m. 70; the second coda functions as the coda's coda. (A few additional abbreviations are present in the diagrams in this chapter. They are '*abbr.*' (abbreviated), '*bs.*' (bass), 'C.S.' (counterstatement), '*embel.*' (embellishing or embellishment), '*ext.*' (extension), '*mel.org.*' (melodic organization), '*trans.*'(transition), and '*w.t.*' (whole tone).)

Main dyad conflicts: Db/D♮, F♮/Fb, Gb/G♮, Ab/A♮, Bb/B♮

Form:	*A*					*C.S. embel.*			*trans.*	*B₁*				
	a	a	b			a	a		c					
Measure:	1	6	9	10	11	13	16	18	19	22	23	27	28	29
Act Sys Pcs:								Fb↗				G♮↗	Db↗	E♮↗ Db↗
System:	5b							8b				5b	5b	2b 5b
													E♮↗	E♮↗
													2b	2b
PCA:	**Db(0)**								**D♮(1)**				**Eb(2)**	**E♮(3)**
PDA/(SDA):	Db		C	Bb	Ab				G♯		F♯			
Harmony:	I				V	I	I	i	V4/3 of bVI	V4/3 of bVI	IV6/4 of bVI	vii°4/3 of III	IIIᵇ6/5	Vᵇ9/III

Form:	*B₂*		*(cadenza)*	*B₃ : dominant prep*			*retrans.*		
Measure:	30	35	37	38	42	43	44	45	46
ASPcs:		E♮↗C♯↗	A♯↗ (G♮/A♯)						
System:		2b 1♯	4♯						
PCA:	**F♮(4)**	**F♯(5)**	**Fx(6)(=G♮)**	**G♯(7)**		**A♮(8)**			
PDA/(SDA):	F♮	F♯		(G♯	F♯	F♯ E♮	D♮, C♮	B♮, A♮	G♯)
Harmony:	III♮			"V⁸—				— 7"	

Diagram 8.1 Liszt, *Trois études de concert*, "Un sospiro"

Form: (cadenza) · *A' (varied)* · *B₃ as coda 1*

Measure	52		53		61	62	66	67
ASPcs:	G♮,	B♭↗, D♭↗			(D♭/E♮)			
System:	1♯	2♭, 5♭						
PCA:	**B♭(9)**	**B♮(10) C(11)**						
PDA/(SDA):	**E♭**		**D♭(0)**			**D♭(0)**		
			D♭			(D♭	C♭	B♭, A♭
Harmony:	V⁷!		I		V⁷	I		(*disjunct dorian tetrachords* =

Form: *coda 2*

Measure:	68	69	70	73
ASPcs:				F♭↗
System:				8♭!!
PCA:				
PDA/(SDA):	*G♮, F♮*	*E♮, D♮)*	**D♭**	
Harmony:	= *octatonic scale*)	I		

Diagram 8.1 Liszt, *Trois études de concert*, "Un sospiro" continued

In Diagram 8.1, note that the PCA does not begin its ascent until the transition to the *B* section is reached in m. 19. In fact, the first D♮ (pc 1) enters dramatically after the unexpected key signature change to A major. At that point, the PDA has already descended to A♭, and at m. 19, G♯, the third of V 4/3 of A major, must be interpreted as an enharmonic reinterpretation of the PDA A♭ in m. 11. Therefore, the application of equal octave subdivision necessitates enharmonic respelling: in the period that prolongs A major, it is necessary that (1) the unfolding diatonic and chromatic octaves continue their respective descents and ascents even in the area of a local harmonic change to integrate the new period firmly into the whole composition, and (2) the foreground melodic events in that new period be respelled to accommodate the local harmony.

There is one element that seems almost to conflict with the foreground appearance of A major, and that is what happens in m. 18 with the change of harmony from D♭ major to D♭ minor and the appearance of F♭, a note that plunges the systems down into an 8♭ system, seemingly in the wrong direction for the upcoming "sharp-key" period (see Figure 8.1).

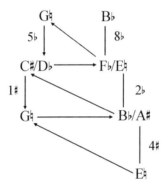

Figure 8.1   5♭ expanded system matrix

Therefore, while the local harmony has been recast as A major, Liszt's system shift implies that the entire expanse exists in the extremes of flat-side tonality, at least on the background level of eleven-pitch-class systems. Obviously, had Liszt wanted, F♭ could have been spelled as E♮; granted, it would have appeared strange in a D♭ chord, but it would have made sense in light of the upcoming enharmonic respellings. Certainly, unusual chordal spellings had appeared around that time which were generally consistent with voice-leading melodic organization but which could be explained from the perspective of vertical spelling. (For example, the tiny, thirteen-and-a-half-measure "Chopin" from Robert Schumann's *Carnaval* incorporates what appears to be a passing second-inversion B♭♭ 4/3 chord between a vi chord and a dominant seventh a measure later; however, the B♭♭ is spelled as A♮ to accommodate a rising chromatic line in the melody.) With respect to vertical alignment, Liszt's spelling of the third of the chord as F♭ instead of E♮ seems a reasonable choice, particularly since one of the primary dyad conflicts of the etude is

F♮/F♭. Therefore, Liszt's chord spelling at the end of the *A* section begs the question of whether the upcoming period in A major is *really* a conveniently renotated B♭♭ major or the notation means *exactly what it says*. (Of course, the next question ought to be, "Is there any way of answering the first question definitively?") The diagram indicates that the continuation of PDA A♭ in the *B* section is expressed as G♯ (m. 19). However, in m. 23, where G♭ would have been the "normal" notation of that pitch in a descending D♭ diatonic array, F♯ must take its place because of the surrounding harmony, and most certainly, notating the third of a D major 6/4 chord as G♭ would be unacceptable in an area of such breadth (Schumann just had to contend with a single measure appearing a bit odd!). We will return to the problems posed by the F♭ and motion into an 8♭ system later.

If we examine the ascending PCA, another chromatic issue arises between mm. 30 and 37. So far, we have been concerned with *dyad conflicts*, situations that crop up with different "versions" of a diatonic note. For example, in Chapter 5, we discussed four dyad conflicts, D♭/D♮, B♭/B♮, A♭/A♮, and G♭/G♮, that created opportunities for developmental processes in Haydn's Symphony no. 84 in E♭. We have seen that as music evolves, composers continue to use dyad conflict as an important tool for both development and compositional rationale through unity. However, with Liszt, we see the dyad conflicts expand into triad conflicts and even tetrad conflicts. In the opening of "Un sospiro," F♮ enters as a note of the tonic chord; however, by the end of the first period, in m. 18, F♮ is displaced by F♭. In m. 30, pc 4 re-enters as F♮ (concurrently with the PDA F♮ below it) and continues to pc 5 as F♯ in m. 35 and then pc 6 as F𝄪 in m. 37. Therefore, as the PCA ascends, we note that Liszt is focusing on variants of the diatonic F♮, including F♭ and, as the etude continues, F♯ and even F𝄪. Of course, dyad, triad, and tetrad conflicts are associated with enharmonicism as well. In the cadenza at the end of m. 37, the previous F𝄪 is enharmonically presented as G♮, that is, until the upcoming G♯ minor sonority enters in m. 38, where, at the end of the cadenza, pc 6 is respelled again as F𝄪. Measure 38 also signals the beginning of a large-scale preparation of the structural dominant which occurs at the retransition in m. 46. The G♯ sonority of m. 38 also signals the arrival at pc 7 and, again, instead of A♭, G♯ must be used in its place. The remainder of the PCA returns to spelling that is consistent with a D♭ major chromatic octave ascent.

Liszt has other strategies for anchoring extended harmonic areas which are not under direct control of the tonic octave, but are extensions from it and, therefore, still associated with the tonic octave on a deeper structural level. From m. 38 to m. 46, a phrase that prolongs G♯ major harmony while contrapuntally moving an upper-register G♯ to F♯ (in the diagram, this is shown as "V$^{8-7}$"), Liszt presents a complete diatonic descent from the PDA G♯ in m. 38 to a prominent G♯ in m. 46. This lower-level *Secondary Diatonic Array* (labeled "SDA" in the diagram and placed in parentheses to demonstrate the boundaries of the entire octave descent) is yet another element of composition that will become more prevalent in the late nineteenth century; we will also see this subordinate structure in the early twentieth century with Debussy's "Doctor Gradus ad Parnassum" as well as the third of his *Estampes*, "Jardins sous la pluie," which, in addition, contains a prominent "Secondary *Chromatic* Array" (SCA). In the Liszt diagram, notice that the notes of the SDA are not specifically those of a descending G♯ minor or major scale since

Liszt has modally inflected the descending array to accommodate the local harmonies of the phrase. Since it is unclear whether F♯ or F♮ is the "correct" diatonic value of the seventh scale degree of the G♯ scale, both are present in the diagram.

The retransition between m. 46 and m. 52 leads us back to D♭ major with the transformation of the G♯7 into an A♭7 (m. 52, cadenza, *pp velocissimo*), and with the arrival of the next PDA note, E♭ (the tenor voice of the dominant seventh, which is bracketed in the diagram to the F♮ from m. 30). In m. 53, with the arrival of D♭ (pc 0), we have the first and only completion of the PCA. Diagram 8.1 depicts how the systems gradually return to 5♭ after having reached 4♯ in m. 37 with the F𝄪 discussed above: G♮ and B♭ as system-shift motivators, followed by D♭, bring us back to a 5♭ system. When the *A¹* section arrives in m. 53, we have returned to D♭ major and all high-level diatonic and chromatic arrays have ended their unfoldings. Even so, Liszt secures the *A¹* section and its two codas by creating another SDA descent. This time, many of the notes of a descending D♭ major scale are modally inflected in the first coda to create an octatonic scale with the disjunct dorian tetrachords D♭–A♭ and G♮–D♮. The second coda restates D♭ at *più lento* (m. 70). Curiously, in m. 73, a B♭♭ major chord enters and its fifth, F♭, forces us back into the same 8♭ system that we saw at the termination of the *A* section in m. 18.

Just a quick word about octatonic scales. These scales of alternating half steps and whole steps (or alternating whole steps and half steps) are seen with increasing frequency in the nineteenth century as composition begins to have a more tenuous relationship to traditional tonality. As mentioned before, the one we see in "Un sospiro" is a product of disjunct dorian tetrachords, which are used in this manner, for example, in the twentieth century by Béla Bartók (particularly in his 44 Violin Duos): since the dorian tetrachord is internally symmetrical, so is the scale created from two dorian tetrachords separated by a half step, that half step becoming the symmetrical axis around which the scale revolves. However, nineteenth- and twentieth-century Russian composers such as Alexander Skryabin would use octatonic scales to organize entire (but short) compositions in the absence of any traditional guiding tonality as a scalar diminution of the diminished seventh chord (see, for example, his Five Preludes for Piano op. 74): in fact, the octatonic scale can be created by juxtaposing the individual pitch classes of any two diminished seventh chords – which of the two is structural, of course, will depend upon the musical context. Following in the footsteps of Liszt, Debussy's application of octatonicism in the third of his *Estampes*, "Jardins sous la pluie," is also used as a scalar diminution of a diminished seventh chord. If we keep in mind that the triad, as a high-level organizational tool, gradually yields to dissonant and symmetrical simultaneities as the nineteenth century progresses, then the increasing prevalence of these scalar and chordal entities becomes the basis of a new normalcy within the ever-evolving chromatic language of the era. In "Un sospiro," the octatonic scale unfolded in the first coda is part of the prolongation of a diminished seventh chord from D♭ to D♭ with the intermediary chord tones B♭–G♮–E♮, the notes present on the downbeats of mm. 67–9. The substitution of octatonic scale steps for D♭ major scale steps resuscitates some of the most important dyad conflicts of the etude so that they can be resolved again in the second coda.

We can now return to the issue of F♭, the missing pitch of the tonic 5♭ system, with regard to its significance in "Un sospiro." (You will recall that the first appearance of the F♭ was in m. 18, before Liszt changed key signatures from five flats to three sharps.) When m. 72 is reached in the second coda, we are in a 5♭ system. Significantly, the last six measures of the piece resurrect some of its most significant dyad conflicts: the B♭♭ chord in m. 73 recalls the A major harmony of the first part of the *B* section, just as the F major triad, a measure before the end, recalls the second part of the *B* section. However, with the A major sonority rewritten enharmonically as B♭♭–D♭–F♭, the dyad conflict of B♭/B♮ is now expanded into a triad conflict, B♭♭/B♭/B♮. Therefore, the question concerning the earlier A major section as a convenient respelling of B♭♭ major returns. Also, the presence of F♭, the missing pitch of the 5♭ system, brings us back down to an 8♭ system, an issue that Liszt may not have considered properly resolved earlier – or, perhaps, *did not want to resolve!* With an 8♭ system now activated, we wait for a G♮ to enter and return us to the tonic 5♭ system. Yet this does not happen: the etude cadences in the 8♭ system. Other issues do resolve, however: the B♭♭ triad in m. 73 is succeeded by a G♭ major triad, whose B♭ (notated with the warning flat) immediately resolves B♭♭. (The B♮ has already resolved to B♭ between mm. 69 and 70.) In m. 76, another of the dyad conflicts is put to rest: the A♮ in the F major triad resolves to A♭ (emphasized by another warning accidental) in the upcoming tonic chord in the concluding measure. Liszt's return to the F♭ in the final few measures of the etude, then, contains a considerable amount of chromatic baggage that raises a host of other questions.

It must be remembered that the transformation of D♭ major to D♭ minor in m. 18 represents a minor-third relationship since the root of the tonic 5♭ system (D♭) is a minor third from the root of the 8♭ system (F♭). Therefore, the minor third that almost seems to hide in the recesses of the etude actually represents a higher level of chromatic organization than the modulations by major thirds that have already been discussed. In fact, any of the compositions we have already described that transpose large areas of material by major thirds – take, for example, Beethoven's "Waldstein" sonata – do so through shrouded minor-thirds progressions that are unfolded in the background and can be viewed in the systems matrix. In the case of the "Waldstein," the relationship revealed in the background of the first movement's exposition is one between a "0" system, the tonic, and a 3♯ system, the system of the second harmonic area. That is, even though the second harmonic area is E major, the relationship that exists between the root of the tonic system, C♮, and the root of the 3♯ system, A♮, represents more of a background relationship than the foreground association of C major with E major. When D♯ enters in the counterstatement/bridge, it does so as the enharmonic transformation of the missing pitch, which was written consistently as E♭ in the opening statement. Again, the relationship of C♮ to A♮ is a minor third, and the intervalic relationship between C♮ and the dividing tritone of the 3♯ system, D♯, is that of an augmented second, an enharmonically respelled minor third. The foreground harmonic organization of "Un sospiro" is very much the same as that of the "Waldstein": the entry of F♭ in m. 18 initiates a minor-third relationship between the tonic 5♭ system and its complementary 8♭ system.

The contention that Liszt took seriously the issues surrounding the tonic 5♭ system's missing pitch, F♭, can easily be demonstrated by examining one of his many substitutions and cadenza-like additions reprinted in the *Neue Ausgabe*. In Bärenreiter's 1971 edition of the new complete works, there is an asterisk at m. 72 that refers to the following paragraph: "Liszt also wrote down ... the following mystically hovering conclusion with major triads on each of the six degrees of the descending whole-tone scale ... to be performed *ad lib.* in place of the conclusion in the text ..."[2]

The seven new measures that are offered as an *ossia* for the last six are reproduced in Example 8.1. Again, at the first measure of the substitute phrase, m. 72, we are in a 5♭ system. The next measure again brings in the B♭♭ major chord with the F♭ missing pitch as it was in the original ending. The next measure, m. 74, has the F major chord with its A♮ third, which is resolved immediately on the second half of the measure. However, m. 75 does depart from the original: the B♭♭ triad enters again with the missing pitch, F♭. B♭♭ is also in the left hand, which is about to descend into a register that has previously been explored in the second part of the *B* section with the F major chords in mm. 30, 32, and 34. However, that B♭♭ in the left hand moves to G♮, allowing us (at least momentarily) to believe that a system-shift up to the tonic 5♭ system is imminent: yet, with F♭ still sustained in the right hand, the F♭/G♮ play of system motivators simply maintains the integrity of the 8♭ system. However, the resolution of A♮ to A♭ occurs twice after that.

In summary, we do not believe that an unequivocal explanation can be offered for all the problems raised by the sharp notation of the *B* section. This is an issue

Example 8.1 Liszt, "Un sospiro," *ossia* (mm. 72–8)

that invariably comes up when an equal subdivision of the octave is used: had B♭♭ been used instead of A♮ for the first part of the *B* section, allowing D♭ to descend a major third to B♭♭, then the second part's opening in F major would have appeared unusual. One of the major thirds needs to be indicated as a diminished fourth because of the peculiarities of our diatonically inclined notational system. Had the etude been notated in C♯ major, the diminished fourth would have come up between F♮ and C♯. In addition, a C♯ major tonic would have defeated the emotional purpose of the piece, whose D♭ tonic projects a darker quality than would have been consistent with a C♯ notation.

---

2   Franz Liszt, *Trois études de concert/Trios caprices poetiques für Klavier*, ed. Zoltán Gárdonyi and István Szelényi (Budapest, 1971), p. 40, repr. from Franz Liszt, *Neue Ausgabe sämtlicher Werke*, ser. I, Werke für Klavier zu zwei Händen, vol. 2, *Etüden II*.

These types of notational concerns are among the many problems with which a nineteenth-century composer had to contend. We believe that the issue concerning notation and enharmonicism in this etude lies within the system-defining potential of a single note, G♮, the missing pitch of the 8♭ system arrived at through the entry of F♭. Liszt's suggestions for an *ossia* final phrase indicates his own personal response to the problem. In the original score, the last utterance of G♮ occurs as part of the descending octatonic scale in m. 68. Although the G♮ is raised to G♯ in the succeeding measure as part of E major harmony (or is it "really" F♭ major harmony?!), G♭ resolves G♮ at the end of m. 70 and in m. 71 as well. The issue is closed. However, in Liszt's seven-measure *ossia*, the G♮ returns in mm. 73 and 75, just when we thought that it might create a system shift back to a 5♭ system. The absence of any further G♭s allows the dissonant G♮ to ring strongly in conjunction with the 8♭ system at the end. If we take the *B* section really to mean B♭♭ major written in A major as a notational convenience, then we should still be looking for one prominent G♮ to return us to our tonic 5♭ system. The most likely place for a significant G♮ would be m. 52, the retransition (cadenza) before Liszt's key signature change back to five sharps.

If you look again at Figure 8.1, the 5♭ expanded system matrix, you will notice that G♮ is one of the pitches that occurs twice: G♮ is not only the pitch that is necessary to return an 8♭ system to a 5♭ one, but also the first pitch necessary to bring the sharp side of the expanded system matrix figure back toward five sharps, which is the path Liszt chose in this etude. Perhaps Liszt's allowing G♮ to remain as a dissonance right up until the end is an indication of his own way of dealing with notational problems, since G♮ is needed by both the sharp side and by the flat side of the matrix to get us back "home." Ironically, home looks very "flat" at the end since the etude ends in the 8♭ system – an 8♭ system with a prominently displayed G♮ that is not resolved except in the traditional manner to A♭. In a way, the opposition of the G♮ with the 8♭ system at the etude's conclusion resolves a very deep-seated problem and a most interesting developmental paradox.

II. Debussy and Chromaticism at the Turn of the Century

Among Franz Liszt's prominent musical "stepchildren," Claude Debussy (1862–1918) must be counted as one of the most significant. "There can be little doubt that Liszt's 'modal effects, whole-tone harmony, pedaling, and various coloristic devices greatly influenced Debussy's piano music.'"[3] A few months before Liszt died, Debussy, having just won the Prix de Rome and living in the nearby Villa Medici,

> visited Liszt on three occasions. We know that Liszt played for him several of his works, including "Au bord d'une source" from *Années*, Book I, which surely must have suggested to Debussy the possibilities for developing piano technique for impressionistic effects. If he did not hear Liszt play "Les jeux d'eau à la Villa D'Este", he certainly came to know it before writing such works as "Reflets dans l'eau" from *Images*, Book I (pub. 1905). Proof

---

3   Derek Watson, *Liszt* (New York, 1989), p. 140, quoted in Kenneth Hamilton (ed.), *The Cambridge Companion to Liszt* (Cambridge, 2005), p. 43.

of his knowledge of the piece is supplied in his "L'isle joyeuse" (1903–4), which virtually quotes the figuration in bars 44–7 of "Jeux d'eau".[4]

We will describe how Debussy's applications of system modulations and diatonic and chromatic arrays create, even in a through-composed piece, both a strong sense of unity and consistency of flow and direction. This is particularly significant in a composition that is so far removed from conventional tonality that hardly a phrase exists in the entire work that is overtly associated with previous musical traditions. What Debussy is able to accomplish in works from his middle period is quite revolutionary, and we believe that only an analysis describing the composer's unique approach to all the kinds of chromatic issues we have discussed has a chance of doing justice in appraising the originality of his style.

Debussy composed his three *Estampes* in 1903. The first of the group, "Pagodes," is a heavily pentatonic composition in a 5♯ system that never uses the missing pitch D♮ (!), a note that finally enters in the next *estampe*, "Soirée dans Granade," with D♮ in m. 7 entering as the first note of the melody and making a wonderful connection from the first composition to the second of the three. The chordal writing, pedal points, pentatonicism, and sheen of high-register, flowing thirty-second notes toward the end are reminiscent of Liszt's "Sposalizio" from Part 2, *Italie*, of the *Années de pèlerinage*.[5] "Soirée" also sounds quite oriental, but has a Spanish flavor with plenty of melodic augmented seconds and a Habañera rhythm. The change from two to three staves is also reminiscent of Liszt's notation for piano.

However, we will discuss the third of the three *Estampes*, "Jardins sous la pluie," which is not as overtly oriental as the other two, but very much more in the style of the "Prélude," the first of the three-movement work *Pour le piano* (1896–1901). "Jardins" makes ample use of Liszt's techniques of thematic transformation and immediate repetition of melodic material. However, like Liszt in his later piano works, Debussy has large sections of music that are quite distant from tonic harmony and entire sections that are prolongations of whole-tone collections where he simply does away with key signatures since none are appropriate. Debussy also enharmonically reinterprets notes from both diatonic and chromatic arrays and organizes his arrays into levels that both unfold the PCA with a substantial SCA and extend the PDA with a segment of an SDA, a technique we saw in "Un sospiro." If one scans the score quickly, it is immediately apparent that "Jardins" begins in E minor and ends in E major and, therefore, the likelihood is that a substantial dyad conflict exists between G♮ and G♯; Debussy does not disappoint. (A few new abbreviations are present in the following diagram. They are '*abbr.*' (abbreviated), '*bs.*' (bass), '*embel.*' (embellishing or embellishment), '*ext.*' (extension), '*mel.org.*' (melodic organization), '*trans.*' (transition), and '*w.t.*' (whole tone).

---

4   James Baker, "Liszt's Late Piano Works: Larger Forms," in Hamilton (ed.), *Cambridge Companion*, pp. 141–2.

5   Excellent voice-leading analyses of "Sposalizio" are present in Howard Cinnamon's "Third Relations as Structural Elements in Book II of Liszt's 'Années de Pèlerinage' and Three Later Works," Ph.D. dissertation, University of Michigan, 1984.

Main dyad conflicts: E♮/E♯, F♮/F♯, G♮/G♯, B♭/B♮

Melodic org. / key:	1st in E mi.						1st in F♯	1st in F♯ mi.			
Measure:	1	4	6	17	18	21	27	31	34	37	41
Act Sys Pcs:		Bb↘		Db↘	E♮↗	C#↗	A#↗				
System:	1#	2b		5b	2b	1#	4#				
PCA/(SCA):	E♮(0)		F♮(1)				F#(2)				Gb(2)
PDA	E♮		E♮						D#	Eb	
Harmony:	*E mi.:* i						II	ii			

Mel.org./key:	1st in C mi.			1st in Db (C mi. key sig.)					
Measure:	43	45	47	50	55	56	60	64	65
ActSysPcs:	G♮↗	Bb↘	Db↘			E♮↗	C#↗	Bb↘	C#↗ (Bb/C#)
System:	1#	2b	5b			2b	1#	2b	1#
PCA/(SCA):	G♮(3)		Ab(4)		(A♮(5)	Bb(6)	B♮(7)	C♮(8)	C#(9) D♮(10), Eb(11), E♮(0), F♮(1)
PDA	Db								
Harmony:	VI —								*(Whole-tone harmonies until m. 71)*

Diagram 8.2 Debussy, *Estampes*, "Jardins sous la pluie"

Mel.org./key:

Measure:	66	68	69	70
ActSysPcs:	(B♭/C♯)	(B♭/C♯)		
System:				
PCA/(SCA):	F♯(2), G♮(3), A♭(4), A♮(5)	B♭(6), B♮(7)	C♮(9), C♯(8), D♮(10), D♯(11)	E♮(0), F(1),
PDA:				
Harmony:				

Mel.org./key:

	2ⁿᵈ in C♯	1ˢᵗ in w. t.	2ⁿᵈ in C♯	1ˢᵗ in B mi. / G♮ bs.
	⌐a	b	a + ext.	l
Measure:	70 (cont.) 71 75	77 83	90	100 103 112
ActSysPcs:	A♯↗		G♮↗	
System:	4♯		1♯	
PCA/(SCA):	F♯(2), G♮(3)) G♯(**4**)		A♮(**5**)	
PDA/(SD4):	C♯⌐		(B♮⌐	
Harmony:	— VI		III	

Mel.org./key: | | | *Abb., varied reprise* | | | | *2nd in B/G♮ bs. 2nd in E* | | *1st in G♯ minor*

Measure:	122	124	125	126	128	133	135	136	137
ActSysPcs:								A♯↗	Fx↗
System:								4♯	7♯
PCA/(SCA):						A♮(5)			A♯(6), B♮(7) — C♯(9),
PDA/(SDA):	B♮	A♮	G♮)	B♮			A♮	G♯	
Harmony:			*E maj.:* V$^{6/4}$ + 6th			I + 6th		iii	

Mel.org./key: | | | | | | *1st in B / F♯ bs.* | |

Measure:	137 *cont.*	139	144	146	147	155	157
ActSysPcs:		E♮↗	Fx↗	E♮↗ , Fx↗	E♮↗		
System:		4♯	7♯	4♯	4♯		
PCA/(SCA):	Cx(10), D♯(11)					D♯(11)	E(0)
PDA/(SDA):					F♯	E♮	
Harmony:					vii$^{\varnothing 13}$	I	

Diagram 8.2 Debussy, *Estampes*, "Jardins sous la pluie" continued

Whereas "Un sospiro" receives an overtly Romantic tempo (and mood) marking, *Allegro affettuoso*, Debussy's application of the French *Net et vif*, "clean and lively," gives the piece more of a sense of Classical lines that shun the typically Romantic inclination to agonize over every melodic turn and change of harmonic direction. Whereas the Liszt etude is in ternary form, Debussy's *estampe* is through-composed with a reprise of primary and secondary melodies in the last period of music: in essence, the composition seems as if it comprises a single extended gesture over its entire course with only a couple of momentary diversions that give one pause to deliberate along the way. In Diagram 8.2, the two basic melodies are indicated as "1st" and "2nd," as are the local harmonies implied by the melodies.

The staccato of the opening left-hand notes and their regularized rhythmic presentation, evocative of a Chopin etude (such as the G♭ major "Butterfly Etude" op. 25 no. 9) or prelude (such as op. 28 no.6 with the B minor melody in the left hand), must represent rain falling on the garden. In m. 4 of "Jardins," the mood is darkened immediately by the entrance of B♭ in the top voice part, which also causes a systems shift to a 2♭ system and produces our first dyad conflict (seeFigure 8.2).

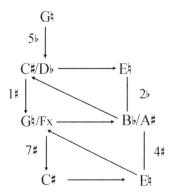

Figure 8.2   1♯ expanded systems matrix

This is followed by another dissonance a fifth away, F♮, that forcefully enters in the bass and creates another dyad conflict, between F♯ and F♮. Although F♮ does not cause another system shift, it does create a typical twentieth-century French modal coloring; in particular, the melodic lines emphasize C against the bass support of A, resulting in a hint of phrygian underpinning to the twisting scalar motion. The F♮ continues, also, to push the mood of the piece into further darkness: in a 2♭ system, C♯ would be necessary to return the systems to the tonic, but no C♯s will enter until m. 21 (see Diagram 8.2). The F♮ is also pc 1 of the PCA.

As the regularity of the *prélude*-style figuration is finally disrupted in m. 16, Debussy continues to introduce more and more flats: E♭ in m. 16 and D♭ in m. 17 – D♭ moves the systems further down to five flats before E♮ brings us back up to two flats again in m. 18. Having encountered D♭, we expect A♭ to come in soon, which it does in m. 19. When G♭ enters in m. 22, the cycle of flats, introduced gradually and, essentially, by fifths, ends. In m. 21, D♭ is respelled as C♯ and the 2♭ system finally returns to the tonic 1♯ system. However, with D♭ having been rewritten as C♯, Debussy now has the opportunity to rationalize motion in the sharp direction: in m. 27, the previous G♭ is reintroduced as the diatonic F♯ and the PCA now moves up to pc 2. With Debussy's change of key signature to six sharps, the "1st" melody (in E minor) that opened the *estampe* is modally altered and transposed to F♯ major, thus reintroducing the first dissonance, the B♭ that occurred back in m. 4, in its enharmonic variant as A♯, whose presence momentarily moves the systems up to a 4♯ system. In m. 31, Debussy alters key signatures again, reducing a six-sharp signature to three; the second note of the descending PDA enters as D♯ in m. 34. However, Debussy must prepare for a harmonic motion in the flat direction so that he can arrive at a rhythmically strong D♭ chord in m. 47. At the change to a three-flat key signature in m. 37, the PDA's D♯ returns as E♭: this is shown in Diagram 8.2 as a dotted bracket in the PDA line between mm. 34 and 37. The dotted bracket is always used here to indicate a tone of either the diatonic or the chromatic array extended by an enharmonic respelling.

With the entry of a C minor sonority in m. 43, Debussy is able to accomplish several tasks. First, the PDA's E♭ is re-emphasized in the tenor voice. Second, the fifth of the C minor chord, G♮, functions as the PCA's pc 3 while simultaneously moving the systems back down to 1♯, a necessary step on the way down to a 5♭ system in m. 47. Notice also that within the intensely chromatic passage between mm. 31 and 43, Debussy had to avoid introducing any G♮s since they would have moved us too soon away from the 4♯ system launched in m. 27. Most interesting is the function of the C minor chord, which acts as a locally verticalized consonant support for a slowly unfolded diminished seventh chord. This is accomplished with the scalar presentation of a segment of a rising octatonic scale through the horizontal space of a major sixth: E♭ to F♮ in m. 37, F♯ to G♯ in m. 39, and A♮ to B♮ in m. 41. The C♮ is the last note in the segment, completing a diminished seventh chord, E♭–F♯–A♮–C♮. This chord is labeled "vii of ... ♯VI" in Diagram 8.2, keeping in mind that D♭ is an enharmonic respelling of C♯.

The arrival at a strongly positioned D♭ major chord in m. 47 has many functions in "Jardins;" as the PCA moves up to pc 4 (A♭) the PDA continues down to D♭. We left a 1♯ system in m. 43, which now continues down to a 2♭ system in m. 45 with the B♭ on the second half of the measure; the D♭ on the first beat of m. 47 moves the systems further down to a 5♭ system, prepared briefly in m. 17 but now extended within a particularly unstable period that begins on the D♭ major sonority. However, without any kind of long-range harmonic progression in D♭ to anchor the harmony, Debussy apparently felt no reason to alter key signatures, and three flats remain throughout this passage. Just as the PCA's F♯ (pc 2, in m. 27) was extended with an enharmonic transformation to G♭ (m. 41), so does the PDA's D♭ ultimately function as a preparation for the motion back into sharps as the *estampe* continues. As one can see in Diagram 8.2, the PDA D♭ in m. 47 is picked up by C♯ in m. 75 with the key signature change to seven sharps. Yet, within this harmonically vacillating transitional period between mm. 47 and 71, Debussy secures the boundaries of the area with a complete double-octave (SCA) rising between the PCA's A♭ in m. 47 and its enharmonic transformation to G♯ in m. 71; this is perhaps the composer's way of anchoring such a lengthy dissonance composed, essentially, of whole-tone collections. The music for this area is presented in Example 8.2.

Example 8.2 Debussy, *Estampes*, "Jardins sous la pluie" (mm. 47–71)

If Example 8.2 is compared with Diagram 8.2, it is apparent that the PCA A♭ is picked up by the SCA A♮ in m. 55, just as Debussy is about to abandon key signatures in m. 56. The line continues to rise by half steps until G♯ is attained in m. 71 with the change of key signature to seven sharps. During the course of this dissonant passage based on whole-tone prolongations, the systems gradually ascend from 5♭ to 2♭ to the tonic 1♯ system, and in m. 77 a 4♯ system is attained. Curiously, even with seven sharps in the key signature, Debussy never has an F✗ in this section and, therefore, the systems never rise to a 7♯ system.

Debussy's diversion into C♯ major between mm. 71 and 99 is organized by a symmetrical formal structure, a short ternary subsection. Measure 75 presents a "new" melody (*a* in Diagram 8.2, actually derived from the "1st" melody), moves into a contrasting section (*b* in m. 83, a melodic transposition of the "1st" melody), and returns to the subsection's opening material with a short extension starting in m. 90 ("*a* + ext." in the diagram). With the change to a seven-sharp key signature, the section's introductory measures on the G♯ octaves (mm. 71–2), and the continuous wobbling between G♯ and F♯ (mm. 73–97), we are led to believe that the G♮ has now moved successfully to G♯ and that the dyad conflict has been settled.

However, in m. 100, Debussy drops key signatures again and G♮ not only returns to re-emphasize the dyad conflict with G♯, but also drags us back down into the tonic 1♯ system. As the section between mm. 100 and 125 unfolds, the G♮ octaves in the bass, a pedal point as significant as the G♯s in the previous seven-sharp section, are asserted forcefully until rapid sixteenths in m. 116 juxtapose G♮ and G♯. Further, G♮ is emphasized with F✗ and G♯ with A♭. (If there were ever a moment in "Jardins" where theories dependent on enharmonic equivalence were proved to be analytically unsatisfactory, this is it!) Debussy has to be careful here: throughout this very chromatic and virtually atonal subsection (mm. 116–25), A♯ must be avoided like the plague since it would prematurely push the systems back up to a 4♯ system and decide the conflict in favor of G♯ – of course, G♯ has to prevail! – too soon. The last gasp of G♮ in m. 125 (part of an SDA which will be briefly discussed below) is settled in the next measure with the final key signature change to four sharps and the return of the wobbling G♯–F♯ in the left hand. G♯s are again present in the reprise of the "2nd" melody in m. 133 and in the reprise of the "1st" melody in m. 136. But the "victory" of G♯ is *uncontested* only after A♯ appears as part of the G♯ minor melodic line and the systems support the final transformation of G♮ to G♯: after the A♯, not a single G♮ appears again.

A little more on the penultimate period between mm. 100 and 125: in m. 103, PCA pc 5 (A♮) enters; it is restated several times, and continues to control the array until a few measures into the last section of the *estampe*, m. 133. This is shown in Diagram 8.2 with an extended bracket between mm. 100 and 133. This section, *1° Tempo (mystérieux)*, starting in m. 100, involves a stabilized PDA B♮ which is prolonged with a short SDA segment between mm. 122 and 125 (SDA B♮, A♮, and G♮ in the diagram). PDA B♮ re-enters at the opening of the final section in m. 126 as part of a B major chord in 6/4 position, and in the diagram, PDA B♮ is bracketed between mm. 100 and 126. Also, since we believe that the (rather significant!) G♯ in the chord at the opening of the last section starting in m. 126 is an impressionistic color tone, it is shown in the diagram as "+6," indicating a sixth above the root of the chord; this notation is used again to describe the E major chord in m. 133 that includes a C♯.

In the final section, from mm. 133 to 157, the 7♯ system is finally raised (in mm. 137, 144, and 146), although only briefly. In fact, it could be argued that the system motivators, F♯ and E♮, simply ensure the integrity of the 4♯ system so that the transformation from E minor to E major can be well underscored: with the arrival of the very low G♮ in m. 125 (the last note of the SDA segment), the motion to E major in the final section is made even more dramatic as G♯s permeate the landscape. The A♯, which is necessary to successfully move the 1♯ system to a 4♯ system (and, therefore, necessary to complete the progress of G♮ to G♯), is first made available in m. 136 during a reprise of the "1st" melody, now stated in G♯ minor. A PCA rise from pc 6 (A♯) to pc 7 (B♮), to pc 9 (C♯) – notice that pc 8, C♮, is absent – to pc 10 (spelled as C♯ – with an F♯ in the vicinity, this is not surprising), and to pc 11 (D♯) occurs rather quickly between mm. 136 and 137. The PCA having attained pc 11 (D♯), we are now watching for the PDA F♯. Both PCA and PDA now create the requisite major sixth to make the final cadence to the E major tonic chord at the end. The PDA F♯ appears in the lowest voice between mm. 147 and 154, while the D♯ which first appears in m. 137 controls the chromatic array until m. 155. In m. 155, E completes the octave descent of the PDA while the PCA's D♯ is momentarily suspended, not reaching the tonic, E♮ (pc 0), until m. 157, the last measure of "Jardins." It is unusual that the two final notes of the PDA, F♯ and E♮, complete their descent in the bass register instead of in the tenor inner voice, but in the absence of a strong V–I cadence in E (the cadence is actually accomplished with a viiφ13 chord to the tonic!) Debussy must make absolutely sure that the cadential major sixth is well defined.

The manner in which Debussy articulates the final cadence is typical of harmonic and melodic motion throughout the composition. By conventional standards of tonality, "Jardins" creates an interesting problem for the music theorist since virtually no phrase is anchored by a full harmonic progression, that is, by a chord progression that moves from the tonic, through an intermediate harmony, to a structural dominant, and then back to the tonic. Even the final cadence does not include the typical dominant-to-tonic formula in the bass. In terms of traditional definitions, aside from a few short melodic statements of the opening melody that generally proceed from the first to the fifth degrees of a scale, there are few (if any!) full harmonic progressions in the whole piece. Therefore, "Jardins," from its beginning until its end, is an experiment in the creation of music that is conceived and executed entirely contrapuntally.

III. Chopin and Debussy Revisit J.S. Bach

For a moment, let us backtrack a little historically. We have seen how Liszt begins a process whereby issues surrounding the missing pitch become the main focus of a composition. We have also seen how Debussy, following in Liszt's footsteps, fully exploits systems organization in his "Jardins" as the foreground function of the triad of conventional tonality fades even further. But the process we are discussing is one that happened gradually over the course of the nineteenth century. To demonstrate this, we will discuss Chopin's and Debussy's musical misreadings[6] of Bach's Prelude in C major from *The Well-Tempered Clavier*, Book 1 (already discussed in Chapter 2) in terms of each composer's use of the inherent implications of the "0" system underlying the C major tonality. Chopin and Debussy were pianists and never lost their interest in Bach's keyboard works, particularly the preludes and fugues of *The Well-Tempered Clavier*. All three composers reflect their unique sensitivity to systems in these three compositions: Bach's treatment of the "0" system's complementary tritone relationships is more implied than realized, whereas Chopin's treatment is somewhat more obvious, and Debussy's response exploits the full potentials of systems with its myriad of musical implications. In a sense, it can be argued that Chopin and Debussy present their own purposeful "misreadings" of Bach's prelude through their own personal early- and late-nineteenth-century reactions to typical eighteenth-century chromaticism. Regarding Chopin's deep interest in Bach's counterpoint, Charles Rosen refers to Chopin as the "greatest master of counterpoint since Mozart:"

> His chief training, in both composition and keyboard playing ... came from a study of Bach, and it was a study that engaged him all his life and which he always recommended to his pupils. His pupils attest to his idolization of Bach. The Well-Tempered Keyboard was the only music he took with him on his famous trip to Majorca with George Sand, and he generally warmed up for concerts by playing some of the preludes and fugues.[7]

In Chapter 2, we discussed the Prelude in C major from *The Well-Tempered Clavier*, Book 1, with respect to the manner in which Bach contrasted E♭, the missing pitch of the "0" system, with F♯, the missing pitch of the 3♭ system. Each of these missing pitches functioned as a system-shift motivator, but their simultaneous appearance consistently had the effect of stabilizing the system in which they occurred, rather than provoking a system modulation, since each prevented the other from moving into a complementary eleven-pitch-class area. Each alone had the potential of causing a system shift, but their appearance together as part of a diminished seventh chord prevented any system shift from occurring. The same situation would have occurred had the system-shift motivators been D♯ and C♮: in a "0" system, the appearance of the missing pitch spelled as D♯ would provoke a system shift to a 3♯ system; however, the simultaneous appearance of C♮, the missing pitch of the 3♯ system, with D♯, would have had the effect of stabilizing the tonic "0" eleven-pitch-class system by pitting the two system-shift motivators against one another.

We begin with Chopin's Prelude in C major op. 28 no. 1, a work that, firstly, pays homage to Bach's C major prelude (note the obvious similarity in the arpeggiated

---

6   The term "misreading" refers to composers of one generation deliberately reinterpreting compositional ideas of composers from a previous generation. For example, the instrumental "chorale" melody of the finale of Brahms's First Symphony would be considered a misreading of the vocal melody (the "Ode to Joy") that informs the finale from Beethoven's Ninth Symphony (see Joseph N. Straus, *Remaking the Past: Musical Modernism and the Influence of the Tonal Tradition* [Cambridge, Massachusetts, 1990]).

7   Charles Rosen, *The Romantic Generation* (Cambridge, Massachusetts, 1995), p. 285. For a discussion of Chopin's attitude of "counterpoint and the single line," see pp. 285–302.

texture) and, secondly, uses the alternative pair of complementary system-shift motivators, C♯ and D♮, in very much the same way that Bach employed E♭ and F♯. In Chopin's prelude, the initial chromatic gesture appears in m. 6, a simple F♯ chromatic passing tone that tonicizes G major and emphasizes the half cadence at the end of the first phrase in m. 8. (Bach's first chromatic, F♯, is also placed in m. 6.) However, F♯, which immediately gives rise to a dyad conflict with its diatonic counterpart, F♮, motivates the appearance of C♯ in m. 13, a note that not only creates a new dyad conflict – this one with the tonic – but also initiates the (PCA (see Diagram 8.3): it must be kept in mind that the consequence of a single chromatic gesture often provokes the introduction of others along the circle of fifths.[8] Chopin punctuates C♯ in the right-hand part with a concurrent C♮ in the left hand, thus producing a rather painful dissonance, even if a short-lived one. Significantly, Chopin's original conception of this measure did not pit C♯ against C♮, but against D♮, a choice that would have avoided the significant dyad conflict between C♮ and C♯. This can be clearly seen in an autograph of the collection of this opus that resides in the Biblioteka Narodowa in Warsaw, Poland.[9]

As one can see in Diagram 8.3, the PCA is unfolded quickly over the course of the next phrase. In the Bach prelude, the first occurrence of pc 3 was spelled as E♭, but its system-motivating potential was neutralized by a concurrent F♯. In the Chopin, however, pc 3 enters as D♯ in m. 14; however, its ability to alter systems is prevented by the C♮ in the left hand. The "0" system is thus stabilized. As the unfolding PCA continues to ascend, the Primary *Diatonic* Array is also set in motion and it begins its descent. The PDA C is picked up at the beginning of the second phrase in m. 9 and continues to B and then to A in an inner voice of m. 13. When pc 3 is reached in m. 13, the PDA reaches G and moves down to F immediately in the next measure, concurrently with the PCA's arrival at F. The convergence on F in both PCA and PDA on a IV6 chord is another reference to the Bach prelude: the primary motivic material in the Bach prelude, E–F–F–E in the upper voice, is draped over its first four measures, and Chopin, as he tips his hat to the master, must find a manner in which the coda of his prelude (mm. 25–34) – which states and restates E and its neighbor note F – may be prepared. In terms of voice leading, that prominent IV6 chord of m. 15 initiates a chromatic voice exchange with the diminished seventh chord in m. 22 (A to A, and F to F♯); in terms of the descending PDA, there is considerable motivation for Chopin to stop the PDA from descending further. The long-range motion from F to F♯ recalls the prelude's first F♯ as a bit of passing chromaticism in the eight-measure opening passage which had the effect of emphasizing F. The PDA F in m. 15 is allowed to ring out until m. 21. The voice exchange creates a dramatic extension of F which is framed by E in mm. 14 and 23.

---

8 See Henry Burnett and Shaugn O'Donnell, "Linear Ordering of the Chromatic Aggregate in Classical Symphonic Music," *Music Theory Spectrum*, 18/1 (1996): 22–50.

9 The manuscript of this prelude can be viewed on the website of the European Library, although the reader will profit greatly by saving it as a picture file and increasing its size and resolution: http://libraries.theeuropeanlibrary.org/Poland/treasures_en.xml. It is a page of an autograph from 1831–39: "24. Preludes pour le pianoforte dediés à mon ami J.C. Kessler par F. Chopin."

Dyads: F♮/F♯, D♮/D♯

Measure:	1	9	10	11	13	14	15
Active System Pcs:	"0"						
System:						(C♮/D♯)	
PCA:	C♮ (0)	---	B		C♯ (1), D♮ (2)	D♯ (3), E♮ (4)	F
PDA:	C	---	B		A	G	F
Harmony:	I	---	V 6/5	I	ii 6/5	V 4/3 of …	IV6

Measure:	18	19	20	21	22	24	25-34
ASPcs:							
System:					(C♮/D♯)		
PCA:	F♯ (6), G♮ (7)	G♯ (8), A♮ (9)	A♯ (10), [B♮ (11)]	-----		B♮ (11)	C♮ (0)
PDA:	-----		[F]	E		D	C
Harmony:	V6	I	V 4/3	I6	Ø7	V7	I (4-3)

Diagram 8.3 Chopin, Prelude in C major op. 28 no. 1

As the PDA continues its descent to E (m. 21), to D (m. 24), and to C (m. 25), the PCA has in m. 20 already reached pc 11 (B), a pitch class that must be sustained while the PDA concludes its descent. The unfoldings of both PDA and PCA are completed with the PDA D moving to C between mm. 24 and 25 and, simultaneously, the PCA rising from pc 11 to pc 0. Chopin's final ten measures parallel Bach's final four.

Concerning the prelude's dyad conflicts, the developmentally motivational significance of the dyads F♮/F♯ and C♮/C♯ has already been discussed. The other outstanding dyad can easily be determined by viewing Chopin's use of the missing pitch, D♯, and its interaction with its diatonic analog, D♮. In the manner of Classical developmental procedures, Chopin resolves all the prelude's dyad conflicts before the close of the work. Thus, the C♮/C♯ conflict resolves with the return of tonic harmony at the coda in m. 25. In a similar manner, the conflict between D♯ and D♮ concludes in favor of its diatonic variant at the structural dominant in m. 24; consequently, the PDA pitch D in that measure both acts as consonant support to the PCA note B (pc 11) and is, at the same time, the final resolution of D♯. However, Chopin reserves the final resolution of F♯ to F♮ for the coda, whose primary purpose is to iterate the neighbor-note relationship between E and F. Thus the restatement of Bach's primary motive has two functions: the first is to accentuate the diatonic neighbor-note relationship, and the second is to resolve a prominent dyad conflict.

There is one other bit of evidence that Chopin deliberately planned his prelude as a homage to Bach; this has to do with the Golden Section. You may recall from Chapter 2 that we pointed out that Bach's carefully chosen placement of the first diminished seventh chord (in m. 22, F♯–A–C–E♭, containing system-shift motivators E♭ and F♯), was at a point that divided the prelude as close to the Golden Section as possible. In the Chopin prelude, the composer makes an eight-measure crescendo and five-measure *stretto* (incidentally, both 5 and 8 are numbers of the Fibonacci series – 0, 1, 1, 2, 3, 5, 8, 13, and so on – which can be used to generate the Golden Section) culminate on a *fortissimo* I6 chord in m. 21 that will give way, in the next measure, to the diminished seventh chord at the other end of the voice exchange that began in m. 15. Bach's diminished seventh chord was spelled F♯–A–C–E♭; Chopin's is enharmonically spelled C♮–D♯–F♯–A. Either way, however, they each stabilize the "0" system around a diminished seventh chord at a physical point that is very close to the 0.618...:1 proportion that closely approximates the Golden Section. Incidentally, while Chopin's placement of his diminished seventh chord is very slightly different both metrically and rhythmically from Bach's (even though Chopin places his diminished seventh chord in *the same measure* as Bach's, m. 22), Chopin's choice of numbers of measures, 34 as opposed to Bach's 35, is indicative of Fibonacci thinking. His choice of 34 measures may also explain the necessity for the unusual notation of the last chord of this prelude, which prevents the prelude from having only 33 measures. (Debussy also used the Fibonacci series to determine the length of sections and periods in his "Jardins sous la pluie.")

To continue our discussion of the attitudes of Chopin and Debussy toward C major, we turn to the opening piece in Debussy's *Children's Corner*, titled "Doctor Gradus ad Parnassum." Debussy's six-piece piano suite, a small collection of character pieces, was composed in 1906–08 and was dedicated to his daughter. Although Debussy's

"Doctor Gradus" may have been written to satirize Muzio Clementi's collection of instructional piano studies called *Gradus ad Parnassum* (in the last number of Debussy's set, "Golliwogg's Cakewalk," he takes aim at Wagner's *Tristan* as well), there are enough similarities among the Debussy, Chopin, and Bach preludes (all in C major) to warrant comparisons. Like Chopin's prelude written seven decades earlier, Debussy's "Doctor Gradus" also appears to have been influenced by J.S. Bach's C major prelude and is in the arpeggiated style of a Bach prelude. Debussy spoke respectfully of Bach and mentioned him often in his essay "Monsieur Croche, the Dilettante Hater"[10] and refers to his daughter Chouchou playing Bach's keyboard works in his letters. Debussy was also quite familiar with the works of Chopin and had been asked by Jacques Durand to create a new Chopin edition. With this request, Debussy was inspired to write his own *Douze études*, which was published in 1915 and was "dedicated to the memory of Frédéric Chopin."[11]

Yet, Debussy's "prelude," with its allegiance to both Chopin and Bach, is also a purposeful misreading, so to speak, of both his predecessors' preludes. Its length, for example, is sufficiently swelled to allow some typically late-nineteenth-century chromaticism that stimulates some quick systems shifts. Whereas neither Chopin nor Bach before him allowed for any extensive system shifts, Debussy's brief key signature changes to two flats and then to five have him expanding on the (unrealized) modulatory system potential of Bach's E♭/F♯ system-motivator dichotomy. Rather, in his "prelude," Debussy explores the very aspect of system modulation that Bach avoided, moving the music into full-blown flat-oriented system modulations. To mark the system shifts, Debussy deliberately constructs a textural change from the constant sixteenth-note figuration that began the "prelude" to that of eighths, before once more regaining his diatonic composure with the prelude-like figuration that started the composition. Both the chromaticism and piece's length – necessary for that degree of chromatic elaboration – take Chopin's and Bach's wholesome, cleaned-and-pressed C major preludes and wonderfully distort them, allowing Debussy to place his unique mark on the whole business, while he thumbs his nose at his own past at the same time.

---

10   Claude Debussy, "Monsieur Croche the Dilettante Hater," in *Three Classics in the Aesthetic of Music* (New York, 1962), pp. 1–71.

11   Roger Nichols, "Claude Debussy" in Stanley Sadie (ed.), *The New Grove Twentieth-Century French Masters* (New York, 1986), p. 47. Cf. François Lesure and Roger Nichols (eds), *Debussy Letters* (London, 1987), p. 296; Debussy revised Chopin's complete works and they were published by Durand between 1915 and 1917. German editions were not available during World War I, but Debussy respectfully acknowledges Ignaz Friedman's Chopin edition published by Breitkopf.

Main dyad conflicts: C♮/C♯, E♮/E♭, F♮/F♯, A♮/A♭

Form: Opening statement   C.S.

Measure:	1	5	6	7	11		21	22	23	24	25
Act Sys Pcs:											
System	"0"										
PCA	C♮(0)							C♮(0)		C♯(1) D♮(2)	
PDA/*SDA:*	C♮	B♮, A♮	G♮	F♮	E♮		D♮	C♮	B♮		
Harmony:	I			ii^{6/5/♮‑♭}	III			"III^7"	I		

Form: Retrans.   Recap

Measure:	25	26	27	31	33	35	37		45	47	51	55	57
ASPcs:						E♭↗ G♭↗			A♮↗				
System:	[C♯(1)D(2)]					3♭, 6♭			3♭				
PCA						E♭(3)			E♮(4)				
PDA/*SDA:*	B♮	A♮	G♮	F♮			E♭		G♮		F♮	E♮	
Harmony:	I^{9/♭7}			♭VII^{8/5/3 ‑ 9/♭6/4}			♭VI^{13}		V		I	ii^{6/5/♮‑♭} Aug.	I

Diagram 8.4 Debussy, *The Children's Corner*, "Doctor Gradus ad Parnassum": systems/PCA/PDA

Form: *Coda* (*"Très animé"*)

	64	65	66	67	68	69	70		73	74	75
Measure:											
ASPcs:					F♯↗		(E♭/F♯)				
System:					"0"						
PCA		F♮(5)			F♯(6), G♮(7)	↙ ↘	A♮(9) B♭(10)			B♮(11) C♮(0)	
PDA/*SDA*:	[D–C		D–C	C]					E♮	D♮	C♮
Harmony:							IV^7			vii$^{\varnothing 4/3}$	I

Diagram 8.4 Debussy, *The Children's Corner*, "Doctor Gradus ad Parnassum": systems/PCA/PDA continued

Diagram 8.4 details a PCA and PDA analysis of Debussy's "prelude." Like Bach and Chopin, Debussy opens with a quick sixteenth-note pattern and establishes an immediate relationship between E and F in mm. 7 and 10. The essence of the next passage, between mm. 13 and 21, is to stress the E in order to play F off against it as a neighboring sonority. However, it is the coloristic portions of the accompaniment harmonizing the neighbor-note relationship that concern us since it is here that the chromatic notes become increasingly prominent: in mm. 9–10, the A that was part of the subdominant harmony's inner voice is flatted to A♭, and it is then enharmonically recalled as G♯ in m. 11 as part of an E major triad (labeled "III" in the diagram). With the presence of A♭ (establishing a dyad conflict with the diatonic A♮), we expect that the introduction of B♭ and E♭ will not be far away. With G♯, however, we expect to see F♯ and C♯, and both notes enter soon in m. 17; the A♯ that enters with these two, instead of fulfilling an expectation of the entrance of D♯, will be enharmonically respelled as B♭: in m. 28, B♭ enters just after A♯ resolves to A♮ in the previous measure. Now spelled as B♭, this note will help to motivate an excursion into the flat side of the circle of fifths. This is significant for two reasons: (1) Bach never explored the flat side of the circle since the modulatory system potential of each of his E♭s had been neutralized by concurrent F#s; and (2) Chopin's choice of D♯ for pc 3 virtually eliminated the possibility of a system modulation in such a short composition since a simple restatement of the tonic C♮ would prevent modulation into a 3♯ system.

The first period of "Doctor Gradus," ending in m. 21, culminates in an unusual chromatic element, A♭, which, on the surface, appears to be a "misspelled" G♯. Also, with the sophistication of compositional layers, a new element appears: an SDA, very much in the style of Liszt. The descent of the PDA (which is in bold letters on the diagram) is frozen momentarily between the opening of the piece and the counterstatement (labeled "C.S." on the diagram) that begins in m. 22. As in the Liszt diagram earlier, the notes of the SDA are italicized so that they can easily be distinguished from the notes of the PDA. In this passage, not too differently, actually, from the organization of a sonata-form opening statement, Debussy anchors C major and simultaneously brings in certain dyad conflicts that will figure significantly as the piece develops. The difference, however, from a standard opening statement of a sonata is that Debussy has provided a high degree of stabilization by including a complete lower-level diatonic octave descent. Notice on the diagram that the PCA has not yet begun to ascend. Bach does this as well: a complete SDA octave descent occurs between mm. 1 and 19 of his prelude. (Chopin included no SDA.)

With the counterstatement in m. 22, Debussy quickly moves away from C major, an option avoided by Bach and Chopin. The pervasive application of B♭ allows a smooth transition to a new key signature, two flats, in m. 33, after which, by m. 35, we find ourselves in a 3♭ system with the entry of E♭, which creates a dyad conflict with E♮. However, Debussy's emphasis on the flat side of the circle is pushed further with the entry of G♭ (just under the E♭) in m. 35. Keeping in mind that G♭ is the missing pitch of the 3♭ system, we now find ourselves in a 6♭ system. This prompts Debussy's alteration of key signature again (to five flats in m. 41), and a pedal point on A♭ ensues, picking up the unusual A♭ that appeared at the end of the prelude's first period (m. 21) and that very same initial chromatic that entered back in

m. 9. As the diagram shows, Debussy's method of stabilizing the area between mm. 33 and 44 is to pick up the PDA note G (m. 31) and allow it to descend further through the application of notes associated with another SDA. In this case, however, with the turn to flat harmonies, Debussy substitutes F♮ and E♭ for the regular PDA/SCA notes F♮ and E♮. Therefore, the regular PDA notes have been modally inflected to accommodate both the E♭/E♮ dyad conflict and a large-scale flat area anchored with a system shift from "0" to a 3♭ system to a 6♭ system.

Until now, the term "dyad conflict," meaning a dissonant relationship between a diatonic note and one of its chromatic counterparts, has been sufficient to describe a certain aspect of a composer's developmental arsenal. However, with this work, we see again the possibility of the *dyad* conflict expanded into a *triad* conflict. In "Doctor Gradus," it would be difficult to find another way of describing the presence and use of three chromatic variants of A (A♭, A♮, and A♯) within the relatively short span of a 76-measure character piece. However, just as the appearance of A♭ allowed us to expect the eventual entrances of B♭ and E♭, an A♯ suggests the eventual appearance of F♯, C♯, G♯, and D♯. If we align the notes used in the prelude in the order of the circle of fifths with the diatonic notes of C major in the middle, the flat chromatics on the left, and the sharp chromatics on the right –

$$G♭–D♭–A♭–E♭–B♭ \; // \; F–C–G–D–A–E–B \; // \; F♯–C♯–G♯–[D♯]–A♯$$

– we can understand why an A♯ should suggest the eventual appearance of D♯. Yet that never happens. Perhaps Debussy avoids D♯, one of the enharmonic versions of the missing pitch and the one used by Chopin, so that E♭, the variant used by Bach, would receive a certain degree of distinction.

At the *1° Tempo* in m. 45, Debussy begins to recapitulate the opening. Also, the A♮ in m. 45 returns us to the 3♭ system that never had a chance to assert itself in m. 35 because of the simultaneous appearance of G♭. However, with the absence of F♯, we stay in the 3♭ complementary system. The second difference from the prelude's opening is the substitution of G♯ (m. 11) by A♭ (m. 55) and the modification of the previous E major chord with an A♭ augmented triad. As A♭ did originally, it motivates the presence of E♭ and reasserts the dyad conflict that initiated the system modulations before. In terms of systems, the E♭ in m. 58 simply confirms the 3♭ system. As the phrase continues to unfold, we find ourselves focused on the E♮/E♭ and A♮/A♭ dyad conflicts, which beg for resolution.

At the *très amimé* race to the finish (m. 67), all dyad (and triad!) conflicts are again stated and now resolved. First, m. 68 contains the F♯, as part of an F♯ major triad, needed to regain the tonic "0" system. But the E♭ still needs to resolve to its diatonic variant. Also, the F♯ that canceled the 3♭ system still needs to resolve to F♮. On top of that, A♯ makes another appearance and, thus, requires resolution as well. To make matters just a bit more complicated, Debussy has also raised the specter of C♯, a note that has not been seen since m. 26. While the arpeggiated C major triad in mm. 71 and 72 helps to restore the tonic, it is actually the IV7 chord in m. 73, the one that Debussy marks *fortissimo* (the only *fortissimo* in the piece thus far), that settles every single conflict that Debussy has raised: F♮ resolves F♯, A♮ resolves both A♯ and A♭, C♮ resolves C♯, and, finally, E♮ resolves E♭.

We would like to make one final observation concerning dyad conflicts in this work and about dyad conflicts generally. The most prominent dyads in the Bach prelude were E♮/E♭ and F♮/F♯; the C♮/C♯ dyad was prominent as well. The F♯–A♮–C♮–E♭ diminished seventh chord raised a prominent dissonant element, but also secured the "0" system by counterposing the system-consonant tritone, C♮–F♯, against its system-consonant complement, E♭–A♮. In the Chopin prelude, the significant dyad conflicts involving C♮/C♯, D♮/D♯, and F♮/F♯, and the tonic matrix diminished seventh chord C♮–D♯–F♯–A♮, played an important role in helping to fix the underlying "0" system firmly by counterposing the C♮–F♯ system-consonant tritone against its A♮–D♯ complement. In Debussy's "Doctor Gradus," the notes of the C♮–E♭–F♯ diminished triad (the most crucial material of m. 68) as well as its more foreground components, A♯ and C♯, both provided a "0" system stabilization and resurrected every dyad and triad conflict previously raised. In the previous chapter, we saw how, in Chaikovsky's Symphony no. 4 in F minor, the pitches F♮, G♯, B♮, and D♮ played a significant role in the way the composer's material was presented, developed, and expanded.

With the eleven-pitch-class system of triadic tonality organized around equal subdivisions of the octave into tritones (ones that yield the system-consonant tritone of the tonic octave) and around minor thirds that bisect the system-consonant tritone at the locus of the missing pitch, it would seem understandable, even logical, that a composer would gravitate toward chromatic conflicts (both dyadic and, eventually, triadic) that are part of the tonic system matrix. More specifically, a composer might be inclined to assemble his dyad and triad conflicts around a diminished seventh chord that includes the tonic pitch. With the increasing of chromatic intensity over the course of the nineteenth century, composers were able immediately to establish a foreground of intense chromaticism and to stabilize that dissonance simultaneously with the use of the diminished seventh chord, particularly one including the tonic. Therefore, the diminished seventh chord begins to play the role of a *functional system stabilizer*. The emergence of a stabilizing diminished seventh chord in the nineteenth century is, of course, on the borderline of being counterintuitive. However, an awareness of this possibility may in the future, or so we hope, provide some insight to the manner in which some twentieth-century composers, such as Béla Bartók, organize their foregrounds.

IV. Schoenberg and the Expressionist Movement

At the turn of the twentieth century, Arnold Schoenberg's first-period works pushed the envelope of common-practice tonality to its limits, but still maintained the compositional features previously discussed. His early compositions from the 1890s suggest influences from both sides of the Romantic-period spectrum, represented by Brahms and Wagner. His indebtedness to grand-scale single-movement composition by Franz Liszt and Richard Strauss is evident in his tone poem *Pelleas und Melisande* (1902–03). The opening of *Gurrelieder* (1900) has an almost Debussyan sense of color and slow harmonic unfoldings as the poetic imagery suggests a sunset. In his songs *Vier Lieder für eine Singstimme und Klavier* op. 2 (1899), Arnold Schoenberg sets German Expressionist poetry that reflects both the anxiety of a world teetering on the brink of conflagration and the obsessive musings of the Viennese on the subjects of sex, eroticism, and nightmares of the subconscious mind. For us, Schoenberg's op. 2 songs are especially significant for their tendencies to apply system shifts as support for extremely vivid poetic images. Whereas a composer from an earlier style period would have introduced non-harmonic tones gradually, Schoenberg presents the entire gamut of chromatic pitch classes immediately. Such is the nature of Schoenberg's rapidly evolving harmonic language that, within the decade, he will become so thoroughly saturated by a fully chromatic foreground that he will dispense with key signatures and functional triads altogether; yet we will discover that the interaction of complementary eleven-pitch-class systems still remains as a vital force even within an atonal harmonic language!

Example 8.1 is the first ten measures of "Erwartung" ("Expectation"), the first song from Schoenberg's four op. 2 *Lieder*. The poem of "Erwartung" concerns a man about to meet his lover. As he stands before her villa, he recalls their last encounter as he examines a ring on his hand whose glistening opal stones mirror the colors of a pond and villa in front of his lover's home. The song is in E♭ major; Figure 8.2 illustrates the 3♭ systems matrix of the piece. On the downbeat of m. 1, the C♭ in the vocal line and upper piano part is a neighbor tone to B♭; the C♭ will be in dyad conflict with the diatonic C♮, the latter pitch *not entering until m. 4*. A similar situation occurs with A♮, a neighbor tone to B♭: its dyadic counterpart, the diatonic A♭, will not enter until m. 3. The G♭ is a neighbor to G♮. Each of these dyadic displacements of notes of the E♭ major scale is part of a diminished seventh chord with E♭ as the tonic, although Schoenberg presents these notes without a straightforward display of a verticalized diminished seventh chord until the middle of m. 9 (this is a voice-leading chord that passes between the boundaries of a chromatic voice exchange between the first chord in m. 8 and the first chord in m. 10, gaining a certain understated quality). The final constituent of the E♭ diminished seventh chord, the tonic E♭, is not contrapuntally destabilized until m. 4, where its dissonant dyadic counterpart, E♮, tripled in the voice and piano parts, initiates the rising PCA.

Example 8.3 Schoenberg, "Erwartung" op. 2 no. 2 (mm. 1–10)

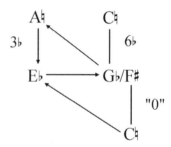

Figure 8.3   3♭ system matrix

In the first chord of m. 1, there is an immediate confrontation of system-shift motivators as G♭ attempts to push the prevailing 3♭ system to a 6♭ system (see Figure 8.1) but is prevented from doing so by A♮. In the poetry, we envision a sea-green pond in front of a red villa ("Aus dem meer-grünen Teiche neben der roten Villa").[12] Perhaps the turn figure around B♭ and neighbors C♭ and A♮ signify the opposition of the red–green complements. Tonally, however, the effect of the G♭ and A♮ system-shift motivators is to secure the 3♭ system. In m. 3, on the word "dead" ("toten"), the G♭ in the piano part is able to move us down into a 6♭ system at the point where the A♮ is superseded by its diatonic counterpart A♭. However, in the next measure, A♮ (the missing pitch of the 6♭ system) returns, restoring the tonic 3♭ system while E♭ is displaced by E♮ toward the end of the measure. Symbolically, the E♮ enters and the 3♭ system returns as we see the moon shining ("scheint der Mond") under the dead oak. With the entry of pc 1 (E♮) and pc 2 (F♮) at the phrase end, we expect some activity. The note D♯ is brought in as an enharmonic variant of the tonic, perhaps to deflect any interference from the previous E♭. Also in the vocal part, the phrase ending on B♮ provides an enharmonic respelling of the previous C♭. Then, in the poetry, "where her dark image reaches through the water," a man stands and removes a ring from his hand: from the 3♭ system, an F♯ enters, in conflict with E♭, trying to push us toward a "0" system. However, the systems are stuck with the continued presence of E♭, just as the man waits momentarily as he anticipates his love, which, at this instant, is as non-progressive as the accompanying harmony. We expect some activity as the PCA rises to pc 3 (F♯), pc 4 (G♮), and pc 5 (A♭) in mm. 6 and 7. Pc 6 (A♮) enters in m. 8 and resolves to pc 7 (B♭) in the next measure. However, the harmony is almost irritatingly stable as E♭ continues to prevent F♯ from accomplishing a system modulation. Expectations abound.

---

12 Walter Frisch has an excellent analysis of the text, particularly with reference to the coloristic aspects of the harmony, in *The Early Works of Arnold Schoenberg: 1893–1908* (Berkeley and Los Angeles, 1993), pp. 92–8, with a translation of Richard Dehmel's poetry.

Dyads/triads: E♭/E♮, G♮/G♭, A♭/A♮, C♮/C♭/C♯

Form (ternary):	*A section*						
Measure:	1	3	4	6	7	8	9...
Active System Pcs:	(G♭/A♮)	G♭ ↗	A♮ ↗		(F#/E♭)		
System:	3♭	6♭	3♭				
PCA:			E♮(1) F♮(2)	F#(3) G♮(4)	A♭(5) A♮(6)	B♭(7)	
PDA:	E♭			D	C		B♭
Harmony:	I	IV♭4/3	V/VI♮	VI♮		passing 6/4	
Text:	Sea-green pond,	dead oak,	shines,	her dark ...	image	reaches, stands a	man

Form:		*B section*		
Measure:	...9	10	12	13	14
ASPcs:	(F#/E♭)		(F#/E♭)		F#↗
System:					
PCA:			B♮(8)...		
PDA:	A♭		G...		
Harmony:	dim 7	ii6/5	V7/VI♮...		"0"
Text:	removes	ring from his	hand.	Three opals glisten,	

Form:					*transition*		*A' section*	
Measure:	17	18	19	20	21	23	24	26
ASPcs:	(D#/C♮)	(G♭/A♮)	E♭↗(G♭/A♮)		(E♭/F#)	(G♭/A♮)		(G♭/A♮)
System:		3♭	3♭					(3♭)
PCA:	C♭(8)	C♭(8)	C♮(9)	[C♭(8), C♮(9)]	D♮(11)		E♭(0)	
PDA:	...G		F			[E♭ ant.]	E♭...	...E♭
Harmony:	"Aug6" of	V6/4			V 6/3	5/3		I
Text:	sink.	And he kisses them,	his eyes glow	like the sea-green	depths:	a window opens up.		From

Diagram 8.5 Schoenberg, "Erwartung" op. 2 no. 2

Form:				
Measure:	26	27	28 — 30	32 — 37
ASPcs:	(G♭/A♮)		G♭ ↘ (C♭/C♮/C♯ triad)	
System:			6♭	
PCA:			[**D♮(11)**	**E♭(0)**]
PDA:			[**F**	**E♭**]
Harmony:			V	I
Text:	a red villa	near the dead oak	a pale woman's hand beckons to him.	

Diagram 8.5 Schoenberg, "Erwartung" op. 2 no. 2 continued

Example 8.3 gives only the first ten measures of "Erwartung," the *A* section of the ternary-form *Lied*; however, Diagram 8.2 provides analytical material for the entire PCA, PDA, and basic harmony for the whole song. You will notice that the *A* section allows the PCA to unfold pcs 1–7, while the PDA descends from E♭ to G. The *B* section, between mm. 12 and 18, freezes both PCA and PDA: this is accomplished by having the systems move from 3♭ to "0" and the foreground events unfold sharp-key harmonies. In the text, the man, instead of immediately proceeding to the villa, delays for a moment as he views the ring that he has taken off his finger, noticing the red and green sparks of the three pale opals. With pc 8 entering as B♮ in m. 12, and the harmony moving into sharps (perhaps representing the glistening of the stones), the next PCA pitch (pc 9), C♮, is unavailable as C♮s local function is to play the role of a system-shift motivator continually clashing against D♯. Therefore, the systems remain in "0" while the man contemplates the similarities of the stones' colors to the sea-green pond and the red villa. Meanwhile the PDA sits on G. In terms of the unfolding chromatic octave at this point, C♮ is not yet able to be activated as pc 9 since it exists only on a secondary level of chromatic structure. The PCA C♮ does not enter (although the note C♮ is often present) until after pc 8, B♮, is transformed into its enharmonic counterpart, C♭, in m. 18. This transformation is prepared on the last eighth note of m. 17, where a B dominant seventh chord is actually an enharmonically respelled augmented sixth chord (B♮, a C♭ "in disguise," resolves to B♭ – of an E♭ 6/4 chord – in the piano left hand while A♮ resolves to B♭ in the right hand). The next vocal note, C♭, our respelled pc 8 (B♮) from m. 12, moves to pc 9, C♮, in the next measure.

In m. 19, as the man kisses the stones and his eyes reflect the sea-green depths, both PCA and PDA continue their journeys and the systems return to a 3♭ system. Pc 9 (C♮) and the PDA F are both attained in m. 19. In m. 21, the song's structural dominant is reached. The F♯/E♭ system-shift motivators secure the 3♭ system, and pc 9 goes directly to pc 11 (C♯, as pc 10 is absent); F remains in the tenor, not having been displaced since its arrival in m. 19. With the return to a 3♭ system and the only unfoldings of the PCA and PDA now accomplished, the woman opens the window and beckons to the man to join her as E♭ appears in the bass, an anticipation of the PDA E♭ that enters in the next measure. We are now in the modified *A¹* of the ternary form, and its return to the tonic assures the imminent rendezvous of the lovers. As if in a glory of chromatic ecstasy, the diatonic C is contrasted with both C♯ and C♭, particularly in mm. 30 and 31, and in very close proximity. The ecstasy of the music at this point is not unlike that at the conclusion of Richard Strauss's *Salome*, composed in the following year (1904–05). At the close of the opera, the C♯ major tonality represents Salome's ecstasy (or, rather, madness), soon to be shattered by C minor at her death.

The aspects of "Erwartung" that are most significant here for our present discussion, however, are the ways in which the diminished seventh chord on the note E♭ is responsible for securing the background harmony. The three pairs of system-shift motivators – E♭/F♯, G♭/A♮, C♮/D♯ – are all essential components of the 3♭ system matrix and ultimately responsible for securing E♭ as tonic. We have seen, also, how in Debussy's "Jardins," which is further down the road toward the abolition of conventional triadic tonality than "Erwartung," system motivators, chromatic and diatonic arrays, diminished seventh chords, and so on play increasingly significant roles in a composition given the absence of the triad as a background structural device, in the voice-leading sense of the term.

It is in relation to the nature of a work such as this that we propose to introduce a new theory to both raise and answer as many questions as we can. However, at this junction, we pose a question about compositions in the early twentieth century that abandoned traditional triadic tonality, even to the point of dropping key signatures. We saw previously how in Schoenberg's "Erwartung" the organization of the song was more determined by long-range unfoldings of minor thirds (augmented seconds) through the opposition of system motivators than by anything having to do with the traditional role of triads; yet there is still a structural dominant in the traditional sense. A little further advanced is Debussy's "Jardins," where an almost total absence of conventional harmonic progression means that the musical landscape must be even more strongly systematized by the structures created by the missing pitch and by dyad conflicts. The presence, too, of Debussy's inclusion of substantial secondary arrays in "Jardins" creates new possibilities for compositional and developmental exploration.

What of later composition? By 1909, Schoenberg and his colleagues in the Second Viennese School realized that triadic tonality had reached its extreme limits and that now, perhaps, the triad could be successfully liberated from its previous position in the formal and structural integrity of a composition. Schoenberg had already internalized the new features of compositions whose use of equal subdivisions of the octave no longer referred to the triad as a high-level structure. Schoenberg himself, during an era of daring experiments at the turn of the century, had suggested that whole-tone scales and quartal harmonies, harmonies based on segments of the chromatic scale ordered as series of perfect fourths, particularly six-note harmonies, would eventually create the language of a new kind of music.[13] The question remains, however, whether eleven-pitch-class systems, missing pitches, and chromatic arrays remain in the "free atonal" music of Schoenberg as the bases for compositional development. We will very briefly examine, then, the opening of the first and most famous of Schoenberg's *Drei Klavierstücke* op. 11 no. 1, from 1909. The same year, Schoenberg also composed his 15-song *Lieder* cycle, *Das Buch der hängenden Gärten* op. 15, based on the Expressionistic poetry of Stefan Georg. Both compositions are totally chromatic and shy away from the overt use of vertical triads, particularly the latter work. In contrast with his technique in the compositions written just before them, Schoenberg completely abandons key signatures, whereas Debussy, toward the end of his middle period, would only dispense with key signatures for short stretches of music, as we saw in "Jardins." However, the approaches taken by Debussy and Schoenberg are not ultimately that dissimilar.

---

13   Arnold Schoenberg, *Theory of Harmony*, California Library Reprint Series (Berkeley, 1983), pp. 390–422, originally published as *Harmonielehre* (Vienna, 1911). The implications of Schoenberg's theoretical writings have been discussed extensively by Henry Weinberg (b. 1931). Weinberg's theories have been explored in Edward Smaldone's "Linear Analysis of Selected Posttonal Works of Arnold Schoenberg: Toward an Application of Schenkerian Concepts to the Music of the Posttonal Era," Ph.D. dissertation, City University of New York Graduate Center, 1986.

Main dyad conflicts: E♭/E♮, F♮/F♯, A♭/A♮

Form:	A₁							A₂					
	a	b	a	c				b					a'
Period:	1		2					3					
Measure:	1	4	9	12	13	14	17	18	19	20	24	25	26
Act Sys Pcs:						D♯↗	C♮↗	E♭↗			F♯↗	E♭↗	
Systems:	"0"					3♯	"0"	3♭			"0"	3♭	
PCA/(SCA)		C♮(0)		C♯(1)	D♮(2)	D♯(3) E♮(4)	D♮(2)	E♭(3)					(E♭/F♯)
PDA		C♮		B♮					A♮				

Form:		b'				B
Period:				4		
Measure:	27	28	30	31	32	34
Act Sys Pcs:	G♭↗	A♮↗	(E♭/F♯)	F♯↗		
Systems:	6♭	3♭		"0"		
PCA/(SCA):		E♮(4)	←——→	F♯(6)	G♮(7) F♯(6)	G♮(7)
PDA:				G♮		

Diagram 8.6 Schoenberg, *Drei Klavierstücke* op. 11, no. 1

Since all atonal music is written without a specific key signature, one would logically infer that the system governing these pieces is invariably a "0" system. For example, if we examine the first period of Schoenberg's op. 11 no. 1 (mm. 1–11), we find that all notes of the chromatic *except for E♭/D♯* are present, indicating that Schoenberg may have considered, consciously or otherwise, that E♭ and/or D♯ was the missing pitch of a prevailing "0" system. In addition, we need to test the hypothesis that a PCA and, even, a PDA or its remnants are operational in this music. While we would not argue that op. 11 no. 1 is in C major, the question arises that if we are in a "0" system, is it also possible that Schoenberg might be unfolding diatonic and chromatic octaves from C to C? We will explore this briefly below.

Further questions are raised with an analysis of dyadic (and/or triadic, and so on) conflicts in the first period of the music. In mm. 1 and 2, within the three beats of the end of m. 1 and the first two of m. 2, Schoenberg presents us with three different Gs: G♯ and G♮ in the melody and G♭ in the bass. As we continue into the second phrase beginning in m. 4, we find dyad conflicts with B♭ and B♮, A♮ and A♯, D♮ and D♭, and F♮ and F♯ between the first and second phrases. Cataloging these chromatic conflicts yields some interesting analytical material, including a potential confirmation of a "0" system in the absence of E♭ (or D♯). However, one other interesting lack of chromatic conflict involves the note C, which also is not immediately associated with a C♭ or C♯. However, in the second period, which begins in m. 12, both the missing pitch, E♭/D♯, and C♮ become chromatically activated: in the thirty-second-note run beginning in m. 12, C♯ stands out since it is the highest note reached in the section and the one that receives the strongest rhythmic emphasis. In Diagram 8.6, we will call this pc 1 (C♯) and the previous C♮ from m. 4 pc 0. Also, we will take the same pc 0 (C♮) as the first note of the descending PDA while the first note that opens the second phrase will become PDA B♮. We will also make the assumption that the G♭ that starts the bass motion in the first period is enharmonically replaced by F♯ in the second phrase, within the rising D major triad in the tenor of mm. 4 and 5 diminished in this way: D♮–F♯–A♮–A♯–B♮. Therefore, for our opening in a "0" system, F♯, the consonant system tritone of a "0" system, sits in the background to stabilize the system. In the second period, starting in m. 12, F♯ and F♮ continue their dyad conflict; also, the continual presence of F♯ prevents the E♭ that enters in m. 12 from modulating systems. Therefore, the system motivators E♭ and F♯ also help to make the "0" system a stable eleven-note entity. However, in m. 14, the entry of D♯ temporarily moves the systems up to a 3♯ system before C♮ re-enters in m. 17 to return us to the tonic "0" system. This allows Schoenberg (1) to explore the sharp side of the "circle of tritones," which does not play a particularly significant role in op. 11 no. 1, and (2) to introduce the system stabilizers C♮ and D♯, that will help to ground the tonic "0" system.

In the third period, beginning in m. 19, the systems move from "0" to three flats with the arrival of an uncontested E♭ already prepared at the end of the previous period in m. 18. The F♯ in m. 24 is not able to return us to our tonic system since E♭ keeps asserting itself. Momentarily, however, the G♭ in the melody of m. 27 brings us briefly into a 6♭ system before the A♮ in the bass of the next measure returns us to a 3♭ system (this balances Schoenberg's short excursion to a 3♯ system at the end of the previous period). Just as F♯ stabilized the "0" system of the opening period of the work, the A♮ that alternates with A♭ in the third period has a similar function of stabilizing the expanded 3♭ system. The A♮ in the bass of this section will also provide the descending PDA with the next note, A♮, which then continues down to G♮ at the end of the period in m. 33.

Measure 34 begins the large central section of the piece: we will call it the *B* section (it is not indicated in Diagram 8.6). Aside from one beat in m. 36 in a 6♭ system, and a couple of beats between the end of m. 41 and the beginning of m. 42 in a 3♯ system, the *B* section basically sways back and forth between a "0" system and a 3♭ system. As the return of the *A¹* section is approached by retransitional material between mm. 45 and 52, we find that this section stays exclusively within three flats; any F♯s in this area are prevented from provoking a system modulation because of the continued presence of E♭s. However, in the measure (m. 52) just before *A* returns, the F♯ in the right-hand part (on the second half of the first beat) moves the systems to "0" with the presence of the "rarer" form of pc 3, D♯. The D♯ sends the systems up to a 3♯ system, preventing the E♭ on the second beat in the right-hand part from returning the systems to a 3♭ system. However, with the D♯ activating a 3♯ system, the high C♮, in the right hand on the third beat of the measure, shifts the system back to its original tonic "0" state just before the *A¹* section begins in m. 53. The final twelve measures go through the following systems transformations: "0", 3♭ (m. 55), 6♭ (m. 56), 3♭ (m. 59), and "0" again (m. 60). Just as the piece ends, however, an E♭ in the very lowest register – recalling the low F♯ in m. 12 – enters and moves the system back down to a 3♭ system, in which the piece ends. Concluding in a 3♭ system actually serves to set up the next piece in the set, op. 11 no. 2, which stays mostly in flat systems. Just before the final cadence of no. 2 (two measures from the end), a very low F♯, in the same register as the one at the end of no. 1, brings the systems up to "0", but the last measure contains uncontested E♭s that end the piece ... almost! The last note in the left hand is the same low E♭ that ended no. 1. However, the last chord (right hand) contains a G♭ in the tenor voice, sending the systems down to a 6♭ system. Where is the A♮ to bring us back to a 3♭ system? The very first note of no. 3 provides the A♮ in octaves, with no other note heard against it! Typical of Schoenberg's multimovement compositions, the pitch material of the next number is set up at the end of the previous one. Op. 11 no. 3 almost (almost, again) ends in a "0" system: the last few measures of the piece reiterate F♯ several times as if to "eradicate" any semblances of the previous 3♭ system. Then, in an almost perverse turnaround, the E♭ returns *ppp* in the penultimate measure, finishing the three-movement cycle in a 3♭ system.

With Debussy's "Jardins," we were able to see how a composition on the precipice of atonality was able to maintain its structural integrity. Here, we have offered a short analysis of op. 11 no. 1 (with some mention of the other two numbers) to suggest that, even in the absence of any semblance of triadic tonality, certain operations that have permeated composition for hundreds of years still seem to be active in the organization of music of later historic periods. And here we come full circle. We note again that the tendencies of composers to treat the total chromatic spectrum as eleven-note system gamuts and to unfold the tonic octave in diatonic and chromatic arrays are ubiquitous and have hovered in the background of composition and its developmental process over the past several centuries.

Bibliography

Aldwell, Edward, and Carl Schachter, *Harmony and Voice Leading*, 2nd edn (New York: Harcourt Brace Jovanovich, Inc., 1989).

Allsop, Peter, *Arcangelo Corelli: "New Orpheus of Our Times"* (Oxford: Oxford University Press, 1999).

Atcherson, Walter, "Key and Mode in 17th-Century Music Theory Books," *Journal of Music Theory*, 17 (1973): 204–32.

Atlas, Allan W., *Renaissance Music: Music in Western Europe, 1400–1600* (New York: W.W. Norton, 1998).

Bach, Johann Sebastian, *Inventionen und Sinfonien*, ed. Georg von Dadelsen (Kassel, 1972).

Bailey, Robert, *Richard Wagner: Prelude and Transfiguration from "Tristan and Isolde"*, Norton Critical Score (New York: Norton, 1985).

Baker, James, "Chromaticism in Classical Music," in Christopher Hatch and David W. Bernstein (eds), *Music Theory and the Exploration of the Past* (Chicago: University of Chicago Press, 1993), pp. 233–307.

——, "Liszt's Late Piano Works: Larger Forms," in Kenneth Hamilton (ed.), *The Cambridge Companion to Liszt* (Cambridge: Cambridge University Press, 2005), pp. 120–51.

Balthazar, Scott L., "Rossini and the Development of the Mid-Century Lyric Form," *Journal of the American Musicological Society*, 41 (1988): 102–25.

Banchieri, Adriano, *L'organo suonario* (Venice, 1605), facsimile edn (Bologna: Forni, 1969).

——, *Cartella musciale* (Venice, 1613–14), facsimile edn (Bologna: Forni, n.d.).

Bent, Ian (ed. and trans.), *Music Analysis in the Nineteenth Century*, vol. 1: *Fugue, Form and Style*, Cambridge Readings in the Literature of Music (Cambridge: Cambridge University Press, 1994).

Bent, Margaret, "Musica Recta and Musica Ficta," *Musica disciplina*, 26 (1972): 73–100.

Berger, Karol, *Theories of Chromatic and Enharmonic Music in Late Sixteenth-Century Italy*, Studies in Musicology, 10 (Ann Arbor, Michigan: UMI Research Press, 1980).

——, "Tonality and Atonality in the Prologue to Orlando di Lasso's *Prophetiae Sibyllarum*: Some Methodological Problems in Analysis of Sixteenth-Century Music," *The Musical Quarterly*, 66 (1980): 484–504.

——, "The Common and the Unusual Steps of Musica Ficta: A Background for the Gamut of Orlando di Lasso's *Prophetiae Sybillarum*," *Belgisch tijdschrift voor Muziekweienschap*, 39–40 (1985–88): 61–73.

——, *Musica Ficta: Theories of Accidental Inflections in Vocal Polyphony from Marchetto da Padova to Gioseffo Zarlino* (Cambridge: Cambridge University Press, 1987).

Boetticher, Wolfgang, "Anticipations of Dramatic Monody in the Late Works of Lassus," in F. Sternfeld et al. (eds), *Essays on Opera and English Music: In Honour of Sir Jack Westrup* (Oxford: Oxford University Press, 1975), pp. 84–102.

Bonta, Stephen, "The Church Sonatas of Giovanni Legrenzi," 2 vols, Ph.D. dissertation, Harvard University, 1964.

——, *The Instrumental Music of Giovanni Legrenzi* (Cambridge, Massachusetts: Harvard University Press, 1984).

Burnett, Henry, "Levels of Chromatic Ordering in the First Movements of Haydn's London Symphonies: A New Hypothesis," *International Journal of Musicology*, 7 (1998): 113–65.

——, "A New Theory of Hexachord Modulation in the Late Sixteenth and Early Seventeenth Centuries," *International Journal of Musicology*, 8 (1999): 115–75.

——, and Shaugn O'Donnell, "Linear Ordering of the Chromatic Aggregate in Classical Symphonic Music," *Music Theory Spectrum*, 18/1 (1996): 22–50.

Burney, Charles, *A General History of Music*, vol. 2 (1789), repr. edn (New York: Dover Publications, Inc., 1957).

Chafe, Eric, *Monteverdi's Tonal Language* (New York: Schirmer Books, 1992).

Cinnamon, Howard, "Third Relations as Structural Elements in Book II of Liszt's 'Années de pèlerinage' and Three Later Works," Ph.D. dissertation, University of Michigan, 1984.

Cohn, Richard, "Introduction to Neo-Riemannian Theory: A Survey and Historical Perspective," *Journal of Music Theory*, 42/2 (Fall 1988): 167–80.

Corelli, Arcangelo, *Historicsh-kritische Gesamtausgabe der musikalischen Werke*, ed. Hans Oesch (Laaber: Laaber-Verlag, 1987).

Dahlhaus, Carl, *Between Romanticism and Modernism: Four Studies in the Music of the Later Nineteenth Century*, trans. Mary Whittall (Berkeley and Los Angeles: University of California Press, 1980).

——, *Studies on the Origin of Harmonic Tonality*, trans. Robert O. Gjerdingen (Princeton, New Jersey: Princeton University Press, 1990).

Danckerts, Ghiselin, *Trattato sopra una diffentia musicale*, c. 1560s, trans. Karol Berger as *Theories of Chromatic and Enharmonic Music in Late Sixteenth-Century Italy*, Studies in Musicology, 10 (Ann Arbor, Michigan: UMI Research Press, 1976).

Daverio, John, "In Search of the Sonata da Camera before Corelli," *Acta musicologia*, 57/2, (1985): 195–214.

David, Hans T., and Arthur Mendel, *The New Bach Reader*, rev. and enlarged Christoph Wolff (New York: W.W. Norton and Co., 1998).

Davidson, A.T., and W. Apel (eds), *Historical Anthology of Music*, vol. 1 (Cambridge, Massachusetts: Harvard University Press, 1959).

Debussy, Claude, "Monsieur Croche the Dilettante Hater," in *Three Classics in the Aesthetic of Music* (New York: Dover Publications, 1962), pp. 1–71.

De la Rue, Pierre, *Opera omnia*, vol. 9, ed. Nigel St John Davison (Neuhausen-Stuttgart: American Institute of Musicology, 1996).

Dreyfus, Laurence, "J.S. Bach's Concerto Ritornellos and the Question of Invention," *The Musical Quarterly*, 71/3 (1985): 327–58.

Drummond, Pippa, *The German Concerto: Five Eighteenth-Century Studies* (Oxford: Oxford University Press, 1980).

Dunn, Thomas D., "The Sonatas of Biagio Marini: Structure and Style", *The Music Review*, 36/3 (August 1975): 161–79.

Epstein, David, *Beyond Orpheus: Studies in Musical Structure* (Cambridge, Massachusetts: The MIT Press, 1979).

Fabbri, Paolo, *Monteverdi*, trans. Tim Carter (Cambridge: Cambridge University Press, 1994).

Fischer, Wilhelm, "Zur Entwicklungsgeschichte des Wiener klassischen Stils," *Studien zur Musikwissenschaft*, 3 (1915): 24–84.

Frank, Joseph, "Spatial Form in Modern Literature," in Mark Schorer et al. (eds), *Criticism: The Foundations of Modern Literary Judgment* (New York: Harcourt, Brace and Co., 1948), pp. 379–92.

Frescobaldi, Girolamo, *Orgel- und Klavierwerke*, ed. Pierre Pidoux, vol. 4 (Kassel: Bärenreiter-Ausgabe, 1963).

Frisch, Walter, *Brahms and the Principle of Developing Variation* (Berkeley: University of California Press, 1984).

——, *The Early Works of Arnold Schoenberg: 1893–1908* (Berkeley and Los Angeles: University of California Press, 1993).

Gagné, David, "Monteverdi's *Ohimè dov'è il mio ben* and the *Romanesca*," *The Music Forum*, 6 (New York: Columbia University Press, 1987), pp. 61–92.

Garratt, James, "Haydn and Posterity: The Long Nineteenth Century," in Caryl Clark (ed.), *The Cambridge Companion to Haydn* (Cambridge: Cambridge University Press, 2005), pp. 226–38.

Gianturco, Carolyn M., "The Operas of Alessandro Stradella," D.Phil. dissertation, Oxford University, 1970.

——, "Caratteri stilistici delle opere teatrali di Stradella," *Rivista italiana di musicologia*, 6 (1971): 236–45.

——, "Evidence for a Late Roman School of Opera," *Music and Letters*, 56 (1975): 4–17.

——, "Music for a Genoese Wedding of 1681," *Music and Letters*, 63/1–2 (1982): 31–43.

——, *Alessandro Stradella (1639–1682): His Life and Music* (Oxford: Oxford University Press, 1994).

Gleick, James, *Chaos: Making a New Science* (New York: Penguin Books, 1987).

Hamilton, Kenneth (ed.), *The Cambridge Companion to Liszt* (Cambridge: Cambridge University Press, 2005).

Harrison, Bernard, *Haydn: The "Paris" Symphonies*, Cambridge Music Handbooks (Cambridge: Cambridge University Press, 1998).

Hepokoski, James, "Beyond the Sonata Principle," *Journal of the American Musicological Society*, 55/1 (2002): 91–154.

——, and Warren Darcy, "The Medial Caesura and its Role in the Eighteenth-Century Sonata Exposition," *Music Theory Spectrum*, 19/2 (Fall 1997): 115–54.

Hübler, Klaus K. "Orlando di Lassus Prophetiae Sybillarum oder Über chromatische Komposition im 16. Jahrhundert," *Zeitschrift für Musiktheorie*, 9 (1978): 29ff.

Hughes, Andrew, *Manuscript Accidentals: Ficta in Focus 1350–1450*, Musicological Studies and Documents, 27 (n.p.: American Institute of Musicology, 1972), pp. 47–51.

Jander, Owen, "Concerto Grosso Instrumentation in Rome in the 1660's and 1670's," *Journal of the American Musicological Society*, 21 (1968): 168–80.

——, 'Let Your Deafness No Longer Be a Secret – Even in Art': Self-Portraiture and the Third Movement of the C-Minor Symphony," *Beethoven Forum*, 8 (2000): 25–70.

Josquin Desprez, *Werken*, ed. Albert J. Smijers (Amsterdam: Alsbach; Leipzig: Kistner & Siegel, 1921–56).

Kamien, Roger, and Naphtali Wagner, "Bridge Themes within a Chromaticized Voice Exchange in Mozart Expositions," *Music Theory Spectrum*, 19/1 (Spring 1997): 1–12.

Katz, Adele, *Challenge to Musical Tradition* (New York: Alfred A. Knopf, 1945).

Kerman, Joseph, *The Beethoven Quartets* (London: Oxford University Press, 1967).

Kircher, Athanasius, *Musurgia universalis, sive Ars magna consoni et dissoni in X libros digesta*, repr. edn, ed. Ulf Scharlau (Hildesheim: G. Olms, 1970).

Koch, Heinrich Christoph, *Introductory Essay on Composition*, trans. Nancy Baker, partial trans. of the *Versuch* (New Haven: Yale University Press, 1983).

Krüger, Walther, *Das Concerto Grosso in Deutschland* (Wolfenbüttel and Berlin: Georg Kallmeyer, 1932).

Kucaba, John, and Bertil H. Van Boer, "Wagenseil, Georg Christoph," in Stanley Sadie and John Tyrrell (eds), *The New Grove Dictionary of Music and Musicians*, 2nd edn (London: Macmillan, 2001), vol. 26, pp. 928–30.

Kurth, Ernst, *Romantische Harmonik und ihre Krise in Wagners "Tristan"* (Berlin: M. Hesse, 1923).

Kurtzmand, Jeffery, "A Taxonomic and Affective Analysis of Monteverdi's 'Hor che'l ciel e la terra'," *Music Analysis*, 12/2 (1993): 169–96.

Lam, Basil, *Beethoven String Quartets 2* (Seattle: University of Washington Press, 1975).

Legrenzi, Giovanni, *Il Giustino* (1683), repr. in *The Opera*, vol. 1, ed. Hellmuth Christian Wolff (Cologne: Arno Volk Verlag, 1971).

——, *Sonate (1655)*, ed. Stephen Bonta (Cambridge, Massachusetts: Harvard University Press, 1984).

Lendvai, Ernó, *The Workshop of Bartók and Kodály* (Budapest: Editio Musica Budapest, 1983).

Lester, Joel, *Between Modes and Keys: German Theory 1592–1802* (New York: Pendragon Press, 1989).

——, *Compositional Theory in the Eighteenth Century* (Cambridge, Massachusetts: Harvard University Press, 1992).

Lesure, François, and Roger Nichols (eds), *Debussy Letters* (London: Faber and Faber, 1987).

Lewin, David, "A Formal Theory of Generalized Tonal Functions," *Journal of Music Theory*, 26/1 (1982): 23–60.

Linfield, Eva, "Formal and Tonal Organization in a 17th-Century Ritornello/Ripieno Structure" *The Journal of Musicology*, 9/2 (1991): 145–64.

——, "Modulatory Techniques in Seventeenth-Century Music: Schütz, a Case in Point," *Music Analysis,* 12/2 (1993): 197–214.

Liszt, Franz, *Trois études de Concert/Trois caprices poetiques für Klavier*, ed. Zoltán Gárdonyi and István Szelényi (Budapest: Bärenreiter, 1971), repr. from Franz Liszt, *Neue Ausgabe sämtlicher Werke*, ser. I, Werke für Klavier zu zwei Händen, vol. 2: *Etüden II.*

Lorenz, Alfred, *Der musikalische Aufbau von Richard Wagners 'Tristan und Isolde'* (Berlin: Max Hesse, 1926, repr. 1966).

Lowinsky, Edward, *Secret Chromatic Art in the Netherlands Motet* (New York: Columbia University Press, 1946, repr. 1967).

——, *Tonality and Atonality in Sixteenth-Century Music* (Berkeley and Los Angeles: University of California Press, 1961).

Lubovsky, Bella Brover, "'Die schwarze Gredel,' or the Parallel Minor Key in Vivaldi's Instrumental Music," *Studi Vivaldiani*, 3 (2003): 105–31.

McCrickard, Eleanor F., "Temporal and Tonal Aspects of Alessandro Stradella's Instrumental Music," *Analecta musicologica*, 19 (1979): 186–243.

Marenzio, Luca, *Il nono libro de madrigali a 5 voci* (Venice: Gardano, 1599).

Marini, Biagio, *String Sonatas From Opus 1 and Opus 8*, ed. Thomas D. Dunn (New York: A-R Editions, Inc., 1981).

Mitchell, William J., "The Prologue to Orlando di Lasso's Prophetiae Sibyllarum," *Music Forum*, 2 (1970): 264–73.

Monn, Georg Matthias, *Symphonies*, ed. Wilhelm Fischer, in *Denkmäler der Tonkunst in Österreich*, xxxix, Jahrgang xv/2 (Graz: Akademische Druck-u. Verlagsanstalt, 1912, repr. 1959).

——, *Five Monn Symphonies*, ed. Kenneth E. Rudolf, in Barry S. Brook (editor-in-chief), *The Symphony 1720–1840*, ser. B, vol. 1 (New York: Garland Publishing, Inc., 1984).

Monteverdi, Claudio, *Tutte le opere*, vol. 7, ed. G.F. Malipiero. Asola: G. F. Malipiero, 1928 (Vienna: Universal Edition, 1966).

Monteverdi, Giulio Cesare, "Dichiaratione della lettera stampata nel quinto libro de suoi madrigali," in Claudio Monteverdi, *Scherzi musicali a tre voce* (Venice: Ricciardo Amadino, 1607), repr. in Claudio Monteverdi, *Tutte le opere*, ed. G. Francesco Malipiero, vol. 10 (Vienna, 1929), pp. 69–72.

Moreen, Robert, "Integration of Text Forms and Musical Forms in Verdi's Early Operas," Ph.D. dissertation, Princeton University, 1975.

Nichols, Roger, "Claude Debussy," in Stanley Sadie (ed.), *The New Grove Twentieth-Century French Masters* (New York: W.W. Norton & Co., 1986), pp. 41–117.

Nitzberg, Roy, "Voice-Leading and Chromatic Techniques in Expositions of Selected Symphonies by Joseph Haydn, Introducing a New Theory of Chromatic Analysis," Ph.D. dissertation, City University of New York, 1999.

Notley, Margaret, "The Chamber Music of Brahms," in Stephen E. Helfing (ed.), *Nineteenth-Century Chamber Music* (London: Routledge, 2004), pp. 242–86.

Palisca, Claude V., "The Artusi–Monteverdi Controversy," in Denis Arnold and Nigel Fortune (eds), *The New Monteverdi Companion* (Oxford: Clarendon Press, 1985), pp. 127–58.

Perle, George, *Serial Composition and Atonality* (Berkeley and Los Angeles: University of California Press, 1977).

——, *Twelve-Tone Tonality* (Berkeley and Los Angeles: University of California Press, 1977).

Pesce, Dolores, "B-flat: Transposition or Transformation," *The Journal of Musicology*, 4/3 (1985–86): 330–49.

Pincherle, Marc, *Vivaldi*, trans. Christopher Hatch (New York: The Norton Library, 1962).

Powers, Harold S., and Frans Wiering, "Mode," in Stanley Sadie and John Tyrrell (eds), *The New Grove Dictionary of Music and Musicians*, 2nd edn (London: Macmillan, 2001), vol. 16, pp. 775–811.

Proctor, Gregory, "Technical Bases of Nineteenth-Century Chromatic Tonality," Ph.D. dissertation, Princeton University, 1978.

Rameau, Jean Philippe, *Treatise on Harmony*, trans. Philip Gossett (New York: Dover Publications, Inc., 1971).

Ratner, Leonard G., *Classic Music: Expression, Form, and Style* (New York: Schirmer Books, 1980).

Riepel, Joseph, *Grundregeln zur Tonordnung insgemein* (Frankfurt and Leipzig, 1755).

Rivera, Benito V., *German Music Theory in the Early 17th Century: The Treatises of Johannes Lippius* (Ann Arbor, Michigan: UMI Research Press, 1980).

Rore, Cipriano de, *Opera omnia*, ed. B. Meier (n.p.: American Institute of Musicology, 1971).

Rosen, Charles, *The Classical Style: Haydn, Mozart, Beethoven* (New York: W.W. Norton and Co., 1971–72, rev. edn, 1997).

——, *Sonata Forms* (New York: W.W. Norton and Co., rev. edn, 1988).

——, *The Romantic Generation* (Cambridge, Massachusetts: Harvard University Press, 1995).

Salzer, Felix, "Heinrich Schenker and Historical Research: Monteverdi's Madrigal *Oimè, se tanto amate*," in David Beach (ed.), *Aspects of Schenkerian Theory* (New Haven and London: Yale University Press, 1983), pp. 135–52.

Sammartini, Giovanni Battista, *The Symphonies of G.B. Sammartini*, vol. 1, ed. Bathia Churgin (Cambridge, Massachusetts: Harvard University Press, 1968).

——, *Ten Symphonies*, ed. Bathia Churgin, in Barry S. Brook (editor-in-chief), *The Symphony: 1720–1840*, ser. A, vol. 2 (New York: Garland Publishing, Inc., 1984).

Schachter, Carl, "The First Movement of Brahms's Second Symphony: The Opening Theme and its Consequences," *Music Analysis*, 2/1 (1983): 55–68.

Schenker, Heinrich, *Free Composition*, trans. and ed. Ernst Oster (New York: Longman, 1979).

Schoenberg, Arnold, *Theory of Harmony*, California Library Reprint Series (Berkeley, California: University of California Press, 1983), originally published as *Harmonielehre* (Vienna: Universal Edition, 1911).

——, *The Musical Idea and the Logic, Technique, and Art of its Presentation: A Theoretical Manuscript by Arnold Schoenberg*, trans. and ed. Patricia Carpenter and Severine Neff (New York: Columbia University Press, 1995).

Schwartz, Judith Leah, "Monn, Matthias Georg," in Stanley Sadie and John Tyrrell (eds), *The New Grove Dictionary of Music and Musicians*, 2nd edn (London: Macmillan, 2001), vol. 16, pp. 945–6.

Smaldone, Edward, "Linear Analysis of Selected Posttonal Works of Arnold Schoenberg: Toward an Application of Schenkerian Concepts to the Music of the Posttonal Era," Ph.D. dissertation, The City University of New York Graduate Center, 1986.

Solie, John E., "Aria Structure and Ritornello Form in the Music of Albinoni," *The Musical Quarterly*, 63/1 (1977): 31–47.

Spitzer, John, and Neal Zaslaw, *The Birth of the Orchestra: History of an Institution, 1650–1815* (Oxford: Oxford University Press, 2004).

Stein, Beverly, "Carissimi's Tonal System and the Function of Transposition in the Expansion of Tonality," *The Journal of Musicology*, 19/2 (Spring 2002): 264–305.

Stradella, Alessandro, *Ah! Troppo è ver*, ed. Remo Giazotto (Milan: Edizioni Curci S.r.L., 1962).

——, *Moro per amore*, facsimile edn reproduced from Vienna, Öesterreichische Nationalbibliothek, Cod 18708 (New York and London: Garland Publishing, Inc., 1979).

Straus, Joseph N., *Remaking the Past: Musical Modernism and the Influence of the Tonal Tradition* (Cambridge, Massachusetts: Harvard University Press, 1990).

——, "Normalizing the Abnormal: Disability in Music and Music Theory," *Journal of the American Musicological Society*, 59/1 (Spring 2006): 113–84.

Talbot, Michael, *Vivaldi* (New York: Schirmer Books, 1992).

Taruskin, Richard, *Defining Russia Musically* (Princeton, New Jersey: Princeton University Press, 2001).

Toft, Robert, "Pitch Content and Modal Procedure in Josquin's *Absalon, fili mi*," *Tijdschrift van de Vereniging voor Nederlandse Muziekgeschiedenis*, 33 (1983): 3–27.

Tomlinson, Gary, *Monteverdi and the End of the Renaissance* (Los Angeles: University of California Press, 1987).

Torelli, Giuseppe, *Op. 8 No. 8*, ed. Ernst Praetorius (London: Ernst Eulenburg Ltd, 1950).

Truscott, Harold, *Beethoven's Late String Quartets* (London: Dobson Books Ltd, 1968).

Vicentino, Nicola, *L'antica musica ridotta alla moderna prattica* (Rome, 1555); Book 3 trans. Rika Maniates as *Ancient Music Adapted to Modern Practice* (New Haven and London: Yale University Press, 1996).

Vivaldi, Antonio, *Opere*, ed. Gian Francesco Malipiero (Milan: Edizioni Ricordi, 1962).

Vitercik, Gregory, *The Early Works of Felix Mendelssohn: A Study in the Romantic Sonata Style* (Amsterdam: Gordon and Breach Science Publishers, 1992).

Vogler, Georg Joseph, *Tonwissenschaft und Tonsetzkunst* (Mannheim: Kurfürstliche Hofbuchdruckerei, 1776; repr. edn Hildesheim: Olms, 1970).

Wagenseil, Georg Christoph, *Symphonies*, ed. Karl Horwitz and Karl Riedal, *Denkmäler der Tonkunst in Oesterreich*, xxxi, Jarhgang xv/2 (Graz: Akademische Druck- u. Verlagsanstalt, 1980).

——, *Symphony in E WV 393*, ed. Bernhard Herzmansky, Diletto Musicale, no. 387 (Vienna: Ludwig Doblinger, 1975).

——, *Symphony in C WV 361*, Diletto Musicale, no. 340 (Vienna: Ludwig Doblinger, 1979).

——, *Fifteen Symphonies*, ed. John Kucaba, in Barry S. Brook (editor-in-chief), The *Symphony 1720–1840*, ser. B, vol. 3 (New York: Garland, 1981).

Watson, Derek, *Liszt* (New York: Schirmer, 1989).

Webster, James, "Schubert and Brahms's First Maturity I & II," *19th Century Music*, 2/1 (1978): 18–35; 3/1 (1979): 52–71.

Wert, Giaches de, *Opera omnia*, ed. Carol MacClintock and Melvin Bernstein (17 vols, n.p.: American Institute of Musicology, 1961–77).

Whenham, John (ed.), *Claudio Monteverdi: Orfeo*, Cambridge Opera Handbooks (Cambridge: Cambridge University Press, 1986).

Willner, Channan, "Chromaticism and the Mediant in Four Late Haydn Works," *Theory and Practice*, 13 (1988): 79–114.

Winter, Robert, "The Bifocal Close and the Evolution of the Viennese Classical Style," *Journal of the American Musicological Society*, 42 (1989): 275–337.

Wolf, Eugene, *The Symphonies of Johan Stamitz: A Study in the Formation of the Classical Style* (Utrecht and Antwerp: Bohn, Scheltema, and Holkema; The Hague and Boston: Nijhoff, 1981).

Zarlino, Gioseffo, *The Art of Counterpoint. Part Three of "Le istitutioni harmoniche,"* *1558*, trans. Guy A. Marco and Claude V. Palisca (New Haven and London: Yale University Press, 1968).

Index